Political Parties, Business Groups, and Corruption in Developing Countries

Political Parties, Business Groups, and Corruption in Developing Countries

Vineeta Yadav

OXFORD
UNIVERSITY PRESS

OXFORD
UNIVERSITY PRESS

Oxford University Press, Inc., publishes works that further
Oxford University's objective of excellence
in research, scholarship, and education.

Oxford   New York
Auckland   Cape Town   Dar es Salaam   Hong Kong   Karachi
Kuala Lumpur   Madrid   Melbourne   Mexico City   Nairobi
New Delhi   Shanghai   Taipei   Toronto

With offices in
Argentina   Austria   Brazil   Chile   Czech Republic   France   Greece
Guatemala   Hungary   Italy   Japan   Poland   Portugal   Singapore
South Korea   Switzerland   Thailand   Turkey   Ukraine   Vietnam

Copyright © 2011 by Oxford University Press, Inc.

Published by Oxford University Press, Inc.
198 Madison Avenue, New York, NY 10016

www.oup.com

Library of Congress Cataloging-in-Publication Data
Yadav, Vineeta.
Political parties, business groups, and corruption in developing
countries / Vineeta Yadav.
    p.   cm.
Includes bibliographical references and index.
ISBN 978-0-19-973590-7 (hardcover : alk. paper)—ISBN 978-0-19-973591-4
(pbk. : alk. paper) 1. Political corruption—Developing countries.
2. Political parties—Developing countries.
3. Business and politics—Developing countries. I. Title.
JF60.Y33   2011
324.209172′4—dc22
2010024689

1 3 5 7 9 8 6 4 2

Printed in the United States of America
on acid-free paper

For my parents, Ramesh and Shashi Yadav

CONTENTS

LIST OF FIGURES

LIST OF TABLES

ACKNOWLEDGMENTS

I would like to gratefully acknowledge and thank the Leitner Institute for International and Comparative Political Economy and the International Security Studies Institute at Yale University for their financial support. The Coca-Cola World Fund and the Smith Richardson Foundation also provided extensive financial support that allowed me to successfully undertake the fieldwork for this project. The Niehaus Center for Globalization and Governance at Princeton University provided me an intellectually stimulating and supportive environment during a year-long fellowship that nourished the analysis and the writing of this book. The Kellogg Institute at the University of Notre Dame and the department of political science at Penn State University have also supported this project. CEBRAP in Brazil and CSDS in India were generous enough to provide me with guidance on the ground.

The political science department at Yale was a wonderful home both intellectually and professionally. I would especially like to thank Frances Rosenbluth, Geoffrey Garrett, and Paul Kennedy for unstinting support and encouragement when I needed it most. I would also like to thank Susan Rose-Ackerman, Helen Milner, Bob Keohane, Paul Bracken, Jim Vreeland, Susan Stokes, Aleksandra Sznajder, David Samuels, Michael Coppedge, Scott Mainwaring, Frances Hagopian, Pierre Landry, John Roemer, Ellen Lust-Okar, Justin Fox, Peter Kingstone, Kurt Weyland, Ben Ross Schneider, Zhiwu Chen, Clive Thomas David Pervin, and Eric Crahan for supporting this project in different ways. In Brazil, David Fleisher, Fernando Limongi, Jose Guilhon, Roberto Troster, and Celina Souza helped me immensely to realize this project there. In India, I benefited from the generous support extended to me by Narendra Jadhav, Susan Thomas, Sasmita Palo, P. M. Patel, G. K. Prasad, Yogendra Yadav, and Sanjay Kumar. At Oxford University Press, I would like to thank David McBride for his support. I would also like to thank three anonymous referees for their comments and encouragement. They helped considerably improve this book. The final errors are, of course, all mine.

Several research assistants were invaluable in carrying out this project. For their outstanding research assistance I would like to thank Sergio Béjar, Chad Evans, Sandra Gomez, Jaqueline Araujo, Welton Luiz, Clarissa Deus, Marcelo Bernardes, Breno Ferreira Cypriano, Marina Brito Pinheiro, Feliciano Guimaraes, Kathakali Chanda, Arva Bhabhrawala, Brinda, and Bhoomi Shroff.

To my parents, brother, and dear friends who took calls from me from any time zone and any life zone—thank you, you have always made me speechless at my good fortune. To my father, you were the best research assistant, hands down! An especially heartfelt thank-you to the Asha gang at UW–Madison. My husband Bumba, who heard every excruciating detail, and many times, you do indeed have more patience than me.

Vineeta Yadav
February 2010

Political Parties, Business Groups, and Corruption in Developing Countries

1

INTRODUCTION

In June 2004, the legislature in Taiwan passed a landmark labor pension reform bill, which changed the level of pension contributions employers had to make and how these funds would be managed. Interest groups from the financial markets industry, the insurance sector, and labor unions lobbied the legislature intensively to influence various details of the bill. Despite a long, hard-fought, high-stakes campaign, no significant allegations of corruption regarding this lobbying process emerged from any source. A stark contrast to the Taiwan example can be observed in events surrounding passage of a controversial labor reform bill by the Argentinean parliament in 2001. Lobbying to influence this bill was marked by allegations of corruption and prosecution of many legislative policymakers on corruption charges. These charges related directly to the legislators' interactions with business lobbies regarding the bill. The resulting scandal almost brought down President Fernando de la Rúa's government. In both countries, the business sector had high stakes in the issue under legislative consideration and lobbying was intense. So why did business lobbying result in highly corrupt transactions in Argentina but not in Taiwan? This particular outcome reflects prevalent trends in each country. Business firms consistently rate the political establishment and public sector in Argentina as more corrupt, and more unduly influenced in its policymaking, than firms do in Taiwan.[1]

These contrasting examples reflect a global puzzle. Even though business interests seems inextricably linked with politics and policy everywhere, their political engagement is associated with much higher corruption in some countries than others.[2] This puzzle leads us to ask the following three questions: Why do some developing democracies experience much higher levels of corruption than others? How does the behavior of business interest groups relate to political corruption? How do legislative institutions governing the policy process promote or restrain corruption through the rules of engagement they provide to political and business actors? This book tries to answer these questions by identifying how legislative institutions establish strategic links among the behavioral incentives of political parties, individual politicians, and business interest groups. The analysis provided in this volume will show how and when these incentives lead to more corrupt behavior.

I argue that legislative institutions, which shape the policy process, play a crucial and neglected role in the corruption drama by shaping the lobbying strategies employed by money-rich business interests. When legislative rules on agenda-setting, amendments, and voting defection costs in a country give control over the substance, timing, and success of policy to political parties, they strengthen parties both in policymaking and politics. In these countries where parties are the influential legislative policymakers, parties rather than individual legislators become the focus of business lobbying. As I discuss later in Chapter 2, such party-focused lobbying leads to higher corruption levels because of the dynamics of both supply and demand factors driving party and politician financing. Therefore, by influencing the political target (or venue) of lobbying strategies, legislative institutions exert significant influence on the corruption profile of a country.

I use two original datasets to test the hypotheses yielded by this theoretical framework. My analysis uses new data on rules of legislative control over agenda-setting, amendments, and voting defection for sixty-four developing democracies from 1984 to 2004, to provide robust support for the hypotheses that party-focused legislative institutions increase corruption levels. Analysis of data obtained from surveys of business groups in two theoretically critical cases, Brazil and India, also provides strong support for the hypotheses that the higher levels of corruption in India compared to Brazil are explained by the differences in the party-focused and individual focused lobbying strategies adopted by business groups in these countries respectively. In contrast to a significant body of existing work, which largely explains corruption as a consequence of *weak* parties, the evidence in this book strongly suggests that *strong* parties can be directly responsible for higher corruption in developing countries.

In this study, I systematically present an alternative theory of corruption for developing country democracies; test the validity of this theory against the full range of existing theories using a time series cross-section dataset; and then provide direct evidence on the posited causal mechanism from detailed studies of two theoretically representative and empirically interesting cases. For reasons discussed later in this chapter, I confine my analysis in this book to developing country democracies, even though political corruption is clearly not exclusive to them. The concluding chapter of this volume, however, reflects on some insights these findings may provide towards an analysis of political corruption in authoritarian regimes as well as developed country democracies.

This chapter introduces the concepts and the structure employed by this book to address the three questions on corruption posed at the beginning of this chapter. I first define what I mean by the terms "political corruption," "corruption," and "lobbying" since these terms have been used to describe a wide range of behaviors in the literature. I then discuss the problem scholars face in measuring corruption and discuss its ramifications for any research on the topic. The second section presents the puzzle motivating this book: the wide variation in the levels of corruption experienced by countries. I then analyze the most prominent theories that have been used to explain corruption and business lobbying, and I follow with a discussion of some of the limitations faced by current theoretical and empirical approaches in understanding these phenomena. I then preview my argument that legislative institutions drive variation in corruption levels by motivating specific patterns of behavior among special interest groups. In the next section, I present a summary of my research design; I also discuss how the theoretical framework and research design used in this project address some of the limitations of other recent approaches to these problems. Finally, I discuss how the remainder of the book is organized to develop these arguments and present the evidence.

DEFINITIONS

In this book, lobbying refers to all *actions*, legal and illegal, taken by groups in their efforts to persuade any political and policy actors of their goals. The corruption level in a country is one of the *outcomes* that can result from such lobbying actions. While corruption is always an illegal phenomenon, lobbying includes actions that do not necessarily have to result in corruption. Importantly, corruption is a multi-causal phenomenon, and legislative lobbying is one of the many behaviors that can contribute to it.

The mostly widely used definition of corruption defines corruption as an "abuse of public office for unauthorized private gain" (World Bank 2000). I expand the scope of this definition in three ways to include situations not covered by this definition in politics. First, political entities need not actually be in office in order to exploit that office. Political agents promising to misuse political office in the future are also engaging in corruption since their transaction is based on the intention to exploit future political office. Second, when funding is directed at parties and used for party purposes, the private gain can be indirect since the investment is in a club good, party reputation, rather than a private good, such as personal reputation. The definition of political corruption articulated by Transparency International Annual Report (2004a, 10) points to an additional aspect of political corruption: "Political corruption is the abuse of entrusted power by political leaders for private gain, with the objective of increasing power or wealth. Political corruption need not involve money changing hands; it may take the form of 'trading in influence' or granting favors that poison politics and threaten democracy."[3]

This definition captures the third aspect of political corruption, the use of *legal* means to deliver favors, for example, by rewriting bills to include or exclude certain sectors from the scope of a bill. Rewriting legislation would qualify as a corrupt practice if money or illegal favors were exchanged between business and political players explicitly in order to facilitate the revisions. The exploitation of future political power and the use of bribes to finance club goods rather than private goods as corruption are exemplified by the actions of both President Jacques Chirac in France and President Roh Tae-woo in South Korea. These leaders claimed that the illegal funds they had raised were for the benefit of their respective parties (Ferdinand 2003, 66). Their actions involved raising money through illegally promising political favors that would be delivered using legal means in the future. Both politicians stood to gain personally from the rise of their parties and thus were willing to invest this money in their parties. Their behavior therefore clearly fits the aforementioned definition of political corruption.

Scholars have further defined several different types of corrupt behaviors, including state capture, patronage, nepotism, influence peddling, and bureaucratic corruption.[4] Since our interest is in explaining what drives political corruption and shapes its links with the overall corruption observed in a country, it is useful to consider the categorization of corrupt behaviors by the types of political agents who engage in these various behaviors. *Grand* corruption has been defined as corruption that "occurs at the highest levels of government and involves major government projects and programs" (Rose-Ackerman 1999, 27). This definition was later extended to cover transactions with other political players (Rose-Ackerman 2006, xix). *Petty* corruption is defined as corruption that "occurs within a framework where basic laws and regulations are in place and implementing officials seize upon opportunities to benefit personally" (Rose-Ackerman 2006, xviii). The *extent* of corruption in a country can be assessed by analyzing whether grand or petty types of corrupt behavior, or both, are prevalent in a country (Gerring and Thacker 2004, 300). As the extent of corruption grows from petty to grand, so does the corruption level prevalent in that country. The highest levels of corruption will therefore be observed in countries that suffer both petty and grand corruption.[5]

"Lobbying" is another term that is widely but variously used in discussions on special interest group behavior. Baumgartner and Leech (1998, 34) define it as "an effort to influence the policy process," while Nownes (2006, 5) defines it as "an effort designed to affect what the government does." Here, I employ a widely used general definition of lobbying provided in a study of lobbying in the European Union by the Public Relations Institute of Ireland, the Chartered Institute of Public Relations, and the Public Relations Consultants Association (Malone 2004). In this report, lobbying refers to "the specific efforts to influence public decision making either by pressing for change in policy or seeking to prevent such change. It consists of representations to any public officeholder on any aspect of policy, or any measure implementing that policy, or any matter being considered, or which is likely to be considered by a public body" (Malone 2004, 6). When lobbying is directed toward elected officials in the legislature, these efforts are referred to as legislative lobbying.

Lobbyists may work in a variety of organizations, including trade associations, firms, public affairs and governmental relations firms, law firms, nongovernmental organizations, public-sector firms, and think tanks. Their actions may include contributing money to election campaigns, volunteering for campaigns, providing technical information to policymakers, mounting public demonstrations of support or opposition, sponsoring media campaigns, donating money legally or illegally to parties and candidates at any point in the political cycle, and so forth. This list includes both legal and illegal actions that are undertaken by special interests in their pursuit of policy objectives.[6] As Norton (2002, 15) observes, both are included in the toolkit that special interests use to forge links with policymakers: "Such links maybe unethical but not illegal . . . they may involve illegal activity (such as bribery) or they may involve activity that falls in a grey area between the two." As a report on lobbying by the OECD (2008,

20) also notes, the relationship between specific lobbying actions and corruption can be subtle in that lobbyists may violate ethical norms of behavior without necessarily violating the law. The report defines a clear criterion for assessing when lobbying actions lead to corruption: "Lobbying activity moves into the category of corrupt practices when something of value to the governmental official is exchanged for official favours" (OECD 2008, 20).

To summarize, for purposes of discussion in this book, lobbying refers to all *actions*, legal and illegal, taken by groups in their efforts to persuade any political and policy actors of their goals. Therefore, lobbying practices may or may not lead to corruption. The corruption level in a country is an *outcome* that can result from lobbying actions, among other things. Aggregate corruption levels range from a low of petty forms of corruption to a high which includes the existence of both political and petty corruption in a country.

PUZZLE

The puzzle motivating this project can be framed as the set of three questions posed at the beginning of this chapter. To restate those questions again: Why do some developing country democracies experience much higher levels of corruption than others? How is the behavior of business interest groups related to corruption? How do legislative institutions promote or restrain corruption through the rules of engagement they provide to political and business actors?

Corruption is a complex, multicausal phenomenon that has roots in many different sources. The deep disputes in the literature about the identity and importance of different sources of corruption are a testament to how little we still know about this widespread occurrence. The rise of democratic forms of government was expected to reduce corruption as were the adoption of market-oriented reforms and the internationalization of developing country economies.[7] These expectations were based on the assumption that corruption stemmed primarily from a lack of competition, whether in the political or economic sphere. Instead, studies have recorded rising levels of corruption in many of the countries that adopted democratic reforms.[8] This disheartening development indicates an urgent need to go back to the drawing board and identify what scholars have missed in their efforts to understand the prevalence of corruption. Therefore, the first question this book addresses is what drives variation in corruption levels in developing country democracies.

One of the most potentially significant omissions in this endeavor is an understanding of the politics of business interests and its potential for raising corruption in a country. Studies of political finance confirm the rising significance of business as a source of legal and illegal political resources in countries around the world.[9] This association of business with political corruption has led to much lamentation in academic, popular, and policymaking circles. It has also inspired substantial investment by policymakers, international aid agencies, and multilateral institutions to develop measures to address the problem. Yet, we do not have a *systematic* theoretical comparative framework for understanding when the influence seeking political behavior of business leads to more or less corruption. The second question this book therefore asks is: How are the strategies of political engagement by business interests linked to the variation in the levels and types of political corruption observed?

This leads us to ask a more fundamental question: On what basis do business interest groups evolve political strategies to engage policymakers across different political systems? Surprisingly, despite the fact that most business lobbying takes place in the legislature—and that such lobbying can potentially affect corruption—the literatures on corruption and legislative lobbying have largely talked past each other. In this book, I consider whether and how legislative policymaking institutions promote or restrain corruption through the rules of engagement they provide to political and business actors.

Why is this puzzle an important one for scholars? The direct and negative impact corruption has on fundamental dimensions of quality of life—poverty, equality, and justice—is, alas, well documented and hardly needs to be recounted as a motive to study corruption.[10] What is even more pernicious is the manner in which corruption can sabotage the success of policies such as democratization and market reforms that were adopted precisely in order to address these problems. Increasingly, citizens around the world feel that the rights granted to them formally by a country's institutions are being undermined in practice by corrupt collusion between business and political elites (Inglehart and Weltzel 2005, 195). They also identify corruption as a bigger cause of lower living standards than bad economic policies (Greenberg and Rosner 2006). These views from the street are echoed by institutions such as the World Bank, whose studies show that countries with higher rates of state capture by businesses experience lower economic growth and lower redistribution (Kaufmann 2006, 25). Both trends point to an increasing and dangerous popular disenchantment with the credibility of these reforms and raise concerns about the threat corruption poses to regime stability.[11]

Political corruption also poses challenges to the continuity and success of economic reforms by jeopardizing support among economic elites. Domestic and foreign firms list corruption as a bigger constraint on business than infrastructure or bureaucratic red tape (World Economic Forum 2004-05, 85).[12] When prominent multinationals such as Siemens, Alcatel, and Halliburton are implicated in bribing local politicians and parties, support for market reforms and globalization is seriously damaged among domestic firms who do not have the wherewithal to compete for political access or influence with rich multinationals.[13] Multinational firms, on the other hand, pay higher costs for doing business in corrupt countries due to the necessity of paying bribes, and they face higher risks of being prosecuted for such corrupt behavior in their home and host countries. Understanding the incentives that lead business groups to lobby for influence using illegal means is, therefore, important to building a strong coalition in support of reforms, implementing sustainable economic reforms, and establishing fair, efficient, and legitimate means of representation to business interests.

Finally, the increasingly significant role of business in financing politics around the world makes understanding the underpinning of political corruption and business's role in it an urgent contemporary issue of burgeoning importance. Studies show that declining party membership and widespread poverty have increasingly reduced the importance of members and grassroots supporters as sources of revenue for parties and candidates in most developing countries, and state funding has proven inadequate in plugging this gap (Hagopian 2009; Bryan and Baer 2005, 10, 21; Austin and Tjernström 2003, 8). These trends of declining alternative sources of funds in a world of increasing political expenses indicate the increasing strategic importance of business donations in politics. Efforts to contain illegitimate, excessive use of this increasing power must begin with an understanding of what determines business influence seeking behaviors and patterns in the first place.

This task is also made urgent by the fact that widespread association of the business community with corruption has led to a pervasive aversion to any business involvement in politics or policy and a flurry of ill-conceived, standardized regulation to curb *all* lobbying. These measures are widely believed to have failed in their goal of containing corruption and introducing transparency into the political engagement of business interests.[14] Unfortunately, they have also restricted the positive benefits of business lobbying from being realized. Business groups can provide valuable technical and political information and expertise to policymakers, inform and mobilize public opinion, and mobilize member support or opposition on policy matters (Norton 1999; Gray and Lowery 2004; Nownes 2006; OECD 2008, 18). They can provide a vital link between policymakers and those most affected and informed about policy consequences, especially in the context of untried economic reforms. Legitimate business lobbying can thus lead to better policymaking. It can also encourage programmatic political competition and enable better citizen monitoring of policy performance, thus creating higher political accountability. Furthermore, the political participation and support of this influential constituency can make a significant difference to the stability of political regimes.[15] Business mobilization and lobbying are therefore both desirable and vital to a well-functioning economic and political system.

For these reasons, organizations such as the UN, USAID, World Bank, and the EU have invested their resources in encouraging the mobilization, organization, and regulation of business interests and their lobbying behavior in many developing countries.[16] Understanding the nature of the incentives that shape the monetary flows of this influential community and its consequences for corruption should therefore be a step in the direction of designing more nuanced measures that limit the negative impact of business lobbying while still allowing for positive externalities. I begin by first summarizing briefly here what we know about the causes of corruption and then analyzing the contributions and constraints of current approaches.

What drives corruption?

This fundamental question has spawned rich literatures in political science, economics, public policy, business, sociology, and other fields. Early work on corruption focused primarily on economic and social factors in order to explain observed variation. This literature consistently identified conditions of low income, weak rule of law, and lack of a free press as important causes of corruption and gave us some leverage on this puzzle.[17] Even with identification of these factors, a large share of the variation in corruption levels remained unexplained. Extensive empirical studies investigating the obvious economic suspects, such as a large government, a closed domestic economy, and high levels of regulation, have failed to confirm a consistent and significant role for these factors.[18] The role of cultural and social factors, including the dominant religion of a country, ethnic diversity, and the identity of colonizers, have not been found to hold up in all samples of countries and periods.[19]

Recent scholarship has thus increasingly come to focus on the political underpinnings of these endogenous policy choices and to investigate the role of political institutions in explaining corruption. In this section, I outline the current institutional debates that speak to questions of corruption. Following that, I will argue that our understanding of the political underpinnings of corruption is not incorrect but is incomplete in three crucial ways.

Political Institutions and Corruption

Political institutions are believed to influence corruption through three channels: by influencing party strength, by establishing lines of accountability, and by creating different levels of political competition.[20] Corruption, it is argued, will be lower when parties are strong because party leaders have longer strategic horizons than individual members and care about long-term returns. Party leaders will therefore curb short-term opportunistic corruption by members in order to establish a brand name that will yield higher political returns in the long run (Manow 2005). If party leaders are corrupt, corruption will still be lower because centralized rent-extraction by strong party leaders is more efficient than decentralized rent-extraction by its members (Shleifer and Vishny 1993; Kang 2002). Political institutions that create strong parties should therefore lead to lower corruption levels relative to systems where institutions create parties too weak to exert such control (Gerring and Thacker 2008, 36).

Both arguments then draw on the insights from the comparative study of institutions to identify which specific institutions weaken or strengthen political parties. Since parties are argued to be stronger in unitary, parliamentary systems with closed-list proportional electoral rules, corruption should be the lowest in countries that have adopted this institutional configuration.[21] By this logic, federal, presidential systems with legislators elected via plurality or open-list proportional rules should create the weakest parties and, hence, should suffer the highest corruption levels. However, empirically, while some studies find that presidential systems do experience higher corruption, others find that they do not.[22] Similarly, some studies find that closed-list electoral systems lead to higher corruption while others do not. Manow (2005) finds evidence that strong parties lead to lower corruption while Panizza (2001) finds that they lead to higher corruption. The evidence linking party strength to corruption directly as well as through its component institutions therefore seems mixed.

Higher accountability to voters is also argued to result in lower corruption. The debate on this link between institutions and corruption seems to hinge on whose accountability is more effective in reducing corruption— that of individual politicians or parties. Voters are believed to hold parties accountable when they are embedded in systems with strong parties but to hold individual legislators accountable when parties are weak. Current theoretical work on this subject has associated both party and individual accountability with both higher and lower corruption. While some have argued that proportional representation electoral (PR) systems with closed lists provide the least amount of individual accountability and should lead to higher corruption (Kunicova and Rose-Ackerman 2005), others have argued that they produce the highest party accountability and should thus produce the lowest corruption (Myerson 1993). Similarly, plurality is argued to be corruption-reducing by some scholars since it provides the highest individual accountability to voters, while others argue that it increases corruption (Birch 2005). Open-list PR systems combine the virtues and vices of plurality and party lists and therefore have been subject to similar debates through their effect on individual incentives to engage in corruption (Kunicova and Rose-Ackerman 2005; Chang and Golden 2004). As discussed above, empirical results on the effects of electoral rules on corruption have also been mixed with studies supporting many contradictory arguments.

Lastly, proponents of political competition argue that systems with institutional structures that lead to higher interbranch and intergovernmental competition should lower corruption.[23] Federal, presidential systems provide the most competition across units of the state and between the executive and legislative branches. Hence, they should provide voters with the most accountability and cultivate a system of political checks and balances across branches and levels by the political agents themselves, thus leading to the lowest corruption levels.[24] Unitary, parliamentary systems, on the other hand, lack robust competition across levels and branches of government and politics and create a unified political structure within both parties and the state. This offers the least accountability to voters and also prevents the development of a robust system of political checks and balances by political agents themselves. Accordingly, countries with these institutions are predicted to experience the highest corruption levels. However, evidence on the competition dynamic has been mixed.[25] Multiple cross-country studies covering most developing countries in the world show that these expectations have not been met in most developing democracies.[26] Moreover, rich developed-country democracies with established market economies show similar variation, casting further doubt on the theoretical foundations of these predictions.[27]

This rich, vigorous debate has yet to be resolved conclusively since the effects of each institution—electoral, executive, and federal—are contested by scholars. Legislatures, which are consistently reported as being sites for corruption, have largely been left out of these analyses (WBES 2005; WEF 2004-05; Transparency International 2009). Though some studies have found that legislative influence has an effect on corruption,[28] little subsequent work has analyzed how the type of legislative institution affects corruption directly or indirectly. This raises the question of whether our current understanding of the political factors driving corruption is incorrect or incomplete. Given the state of the debate, legislatures seem ripe for study as a potential source of corruption in developing democracies.

How is business interest behavior related to corruption?

Business has the means and the motive to engage in influence seeking in developing democracies. Study after study documents their role as one of the primary sources of political funds in these countries.[29] Scholars have therefore begun to fruitfully analyze how the manner of business organization and the strength of business interests relative to the state interact with the political establishment to create different types and levels of corruption (Kang 2002; Johnston 2006). Yet, few studies of corruption analyze whether there are any systemic *institutional* elements that link the patterns of political engagement of business interests with the level and type of corruption observed in a country. On the other hand, the rich literature on special interest behavior that explores patterns of political behavior exhibited by business groups does not examine their links to corruption. A small emerging literature has now begun to explore a specific aspect of this question, that is, the links between political lobbying by business and bureaucratic corruption. Each of these three bodies of work offers some insights relevant to our research question.

The extensive body of work on special interest groups in political science, economics, business, and public policy addresses two questions pertinent for studying corruption: (1) what causes business interests to choose particular types of tools in a given country, and (2) how do business interests choose who the lucky recipient of their resources will be. Special interest groups can employ a variety of resources, including electoral campaign contributions and legislative lobbying during the legislative term using money, information, media campaigns, and demonstrations. They may choose to target their resources to individual legislators, party leaders, the executive the judiciary, the bureaucracy, or subnational actors of any of these types. Their specific venue choice can depend on a range of political and nonpolitical factors. Political institutions are one of the key political factors in influencing decisions about venue and resource choices (Hall and Deardorff 2006; Lowery 2007; Bennedsen and Feldman 2002a, 2002b, 2006a, 2002; Holyoke 2003).

Arguments linking electoral rules to lobbying behavior have focused on the incentives these rules provide politicians to develop party-based or individual political reputations for advancement (Carey and Shugart 1995).[30] These rules, it is argued, establish incentives for party- or individual-centered behavior by legislators in the legislature (Cain, Ferejohn, and Fiorina 1987; Katz and Sala 1996) and, hence, provide the foundation for understanding the role of electoral institutions in establishing legislative lobbying behavior. According to institutional theory, PR systems should motivate party-directed lobbying by business groups while plurality rules should cause legislator-directed lobbying (Grossman and Helpman 2001; Persson and Tabellini 2002; Naoi and Krauss 2009).

Arguments based on executive-legislative regime types argue that parties in parliamentary regimes can exert strong party discipline in the legislature and hence should attract lobbyist efforts, whereas a lack of similar party abilities should lead groups in presidential regimes to lobby individual legislators instead (Cowhey and McCubbins 1993; Rockman and Weaver 1992). Groups should be more likely to lobby politicians in presidential systems and bureaucrats in parliamentary ones because the fused political power of the executive branch and the legislature in parliamentary systems leads to relatively more delegation.[31] Additionally, scholars have argued that centralized legislatures should attract party-focused lobbying for reasons of high party discipline and that decentralized legislatures should lead to individual-focused lobbying (Bennedson and Feldman 2002a, 2002b). However, these theories leave unexplored the institutional mechanisms that lead to such centralization. Finally, it is argued that groups in their lobbying efforts are more likely to use information in presidential systems and money in parliamentary systems.[32] Empirical evidence on lobbying behaviors across countries, however, does not support these predictions on lobbying behaviors. Lobbies in both parliamentary and presidential systems are found to exhibit considerable variation in their choice of venues and tools.[33] These results point to potential omitted variables.

These studies do not extend their arguments to the analysis of corruption caused by lobbying. So we do not know, for example, whether lobbying parties in parliamentary systems is more likely to lead to higher or lower corruption than lobbying individuals in presidential systems; nor do we know whether more lobbying of bureaucrats in parliamentary systems will lead to higher or lower corruption compared to presidential systems. A recent strand of work has begun looking at one piece of this larger puzzle by studying the relationship between political lobbying and bureaucratic corruption across countries (Harsstad and Svenssen 2009; Campos and Giovannoni 2008; Damania, Fredriksson, and Muthukumara 2004).[34] The mixed empirical evidence found on the nature of this relationship further emphasizes the importance of understanding the larger context in which these specific behavioral choices are embedded.

These findings on lobbying and corruption invite an integrated theoretical framework that includes an analysis of how particular strategic lobbying choices, such as those regarding who is lobbied and how, might be linked to the observed patterns and/or levels of corruption. As I discuss next, any such analysis would be incomplete without addressing how variation in the institutions that are arguably the most relevant for the calculus of policy-seeking business groups—legislative rules on policymaking—affects lobbying and corruption.

What is missing?

Despite a general consensus that business involvement in politics can be a significant source of political corruption in developing democracies, there is still little theoretical work that systematically relates institutional features of a country's political system, especially its policy system, with corruption-inducing business behavior. There is also scarce comparative analysis of variations in the timing and patterns of business contributions across different stages of the political cycle or of their rationale for doing so. The neglect of legislative institutions in this context goes to the heart of arguments relating corruption levels and lobbying to political institutions.

Legislatures in developing countries have traditionally been characterized as marginal or rubber stamp institutions and discounted as effective sources of political or policy power.[35] This stylization has led to three important consequences for the study of corruption. *First*, legislative lobbying has been dismissed as an influential or popular mode of political engagement by business interests in developing democracies. Consequently, it has not been treated as a potentially significant source of corruption in these countries either. The empirical evidence we have, however, contradicts these stylizations. Studies show that business interests in developing countries frequently attempt to exert influence through their legislatures (World Bank 2000, 2005; World Economic Forum 2004–2005), and that legislatures are consistently identified as being among the most corrupt institutions by both business firms (World Bank 2000, 2005; World Economic Forum 2004–2005) and citizens (Transparency International 2004). Figure 1.1 shows the distribution of results from a global survey of 6,099 firms in 104 countries asking firms how much influence they felt they exerted on the national legislature (World Bank 2000). As can be seen clearly, the distribution of influence levels reported by firms in developing country democracies (represented by the non-OECD category bar in fig. 1.1) is comparable to those in developed country democracies (the OECD category bar). These figures collectively suggest that the neglect of legislative politics and legislative institutions has been an expensive analytical choice in understanding both corruption and lobbying in developing democracies.

To see how legislative influence varies with corruption levels, figure 1.2 combines this data with the corruption scores assigned by the international corruption watchdog agency Transparency International (TI) for a representative sample of countries. Rather than being consistently low, figure 1.2 shows that there is considerable variation in how much success firms have enjoyed in exerting such influence across developing countries. The evidence also shows that the relationship with corruption is complex. Countries where firms exert higher legislative influence are not necessarily the more corrupt ones. Therefore, corruption is not *necessarily* associated with legislative lobbying in developing democracies. These findings invite inquiry into business engagement with legislative politics and policymaking. In this book, I put forward a theoretical framework that explains why we see this variation in the relationship between lobbying and corruption.

Second, the assumption of marginal or rubber stamp legislatures has also led to the dubious assumption that legislative rules do not significantly affect party strength in developing democracies. Studies of party strength have focused largely instead on electoral rules, executive regime types, and federalism and ignored the tremendous variation to be found in legislative rules in developing democracies (Shugart and Carey 1992). Recent scholarship, however, shows that legislative rules affect the timing, substance, implementation, success, and consequences of policy.[36] Furthermore, by influencing whether party leaders can constrain the manner and degree to which members engage with policymaking, as well as with their parties, they also influence the political foundations of party strength (Laver 2006; Cheibub 2007).

The presence of party coalitions in politics strengthens both channels of impact by changing the political costs to members of disobeying the party. Legislative rules can be used to enforce policy bargains with coalition partners as well as to sustain coalition partners in government.[37] Whether these dynamics favor party leaders or their members

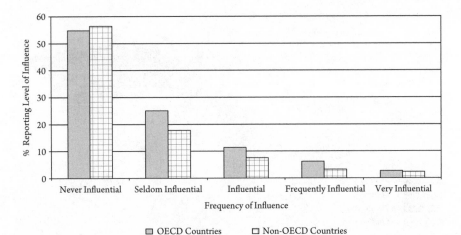

Figure 1.1. *Business Influence on Policy in the National Legislature: Developed and Developing Countries (6,099 Firms)*
Source: WBES 2000 Survey Question # 10—When a new law, rule, regulation, or decree is being discussed that could have a substantial impact on your business, how much influence does your firm typically have at the national level of government on the content of that law, rule, regulation or decree? Would you say "very influential," "frequently influential," "influential," "seldom influential," or "never influential"?

will depend on the nature of the rules themselves. Current theoretical arguments that relate institutions to corruption and lobbying through their impact on party strength, therefore, face the possibility of a serious omitted variable bias in their analysis. This could be causing incorrect inferences about the impact of other institutions on party strength and, hence, on corruption. I explicitly address this issue by considering how specific legislative rules governing policymaking affect the interactions between party leaders and backbenchers and thus influence party ability to forge discipline in the legislature.

Third, as a consequence of assuming legislative impotence, scholars have strongly emphasized the importance of bureaucratic rather than legislative lobbying by business as a source of high corruption *especially* in developing democracies.[38] However, as recent work in the delegation literature has argued, the degree of bureaucratic and judicial policy delegation is also a function of institutional design. Specifically, these scholars have argued that the levels and types of delegation are also a function of *legislative* institutions.[39] The choice of the bureaucracy as an alternative lobbying venue is thus embedded in the context of legislative institutions as well. In some contexts, business lobbies may act successfully as fire alarms for bureaucratic corruption thus lowering it, whereas in others they may be co-opted into their rent-seeking networks thus raising corruption levels.

Similarly, the influence of the judiciary over policy and its attractiveness as a target or venue for business lobbies will be embedded in its institutional context as well.[40] Without embedding these delegated relationships in their institutional context, we cannot say how bureaucratic or judicial corruption will be affected by business lobbying of political principals in a given country. The behavior of these public officials

a

Country	Average Level of Influence Over Legislature	Transparency International Corruption Perception Index
Argentina	2.43	3.5
Brazil	2.53	3.9
China	2.82	3.1
Chile	2.63	7.4
India	2.89	2.8
Indonesia	3.19	1.7
Malaysia	3.28	4.8
Mexico	2.52	3.3
Philippines	3.75	2.8
Poland	1.94	4.1
Russia	2.10	2.1
Turkey	2.37	3.8

b

Figure 1.2. (a) and (b) *Transparency International's Corruption Perceptions Index [CPI] for 12 Selected Countries in 2000: 1 (high) to 10 (low).*

defines the extent to which the larger society, outside of the political and economic elite, is subjected to corrupt practices. Therefore, it links political corruption to general corruption and is important for understanding the *extent* of corruption in any country. The theoretical framework presented in this book addresses these concerns by embedding delegation relationships in their institutional context.

Lastly, this literature faces considerable empirical challenges. The empirical literature on corruption suffers from a problem of observational equivalence due to a lack of micro-level data on causal mechanisms. Rarely have institutional theories of corruption presented systematic evidence directly documenting the causal mechanism at work. Such micro-level behavioral data are essential for corroborating any specific causal story linking institutions to corruption. Unfortunately, such behavioral data has been scarce and thus rarely used in analyses.

In the comparative context, comparable data on lobbying is extremely scarce. The paucity of basic data on institutional knowledge of business groups, their interactions with the political establishment, and their decision-making calculus poses a significant hurdle to understanding lobbying behavior and its link with political corruption. The Business Environment and Enterprise Surveys (BEEPS) and the World Business Environment Surveys (WBES), conducted by the European Bank for Reconstruction and Development and the World Bank, have made a strong beginning in this direction by collecting some characteristics of membership and some interactions with institutions. However, there are significant gaps on important basic political behaviors such as who is lobbied, how frequently, at what stage of policy or with what resources.

Many facets of lobbying are fundamentally harder to observe and document and present a tougher challenge to researchers. As Johnston (2006, 10) summarizes, "At the elite level, a range of informal favors for contributors and an active trade in access lies beyond the reach of any conceivable, much less desirable, system of disclosure." Business interest groups may not wish to reveal the intensity or details of their lobbying campaigns even when using perfectly legal means to do so in order to preserve their strategic advantage over their rivals. Illegal behavior is, of course, kept even more secret. There are single country studies that analyze some of these behaviors but unfortunately their data is not comparable.[41] To the best of my knowledge, there is no cross-country dataset that records in detail the political interactions of business interests with the political establishment. This book addresses some of these issues by using data from a survey of business groups in Brazil and India that provides exactly such micro-level evidence on their lobbying patterns.

To summarize, the neglect of legislative institutions in the corruption literature has led to the neglect of legislative lobbying as a source of corruption, a potentially incomplete assessment of the sources of party strength and its affect on political corruption, and an undertheorized relationship between political corruption and administrative and judicial corruption due to the neglect of the institutional foundations of political delegation. Furthermore, empirical testing of the micro-mechanisms generating corruption has been less frequent and testing of the micro-mechanisms underlying lobbying have been very rare. Therefore we lack a theoretical framework that frames the institutional contribution to the relationship between legislative lobbying and corruption as well as empirical studies testing it. In the next sections, I first preview how this book addresses some of these concerns by presenting the central theoretical argument offered in this book and then discuss the research design I have adopted to test its predictions.

THE ARGUMENT IN BRIEF

In this book I explore theoretically and empirically, the links between the incentive structures created by legislative institutions, the strategic lobbying decisions made by business groups, and the corruption level in a political system in a comparative context. I present a theoretical framework arguing that the identity of the political player targeted by business interest groups in the legislature is a significant determinant of the level of corruption and that legislative institutions influence who this target will be. Specifically, I argue that countries with legislative rules that create party-focused lobbying will experience higher corruption compared to countries where business interests lobby individual legislators.

When legislative rules give parties the prerogative to set the agenda and control the introduction of amendments, parties rather than individual legislators control the timing and substance of bills. When these rights are supplemented with the ability to expel party members for voting and acting against party wishes, parties control the voting process as well, thus establishing firm party control over the entire policymaking process. I refer to countries with these types of legislative institutions as *party-focused systems* and countries where legislative institutions give individuals these policymaking privileges as *individual-focused systems*. Business interest groups, who are rational actors, will respond to the political locus of policy control they observe in their country. Therefore, they will lobby parties at all stages of the political cycle in order to win influence over policy outcomes in party-focused systems, and they will lobby individual legislators at all stages in individual-focused systems.

Party-focused lobbying results in higher and more pervasive corruption due to four dynamics. First, parties need to raise more funds than legislators, and second, they prefer fungible money over other political resources. These two demand-side mechanisms raise the relative demand for corrupt money in party-focused systems. Two supply side dynamics—party ability to capture state institutions such as the bureaucracy and the judiciary via legislative delegation and to protect corrupt financing practices—increase party ability to supply their higher demands. The result is higher and more pervasive corruption in countries where legislative rules allow parties to wield policy influence in the legislature. Legislative rules governing political control over the policy process in a country, therefore, link the incentives of political players and business interest groups through mechanisms that directly affect the levels of corruption we observe there.

The book's main theoretical argument therefore leads to three main hypotheses. Party control over agenda-setting, amendments, and voting should all lead to higher corruption levels. Table 1.1 summarizes the main hypotheses presented and subsequently tested in this book.

This allows us to explain how legislative variation across electoral and executive regimes affects the incentives those institutions provide for corruption as well. Studies of corruption consistently report that corruption is higher and more pervasive in Argentina than in Taiwan for example, both presidential democracies.[42] The argument here provides one key reason for Argentina's higher level of corruption. Legislative rules on policymaking favor parties in Argentina but individual legislators in Taiwan.[43] Even in a young democracy like Taiwan, which has a historical legacy of strong parties, this has increasingly motivated business lobbies to move their lobbying strategies away from targeting political parties and toward directly lobbying legislators.[44] In Argentina, which also has a presidential system, party dominance through legislative poli-

Table 1.1. Testable Hypotheses: Lobbying, Institutions, and Interest Group Behavior

Lobbying Venues and Corruption Levels	
H_0	In countries where interest groups lobby parties, corruption levels should be higher relative to where they lobby individuals
Legislative Rules and Lobbying behavior—Tested for Brazil and India	
$H1_A$	When parties control agenda-setting, groups will be more likely to lobby parties
$H2_A$	When parties control introduction of amendments, groups will be more likely to lobby parties
$H3_A$	When parties control postelection chamber membership, groups will be more likely to lobby parties
Legislative Rules and Corruption—Tested for 64 countries, 1982–2004 and for Brazil and India	
$H1_B$	Where parties control agenda-setting, corruption levels should be higher
$H2_B$	Where parties control introduction of amendments, corruption levels should be higher
$H3_B$	Where parties control postelection chamber membership, corruption levels should be higher

cymaking procedures has created and sustained patterns of party-focused lobbying.[45] Thus, legislative lobbying is contributing significantly toward the higher corruption levels in Argentina.

RESEARCH DESIGN

In order to test the hypotheses presented in this book, I needed data that operationalized both the dependent variable (national corruption levels) and the independent variables (the choice of political venue by business groups across countries, whether or not legislative rules give parties control over agenda-setting, introduction of amendments, and the ability to expel dissidents who vote against them). Cross-country corruption data has been collected by Transparency International, the International Country Risk Group, and the World Bank for the last two decades. However, there did not exist any cross-country data recording who business groups target politically in their lobbying efforts for any year. Similarly, no dataset recorded the details of rules on agenda-setting, amendments, and party ability to expel members for antiparty voting across countries for any time period.

To address these formidable challenges, I employed a two-pronged research strategy. I constructed a new dataset on the relevant legislative rules for sixty-four developing democracies from 1984 to 2004 directly from the primary procedural documents of various chambers. This gave me the ability to test the theoretical links between legislative institutions and corruption for a large set of countries. This strategy maximizes the robustness of the results and ensures that they are not subject to any biases resulting from a specific choice of cases. Furthermore, the careful use of control variables operationalizing electoral rules, federalism, executive regimes, and socioeconomic factors allows me to assess the theoretical validity and contribution of legislative rules to corruption in the context of alternative explanations.

I then combined this analysis of the *macro*-level links between institutional rules and corruption levels with the analysis of interest group level survey data from two theoretically crucial cases to directly test the *micro*-level causal mechanism of lobbying. Table 2.2 summarizes this strategy. As this table illustrates, this strategy requires using micro-level behavioral data from carefully selected cases to address the problem of observational equivalence and offer evidence that institutionally motivated lobbying strategies, rather than other factors, are driving the results on corruption levels. To get these data I selected two cases using Mills's "method-of-similarity" and conducted surveys of business groups there using a multistage, stratified, clustered, random sampling design. Brazil, with 158 groups surveyed, represents the category of countries with individual-focused legislative institutional rules, whereas India, with 179 groups surveyed, represents the institutionally party-focused category of countries. Chapter 3 provides all the details of this research strategy and case selection.

In addition to the survey data, I also used process tracing to carefully assess the empirical accuracy of the causal mechanism underlying my theoretical arguments for these cases. Evidence from more than one hundred open-ended interviews of government officials, political parties, politicians, journalists, scholars, and leaders of business and labor groups from Brazil and India is also used to corroborate the causal story that is posited in the book's theoretical chapter along with secondary evidence from a variety of sources.

WHY THE FOCUS ON DEVELOPING COUNTRY DEMOCRACIES?

As frequent and public political scandals testify, political corruption is hardly unique to developing country democracies. So why focus only on this set of countries in this book? There are a number of reasons relating to the political environment in developing democracies that guided this decision.[46] As scholars have argued, institutions matter for explaining corruption in developed democracies as well.[47] However, the level of corruption and the challenge it poses to society in developing democracies is very different. Here I focus on a select few differences in institutions, parties, interest groups, and exogenous factors that pertain directly to the analysis undertaken here. However, there are more reasons as well.

Institutions in developing democracies are typically at various stages of consolidation. This affects key aspects of the behaviors of political and economic elites and the relationships between them. For example, unconsolidated legal systems create personal and systemic political risks unique to developing democracies. The stakes of losing elections are much higher in countries that have politicized police and legal systems. Opponents may find that the physical and financial safety of their families and friends is jeopardized with no recourse to neutral state institutions. This changes the nature of the goals of office, the manner in which campaigns are run, and the nature and magnitude of funds required for campaigns. Illegal political tactics stemming from such concerns are the norm in many developing democracies but are rare in other democracies. Furthermore, these tactics affect the relationship between political elites and public institutions. While delegation decisions by the legislature to the bureaucracy and the judiciary may be dominated by concerns about policy expertise and information in developed democracies, in developing democracies these decisions may be substantially driven instead by security and financial considerations.

Another example that illustrates the difference in the social stakes involved is the threat to regime survival. While corruption may lead to changes in the governing elites or the rules governing democratic competition in developed country democracies, it does not pose a systemic risk to the survival of the democratic regime itself in these countries. Their institutional and economic capacity allows them to handle these problems without resulting in the regime's failure. In contrast, in the environment of high political uncertainty and weak institutional capacity found in many developing democracies, corruption can pose a substantial systemic risk to the regime itself.[48] In the past, such disillusionment with corrupt democratic performance facilitated military coups such as those in Brazil in 1964, Ghana in 1979. and Pakistan in 1999. In the contemporary world, the extraordinary street battles Thai citizens waged in 2008 demanding an appointed legislature to replace their corrupt elected one demonstrates that the potential of corruption to cause democratic regression and social chaos in these countries is always present (Financial Times, September 3, 2008).[49] Thus, the weakness of institutions affects many dimensions of politics in these countries and requires specific analysis.

The second set of factors that demand a different analysis relate to the nature and operation of parties in developing countries. Not only do developing democracies exhibit a much wider range of party types (Diamond and Gunther 2001), parties there also operate under very different legal regulations. While parties in most developing democracies must operate under the constraints of constitutional laws that govern most aspects of their formation and operation, such regulation is rare in rich democracies (Janda 2005). These factors, among many, suggest that political parties in these countries might be strategizing in political and competitive environments that are fundamentally different than those found in developed country democracies. Third, interest group communities in developing democracies come from a wider range of political and economic experiences and legacies, and they operate in an information and media context quite different from that of developed countries. This can affect the range of tactics they might consider, the value of insider and outsider lobbying tactics, and the salience of public opinion.[50] Combined with the differences in institutions and political competition, these factors define a strategic environment that is distinct from that of developed democracies.

Finally, factors such as low income and external intervention are specific only to developing democracies. Low income affects state ability to subsidize political expenses, raises the incentive for all public officials to engage in corruption, and creates underfi-nanced regulatory institutions. The active engagement and intervention of interna-tional institutions such as the IMF and the World Bank in the design of key domestic institutions such as the judiciary and the central bank affects the strategic incentives of both political and economic elites to engage with these institutions as well. In the con-cluding chapter of the book, I assess the insights this book offers to see which may be applied fruitfully to developed countries. However, the analysis here is restricted to developing democracies only.

In the conclusion, I also discuss how the political dynamics underlying corrupt behavior and business lobbying may be very different in developing countries with authoritarian political systems. Authoritarian countries display considerable institu-tional variation, especially in the type of institutions they adopt, the power these insti-tutions are given formally, and the powers they genuinely command (Wright 2008; Przeworski and Gandhi 2004). Similarly, political parties and constitutions in these countries, if they exist, may serve very different functions (Boix and Slovik 2009; Johnston 2006). While many of these countries have adopted legislatures and formal procedures to pass policy legislation, the nature of their influence is poorly under-stood. Therefore, despite the deceptive similarity of institutional forms in many of these countries, the differences in the political calculations of leaders and followers are significant enough to require a very different analytical framework to study them (Chang and Golden 2010). It is for these reasons that I chose to focus only on the analysis of corruption in developing country democracies in this book.

BOOK ORGANIZATION

The book is organized as follows. In chapter 2, I develop the book's central theoretical framework, which links the legislative structure of policymaking in a country with the incentives to engage in high or low corruption. I provide the strategic context for the importance of business funds in political finance. In doing so, I first analyze why key legislative institutions—agenda-setting, introduction of amendments, and the ability to expel anti-whip voters—drive the political venue choice of special interests attempt-ing to influence policy outcomes. I then analyze the four dynamics of party politics that link party-focused lobbying to higher corruption levels. I formulate the hypotheses linking legislative institutions to corruption levels and put them in the context of alternative theoretical hypotheses. Finally, I present the research design adopted for empirical testing of these hypotheses in the context of available data.

Chapters 3, 4, and 5 present the case study analysis that tests the causal mechanism directly. Chapter 3 discusses the methodology employed in selecting the appropriate cases and the types of within-case analysis undertaken for testing the causal mecha-nism at the micro-level. Next, I discuss in detail the institutional design that makes India representative of the category of party-focused systems and Brazil representative of individual-focused systems along with the limitations posed by these cases. In chap-ter 4, I test the first set of hypotheses relating legislative institutions to lobbying behav-iors. I first outline the sampling design and sampling frame used for collecting data on lobbying, political corruption, and corruption in Brazil and India and present some sample characteristics. I then use a combination of data from this survey, open-ended interviews, and process tracing of legislative bills in each country to test the hypotheses that parties should be lobbied in India and legislators in Brazil.

Chapter 5 tests the second set of hypotheses relating legislative lobbying behaviors to corruption levels. I use data from the two country surveys; open-ended interviews; secondary sources; and the ICRG, TI, and WB surveys to test whether business lobbying leads to higher political and overall corruption in India relative to Brazil and to all individual-focused countries in the sample. I also provide evidence on the conditional nature of the strength of the political links between political and overall corruption and show that these are stronger in party-focused India.

In chapter 6, I report results from the large-n analysis that is employed to evaluate the three hypotheses regarding the impact of legislative rules on corruption for a sample of sixty-four developing country democracies from 1984 to 2004. I discuss in detail the operationalization of the independent variables and then present the statistical results obtained from testing the effects of three legislative rules on corruption. I illustrate the substantive effect of party control of agenda-setting, amendments, and voting on bills on corruption. The results from the large-n empirical analysis provide robust support for the broader implications derived from my theoretical arguments.

In the final chapter, I summarize the theoretical, empirical, and methodological contributions that this book makes to our understanding of corruption and lobbying in developing countries and discuss some of its limitations. I then discuss some of the consequences of these findings for the study of corruption, institutions, interest group politics, political parties, and the impact of globalization on domestic politics. I conclude by recognizing that this is one of the first systematic, comparative study of the relationship between lobbying and corruption and that a fruitful area of future research would be to develop a more unified theory that incorporates the incentives generated by both electoral and legislative institutions.

2

INSTITUTIONS, LOBBYING, AND CORRUPTION:
A THEORETICAL FRAMEWORK

"It is important to clarify the policy-making role of legislature because the strength of a nation's legislature is often viewed as directly related to the strength of that nation's commitment to democratic procedures. The connection, though simplistic, is understandable because the legislature, more than any other political institutions, stands at the confluence between democratic theory and democratic practice." Olson and Mezey (1991, xi–xii)

". . .the potential of policy prescriptions to deliver better outcomes ultimately depends, to an important extent, on the *quality* of the policymaking process through which policies are discussed, approved, and implemented." Spiller, Stein and Tommasi (2009, 2)

The above statements stress the importance of legislatures as institutions that establish the very nature of a country's politics and wield the ability to improve the lives of its citizens through their policymaking prowess. Unfortunately, legislatures in most developing democracies have rarely reached these lofty yet essential goals. The typical experience in these countries is reflected instead in the following characterizations of legislative policymaking. A Ugandan MP lamented how parliamentarians were failing to represent their voters, "candidates are literally prisoners of the sponsoring individuals, interest groups or corporate organizations who they expect to do their bidding once they are in parliament . . . such politicians vote according to the wishes of their masters" (quoted in Bryan and Baer 2005, 19). In another example, Romanian ex–Prime Minister Mugur Isarescu commented on the abuse of one the most important legislative policy powers of parliament by parliamentary parties in Romania in saying, "The situation of the budget is devastating. Practically, there are no budgets anymore. There are only exceptions, facilities, tax-exemptions—an overwhelming corruption that originates in the very text of laws. And this is because everything is discretionary, everything is nego-tiable" (quoted in OSI 2002, 509).

These pessimistic statements reflect a widely held view of policymaking in devel-oping democracies—that it has been captured successfully by business interests with the welfare of citizens being only a distant concern for parties and politicians.[1] Yet, as figures 1.1 and 1.2 (a) and (b) in chapter 1 and the report of bribery by firms in the WEF (2003, 2005) surveys illustrate, this is not the reality in all developing countries. Busi-ness groups can exert policy influence without engaging in extensive corruption. Na-tions can benefit from the technical expertise and performance accountability that business interests provide without incurring the heavy cost of endemic corruption. This raises the question of why some countries seem more prone to corruption through legislative lobbying by business interests. As discussed in the introduction, current studies of lobbying and corruption have largely talked past each other and thus have not addressed this question directly, theoretically or empirically.

In this chapter I present a theoretical framework that (a) analyzes how differences in the lobbying strategies of business interest groups emerge from differences in their legislative institutions, (b) establishes the link between these institutionally inspired lobbying strategies and patterns of corrupt behaviors, and (c) analyzes which of these patterns is more likely to lead to higher political and aggregate corruption. I will argue that countries with legislative institutions that incentivize lobbying directed at polit-ical parties will experience higher corruption than those countries that incentivize lobbying directed at individual legislators. This is the central hypothesis of this book.

This hypothesis is based on a two-step analysis of the institutional drivers of legisla-tive lobbying behavior and the link between lobbying choices and corruption. Figures 2.1(a) and (b) summarize this argument. In order to influence policy, business lobbies target the political principals they perceive as exercising influence over the legislative policy process. I argue that when legislative rules on agenda-setting, amendments, and voting expulsions give parties control over the policy process, they incentivize business lobbies to lobby parties for policy influence. Party-focused lobbying, however, results in higher and more pervasive corruption due to four dynamics. Two demand-side mechanisms—parties need to raise more funds, and they strongly prefer money over other political resources—raises their relative demand for corrupt money. Two sup-ply-side dynamics—parties' ability to capture state institutions such as the bureau-cracy and the judiciary via legislative delegation, and their ability to protect corrupt financing practices—increase the ability of parties to supply their demands in party-focused systems. The result should be higher and more pervasive corruption in coun-tries where legislative rules allow parties to wield policy influence in the legislature.

This chapter is divided into four sections to present this argument. In section 1, I put the potential significance of business lobbying in corruption in context by assessing how important business funds are in financing politics in developing democracies. This discussion also demonstrates why corruption in developing democracies requires an analytical framework distinct from that needed in developed democracies. In sec-tion 2, I analyze how legislative institutions influence the lobbying strategies of policy-seeking business interests. I present three hypotheses linking legislative institutions to lobbying strategies. In section 3, I present four dynamics that link party-focused lobbying patterns to higher corruption and then present the hypotheses linking lobbying patterns to corruption and also linking legislative institutions to corruption. In section 4, I present the research design adopted to test the hypotheses in this book. Chapters 3, 4, and 5 will present evidence from two case studies, and chapter 6 will present empirical evidence from the statistical analysis of a 64-country, 20-year time series cross section (TSCS) dataset to test these hypotheses. They strongly support the theoretical framework presented in this chapter.

(I)   THE STRATEGIC POLITICAL IMPORTANCE OF BUSINESS FUNDS

In order to understand whether legislative lobbying by business interests can be a significant source of corruption in developing democracies, it is instructive to consider the financial context in which business interests offer policymakers financial inducements to influence policy on their behalf. If business funds comprise only a small share of political expenditures in developing country democracies, then their contribution to corruption in these countries will be small as well. As I will discuss below however studies show that this is not the case. Business funds are typically indispensable to the conduct of political campaigns and the management of political office for both parties and politicians in all these countries. Indeed, in many countries, business interests are the most significant and reliable source of funds for parties and politicians. Therefore, policymakers in these countries have strong incentives to use legislative policy influence, which is highly valued by business interests, to raise these much-needed funds.

Both political parties and their members rely on the same set of sources—voters, interest groups, and the state—for necessary funds. Parties can tap into two additional sources of revenue: member subscriptions to their party and party-run businesses. These sources can be broadly classified into categories of public financing, business financing, and others. Members can sometimes rely on party funds. In the absence of reliable global data on political finance, recent studies have used a combination of legally filed reports, elite surveys, and interviews to identify the following trends on the relative importance of these various financial sources to political parties and politicians.[2]

First, the importance of member dues as a source of revenue is declining and has ceased to be significant in most polities around the world.[3] For example, in Bulgaria in 1999, member dues only provided 0.078% and 4% of total income for the leading parties there. In Estonia in 2000, they ranged from 1.81% to 7.15%, while in the same year in Hungary the Socialist Party received the highest amount in membership dues at 3.27% of total income (Walecki 2003, 77). Party levies imposed on members do not yield a significant share of resources for most parties, though leftist parties can sometimes be exceptions to this.[4] Party-run businesses are not a common source of significant revenues in many countries as parties are generally restricted in the profitable activities they are permitted to undertake (Bryan and Baer 2005; USAID 2003).

Second, voter contributions have been equally dismal around the developing world and have been declining as well for many reasons including poverty (Nassmacher

2003; Pinto-Duschinsky 2001). As Johnston (2006, 3) points out, "Parties in these societies typically confront pervasive scarcity." In Romania, for example, this has meant
that parties traditionally have not even tried to collect membership dues (Walecki
2003, 79). Distrust of political parties and politicians further inhibits public participation (IDEA 2003, 36; Bryan and Baer 2005, 15). Duverger's (1954, 63) idealist concep-
tion of mass parties as being "essentially based upon the subscription by its members"
is therefore not a feasible reality today in most of these countries.

The *third* trend identified is that public funding has largely failed both to reduce the
levels of financing raised from other sources and lessen the practice of resorting to illegal financing options in these countries.[5] In a detailed study of 111 countries, scholars
found that only 64% of developed and developing countries had *any* level of direct or
indirect public financing directed toward political agents, whether they were parties or
individual politicians (Austin and Tjernström 2003, 187–189). These numbers over-
state the role of state financing since many countries with these rules have been too
financially strapped to actually dispense significant state funds or sometimes any
funds at all (Nassmacher 2003, 25; IFES 2002; Pinto-Duschinsky 2001; van Biezen
2000). For example, of the 14 countries in Africa which had public funding rules on
the book, only 4 were in a fiscal position to afford providing it in significant amounts
(Saffu 2003, 25).[6] Furthermore, the various constraints typically placed on the use of
public funds and the strategic political perception of them as supplements to rather
than substitutes for private funds (van Biezen 2000) reduces their strategic value.[7] For
example, in Guatemala and Honduras, state funding was estimated only at about 5%
and 10% of all expenditures incurred by parties (Casas-Zamora 2004). In-kind subsidies, typically offered in terms of media time, do not reduce such demands significantly because free time may be offered on state media with low ratings and also
because campaigning may still be done largely by face-to-face contact (Bryan and Baer
2005; Casas-Zamora 2004; Pinto-Duschinsky 2001).

At the same time that member and voter financing levels have been falling, legal expenses to run campaigns for office and to maintain tenure in office have been steadily
rising globally.[8] The trends discussed above demonstrate the scarcity of legitimate
sources of funding to finance *legal* political expenditures. Additionally, as I discuss in
detail later, there are a wide range of illegal political tactics that are routinely employed
by political parties and politicians in many of these countries in order to survive and
succeed politically during campaigns and while holding office. These tactics, which
include vote buying, bribing electoral officers, bribing legislators, hiring thugs, and so
forth are blatantly illegal, expensive, and specific to developing country democracies.
Financing these illegal practices requires considerable levels of untraceable funds.
Thus they exacerbate tremendously the incentives to raise illegal funds by any means
in developing democracies.

This raises the question of where the money to supply these increasing expenses is
coming from, especially in countries where there are comparatively fewer and poorer
legitimate sources of fundraising. The last clear trend that these studies identify gives
us the answer—the increasing salience of business money in developing country democracies. Business interests possess and can provide to the political establishment

many politically valuable resources including money, votes, technical expertise, volunteers, a public profile, and media access.[9] However, when it comes to the ability to supply money, business groups dominate other interest groups and financial sources in society.[10]

Based on a growing body of evidence, the consensus that has emerged among scholars, practitioners, and observers is that business interests have become increasingly important to political finance in most countries and dominant in many.[11] Bryan and Baer (2005, 10) report that 16% of all elites in their 22-country survey reported that business was the single biggest source of funds for the political establishment in their countries. This made business the second most important source of funding identified by respondents after the *sum total* of revenue raised through membership dues, party-owned businesses, levies on party office holders, and donations by party members (34% of respondents). In numerous countries such as Nepal, Zambia, Bulgaria, Bangladesh, Latvia, South Africa, and Indonesia, business funds dominate political financing.[12] Ukraine and Indonesia provide illustrative cases. In Indonesia, 64% of 2004 campaign funds for Megawati Sukarnoputri's presidential bid came from the business sector (Mietzner 2007, 248). In Ukraine, leaving aside the Communist parties, the share of corporate contributions to party incomes in 1999 ranged from an astonishing low of 80% to a high of 99.99% (Walecki 2003, 81).

Studies of business elites confirm their high participation in political financing. In a global survey of business executives (World Economic Forum 2003), the authors found that 41% of business leaders reported that illegal political donations were common or fairly common and, only 18% had never donated to political parties and politicians. Furthermore, these trends seem set to continue and in many cases gain strength in the context of widespread poverty and increasing political costs. For example, Saffu (2003, 23) observes for Zambia that even when member donations are forthcoming, the realities of political financing ensure business dominance: "But, useful as such donations were, they usually fell short of the huge sums required to put up a credible show in elections. The really huge donations, counted in thousands and millions of dollars in an economic environment of desperate poverty where gross domestic product (GDP) per capita might be only USD 300, or even less, could be made only by business tycoons." As the trends above indicate, this reality is common across most developing democracies. Evidence from studies of political, civic, and economic elites, therefore, all confirm the trend that business is increasingly becoming the backbone of the political financing system in developing democracies.

Collectively, these trends suggest strongly that the political rewards for generous business donors in these countries should be very high. As the 2009 Transparency International Report states, "Companies whose turnover dwarfs the national income of entire countries command a level of financial firepower that it is impossible for any other voice to match in the competition for political visibility and persuasion" (Zinnbauer 2009, 33). Saffu (2003, 23) summarizes the attitude of business donors in Zambia: "There was a marked tendency on the part of the tycoon donors to regard politics as business by other means and political parties as appropriate investments." Similarly, business interests in Kenya stated that "politics is a 'Savings Club': you get what you put in" (Africa Confidential 1997).

Therefore, if a country suffers from high corruption, it behooves us to take a deep look at the incentive structure that exists for business interaction with the political community there. Conversely, if a country does not experience high corruption despite business lobbying, we need to understand the factors that constrained the business sector from breeding corruption. In the next section, I analyze the first part of this puzzle by considering how legislative rules create two distinct lobbying patterns that are connected to different patterns of corruption. In the section after that, I complete the causal chain by analyzing which of these lobbying strategies leads to higher and more pervasive corruption. Collectively, these two steps allow me to specify the institutional conditions under which, ceteris paribus, we should expect to see higher corruption levels due to the behavior of business lobbies.

(II) LEGISLATIVE INSTITUTIONS AND INTEREST GROUP STRATEGIES

As Huber and Shipan (2002, 1) state, "Legislative statutes that politicians adopt provide the most important and definitive mechanism for defining policy on most issues." Since interest groups engage in lobbying primarily to influence policy outcomes, they should be lobbying the players they perceive can successfully exert influence over the passage of bills in the legislature (Hall and Deardoff 2006; Baumgartner 2002). This question of venue choice for interest groups thus boils down to analyzing *who* is able to influence policy outcomes successfully in the legislature under different institutional conditions. In this section, I first analyze the theoretical arguments and empirical evidence in the literature on institutions and comparative lobbying that address this question to identify the missing pieces of this puzzle. Next, I proceed to argue that *legislative* institutions are crucial in determining whether or not parties command the discipline required to exert such legislative policy influence and hence in determining whether they are targeted by business lobbies seeking policy influence. I then focus on three specific legislative rules crucial to policy influence—agenda-setting, amendments, and voting.

Parties will be influential policymakers in the legislature when they can exercise discipline over the legislative behavior of their assembly members. Party discipline is defined to exist in a party when "followers regularly accept and act upon the commands of the leader or leaders," and when the leader has "ways and means of inducing recalcitrant members to accept and act upon . . . commands" (Ozbudun 1970, 305). When individual members attempt to reconcile differences in the preferences expressed by their constituents, their party leaders, and their own values and policy goals, they weigh the costs and benefits of supporting or compromising each category of preferences (Kingdon 1984; Laver 2002, 2006). When party leaders have the capacity to impose significant costs on their members for not following party wishes and benefits for doing so, party preferences should dominate these calculations. This is the case in which party influence in the legislature should be high and parties should attract business funds. Factors that affect the ability of political parties to impose costs and endow benefits are therefore central to parties' ability to successfully induce legislative discipline among party members and hence are also central to their ability to attract business lobbies.

Scholars have argued that because institutions determine many of the carrots and sticks available to party leaders for this purpose, legislative party discipline is endogenous to the strategic environment created by political institutions.[13] Arguments linking electoral rules to party discipline have focused on the incentives they provide politicians to develop party-based or individual political reputations (Carey and Shugart 1995), which then lays the foundation for their party- or individual-centered behavior in the legislature as well.[14] This connection has provided the foundation for understanding the role of electoral institutions in establishing lobbying behavior (Grossman and Helpman 2000; Persson and Tabellini 2004; Naoi and Krauss 2009).

Arguments based on executive–legislative regime choices argue that parties in parliamentary regimes can exert strong party discipline in the legislature and hence should attract lobbyist efforts, whereas a lack of similar abilities should lead groups in presidential regimes to lobby individual legislators instead (Cowhey and McCubbins 1995; Rockman and Weaver 1993). Finally, scholars have argued that centralized legislatures should attract party-focused lobbying and that decentralized legislatures should lead to individual-focused lobbying (Feldman and Svenssen 2001, 2002). However, these theories leave the institutional mechanisms that lead to such centralization unexplored. All these theories of comparative lobbying have thus been built on the foundation of institutional theories of legislative party discipline. These arguments linking political institutions to legislative party discipline have come under increasing theoretical and empirical scrutiny by scholars in the light of new theoretical and empirical findings. Therefore, these predictions of lobbying behavior also need to be reexamined.

Recent findings on electoral rules suggest that without elaborating on the factors that give party labels value in the eyes of voters and backbenchers and make party affiliations in the legislature useful for fulfilling legislator ambitions, a discussion of how electoral rules influence party discipline in the legislature is incomplete. For example, the prevalence of party switching in practice throughout the legislative cycle in some legislatures (Agh 1999; Heller and Mershon 2001; Mershon and Shvetsova 2002, 2009; Desposato 2006; Janda 2008) raises questions about the basis for legislative behavior (Laver and Benoit 2003) and the extent to which electoral incentives influence the subsequent behavior of legislators and parties in the legislature.[15] Membership in coalitions can affect the extent of party loyalty expressed by legislators as it raises competition for legislative and executive positions and potentially dilutes the electoral value of party labels.[16] These theoretical challenges find support in the mixed evidence linking electoral rules to legislative party discipline, especially on voting (Haspel, Remington, and Smith 1998; Morgernstern 2004; Thames 2006; Desposato 2006; Carey 2007; Tavits 2009).

The most-contested dimension of the debate on legislative party discipline and hence of comparative lobbying has been the significance of the distinction between parliamentary regimes and the separation of powers embodied in presidential systems for party discipline.[17] While scholars agree that the choice of executive regime exerts a strong influence on the incentive structure facing party leaders and their members, they have increasingly emphasized the extent to which the differences in these incentives can be overcome or subdued considerably by other institutional and organizational factors. Empirically, scholars have found that the vote of confidence is not frequently used by party leaders in parliamentary regimes[18] and its presence does not exclusively determine the legislative unity exhibited by parties.[19] Evidence that voters associate the performance of legislators with that of the president, and vote on the basis of that association, undermines the argument that party discipline in presidential systems will be weak because the electoral performance of presidents and congress members are independent of their policy performance.[20] So, too, does evidence of the frequency of coalitions in presidential systems. Therefore, both levers of control—mutual independence of origin and survival—have not been found to be poison pills in presidential systems nor have they been the panacea for many disciplinary problems in parliamentary systems.

Cheibub (2007, 123) summarizes the cumulative impact of these findings: "Partisan linkages exist in presidential systems in the same way that individualistic linkages exist in parliamentary ones. We must therefore conclude that the form of government is not itself sufficient to drastically differentiate parliamentary and presidential systems when it comes to party discipline." Haggard and McCubbins (2001, 4) similarly conclude that "this distinction between macro institutions is inadequate" and argue that "explaining political outcomes often required greater focus on the details of institutions' structure." Scholars also find that the policymaking process itself varies substantially within executive regimes (Spiller, Stein, and Tommasi 2009, 23). Scholars have thus questioned whether the choice of parliamentary regime is necessary or sufficient for party discipline in the legislature.[21] This evidence on the complexity of legislative strategies adopted by party leaders and backbenchers suggests that the form of government should be insufficient to explain the lobbying behavior of business groups as well.

Evidence from various studies supports this hypothesis. A study of 19 Western European parliaments by Liebert (1995) shows that some parliamentary democracies exhibit cross-party individual-focused lobbying patterns rather than the party-focused lobbying predicted. Similarly, Saalfeld (1999) and de Winter (1999) report that interest groups in Germany and Belgium target parties while Norton (1999) and Della Salla (1999) report that interest groups in the United Kingdom and Italy spend substantial resources on lobbying legislators. Cross-country studies of lobbying in developing democracies are scarce; however, evidence from single-country studies shows that the constitutional form of government is insufficient to explain lobbying behaviors. For example, legislative lobbying in Argentina, a presidential system, is party-focused while lobbying in the Czech Republic, a parliamentary regime, focuses largely on legislators.[22]

Collectively, these empirical findings and conclusions therefore invite us to reassess the relationships among institutions, legislative discipline, and special interest behavior and to identify and analyze additional factors driving these relationships. In the rest of this chapter, I will argue that legislative institutions play a significant role in explaining when and why parties gain the ability to enforce legislative party discipline successfully and thus become the purveyors of legislative policy influence to business groups.

By governing the passage of legislation, legislative institutions directly influence which policies are implemented (Aldrich 2007; Cox and McCubbins 1993; Döring 1995), who benefits from them (Spiller, Stein, and Tommasi 2009; Milner 1997; Cox 1987), and who gets political credit for the successes and blame for the failures (Cox 2000; Rasch 1995). Legislative rules influence the ability of party leaders, presidents, and prime ministers to sustain coalitions (Volden and Craig 2004; Heller 2001) as well as to ensure that coalition partners deliver policy benefits to parties, party members, and their constituents in both types of regimes (Thies 2001; Martin and Vanberg 2004).[23] These outcomes directly affect the electoral security of parties and members by influencing how attractive they look to their constituents at the next elections. Influence over legislative policymaking also allows influence over policy implementation and oversight since powers of delegation to the bureaucracy and judiciary are determined via the legislative policy process as well (Bawn 1999; Epstein, O'Halloran, and Shvetsova 2002; Mishra 2006; Huber and Shipan 2002, 2008; Vanberg 2008; Ginsburg 2008; McCubbins and Rodriguez 2008).

Business interests care about policy outcomes, implementation, and adjudication and should therefore be strongly motivated to lobby the political principals they perceive are in charge of this policy process. This implies that their decisions about which political principals—parties or legislators—to donate money and resources to should be significantly influenced by legislative rules as well. As discussed earlier, business funds are increasingly crucial to the political prospects and payoffs for parties and politicians. Legislative influence over policymaking is therefore a very valuable resource for the political principals who command it.

I now explore the legislative influence blackbox by investigating the impact of three specific legislative rules—agenda-setting, amendments, and antiwhip voting—on legislative party discipline and interest group lobbying behavior. These legislative rules govern which bills make it to the business agenda in a given session, the timing of different legislative stages, the final substantive form of the bill before it comes up for a vote, and the nature of political support that needs to be mustered in order to win votes or impose losses, respectively. Each rule is a source of policy influence. Hence, each rule should be a source of party discipline and thus an input into lobbying venue decisions.

Interest groups thus have both the incentives and resources to invest in acquiring knowledge about these legislative procedures. Their lobbying decisions should therefore be highly influenced by their perceptions of the locus of political control over these policy stages. Variation in the legislatively allocated degree of party control over these three policy stages across countries should therefore drive variation in strategic lobbying choices by business groups. Step 1 in figures 2.1 (a) and 2.1 (b) summarize this part of the theoretical framework. In the next section, I discuss the four mechanisms that translate this higher party influence over the legislative policy process into higher corruption, thus linking these three legislative rules to higher corruption.

Agenda Control: Tsebelis (2005, 3) defines an agenda setter as "a politician who is able to control the agenda during the deliberations and make proposals to the decision-making body." The political actors who exercise agenda-setting powers decide how

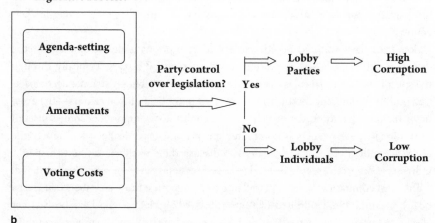

Figure 2.1. (a) and (b) *Legislative Rules, Business Groups and Corruption Levels: A Causal Diagram*

many bills make it to the business agenda of the house for consideration and when, which bills are included in this slate and which are not, and the substantive and ideological nature of the bills that do make it to consideration (Tsebelis 2005, 7; Döring 1995). Finding a spot on the crowded business agenda and the ability to block undesirable bills and motions from being put on the agenda are both highly valuable powers as is the ability to influence timing (Blondel 1972; Cox 2000, 173). Since agenda-setters may select among alternative drafts of bills, their agenda-setting powers also allow them to influence the substance of legislation and set the terms of policy debate (Tsebelis 2005, 4).

Kingdon (1984, 2) summarizes the advantage these abilities give agenda-setters in the policy process: "The patterns of public policy . . . are determined not only by such final decisions as votes in legislatures or initiative and vetoes by president, but also by the fact that some subjects and proposals emerge in the first place and others are never seriously considered." In addition, Cox (2000, 184) states that "the power to decide which bills make it to the floor is arguably the least appreciated but most fundamental power in terms of influencing final (policy) outcomes." Empirical evidence across political systems confirms that agenda-setters enjoy an edge in determining the composition of floor business and rarely get rolled on agenda-setting votes.[24] For all of these reasons, agenda-setting influence should be very valuable to business donors.

Anecdotal evidence from various countries supports this. For example, the gambling industry in Brazil contributed money to legislators so they would sponsor bills related to their industry for introduction on the floor agenda (LatinNews.com, April 19, 2007).

Studies of policymaking in Poland report that the business practice of paying policy-makers to place or block new laws from the agenda has become increasingly common there (OSI 2002, 7). In Indonesia, even bureaucrats and judicial officials joined busi-nesses in bribing parties to introduce the versions of bills they favored to the floor (Assegaf 2007, 16). These examples suggest that business interests put a high value on agenda-setting influence, and in order to obtain it they are willing to fund the polit-ical players—parties or individual legislators—who control agenda-setting in their country.

Countries have adopted a wide variety of institutional rules to implement the distribution of agenda-setting powers over these political players. Typically, through the specific institutional rules they adopt, different assemblies distribute agenda-set-ting powers in different combinations over four potential political centers—the exec-utive, the president or leader of a chamber, a committee composed of some subset of institutional leaders (such as committee chairs) and party leaders, and finally the entire assembly itself. The sample of cases discussed below illustrates how the party-individual perspective would be used to classify cases as party- or individual-centered.

The most common arrangements fall into two categories: those chambers that elect a board or committee composed of some subset of legislators who have been either elected to this position by the floor, and those chambers that have boards and commit-tees headed by their party leaders or by those directly appointed to them by their party leaders. In the first case, members' ability to access these positions is not contingent upon party goodwill. Their election to these positions will depend on their personal reputations and their ability to credibly promise access and/or agenda favors to all, not just to co-partisans. Hence, their loyalties will not lie entirely with their parties and they may act according to their own preferences. Furthermore, the existence of multiple mem-bers provides multiple alternative points of access to those seeking to influence the agenda. In this case, individual members can have a direct say in establishing the agenda of the house, and the party cannot use agenda access as an exogenous form of carrot or stick with its own members. This is a case where individuals are likely to have the most control over the agenda and party leaders the least. Groups should target individuals in this case either in their capacity as board members or as ordinary members who can access the agenda through the board. Examples include Ecuador, El Salvador, and Nicaragua.[25]

In the second case, party leaders can choose to reward or deny these valuable posi-tions to selected members at their will. Party leaders commonly influence board selec-tion, either by promoting members to positions in the executive; by serving as committee chairmen, which entitles them to hold these positions; or by directly nom-inating members for their share of the board seats. Party leaders may be required to be board members themselves if the rules specify an agenda steering committee com-posed of parliamentary party leaders. Both these arrangements give parties consider-able agenda influence, which they use to their own political and policy ends. In these cases, parties will be strengthened by the legislative rules governing this legislative function. This should be the case in Argentina, Mexico, and, Costa Rica, for example, since they have arrangements corresponding to these agenda-setting configurations. In these countries, therefore, ceteris paribus, groups should target parties.

Rules that allow subsets of legislators to introduce discharge petitions to bring bills to the consideration of the floor may reinforce or undermine these powers. When they demand a qualified 2/3 majority as in Argentina or Bolivia, or if they must be challenged through the party leadership itself as in Mexico, they further reinforce party control over the agenda. When they demand simple majorities, as in Chile, or just require the signature of a few legislators, such as in Brazil, they undermine party influence on the agenda.

The other extreme is that of a single chamber official elected to his position by his party leaders in their capacity as leaders of the majority party. Here the entire recruitment procedure for this position is highly partisan, hence party leaders control the agenda of the chamber through their appointed member. While he consults all party groups, his decision once made cannot be challenged. Therefore, his party is able to control the agenda through his office. This is the case in Honduras. Groups should lobby parties in such a political system. Countries such as South Africa combine the prominent role of a partisan speaker with consultation with committees composed of party leaders. This maintains the hold of party leaders over the agenda.

Finally, some countries also put in place speakers who are constrained by procedures and elected with the support of the entire floor. In these arrangements, speakers are prominent agenda-setters as well but tend to command influence independent of their party leaders (Rasch 2002, 279). These arrangements create environments where individual legislators find it feasible to obtain spots for their bills and amendments on the agenda independent of their party's wishes. Individual legislators may also negotiate freely with other assembly agents in a manner suited to their priorities. In some cases consultation with party leaders may be required, but it is nonbinding and hence results in little increase in party leaders' influence over the agenda. In countries with either of these arrangements, legislators should be the most frequent target of choice for special interests since most groups will not have the resources necessary to influence the speaker directly. For groups which do have resources, speakers will be targeted in their individual capacity rather than as representatives of their parties. Poland, the Dominican Republic, and Chile fall into this category of countries. Where the agenda is set directly by the entire floor, parties will have minimum control over it since legislators can logroll on agenda-setting as well.[26] The Netherlands is one of the few examples of this arrangement.

In summary, agenda-setting rules in the legislature determine which political actors control the placement, timing, and initial substance of bills on the agenda of the house. Since business interest groups value the ability to influence the agenda, they should lobby the political agent with this influence. When party leaders are institutionally empowered in agenda-setting, they are the ones with agenda influence. Hence, they will increase legislative party discipline by controlling member access to it as well as by using it to raise funds from business sources. This should further enhance the ability of parties to enforce discipline since their members must depend on party leaders to access the funds business lobbies have contributed. We derive the following falsifiable hypothesis:

H_{1A}: When agenda setting rules endow political parties with agenda control, ceteris paribus, groups should be more likely to lobby parties.

Amendments: Whether or not a group wanted a certain piece of legislation to make it to the floor agenda and whether or not it succeeded in placing its preferred draft on the floor, the next strategic battle is to influence the substance of the draft under floor consideration. This is done via the introduction of amendments that modify the substance of the original draft of the bill under consideration. As Milner (1997, 104) points out, amendments offer a considerable advantage, "The one amending can alter the agenda-setter's proposal to bring it closer to the former's ideal point; maximally the amender can change the proposal to its ideal point." The initial grounds of the legislative debate are laid down by the original draft of the bill on the agenda. However, by allowing amendments to be introduced at different times in the process, amendment rules give policymakers the ability to redress lack of agenda powers and increase their access to the bill drafting process. Thus, Di Palma (1977, 59) states, "Both the initiation of bills and the proposal of amendments must, therefore, be seen as resources that Members of Parliament employ in different ways to negotiate decisions and influence legislation."

Furthermore, institutional barriers for introducing amendments generally tend to be lower than those for getting a bill on the agenda (Mattson 1995; Heller 2001). The constraints of time as well as the technical skills needed to add an amendment to a previously drafted bill are also less stringent. As Mattson (1995, 473) points out, "The right to initiate amendments is generally related to the right to initiate laws, since an amendment can be regarded as a limited form of initiation of legislation. However, despite the close relationship of the two, the right to initiate amendments is generally less restrictive than the right to initiate legislation." Thus, amendments provide a more accessible method for influencing the substance of legislation. Amendments are also frequently used strategically to influence the timing of bills at various stages since consideration of amendments delays the progress of bills, and even sometimes to scuttle them entirely under the weight of too many amendments.

Finally, the versatility in content provided by amendments provides party leaders, legislators, the executive, and various interest groups with a wider set of bargaining tools that can be used to strike bargains across many dimensions of policy. They are frequently used to influence the scope of a bill, the structure of supervision and implementation, the identity of affected groups, the distribution of costs and benefits among affected groups, and the schedule of implementation, among other things. As Baron and Ferejohn (1989, 1200) point out, this "reduces the power of the member recognized first and results in an outcome that more evenly distributes the benefits among the winning majority." Party leaders can thus use amendments to buy support for the general substance of a particular bill by granting exceptions for the constituents and donors of particular legislators. This allows better deals to be struck within parties, thus enhancing party ability to enforce legislative discipline, as well as across parties, enhancing the strength of coalitions (Volden and Craig 2004; Heller 2001).[27] Similarly, individual legislators can use amendments to increase their capacity to build a coalition for their bill by striking deals with other legislators to logroll. Their strategic utility can be seen from the sheer volume of amending activities in various developing democracies. For example, over the 1997–2004 period, 59% of all legislative laws in Slovakia, 58% in

Poland, 52% in the Czech Republic, and 46% in Hungary were amendments to existing laws rather than new laws (Zubek 2005, 8).

The ability to influence legislative amendments to bills therefore provides interest groups with an especially effective procedural tool to affect changes in the substance, scope, and timing of legislation as well as to forge bargains. They can use this legislative tool to water down the harmful provisions of a bill that affects them negatively and to increase the share of benefits they obtain from a bill that affects them positively. Thus, they should be willing to pay handsomely for the ability to influence amendments and direct their lobbying efforts to the policy actors who can deliver such influence on their behalf.

Lobbying patterns from several countries confirm that they do. For example, in Poland, Siedliecka (2004) and Zubek (2005, 32) find that the most common method adopted by the executive and parliamentarians to accommodate interest groups' demands is to introduce laws and amendments tailored to their specific cases in the Sjem.[28] The World Bank reports that on some issues Polish businesses were willing to pay as much as $3 million to legislators for individual amendments to bills affecting them (World Bank 1997, 427). In the Czech Republic, legislators report that amendments to commercial bills, such as a 1998 bill on lotteries and a 2001 bill to abolish duty-free shops, were subject to heavy lobbying using dubious tactics (OSI 2002, 166).

The legislative process for the European Union (EU) legislation called "Reach" (which stands for registration, evaluation, and authorization of chemicals) demonstrates how all the advantages that amendments offer can play a crucial role in lobbying strategies and policy outcomes. The initial 2003 draft would have imposed labeling, testing, and reporting requirements on the use of 30,000 chemicals affecting industries ranging from primary commodities, such as metals, to user industries. such as textiles and detergents, in all EU countries (Financial Times, November 18, 2005). Business opposition to the bill was manifested in intense lobbying by various industry associations while environmental and consumer groups such as World Wildlife Fund and Greenpeace mobilized in intense support of the safeguards in the bill. The legislative fight between these competing special interests was played out over the next two years primarily through the tabling of 5,000 amendments. The bill that was eventually passed two years later watered down the requirements on registration, testing, and reporting data; reduced the obligations to provide acceptable substitutes of potentially harmful chemicals; and reduced the number of chemicals targeted from 30,000 to 10,000 all via the use of amendments to the original bill. As this example demonstrates, amendments can be used to great policy effect to serve one's interests and hence are the subject of intense lobbying attention. Therefore, political influence over them should be very valuable to business interests and thus to the political players who have such influence.

While most analyses of amendment rights have focused on the rights of governments versus opposition groups to introduce amendments, the theoretical framework of this project requires an examination of these rules in light of how they allocate influence over this stage to parties and legislators. Countries differ regarding the identity of who can introduce amendments and at which stage of the process they can do so.[29] If legislative rules in a given country allow legislators the right to introduce amendments at any stage of the process without procedural vetting or interference from party leaders or their direct appointees, then legislators are considered to have the right to introduce amendments for the purposes of this study. In these countries, amendment rights should weaken party discipline. Otherwise the country is considered to be party-focused in its amendment rights. In these cases, party leaders will be able to use their influence over amendments to forge party discipline and deliver outcomes to lobbies in exchange for funds. As the data in chapter 6 will show, there is substantial variation across countries in the ability of individual legislators to introduce amendments and the capacity of parties to constrain them in this task.

In both systems, business interest groups should value these strategic benefits of influence over amendments and lobby the political actor with control over this stage. They should therefore be willing and able to pay individual legislators for the opportunity to exert such influence when they perceive individual legislators to be in charge of amendments. This should be the case, for example, in Poland and the Czech Republic. When groups observe that legislative rules give political parties influence over amendments, they should lobby parties instead. Thus, the rules in South Africa and the Philippines lead us to expect that political parties should be lobbied in these countries. We get the following falsifiable hypothesis:

H_{2A}: When amendment rules endow political parties with control over amendments, ceteris paribus, groups should be more likely to lobby parties.

Voting Dissidence: At the end of the legislative process, a bill finally comes up for the vote, which will determine whether or not it becomes law. Irrespective of their level of influence at the agenda stage, business groups who support or oppose this bill must now muster enough votes to support their position. Therefore, business interests should seek to influence the votes of lawmakers in their favor at this stage. Various studies confirm that they do. A 2005 EBRD–World Bank study found that 46% of 185 firms in Albania, 37% of 314 firms in Armenia, and 24% of 268 in Bulgaria reported being affected by the sale of parliamentary votes to private interests in their countries (BEEPS 2005). In Ukraine, for example, IFES (USAID 2006, 45) study reports that "protectionism, at least within some markets (vehicles, sugar, vegetable oil), was allegedly lobbied with massive buying of votes in parliament." Others report that legislative votes in Poland and Indonesia were frequently subject to bribery by business interests (OSI 2002, 426–427; Mietzner 2007). Given the high value of such votes and the active market for them in developing democracies, the ability to control and deliver them will be very valuable for politicians and political parties.

Parties, however, will only be able to ensure that business financing to influence votes flows to party coffers rather than to the private funds of legislators, if they can commit ex-ante to delivering the votes of their legislative delegation to business groups. Party ability to do so will depend on their ability to impose sufficient costs on voting dissenters. These costs can include minor wrist-slaps, such as denying staff support; denying desirable committee seats; to the heaviest penalty possible, withdrawing the members' party affiliation. As Laver (2006, 132) points out, "If a party's decision-making regime can credibly threaten to withdraw the party label from legislators who fail to abide by party decisions about legislative behavior, then this makes such decisions easier to enforce." Typically scholars have looked at party denial of nominations to party tickets in subsequent elections or votes of confidence as the mechanisms through which parties can implement this punishment. However, many legislatures provide parties with an even more effective tool—the ability to strip members *immediately* of their legislative mandate if they vote against party wishes. I call this "voting dissidence control."

Several factors make this threat especially effective. Parties can use this threat to credibly threaten the only term legislators are guaranteed to have—their current one—and deprive them immediately of all benefits of office. Additionally, they can be surgical and expel only the offending members from the legislature. These advantages allow parties to impose the maximum cost on dissenters while minimizing the cost to the party itself, and they also discourage building antiparty voting coalitions. Unlike the vote of confidence in parliamentary systems, even governing parties can threaten expulsion more credibly since the party's tenure in government will not necessarily be tied to such expulsions. Parties can thus wield this threat more effectively as a modus operandi for producing voting discipline rather than using the nuclear vote of confidence.

For these reasons, when a legislature gives party leaders this ability to control dissident mandates, parties should be able to credibly commit ex-ante to delivering the desirable policy votes to businesses and thus attract their donations. In countries like Turkey, Trinidad and Tobago, and Nepal, where parties have this legislative power, we expect parties to exert influence over voting and to attract business funds at this stage. In countries like Poland and Brazil,[30] where parties are not given this legislative privilege, individual legislators will be free to vote their own preferences and will present more attractive lobbying targets to interest groups.

From this discussion, I derive the following falsifiable hypothesis:

> H_{3A}: When legislative rules allow political parties to expel members from their legislative seats for antiparty voting, ceteris paribus, groups should be more likely to lobby parties.

Each of these three legislative rules affects whether or not parties are in a position to extract corruption rents from business donors in exchange for exerting strong influence over the legislative policy process in their favor. I now discuss the four mechanisms that cause such party control over legislative policy influence to generate higher corruption in developing countries compared to countries where they are unable to do so.

(III) PARTY POLICY INFLUENCE AND CORRUPTION: FOUR MECHANISMS

Legislative policy influence is a lucrative asset for both parties and politicians. However, two demand-side mechanisms—parties' need to raise more funds and their stronger preference for money over other political resources—raise the demand for corrupt money. Two supply-side mechanisms—party ability to capture state institutions via legislative delegation and to protect corrupt financing practices—increase their ability to supply their demands in party-focused systems. The result, as shown in the second step of figures 2.1 (a) and 2.1 (b), is higher and more pervasive corruption in the countries where parties wield policy influence in the legislature compared to systems where they do not wield such influence.

Demand Side Mechanisms—Scale and Fungibility

As discussed in section 1, both parties and politicians in developing democracies face chronic problems in raising sufficient money to finance their political expenses. Parties, however, face a more severe cash crunch because they serve several additional roles in society that individual politicians do not (Key 1964; Aldrich 2008). These include operating as organizers and financiers of party and candidate election campaigns, as managers of party organizations, and as managers of legislative offices for the party. As organizations, parties must incur additional expenses to maintain a network of offices and staff at all times and to conduct rallies, events, and other actions geared at building the value of the party brand. In office, parties need to maintain a secretarial and research staff that supports legislative work by the party and its members, since states in developing countries do not usually provide adequate staff support for legislators (Fish and Kroenig 2008; Ames 2002).

As campaign managers, parties must finance complex campaigns that cater to local, regional, and national constituencies. The scale of election expenses this requires is significantly higher, especially for transportation and media campaigns (Bryan and Baer 2005, 14–15). The more ethnically and linguistically diverse a country is, the higher the expenses parties will incur in designing and airing campaign ads. Additionally, parties may provide various levels of financial support to their candidates. As discussed earlier, low incomes and low political participation in developing democracies typically means that funds raised from voters, party members, and the state are insufficient to finance even these legal expenses, which are necessary for parties to perform their roles adequately.[31] At the same time, parties in these countries must finance a variety of illegal political tactics to stay competitive and to prosper at all stages of politics (Johnston 2005, 5; Carothers 2002; Bleichinger 2002).

During elections, parties commonly finance a wide range of illegal tactics, including vote-buying, hiring goons to intimidate opponents, stuffing ballot boxes, and bribing election and police officials to ignore various campaign violations.[32] For example, in Thailand, parties spent an estimated $460 million in 2001 buying votes across the country (Schaffer 2004, 23); in Kenya, parties spent about 50% of their campaign funds on vote-buying; and Bangladeshi parties reported this activity as their biggest expense as well (Bryan and Baer 2005, 76, 33). In Armenia, experts judged vote-buying to be the single most important determinant of the 2008 election outcome (Hoktanyan 2008, 7). In Nepal, a prominent party leader stated the importance of hiring thugs on a large scale for parties during elections: "Money, muscle and mafia are what determine the outcome of elections."[33] In Botswana, parties bribed opposition candidates to withdraw from the race so that their own candidates could get elected unopposed (Bryan and Baer 2005, 18), while parties in Nepal, Bangladesh, Zambia, and Kenya reported buying registration cards to prevent voters from voting at all (IFES 2008; Bryan and Baer 2005; USAID 2003; Austin and Tjernström 2003).

While politicians engage in some of the same tactics, not all candidates have the funds to carry out these tactics and their actions are restricted to their own districts. Both lower the aggregate impact of these tactics on corruption. For example, in Ukraine, a well-financed candidate spent $100,000 dollars on distributing live piglets to his constituents (USAID 2003, 23), while in Taiwan, candidates in urban areas distributed as much as $3 million to buy votes (Schaffer 2004, 84). In Nigeria, rich candidates who could afford it hired muscle to intimidate voters and stuff ballot boxes in their own districts during elections (IFES 2008, 41). Parties, on the other hand, must employ these tactics on a much larger scale and finance such electoral tactics at the regional and/or national level, which raises the magnitude of expenses considerably.

During their term in office, party leaders must amass a war chest of untraceable funds to purchase votes for enacting policies, influencing votes of confidence, and approving appointments. For example, in Nepal, ruling parties paid legislators from the opposition and their own party a "Dashain allowance" in order to maintain their support for their agenda (TI 2006, 207), while parties in Angola paid an annual "Christmas bonus" of $30,000 to friendly parliamentarians (TI 2004, 61, 64). In Ukraine, party leaders paid many legislators from their own party as well as from opposition parties monthly allowances of roughly $5,000 plus a lump sum bonus ranging from $20,000 to $50,000 per legislator to vote with them on key issues (Walecki 2003, 81). Leaders also raise funds to bribe legislators to switch party affiliations. For example, in Zambia, Peru, and Botswana, party leaders paid opposition members to switch to their parties or to become independent and vote with them (Bryan and Baer 2005, 18; Walecki 2004, 1).

These are expenses that are specific to party strategies to maintain office and legislative influence during their tenure in office. Individual legislators do not need to raise funds to finance such strategies since they do not need to practice them. In a party-focused country where parties are the influential political actors, party leaders must actively create and continuously maintain a large war chest to ensure the continuing level of party loyalty required for legislative success. As the figures from Angola and Ukraine cited above show, the amounts required for such purposes by parties is considerable by any standards. They are astonishingly high considering the low income level of these countries and the level at which voters and members can legally fund their parties. Some scholars have argued that when parties are strong and campaigning is organized by parties, corruption should be lower because parties can realize economies of scale in their campaigns that individual candidates cannot. However, as the discussion above shows the many additional practices and tactics that parties must employ in their bid to win office and hold it raise the demand for money that parties face relative to individual legislators considerably. These tactics are rarely employed in developed democracies and thus they demonstrate one important reason why developing country democracies require a distinct theoretical framework. This is the *first demand dynamic* that should raise corruption levels in party-focused countries relative to that in individual-focused countries.

This discussion also brings out a *second* dimension of political finance that is specific to political parties—their strong preference for fungible resources, especially money over nonfungible resources. Financial contributions are undoubtedly welcomed by all participants in politics. However, there should be a significant difference in how parties and individual politicians assess the *relative value* of resources in party- and individual-focused systems because of the differences in the nature of campaigns they must run and the kind of office-management tasks they perform. Both candidates and parties value the ability to transfer donated funds to finance different activities such as vote-buying, advertising, and so forth. However, given the multidistrict nature of the electoral campaigns they run, parties have a higher need for resources that can be transferred across electoral districts to maximize the party's electoral goals. This privileges fungible resources such as money, which retains value across districts, over more district-specific resources such as information and volunteers. While money is attractive to individual candidates as well, other resources such as constituency-specific voter information, free space to hold rallies or host offices, or local volunteers may be valued more highly by them than by parties due to their geographic specificity.

Similarly, the need to finance illegal tactics such as bribing legislators for votes and seats during their legislative term leads parties to value money more than resources such as technical information or drafting skills on policy issues. This is reinforced by the fact that since they have a larger base of supporters and members, parties are more likely to have access to in-house technical skills on policy issues, thus lowering their value even further. Therefore, the marginal value of these resources is significantly different for parties and individual politicians. Fungible resources, though valued by all, have higher relative value for parties. Business interests should respond to these incentives by using money more frequently when lobbying parties compared to when they lobby legislators directly. Thus, fungibility of money creates a *second dynamic* that should cause corruption to be higher in party-focused systems.

When parties control the legislative process, they can use their legislative capacity to successfully meet these higher demands by engaging in various illegal financing practices involving policy quid pro quos with business groups. For example, in Tanzania, parties passed a legislative bill that legalized the practice of *takrima*, giving and receiving gifts in good faith. This was then used to justify both obtaining such gifts from businesses and giving them to voters in exchange for votes during elections (Bryan and Baer 2005, 17; U4 2006). In Romania, faced with voters and members too poor to contribute significantly to party coffers, party leaders went through the accounts of state banks, identified businesses who had borrowed from them, and then extracted donations for passing legislative bills and decrees rescheduling their debt (OSI 2002, 501; Bryan and Baer 2005, 19; Gryzmala-Busse 2007).

In contrast, Polish legislators on the Parliamentary Committee on Cultural Matters used their amendment powers on this committee to obtain financing from media companies for their personal campaigns (OSI 2002). These legislators benefited substantially from their legislative powers, but other party members who did not hold legislatively important positions did not benefit from this at all. Thus, the extent of corruption caused by their manipulation of legislative policy influence was limited to a few specific individuals. Since such positions are occupied by a substantially smaller subset of the entire membership of a parliament, this caps the number of policymakers who can successfully use such fundraising strategies. Aggregate corruption generated from such legislative lobbying is therefore restricted to such positions and capped at a much lower level.

Lacking the capacity to assure passage of suitable legislation similar to those that allow parties to innovate multi-institutional schemes, individual legislators cannot make ex-ante promises to business donors for devising and implementing such complex corruption schemes. Aggregate corruption through lobbying motivated by such schemes should therefore be lower in individual-focused systems. These examples illustrate how higher demands on a party for operating funds motivates party leaders to meet those demands through the active use of their power to influence legislation at the cost of higher corruption levels.

Supply Side Mechanisms

When parties are located in party-focused legislative systems, two supply-side mechanisms—party ability to use legislation to capture state institutions, which exercise delegated policy powers, and to protect corrupt financing practices—increase their ability to raise illegal funds so that they can meet these higher demands. These supply-side dynamics therefore raise corruption in party-focused systems beyond that in individual-focused systems.

Legislative Delegation

Businesses must deal with bureaucratic and regulatory officials during various stages of policy implementation and regulation as well as in the course of their operations. Decisions by these public officials can affect almost every aspect of a firm's bottom line in the short and long term. Therefore, business interests should place a very high value on influence over policy implementation and regulation outcomes. Similarly, judicial decisions can exert enormous impact over how businesses are affected by legal and bureaucratic procedures on issues such as bankruptcy, debt recovery, dispute resolution, intellectual property rights, and the creation of special commercial courts (World Bank 1995, 17; Hammergren 2007, 90–96). For these reasons, business interests place a high value on attributes of the judicial system such as its powers to review the constitutionality of legislative statutes, to consider business challenges to administrative decisions of bureaucratic officials, and to challenge implementation decisions by elected officials. The scope of manner in which the bureaucracy and the judiciary make these decisions regarding policy implementation and oversight is determined by the powers that are delegated to them by the legislature via legislative statutes.

Decisions regarding the degree of discretion given to public officials, the identity of the state agencies in charge of implementation, their budgets, rules regarding appointments and dismissals, and supervision of public officials during implementation and regulation are frequently made via legislative statutes.[34] By pulling their *legislative* strings, legislatures can manipulate bureaucratic procedures, appointments, and decisions to create either a politicized and captured bureaucracy or a truly independent one. Similarly, decisions about the jurisdiction and powers of courts, the method for appointments and dismissals to high courts and supreme courts, and budgets for these activities are made via legislative statutes. By manipulating these details strategically, a legislature can establish an independent court with powers of constitutional review and autonomous jurisdiction or it can establish a weak, politicized court that operates as an extension of the political establishment.[35] Political control over the judiciary can also be used by political principals to enhance their control over policy implementation by the bureaucracy through granting a politicized judiciary the powers to enforce and invalidate administrative procedures and decisions (Spiller 1996; Rodriguez 1994; Ferejohn and Shipan 1990).

Since these institutional characteristics are established via legislation, the level of political control over legislation will be one of the key factors that strongly influences whether the bureaucracy and judiciary are politicized and used as political tools for influence-peddling or whether they are effective independent institutions.[36] This in turn will influence whether business interests lobby parties and politicians or bureaucrats and judges directly to gain influence over administrative and judicial decisions regarding policy. When party leaders control agenda-setting, amendments, and voting, they will be able to lead disciplined legislative parties into making delegation decisions that favor the parties' goals. Political influence over the legislative process in these countries allows parties to extend their influence from policy design in the legislature to aspects of policy implementation, oversight, and adjudication. Therefore, in order to influence which agencies and institutions exercise implementation authority, what the scope of this authority is, who should be supervising them, and even which specific officials should be involved in the process, business interests can lobby parties during the legislative policy process itself. Furthermore, influence over the legislative policy process increases the ability of both parties and businesses to design and sabotage the entire life-cycle of policies to suit their interests, whether through obtaining a specific policy goal or extracting illegal rents. Accordingly, when business interests seek influence at these institutions, they will lobby parties rather than the bureaucrats and judicial officials themselves.

In contrast, in individual-focused systems, even influential legislators do not command the legislative influence necessary to consistently deliver the blocs of votes required to capture these institutions and influence their ongoing behavior. As a result, while ad hoc collaborations between corrupt officials and politicians will occur in these countries, they should not experience the *systemic* corruption that widespread partisan influence-peddling generates in party-focused countries. In party-focused systems, on the other hand, not only are parties able to peddle influence over a wide range of state institutions, they are also able to devise new schemes and offer new influence products to business donors by leveraging their control over state institutions creatively. Thus the ability of parties to translate their legislative policy influence into partisan influence at various institutions should raise the level of corruption through influence-peddling beyond that possible in individual-focused countries. The examples below illustrate this argument.

In November 2004, the Nicaraguan assembly passed a bill placing a number of important state institutions, including the supervisory bodies for social security and public services, directly under its control. By 2006, journalists had already uncovered the first massive corruption scheme exploiting this newly gained legislative influence. The Sandinista National Liberation Front (FSLN) party was found to have manipulated the public welfare body to deliver the first public contracts to some of its business supporters. It then pressured the national social security and pension funds to supply these donors with cheap credit to meet these contractual obligations (TI 2006, 16; TI 2004, 215). Hence, the ability to pass legislation was used successfully by the FSLN party to enact a complex multiinstitutional scheme that then enabled its business donors to obtain various lucrative benefits in exchange for their financial support of the FSLN.

In Argentina, legislation was used multiple times to change the rules for appointing judges in order to facilitate party control over the judiciary (TI 2009; Hammergren 2007). During Carlos Menem's tenure, the Justicialist Party successfully increased the size of the judicial commission responsible for appointments and stacked it with friendly legislators and judges (Cárdenas and Chayer 2007, 47). During President Nestor Kirchner's term, partisan control over the commission was extended further by legislating changes to its composition again so that seven of thirteen commission members were now political appointees from the executive and the legislature. This ensured that parties could veto any judicial appointments they did not approve of. At the same time, legislation was passed to formally waive the requirement of entrance exams for judges as well (TI 2009, 212). This allowed parties to appoint judges willing to be friendly to important party donors while uncooperative judges were fired. The result has been an explicitly partisan and accommodating judiciary (Hammergren 2007, 101; Helmke 2005; TI 2007, 46). These kind of multi-institutional influence-peddling schemes are beyond the capability of individual legislators no matter how influential they are. Thus, the legislative ability of party leaders to deliver desirable delegation outcomes to donors via legislation is an indispensable cog in the process of converting partisan legislative strength into partisan rents.

The operational independence of these institutions can also be effectively compromised through manipulation of their personnel and budgets if these require legislative approval.[37] When appointments are endogenous, the entire bureaucratic structure is more likely to be co-opted into creating a vertical system of graft with political principals at the top of the pyramid (Basu 1992; Bac 1996; Mishra 2006; World Bank 2007). Parties with legislative policy discipline have the power to effectively endogenize these appointments and use it to reconfigure the bureaucracy and judiciary to establish rent-extracting networks at these institutions. The Argentinian manipulation of the judiciary discussed above provides one such example. Therefore, instead of having no mechanism with which to punish recalcitrant bureaucrats (Naoi and Krauss 2009, 887), business interests in party-focused countries can use party influence to exert strong pressure on bureaucrats to accommodate their interests. This kind of co-optation of public officials into party rent machines allows parties to steal resources from state coffers directly as well as to raise revenue by extracting bribes from citizens through vertical graft schemes.

For example, Kenyan bureaucrats who wanted to stay in their positions were pressured to organize *harambees* or get-togethers in order to raise funds for their political supervisors (Bryan and Baer 2005, 17). They commonly responded by collecting money from donors and arranged for future public contracts in exchange. In Indonesia, the Golkar Party used its partisan influence over central bank officials to bail Bank Bali out of financial trouble in 1991 in exchange for a payment of $70 million from them (Assegaf 2007). In Bulgaria, officials were similarly co-opted in the process to funnel most of the revenues from the privatization of state firms directly into funds controlled by political parties (Grzymala-Busse 2007, 194). Privatization processes in Cote de-Ivoire, Zambia, and Malawi were similarly exploited by parties for their own purposes (Bryan and Baer 2005; Saffu 2003). The scale on which parties can organize such schemes is again unmatched by individual legislators since only parties can credibly wield the legislative stick.

These examples also illustrate how partisan co-optation of state institutions raises petty corruption because parties instigate, tolerate, and encourage bureaucrats and judges to run their own bribery schemes as long as the revenues are shared. In a study of party financing in Indonesia, a party official of the Partai Demokrat described a scheme commonly used by parties in collaboration with businesses to raise funds (Mietzner 2007, 248). The party would establish an enterprise that developed business proposals, which were then circulated among its own governors and district chiefs. Businesses who had been given public contracts then hired the Partai Demokrat–affiliated firm as a subcontractor allowing the party to funnel some of the contract money back to its own coffers. It is due to partisan behaviors and networks such as this that experts argue that in Indonesia "hierarchical, systemic corruption became one of the central features of the New Order political economy" (Davidson et al. 2006, 9).

Similarly, the World Bank (2007, 409) notes, "lack of judicial independence and judicial corruption go hand in hand." Studies of the judiciary in Sri Lanka (TI 2007) and Romania (EU 2008) have found that judges who exhibited too much political independence and did not cooperate with parties were routinely transferred or subjected to early retirement or bogus charges. Such political interference has turned these systems into sites for influence-peddling to the friends of political parties. Rose-Ackerman (2007, 21) describes how a politicized judiciary increases the level of petty corruption as well: "If top judges are corrupt or dependent on political leaders, they can use promotions and transfers of judges to discipline those unwilling to play the corruption game. Lower level judges might then collect bribes and pass on a share to those above."

For example, in Ukraine, partisan control over judicial appointments and the dismissals process allowed parties to use the judiciary to construct such a lucrative vertical graft scheme. The Heads of Courts, who are politically appointed, extracted bribes from judges seeking positions in urban areas and then passed them up the ladder to their political patrons (USAID 2006, 26). These judges in turn recouped their losses by extracting bribes from litigants and their lawyers during the course of carrying out their judicial duties. The result, as the USAID (2006) report notes, is that "interference in judicial decision-making by the executive and parliamentary branches, higher level judges, and businesspeople is common." Thus, by facilitating state capture, the powers of legislative delegation created incentives for state officials to engage in corruption themselves as long as they shared the gains with their political masters. Behaviors such as these substantially increase the extent to which politically induced petty corruption pervades larger society and raises grand and petty corruption.

Since bureaucrats and judicial officials are co-opted into partisan networks to generate rents, they also experience and in many cases come to share the norm of exploiting their positions for personal enrichment. These dynamics are more likely to attract corrupt individuals into public institutions rather than honest citizens who would not be ethically comfortable with participation in such graft systems (Diamond 2003; Krueger 1997). This should also raise the frequency with which such independently run corruption schemes by these public officials emerge and succeed. Their cooperation with party officials can further facilitate such petty corruption by affording them protection from prosecution as long as they cooperate with their political principals.

This discussion illustrates how parties can use their control over delegated powers to capture state institutions and then use them to *routinely* produce rents that influential individuals can rarely access. While influential legislators will collude with willing officials in ad hoc schemes leading to corruption in individual-focused systems as well, only parties with captive state institutions can ex-ante peddle influence over a wide range of functions associated with these institutions to business interests. Business interests will lobby parties to peddle influence at state institutions in support of existing policies and additionally to design entirely new rent schemes whose revenues can be shared among parties and businesses. This is the *third dynamic* that should cause business lobbying to lead to higher corruption in party-focused countries relative to individual-focused countries.

Transparency, Creative Accounting, and Donor Protection

The institutional ability of a country to audit the finances of its political establishment is crucial to the task of limiting corruption. Ward (2004, 39) sums up the implications of institutional weaknesses in these agencies for corruption succinctly by stating that "disclosure is to politics what financial statements are to business." Neither parties nor politicians have an incentive to be honest in their declarations since money not declared to the authorities can boost expenditures on legal and illegal political tactics. Unsurprisingly, therefore, illegal financing, poor reporting, and weak auditing can be found in both party-focused and individual-focused legislative systems in developing democracies. However, as I argue below, the higher legislative ability of parties to compromise these institutions increases their ability to protect fraudulent financing practices. This creates the *fourth dynamic* that causes corruption to be higher in party-focused legislative systems.

Parties raise money from a diverse range of donors who are geographically distributed and can contribute to them at local, state, or national levels. Parties must also spend on a broader range of legal functions distributed across all of their districts. Party accounts consolidate these revenues and expenses across all geographic levels for all these functions and sources. Hence, they are considerably more complex than the accounts of legislators who must do so only for a single district (Walecki 2004; USAID 2003; Pinto-Duschinsky 2001). This complexity demands a considerably higher caliber of technical accounting skills to audit them successfully. However, matters are made worse by the fact that both parties and individual politicians in these countries accommodate illegal expenditures in their accounts as well.

While both will cook their accounts to camouflage such expenses, the severity of the challenge this poses for auditors will be higher for party accounts. Even illegal expenses are incurred through a more diverse range of illegal tactics by parties, including those specific to them, such as vote-buying in parliament. Therefore, by their nature, party accounts in *all* countries offer a considerably harder challenge to auditors than the accounts of individual candidates. In countries where parties can manipulate the operations of appropriate accounting agencies, political accounting fraud should cause much higher corruption. This ability is a direct consequence of the legislative influence parties exercise over the appointments, budgets, and powers of state agencies charged with auditing and overseeing political accounts in a country.

As Walecki (2002, 9) notes, "Any enforcement agency's autonomy must result from many factors, including its membership, terms of appointment, funding and administrative jurisdiction. . . . The enforcement agency should have specialized personnel and should be unconditionally supported by the judiciary, policy and other anti-corruption bodies." In party-focused systems, all of these dimensions are vulnerable to legislative capture by parties. When parties can exercise influence over the legislative process, they can manipulate the jurisdiction, powers, appointments and dismissals, and budgets of these agencies in order to ensure they have inadequate budgets, are understaffed or staffed by technically underqualified people, and have little power to initiate investigations or enforce penalties. This environment then enables parties to falsify accounts and underreport funds to suit their needs with less fear of exposure or punishment by politically compromised auditors.

Business donors to parties in such systems can in turn rely on similar agency weaknesses in oversight and on party capture of these institutions to protect them from prosecution for making illegal party donations. This undermines the potential of auditing donor accounts to identify corrupt practices as well. Since most political funds flow to parties in party-focused systems, this effectively ensures that a higher share of ongoing political financial transactions in the country is now opaque, inaccessible, and illegal. Furthermore, since both parties and business interests face a lower legal cost for illegal financial behaviors, they are more likely to engage in these behaviors more frequently.

In contrast, in individual-focused systems, politicians cannot produce many of these corruption-facilitating benefits since they do not have the legislative influence to *systemically* capture auditing and oversight agencies or the judiciary. This reality of a less politicized enforcement system should lead to more independent and better resourced auditing agencies. Furthermore, individual accounts are significantly less challenging technically than party accounts since both revenues and expenses are geographically and functionally more limited. Thus their technical scope for fudging accounts is more restricted than that of parties. On the other hand, the chances of any individual candidate being audited is significantly lower since the number of candidates is vastly greater than the number of parties in any country. However, the technical ease of auditing individual accounts combined with the reality of operating in an institutional environment that is less politicized and partisan, should make it more likely for accounting violations to be successfully detected and penalized if they are audited. Under these conditions, legislators will not be able to offer their business donors institutional protection from prosecution for illegal financing.

The political and financial costs of being caught are therefore higher for both legislators and business donors as are the chances of being caught in individual-focused systems. While this certainly should not stop donors or politicians from engaging in monetary exchanges, it should limit the extent to which these behaviors will be common in practice. Thus higher chances of detection should depress the boost that a lower accounting capacity can give to corruption in individual-focused countries, leading to lower corruption levels. At the same time, as discussed above, while party capacity to falsify accounts will always be higher than that of individual legislators, its impact on corruption should be substantially higher only when parties are situated in party-focused legislative systems.

Studies show that the awareness of this asymmetry in resources and the strategic opportunity it offers is widespread among parties in developing democracies and that they have evolved many financial practices to exploit this advantage (Nassmacher 2003,140; USAID 2003, 48; IDEA 2003). Fewer than a third of 430 elite survey respondents from 22 countries reported that their party actively maintained an accounting system in place for external review, and an even smaller subset reported the existence of any kind of internal auditing mechanism (Bryan and Baer 2005, 11). Importantly, interviews with party officials and candidates reported party motives for such practices ranging from the less frequent benign explanation, a lack of capacity, to the more frequent one, concealing sources and expenditures from authorities (USAID 2003, 43–48; IDEA 2003; Bryan and Baer 2005, 12). In Indonesia, for example, NGOs reported that few parties expressed any interest in the accounting training being offered to them (IFES 2004). Financial transactions were typically conducted secretly within a small coterie of top party leaders, and they were conducted in cash in Turkey, Bulgaria, Romania, Bangladesh, Argentina, Indonesia, Armenia, South Africa, and Zambia among others (USAID 2003, 48; Bryan and Baer 2005, 10–12). It is unlikely that parties in such countries who are enjoying the advantages offered by weak agencies would then invest in building up the autonomy and technical capacity of these agencies in these countries. Studies show that this is indeed the case.

Agencies tasked with auditing political accounts in party-focused legislative countries rarely received the budgetary support, institutional independence, authority, or trained personnel required to perform their tasks effectively.[38] For example, in Bulgaria, appointments to the Chief Electoral Commission, which is responsible for auditing political accounts, are actively manipulated by parties via their legislative powers to suit their convenience (IFES 2002, 27). Parties there have thus successfully managed to escape any violations for illegal funding by businesses despite the widespread knowledge that they rely almost exclusively on such funds for their operations (IFES 2002, 28).

In Indonesia, the anticorruption body, the Komisi Pemberantasan Korupsi (KPK), has constantly struggled to carry out its mandate in the face of threats to deny legislative approval of its budgets and dismissals and framing of senior officials who dared to pursue politically sensitive corruption cases (Jakarta Times, March 12, 2010). Despite that fact that only 9 out of 50 registered parties filed annual reports with them in 2004 and only 4 complied with accounting requirements, no penalties were imposed on any parties (Dahl 2004, 10). The professional accountants association in Indonesia has frequently questioned the technical competence of the KPK to carry out their mandate and, as an example, pointed to events such as the fact that three out of five accountants assigned to audit political accounts during presidential campaigns were not actually qualified to do so (Dahl 2004, 14; TI 2009, 263). Despite popular support for the KPK, partisan control over legislative instruments has thus been very effective at ensuring few politically inconvenient investigations have been undertaken (Dahl 1999, 5). Similar patterns of underfunding and manipulation of personnel are observed in Armenia, Georgia, and Turkey as well (IFES 2002, 2008).

Partisan capture of the judiciary further enhances party ability to engage in accounting fraud in party-focused developing democracies by allowing manipulation so cases can be easily dismissed or resolved in their favor. For example, when NGOs challenged party accounts in court in Bangladesh, the supervising judge, appointed under a partisan patronage system, absolved the parties of any guilt despite overwhelming evidence to the contrary (TI 2009, 17). In Argentina, a crusading judge was fired when he refused to drop investigations of suspicious campaign donations to parties by businesses (TI 2004, 148). Faced with considerable evidence of party connivance, a more politically compliant judge declared that parties could not be penalized for excessive expenditures if they were unaware of them (TI 2007, xxiii). In contrast, in Poland and the Czech Republic, countries where legislatures are individual-focused, several legislators and party leaders were successfully identified as violators and prosecuted in the wake of scandals surrounding their financial accounts (OSI 2002; IFES 2002; Walecki 2002). These examples illustrate how party strength in legislation translates to higher corruption because it gives parties the ability to successfully manipulate their financial accounts and protect fraudulent fundraising practices.

I expect that in addition to the two demand-side mechanisms, these two supply-side dynamics will be activated when parties control the legislative process. Each of these mechanisms specifies particular incentives underlying party–business collusion, which result in higher levels of corruption in party-focused systems. Legislative institutions are key to this argument because they specify when parties have the ability to realize their higher demands for funds and when they do not. Thus, they identify the institutional conditions under which business lobbying will lead to higher levels of corruption. Collectively these four dynamics provide us with the following testable hypothesis:

H_o: When business interest groups lobby parties, ceteris paribus, corruption levels should be relatively higher.

As illustrated in figures 2.1 (a) and (b), combining H_o with the insights from H_{1A}, H_{2A}, and H_{3A}, we therefore get the following 3 testable hypotheses linking legislative institutions to corruption:

H_{1B}: When agenda-setting rules endow political parties with agenda control, ceteris paribus, corruption should be higher.

H_{2B}: When amendment rules endow political parties with control over amendments, ceteris paribus, corruption should be higher.

H_{3B}: When voting rules endow political parties with control over voting expulsions, ceteris paribus, corruption should be higher,

(IV) RESEARCH DESIGN

There are three sets of hypotheses that need to be tested empirically in order to systematically test the entire theoretical framework. The first set, consisting of H_{1a}, H_{2a}, and H_{3a}, tests the first link of the causal mechanism identified in this framework that party-focused agenda-setting, amendments, and voting defection rules lead to party-focused lobbying by special interest groups. The second set consisting of H_o would allow us to directly test whether party-focused lobbying is causing higher corruption levels, the second link in the causal chain linking institutions to corruption. Lastly, H_{1b}, H_{2b}, and H_{3b} tests the corruption implication of institutionally induced, party-focused lobbying by testing whether countries with party-focused legislative institutions experience higher corruption levels.

As I discussed in the introduction, with a few exceptions, many studies of corruption test theories at the level of H_{1b}, H_{2b}, and H_{3b} without directly testing the causal mechanism embodied by H_{1a}, H_{2a}, and H_{3a} and also H_o here. This common empirical strategy does not allow us to distinguish between the legitimacy and contribution of alternative theories, especially in the context of a multicausal phenomenon such as corruption. This causes serious observational equivalence problems since we cannot conclusively reject any of several explanations linking institutions to corruption. In this section, I discuss how the research design adopted by this book addresses these concerns and what its limitations are.

Table 2.1 summarizes the research design problem faced by this project. Row 4 in Table 2.1 details the ideal data required to perform the tests corresponding to the three sets of hypotheses discussed above. The required data would include comparable measures of corruption and individual institutions across as many countries as possible, enabling large-n statistical testing. It would also require qualitative data, which allows us to check the veracity and robustness of our operationalization as well as to test these results for individual countries in more detail through various case studies. However, as row 5 demonstrates, this strategy is infeasible due to a lack of data on both key dependent and independent variables.

Table 2.1. Testing Hypotheses: Research Design Problem

		Legislative Institutions	Legislative Lobbying	Corruption
1	H_o		Independent Variables	Dependent Variable
2	H_{1a}, H_{2a}, H_{3a}	Independent Variables	Dependent Variable	
3	H_{1b}, H_{2b}, H_{3b}	Independent Variables		Dependent Variable
4	Ideal Testing Data: Level, Type	Country Level, Panel Data	Interest Group Level, Survey Panel Data	Country Level, Panel Data
5	Available Data, Type	Missing Panel, Some Cross-Sections	None	ICRG, TI, WB Time Series Cross Section (TSCS)
6	Potential Sources	Constitutions, Primary Documents	Do Original Country Surveys— Myself	ICRG, TI, WB
7	Feasibility	Feasible	Limited	Available
8	Strategy	Construct TSCS	Selected Case Studies	Use Existing TSCS

The choice of political lobbying venue at the level of individual interest groups in a given country, which is the dependent variable required for testing H_{1a}, H_{2a}, and H_{3a}, (row 2) and the independent variable for testing H_o (row 1), is simply not available for many countries. This decision choice can only be captured by surveying interest groups around the world on their lobbying decisions. Currently, no existing survey does this. Therefore, there are no existing studies from which I could code this decision variable. This is the first very significant hurdle facing any study of comparative lobbying behavior. Second, the independent variables required for testing $H_{1a,b}$, $H_{2a,b}$, and, $H_{3a,b}$—whether legislative rules empower parties or individual legislators to set the agenda, introduce amendments, and allow parties to expel dissenting voters—has also not been coded for a large set of countries across time. This is the second significant challenge to the ideal strategy.

Row 6 shows the potential strategies that can be adopted for overcoming these challenges and row 7 summarizes their feasibility. The public availability of constitutions and rules of procedure for the assemblies of various countries makes it possible to code party or individual control over agenda-setting, introduction of amendments, and party ability to fire dissenting legislators from the chamber directly from these documents. Therefore, the second challenge can be overcome in a manner that facilitates cross-country large-n analysis. Chapter 6 discusses how this strategy allows me to construct a time-series cross-section (TSCS) dataset of 64 developing democracies from 1984 to 2004. This dataset lends itself to statistical techniques of inference and testing and allows me to perform robust tests of the impact of legislative institutions on corruption levels.

However, the first challenge, lack of group level data on venue choice, can only be overcome by conducting group level surveys in a large number of countries. While eminently desirable, this is unfortunately beyond the resources of any individual researcher. Therefore, to address the challenge of testing the causal mechanism directly in the absence of this data, I adopted the strategy of conducting a detailed case analysis of two selected cases, Brazil and India, to obtain the required data. Table 2.2 summarizes this research strategy. In sum, I use a combination of case-analysis of two most-similar cases, Brazil and India, to directly test the causal mechanism specified in H_{1a}, H_{2a} and H_{3a}, and also H_0 and apply statistical analysis techniques to a set of sixty-four developing democracies from 1984 to 2004 to test the large-n implications of the theory, H_{1b}, H_{2b} and H_{3b}, connecting legislative institutions and corruption. This allows me test the specific causal mechanism directly for these two theoretically crucial cases and to test if the implications of this causal mechanism are generalizable beyond these cases.

Clearly, evidence from two cases cannot prove that this causal mechanism is what links legislative institutions to corruption across all sixty-four countries. Importantly, if the survey data from the two case studies do not support H_{1a}, H_{2a}, and H_{3a} and H_0 in these theoretically crucial cases, then it makes it unlikely that legislatively induced lobbying is the causal mechanism driving corruption in these countries. If they are supported, then the case analysis does justify the collection of further lobbying data in these countries to test it more thoroughly over a diverse set of countries.

Consider figures 2.1 (a) and (b). If the large-n analysis still finds support for higher corruption in party-focused countries, then in the absence of case support for it, it would imply that a causal mechanism other than lobbying connects legislative institutions to corruption. If the large-n analysis does not find support for higher corruption in party-focused countries, in the presence of case study support for lobbying (H_{1a}, H_{2a}, and H_{3a}), it implies that legislative lobbying is not significant as a cause of corruption across countries. If the large-n analysis does not find support for higher corruption in party-focused countries, in the presence of case study support for corruption (H_0), it implies that legislative institutions do not drive lobbying. If the large-n analysis does not find support for higher corruption in party-focused countries, in the absence of case study support for lobbying or its link to corruption, then neither legislative institutions nor lobbying are linked and neither do they individually affect corruption.

This combination of data and testing strategies therefore allows us to comprehensively test the individual links in the causal argument presented in figure 2.1 (a) and (b) and articulated in the three sets of hypotheses presented in this chapter. In the next chapter, chapter 3, I discuss how and why these particular cases were selected and the

Table 2.2. Research Design Strategy

	Legislative Institutions	Legislative Lobbying	Corruption
1	*Ho*		**Independent Variables**	**Dependent Variable**
2	*Analytical Strategy*	• *Select Most-Similar Cases: Brazil (Individual-Focused), India (Party-Focused)* • *Within-Case Analysiso Statistical testing using data from interest group surveyso Secondary evidence from open-ended interviews, other studies, and anecdotes*		
3	Data	From Two Case Studies—Brazil, India: • Interest Group Survey Data • Open-ended Interviews • Secondary studies and data from surveys by other organizations		
4	H_{1a}, H_{2a}, H_{3a}	**Independent Variables**	**Dependent Variable**	
5	*Analytical Strategy*	• *Select Most-Similar Cases: Brazil (Individual-Focused), India (Party-Focused)* • *Within-Case Analysiso Statistical testing using data from interest group surveyso Process tracing through passage of bills, interviews*		
6	Data	From Two Case Studies: Brazil, India: • Interest Group Survey Data • Open-ended Interviews • Analytical Narrative from Passage of Legislative bills • Anecdotal Evidence		
7	H_{1a}, H_{2a}, H_{3a}	**Independent Variables**		**Dependent Variable**
8	*Analytical Strategy*	• *Time-Series Cross-Sectional Country-Level Analysis*		
9	Data	• *Analysis of secondary data and evidence, interviews* Times-Series Cross-Section Analysis of 64 Countries 1984–2004		

various kinds of within-case analytical strategies that were adopted in order to provide robust tests of all the hypotheses.

CONCLUSION

This chapter laid out a theoretical framework that specified why and how the strategic incentives of parties, individual politicians, and business interest groups to engage in corruption were linked. Since business interest groups are a key source for many politically valuable resources especially money, the incentives for policymakers to cater to their policy goals are strong in both party- and individual-focused legislative systems. However, when parties are institutionally enabled to influence the legislative policy process, their capacity to cater to business goals will be much higher. Thus, the legislative locus of political power over policymaking should influence business lobbying strategies and through them determine the level and extent of corruption in a country.

Specifically, I argued that when legislative rules on agenda-setting and amendments favor parties and rules on voting allow party leaders to strip antiwhip voters of their legislative mandate, ceteris paribus, legislative party discipline would be high. This would make political parties, not the legislators, the brokers of policy outcomes and as a result parties would attract business funds. Otherwise, legislators will be the influential policy brokers in the legislature and, accordingly, business interests will lobby legislators instead. Party-focused lobbying, however, should result in higher and more pervasive corruption due to four dynamics.

Two demand-side mechanisms—parties need to raise more funds and they prefer money over other political resources—raise the demand for corrupt money in party-focused systems. When parties control the legislation process, two supply-side dynamics—party ability to capture state institutions such as the bureaucracy and the judiciary via legislation and to protect corrupt financing practices—increase party ability to supply their higher demands successfully. The result should be higher and more pervasive corruption in countries where legislative rules allow parties to wield policy influence in the legislature.

The analysis in this chapter yielded three distinct sets of hypotheses: first, hypotheses linking party agenda-setting institutions to party-focused lobbying and higher corruption; second, hypotheses linking party ability to introduce amendments to party-focused lobbying and to higher corruption; and third, hypotheses linking party ability to expel legislators from their legislative mandate for voting against the party to party-focused lobbying and to higher corruption. If correct, these hypotheses should allow us to refine our analysis of the incentives institutions offer business and political elites to engage in corruption and explain why we see variation in corruption levels across countries with similar electoral rules and executive regimes.

The research strategy outlined for testing these hypotheses needs to wrestle with the lack of cross-country data on lobbying and on legislative institutions. Therefore, I outlined a strategy that combines using original TSCS data on legislative institutions to test their implications for corruption with survey data from a controlled comparison of two most-similar cases in order to directly test the causal mechanism of legislatively induced lobbying. Chapter 3 outlines the case selection process, establishes the institutional parameters for the two cases of Brazil and India, and assesses their suitability to represent the underlying theoretical categories of individual-focused and party-focused legislative systems, respectively. Chapter 4 uses data from surveys of business interest groups in Brazil and India and analyzes the passage of four bills to test the three hypotheses on legislative institutions and lobbying. Chapter 5 uses data from the surveys, anecdotes, and evidence from interviews to test the hypotheses on lobbying and corruption levels. Chapter 6 then presents the time-series cross-section analysis testing the links between legislative institutions and corruption levels for sixty-four developing democracies from 1984 to 2004.

3

CASE STUDIES: LEGISLATIVE INSTITUTIONS
IN BRAZIL AND INDIA

Most institutional theories of corruption posit a specific causal link between national institutions and levels of corruption. In order to test their predictions regarding the corruption implications of these institutions, they conduct panel or cross-country tests at the macro level of institutions without testing the causal mechanism itself directly. Unfortunately, this country-level macro-analysis cannot rule out the possibility that the predicted outcomes of corruption may be linked to institutions by a causal mechanism different from the one being proposed. As discussed in the introduction, this has been a common constraint in the study of corruption. Given the illicit nature of corrupt exchanges, scholars have been hampered in this effort by the severe challenges of collecting the data required to directly test various causal mechanisms. In this chapter, I discuss how the research design adopted in this book addresses this problem of micro-level empirical testing of the causal mechanism by adopting a strategy of comparative case analysis and studying two theoretically important cases—Brazil and India. I discuss the logic for selecting these specific cases and present relevant details on their legislative institutions and lawmaking process.

As discussed in chapter 2, table 2.2 summarizes how this research design meets the research goals of this study by combining the analysis of a large number of countries over time with in-depth study of two cases. Data from a time-series cross-section (TSCS) dataset of sixty-four developing democracies from 1984 to 2004 will be analyzed in chapter six to robustly test hypotheses H_{1b}, H_{2b}, and H_{3b}, which state that each of the three party-focused legislative institutions lead to higher corruption levels. In order to address the challenge of testing the causal mechanism directly, I adopted the strategy of conducting a detailed case analysis of two selected cases. Fearon and Laitin (2008, 757) argue that case studies are powerful tools for evaluating whether the causal arguments proposed to explain empirical regularities in large datasets are in fact plausible. They state that "one typically uses additional data about the beliefs, intentions, considerations, and reasoning of the people who made the choices that produced the outcome in order to test whether the 'higher-level' general story told about many cases is discernible in particular, concrete cases." A strategy of comparative case analysis thus allows one to feasibly acquire previously unavailable data at the level of detail required for a limited number of theoretically appropriate cases and then to use it for testing theory. Since data on political lobbying by businesses is unavailable for most countries, case studies offer a feasible method for testing the causal theory posed in this book.

There are several additional methodological advantages of this strategy as well. Gerring (2007, 84) summarizes the scope of case studies in a larger strategy of empirical testing as follows: "Cross-case arguments draw on within-case assumption, and within-case arguments draw on cross case assumptions. Neither works very well when isolated from the other. In most circumstances, therefore, it is advisable to conduct both types of analysis." Case studies, therefore, complement large-n analysis by offering the opportunity to verify concepts, elaborate nuances, and detect flaws in the causal logic being employed. Furthermore, as Gerring (2007, 45) points out, " . . . when studying decisional behavior, case study research may offer insight into the intentions, the reasoning capabilities, and the information-processing procedures of the actors involved in a given setting." Since the key dynamic in this project is the behavioral response of special interest groups to legislative incentives, case studies should be an especially potent tool for this project. In this chapter, I first discuss the logic for selecting these particular cases, the goodness of their fit with the strategy outlined in chapter 2, the limits their selection poses, and the various kinds of within-case analytical strategies that were adopted in order to provide robust tests. I then present a detailed discussion of the two cases, Brazil and India, outlining their characteristics, their legislative rules on agenda-setting, the introduction of amendments and voting dissidence, and the values they take on in the case selection strategy.

CASE SELECTION

There are three sets of hypotheses that need to be tested empirically in order to systematically test the entire theoretical framework. The first consists only of H_o and tests directly whether party-focused lobbying lead to higher corruption levels. The second set, consisting of H_{1a}, H_{2a}, and H_{3a}, tests the first link of the causal mechanism identified in this framework, whether party-focused agenda-setting, amendments, and voting defection rules lead to party-focused lobbying by special interest groups. The third set, consisting of H_{1b}, H_{2b}, and H_{3b}, tests whether party-focused legislative institutions lead to higher corruption levels. Therefore testing the hypotheses H_{1a}, H_{2a}, and H_{3a} and H_o using cases would allow a direct test of the 2-step causal mechanism, whereas testing H_{1b}, H_{2b}, and, H_{3b} allows a test of the resulting implications of institutional design for corruption levels for the full sample.

In this book the selected case studies need to primarily serve the research objective of theory testing.[1] In order to accomplish this goal successfully, the cases selected must be appropriate, and within-case analysis must be as robust as possible.[2] Scholars have suggested several strategies for achieving these goals and for reducing the cost of non-ideal case selection.[3] I drew on this body of techniques to adopt the case selection strategy known as "most-similar" design by Gerring (2007) and as "different design" by Mills (1834) and selected Brazil and India as the theoretically appropriate cases for this project.

This case selection strategy requires three important characteristics.[4] First, the se-lected cases must be representative of their underlying categories. Second, they must be matched on aspects that are irrelevant to the theory so that unit homogeneity is maximized. This ensures that any differences in our findings are not driven by differ-ences in these extraneous factors. Third, the cases must be such that the explanatory variable assumes the most distinct values possible on the range of possible values. Cases that satisfy these three criteria allow a robust test of the predicted outcomes. As I argue below, table 3.1 and 3.2 show that the cases of Brazil and India meet all three criteria well and thus they allow us to conduct a robust and transparent test of hypo-thesis H_o and H_{1a}, H_{2a}, and H_{3a}, as well as H_{1b}, H_{2b}, and H_{3b}.

The universe of cases here is the full set of sixty-four developing democracies in the full sample. The *first* concern about the 2 selected cases, Brazil and India, is whether they are typical of the theoretical categories they are meant to represent. In this study, there are two relevant categories: cases where legislative rules favor parties leading to stronger parties, the party-focused cases; and cases where legislative rules do not favor parties leading to weaker parties, the individual-focused cases. Rows 1, 2, and 3 of table 3.1 show the distribution of the 3 key independent variables for the full TSCS sample of 64 developing countries as well as for the 2 cases. Row 1 shows that 56% of all obser-vations are from cases where parties, not individuals, are empowered to set the agenda; row 2 shows that 53% of all observations represent cases where rules empower parties to introduce amendments; and row 3 shows that 39% of observations come from cases where parties have the ability to deprive dissenting members of their mandate. As I show in detail in the next section in this chapter, in 2005–2006 the Indian case repre-sents the institutional case, where all three rules empower parties, and the case of Brazil represents the case where all 3 legislative rules empower individual leaders at the expense of party leaders.[5] Therefore, both these cases are typical of the 2 categories they are meant to represent on the explanatory factors of interest in this project— party- and individual-focused legislative systems.

The *second* criterion these cases must satisfy is that they must match on other fea-tures and factors that are irrelevant to the theoretical mechanism we want to test. This is the "most-similar" aspect of this strategy. In chapter 6, differences in such factors will be allowed for in the statistical analysis through their inclusion as control variables. However, in our selection of cases, we must pick cases which "match" on these other variables. The full list of potential matching variables is given in rows 4–12 of table 3.1 and rows 1–5 of table 3.2. The list in table 3.1 includes factors that are identified as driving corruption in other institutional theories, such as electoral rules, electoral par-ticularism, district magnitude, executive regime, and federal or unitary system. The list in table 3.2 includes socioeconomic factors such as per capita income, rule of law, ethno-linguistic fractionalization, and civil and political liberties, which are theorized

Table 3.1. Institutional Rules for Sample and Cases

		Full Sample (64 Developing Country Democracies, 1984–2004)				Brazil	India
		Mean	Standard Deviation	Minimum	Maximum Value		
Legislative							
1	Agenda-Setting	.56	.31	0	1	0	1
2	Amendments	.53	.41	0	1	0	1
3	Voting Defections	.39	.27	0	1	0	1
Electoral							
4	Particularism	5.7541	4.0698	1	12	7	10
5	Average Ballot	.9540	.8445	0	2	2	2
6	Average Pooling	.7515	.8709	0	2	0	2
7	Average Voting	.6748	.5927	0	2	1	1
8	Average District Magnitude	36.700	113.5248	0	480	11	5
9	Plurality	.5423	.4984	0	1	1*	1
10	Closed List	.4813	.4999	0	1	0	0
11	Presidential	.56	.73	0	1	1	0
12	Federal	.56	.49	0	1	1	1

*Brazil has two elected chambers, the Senate and the House of Representatives. The Senate is elected via plurality rules while the House is elected via open-list proportional rules.

Table 3.2. Social, Economic, and Political Profile for Sample and Cases

			Full Sample (64 Developing Country Democracies, 1984–2004)				
		Mean	*Standard Deviation*	*Minimum*	*Maximum Value*	*Brazil*	*India*
1	*Log GDP per Capita*	3.86	4.07	1.91	11.25	8.71	7.47
2	*ELF*	.48	.25	.002	.88	0.57	0.88
3	*Rule of Law*	-.09	1	-2.5	2.29	3.68	2.73
4	*Civil Liberties*	3.5722	1.4039	1	7	3.1429	3.3333
5	*Political Liberties*	3.2446	1.7878	1	7	2.3810	2.3809

as being important in driving corruption by other theories. Since our focus is on corruption, matching our cases on these dimensions allows us to focus our analysis on factors driving the outcome of interest—legislative institutions.

As these data show, Brazil and India are better matched on some factors than others. With regards to electoral incentives, these cases provide a good match. Neither country employs closed-list proportional rules, the electoral system most closely associated with creating strong parties (Carey and Shugart 1995; Hix 2004). India elects members through plurality in single member districts to its lower chamber, a system Brazil uses to elect three members per district to its senate. As scholars have pointed out while plurality systems are more party-oriented than open-list PR, they do not generate strong parties which afford party leaders strong control over rank and file members (Hix 2004; Hicken 2009). The political capital that candidates bring to the ticket in plurality systems is considerable and voter identification with individual candidates is high, therefore plurality rule provides candidates with incentives to cultivate a personal vote (Hix 2004; Lindberg 2005; Gallagher and Holliday 2003; Curtice and Shively 2000). Hence, in these systems, while the party label does have some value, it does not have a decisive influence on voters (Gallagher and Holliday 2003, 114). Additionally, members to the lower house in Brazil are elected via open-list proportional system (PR) in statewide districts, a combination widely associated with weak parties and strong incentives to develop personal votes in the countries which employ them (Carey and Shugart 1995; Mainwaring 1992). Hence, the configuration of electoral rules in Brazil and India predict that parties should not be strengthened by them in either country.[6]

Therefore both countries have electoral systems that should give party members strong incentives to take actions which invest in their own reputations rather than that of their parties. Their choice as cases thus allows us to match them on this crucial element and control for the impact of electoral rules on corruption. However, on the dimension of executive regime type, these cases are somewhat different.

India has a parliamentary system where the executive relies on the legislature's vote of confidence to stay in office whereas Brazil, has a presidential system with a directly elected president. Despite this difference, two factors make these cases suitable for a comparative study of legislative policymaking. First, Brazil is considered to be among the strongest presidential systems in the world in terms of legislative powers, and second, both countries have operated in the context of coalition politics for the last two decades. Shugart and Carey (1997, 155) score the Brazilian president as a 12 on a 16-point scale, which puts it in the category of the strongest executives among the presidential systems of the world along with Argentina and Chile. This makes the policy-making role of the executive, and his influence on the legislative process more comparable to the strong executive typical of a parliamentary system including India's. Furthermore, politics in both countries since the 1980s has been characterized by coalition politics with ruling and opposition alliances being consistently composed of a high number of ideologically and politically distinct parties. Executives in both these countries have therefore had to work hard under conditions of political uncertainty to build legislative coalitions in order to sustain their political influence and pass their policy agendas. Therefore with regards to the policymaking environment, Brazil and India both have strong executives who enjoy considerable institutional advantages in legislation but must operate under the constant political threat posed by the fragile legislative coalitions they have to rely on. Thus, while these cases do not allow us to perfectly match the incentives created by the independence of the executive, they do capture the real political constraints placed on the executive's effective power to make policy. As the data in tables 3.1 and 3.2 show, Brazil and India are well matched on most potentially confounding dimensions but not on all.

As table 3.2 demonstrates, the assumption of perfect unit homogeneity holds reasonably well for these two countries. However, developing democracies exhibit a very wide range of values on socioeconomic factors including those frequently identified as important by alternative theories of corruption such as per capita income, rule of law, and civil liberties. It is unfortunately not feasible to find countries from the set of developing democracies which match perfectly given how many dimensions are relevant to the study of corruption. While these two cases are good representatives of developing countries on many dimensions—being close to the average or within one standard deviation on many socioeconomic dimensions—they both have substantially higher scores on rule of law. Therefore, perfect homogeneity is unavoidably violated in practice with respect to the underlying categories to some extent, as in many other studies. The large-n analysis in chapter six which allows us to account for differences on all of these institutional and socioeconomic dimensions across countries is therefore crucial in allowing us to understand the extent to which the results from this case analysis of Brazil and India can be generalized successfully to all developing country democracies.

In order to deal with such violations of unit homogeneity or perfect matching, scholars have suggested using process tracing to conduct within-case analysis.[7] This project is especially suited for process tracing because the sequential links in the causal chain are well defined, the falsifiable hypotheses for each stage are clearly articulated, and the alternative theories are well understood. Therefore to collect the independent bits of evidence required for conducting process-tracing successfully, I adopted a multipronged strategy.

First, I collected data on the lobbying behavior and corruption perceptions of business interest groups in both countries through a survey using a multistage stratified random sample design. Second, I conducted extensive open-ended interviews with relevant actors to gather qualitative evidence on these behaviors. Third, I analyzed the passage of specific legislative bills through the legislative chambers in Brazil and India. Fourth, I gathered data from surveys conducted by other institutions and organizations on lobbying and corruption in these countries.

As table 2.2 detailed, analyzing these independent sets of evidence as part of the within-case analysis should allow me to do process tracing and compensate somewhat for the limitations of the matching process in selecting cases. Despite imperfect matching on some of these factors, Brazil and India are well matched on many important factors and should therefore represent a good set of cases to implement the most-similar design for the universe of developing democracy cases under study.

The *third* and final criterion for implementing the most-similar design is to select cases that offer the clearest contrast on the independent variables, that is, cases that are most different on the explanatory variables. As I discuss in detail in the next section, Brazil and India represent cases where all three rules favor either parties (India) or individuals (Brazil). Therefore, they provide the most different values on the independent variables. Thus, they fulfill the final requirement of Mills's most-different design as well.

These two countries also share some trends and features common to most developing country democracies during this period thus enhancing their ability to represent their theoretical categories. Both countries moved to truly competitive multiparty democracies at roughly the same time. In Brazil's case, the 1988 transition was from a military dictatorship with an ineffective legislature to a presidential democracy with multiparty coalitions. In India, the transition was from an effectively one-party dominance by the Congress Party at the center to sustained multiparty coalition governments at all levels. Political and economic elites in both countries, therefore, made the shift to operating in a significantly more competitive political environment with a high degree of political uncertainty at roughly the same time. This experience of increasing competitiveness, electoral costs, and political learning by elites is shared by most developing country democracies and makes them especially good examples of their categories.

On the economic front as well, Brazil and India share the experience common to many developing countries of adopting and then abandoning models of state-led development policies, which emphasized import substitution and publicly owned enterprises in favor of market-led economic models that emphasized exports, foreign investment, and private ownership. They also have economic structures, strengths, and weaknesses that are fairly similar (IFC 2004, 15). Therefore, the kinds of policy challenges and issues that businessmen and politicians in these two countries grappled with were shared by other developing democracies as well. These two countries are also important players in global markets and at international institutions, which increases their comparability. However, as two of the biggest emerging markets, some of the issues and problems business and political elites face in these countries may not be shared by elites in countries with small, less internationalized economies. Additionally, both countries have for several decades had interest group communities that consisted of both state-sponsored organizations and voluntary organizations. This allows us to minimize the chances that any differences found in the lobbying and corruption outcomes may be driven by differences in policy issues or economic structures or the experience of their interest communities.

These two countries, which have the critical institutional features required for them to be good cases for theory testing, thus also make good representatives of important trends common to developing democracies. The results obtained from the analysis of these two countries therefore should be strongly representative of developing democracies and should be devoid of any systematic biases. However, as Fearon and Laitin (2008) and Gerring (2007) among others point out, two cases can only be suggestive, not definitive. These cases will not perform well in representing countries dissimilar to them on key features. This is where the large-n analysis is critical because it checks if these results hold when countries differ on these features. The results yielded by these case studies can therefore be understood only in the theoretical and empirical context of the large-n analysis that chapter 6 provides.

Chapters 6 and 7 discuss some of the potential implications and limitations of using the case study strategy and the empirical strategy outlined here for this project. Until such time when an institution or researcher with sufficiently deep resources conducts a global survey of interest groups and collects the required data on lobbying to conduct large-n as well as a large number of case studies, further work by other scholars should systematically expand this set of cases beyond India and Brazil in order to overcome these limitations. This would enable further testing of the causal mechanism under a broader set of control factors and would facilitate the systematic exploration of further nuances and variations in these findings. For the purposes of this book, however, Brazil and India provide an appropriate set of cases to robustly test whether institutional differences in the legislature motivate different lobbying strategies by influencing party strength, and whether these different lobbying strategies in turn lead to significantly different corruption levels. I now discuss in detail the institutional rules of the Brazilian and Indian legislatures and the political behaviors they generate.

LEGISLATIVE RULES IN THE INDIAN PARLIAMENT

At its independence in 1947, India adopted a bicameral, federal, parliamentary system of government. India's 543 members are directly elected to the lower house, the Lok Sabha (LS), for five-year terms by first-past-the-post rules in single member districts. Members to the 250-seat upper house, the Rajya Sabha, are indirectly elected for six-year terms in proportion to seats held by political parties across national and state legislatures. Nominations are made by political parties.[8] The two houses do not have equal legislative powers. While policy bills and constitutional amendments may be introduced in either house, money bills can only be introduced in the lower house and vetoed by it. Therefore, in practice the lower house has wielded more influence. The Upper House is a valued political asset for parties since it allows senior leaders to be nominated to the parliament directly by the party without standing for elections. This can be important since being an MP is a legal requirement for holding a cabinet position. For example, Prime Minister Manmohan Singh became eligible for the prime ministership only because he was nominated to the Rajya Sabha by the Congress (I) after losing in the general elections.

The legislative law-making process in India consists broadly of three stages—introduction, consideration, and passing. Subsequently bills must be notified if passed and are allowed to lapse if they fail. Figure 3.1 outlines the details of this process. During

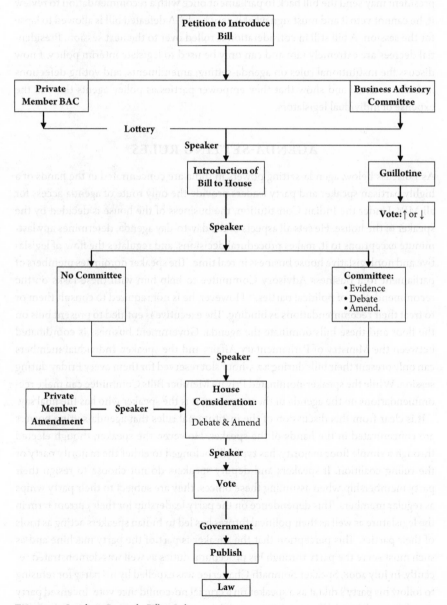

Figure 3.1. *Legislative Process for Bills in India*

introduction, the bill is introduced and its principles and goals are discussed in the chamber. The speaker then decides whether the bill should be referred to any committees, circulated for public opinion, or voted on in the floor. After any committee modifications, the bill is brought to the plenum for final *consideration*. Here it is debated clause by clause and can be amended by any member who has managed to get on the agenda. After this process has been completed, the bill is voted on. If passed, the process is repeated in the other chamber. After approval by both houses, a bill has to be approved by the president and officially notified in order to take effect. While the president may send the bill back to parliament once with a recommendation to review it, he cannot veto it and must sign what is sent back.[9] A defeated bill is allowed to lapse for the session. A bill still in consideration is rolled over to the next session. Presidential decrees are extremely rare and can only be used to legislate interim policy. I now discuss the institutional rules on agenda-setting, amendments, and voting defections in India in detail and show that they empower parties as policy agents there at the expense of individual legislators.

AGENDA-SETTING RULES

As I discuss below, agenda-setting powers in India are concentrated in the hands of a highly partisan speaker and party leaders provide the only route of agenda access for all MPs. Under the Indian Constitution, the business of the house is decided by the speaker of the house. He sets all aspects of the day-to-day agenda, determines any last-minute exceptions to it, makes procedural decisions, and regulates the flow of legislative and nonlegislative house business in real time. The speaker nominates members of parliament to a Business Advisory Committee to help him with these tasks on the recommendation of political parties.[10] However, he is not required to consult them or to treat their recommendations as binding. The executive is entitled to present bills on the floor and these bills dominate the agenda. Government business is coordinated between the Ministry of Parliamentary Affairs and the speaker. Individual members can only present their bills during a 2.5-hour slot reserved for them every Friday during session. While the speaker-nominated Private Member Bills Committee can make recommendations on the agenda of these sessions, it is the speaker who has the final say.

It is clear from this discussion of the institutional rules that agenda-setting powers are concentrated in the hands of the speaker. However, the speaker, though elected through a simple floor majority, has typically belonged to either the majority party or the ruling coalition. If speakers and deputy speakers do not choose to resign their party membership when assuming these offices, they are subject to their party whips as regular members. This dependence on the party leadership for their current term in the legislature as well as their political futures has led to Indian speakers acting as tools of their parties. This perception that the speaker is part of the party machine and as such must serve the party through his procedural duties as well was demonstrated recently. In July 2008, Speaker Somnath Chatterjee was expelled by his party for refusing to follow his party's diktat as a speaker on a crucial no-confidence vote. Incensed party members exclaimed (Financial Express, July 17, 2008), "He is a senior member who led the party in Parliament for more than fourty years. No body expected such a behavior from him."

Soli Sorabjee (Kashyap 2003, vii), who has the rather unique perspective of being a former attorney general of India, president of the United Lawyers Association, and head of Transparency International in India, commented on this reality, "Unfortunately they [Speakers] regard themselves as the spokesmen or the hatchet men of the political party which has been responsible for their election as Speakers. . . . Many orders of the Speakers which have been challenged before courts reveal absence of fairness and objectivity, betray a high degree of partisanship." For example, speakers have interpreted the rules on the expulsion of party-switchers liberally to produce outcomes favored by their party leaders.[11] For example, in 1990 Speaker Rabi Ray ruled that a party split was a one-time affair and disqualified all congress legislators who joined a splinter group belatedly. His immediate successor, Shivraj Patil, made the opposite interpretation and ruled that a split was a continuous process and extended legal protection to all members who left the Janata Dal at various points of time during 1992–1993 to join the ruling Congress Party to which he belonged (Mitra 1998, 103–107; Ventakesan 2001, 16). The relevant set of agenda-setting agents in India is thus very limited and includes the speaker, his own party's leaders, and leaders of other parties.

This reality is also reflected in the process that parties have evolved to handle agenda-access requests internally at the party level. All parties in India centralize the process of bargaining for agenda access internally and negotiate directly with the current speaker on behalf of members. The right-leaning Bhartiya Janata Party (BJP) and the leftist Communist Party of India-Marxist (CPI-M) leaders, for example, hold regular formal party meetings during sessions and finalize their party's business agenda for the day including requests to the speaker.[12] Individual legislators must go through party leaders as the only channels of access they have. The Business Advisory and Private Member committees rarely meet, are poorly attended, and have no influence. For example, in three sessions of the 14th Lok Sabha (LS) held in 2005, the Business Advisory Committee spent on average 4.62 minutes arranging the agenda for each of LS's 85 sittings while the Private Committee on average dispatched the business of 22 Friday sessions in 12 21-minute meetings![13] These numbers, typical of these committees, show their irrelevance to the policy process. In order to access the agenda in order to introduce bills, amendments, motions, or to obtain time for debate or questions, legislators must largely rely on the goodwill of their party leaders.

Former Minister and Parliamentarian Arun Shourie (2007, 82) sums up this situation succinctly: "What is to be done that day in the legislature, for instance, is decided by two or three individuals. . . . In fact, he, the average legislator, that is every member except those two or three controllers, does not contribute anything substantial to the decision; indeed, most often he learns about what is to happen only after he enters the house." The extent of partisan agenda control over policy was powerfully demonstrated on March 18 and 19, 2006, when the Speaker Somnath Chatterjee, a legislator from the ruling coalition, revised the floor agenda with no prior warning or consultation and changed committee oversight procedures to favor his allies.[14] The ruling affected the consideration of the budget by one of the most prestigious committees in the parliament, the budget committee. Analysis of the legislative business reports shows that the only legislators able to successfully obtain time to raise questions and introduce motions and bills are those MPs who are known to be rising stars in the good graces of the party leadership (Lok Sabha Bulletin, various issues; PRS 2009).

As the discussion above details, the speaker and party leaders are the only institutional actors who determine when to put a bill on the floor agenda, whether or not to recommend it to any committees for consideration, the choice of committee assigned to consider a bill, if and when to allow amendments to bills, when to schedule the final bill for a vote, and the voting procedure itself. According to hypothesis H_{1a}, business groups should observe this concentration of agenda power in the speaker's hands, and importantly its partisan roots and complexion, when they mull over their choices to influence the policy agenda. In India, therefore, their choice for obtaining influence over the agenda should be the leaders of political parties.

AMENDMENTS

As I discuss below, the rules on amendment of bills in India favor parties over legislators as well. Amendments to bills may address the substance of a bill, its scope, its implementation schedule, or the procedure it must follow. Private members in India have no constitutional privileges in terms of reserved time or the right to introduce amendments to the agenda.[15] Private amendments can only be allowed if and when the speaker permits, and if it is tabled successfully the cabinet must approve it before the plenary vote. Moreover, once an amendment has been taken into consideration, during consideration, the legislator who moved the amendment does not enjoy any precedence in its debate. Private amendments can be offered to committees; however, they are not binding on the house.

This channel for introduction and approval of amendments has meant that individual legislators in India are not able to effectively access the floor to influence bills on their own. They must go though their party leaders in order to put their amendment on the agenda and get approved by the cabinet. Both are influenced through party leaders. In practice this has meant that only amendments whose substance is agreeable to and sanctioned by the party may be introduced into either house. Even for issues on which individual legislators have significant ideological differences with their party leaders, and when public discussion of the bill ensures constituents are following their MP's actions, legislators have been unable to table their own amendments.

For example, when the Insurance Regulatory and Development Authority Bill 1999 was being debated in parliament, the only amendments that were in fact introduced and discussed in the house where those shepherded through by various party leaders.[16] This bill was highly unpopular with many voters as well as organized groups and thus provided dissenters with a chance to establish their personal reputations with these constituents based on their position on this bill. Despite the fact that dissenting legislators from all parties publicly stated their opposition to the bill, none of the individual amendments they introduced were tabled. This lack of ability by legislators to influence policy bills through amendments and the complete dominance of this process by parties should be clear to all special interests in India. According to hypothesis H$_{2a}$, business groups in India should therefore respond by lobbying party leaders, not individual legislators, when they wish to amend bills under consideration.

VOTING DISSIDENCE

As I discuss below, in India, legislative rules allow political parties to control the voting behavior of their legislators completely. Under the 10th Schedule of the 52nd Constitutional Amendment 1985, a member may be disqualified from his membership in parliament under two conditions.[17] The first condition is if he has expressly gone against his party's whip on any motion either by voting against it or by abstaining to vote. The only exceptions to such disqualification are if the member has obtained the party's prior permission to vote against it or if he subsequently obtains it within fifteen days of his action.[18] Second, a member is disqualified if he gives up his party membership voluntarily in order to switch parties or become independent. Independent legislators choosing to affiliate with a party in parliament are also disqualified but mergers are deemed not to affect membership. Importantly, expulsion from the chamber is *not* automatically triggered but must be formally requested by the offended party and then granted by the speaker. This is an important point since no proceedings are initiated if the party does not request it. This discretion has provided party leaders with a very effective threat, and they have used it to enforce absolute voting discipline in their legislative delegations irrespective of the member's popularity or standing.

The following view expressed by a senior party leader of a major national party was voiced and shared by many leaders of other parties: "Anti-party voting in committees or on the floor will get an MP in serious trouble with his party. A fellow committee member came to me and told me that he agreed with me ideologically and sympathized with my constituents but could not vote with me for fear of his party. This was a very senior party member with his own voter base. We don't tolerate such behavior also."[19] Party control over voting has been further enhanced by the partisan capture of the speaker's position. In a rather striking example, G. K. Moopanar and Jayanthi Natarajan, who quit the Congress (I) in 1997 to start the Tamil Manila Congress Party, voted repeatedly with the Congress Party in parliament under this threat of expulsion (Mitra 1998, 139–140). Despite campaigning against the Congress (I) publicly, they followed party discipline because they did not want to lose their parliamentary seats. Such voting behavior is not uncommon and may be readily observed by the media and interest groups.

Even on issues where legislators have strong ideological objections and can draw on substantial public support, such as in the passage of the IRDA and the Patents Amendment bills discussed in chapter 4, legislators vote along party lines. With 10 candidates standing for every parliamentary seat and legislative turnover averaging over 50%, reelection is by no means assured even at the best of times. Without party support, the chances of success are much slimmer. Therefore, members cannot afford to lose their seats by voting their conscience or voting with their constituency interests if it goes against the party writ. The ability of parties to strip any members who vote against them of their legislative mandate gives party leaders an immense capacity to ensure voting discipline in the chamber and the ability to deliver voting outcomes on bills to interest groups. According to hypothesis H_{3a}, business lobbies should recognize the influence that party leaders are able to exert over the voting behavior of their party legislators and lobby parties in India to influence voting.

LEGISLATIVE RULES IN THE BRAZILIAN PARLIAMENT

Brazil has a bicameral, federal system of government with a directly elected president.[20] The Brazilian president is elected by plurality in a two-round runoff system. Only the top two vote-getters from the first round compete in the second round. The Federal Senate and the Chamber of Deputies make up the National Congress. The Chamber of Deputies with 513 members represents the people. Deputies are elected via an open-list proportional system for four-year terms. District magnitude varies with a minimum of 8 (Amazonia) and a maximum of 70 (So Paolo) deputies for every province. Turnover in the Chamber has been high running between 50% and 60% for legislators since 1988. The number of parties represented in the Chamber has also been high and has ranged from a low of 4.1 in 1989 to a high of 9.4 in 1992 over the last 20 years (Morgenstern and Nacif 2000, 59). The Federal Senate represents the 26 states and the federal district. Senators are elected through a first-past-the-post principle for eight-year terms. Three senators are elected per state, along with two substitutes. One-third and two-thirds of the Senate seats are rotated in elections every four years. Senior political figures in Brazil tend to run for the Senate rather than the Chamber of deputies. Both chambers elect their own governing boards.

THE BRAZILIAN LAW-MAKING PROCESS

The law-making process is comprised broadly of seven steps: initiative, debate, voting, passing, sanction or veto, enactment, and publication. Figure 3.2 provides an overview of the various stages in the process. Of these stages, the first five take place within the executive and the legislative branches, whereas the last two are the responsibility only of the executive. The legislative process begins when a bill of law is introduced in one of the houses—the Chamber of Deputies or the Federal Senate, which is then called the "originating house." Bills originating from the president of the republic, the supreme federal court, the higher courts, a federal deputy, the federal prosecutor-general, or citizens are taken up first in the Chamber of Deputies. Those originating from a senator or a state legislative assembly start life in the federal senate.

Within the originating house, the bill of law is submitted to technical, material, and formal analyses, which are carried out by corresponding committees of that house.[21] If the bill of law is approved by the competent committees, it is then forwarded to the plenum for a vote. Floor members may take a bill out of committee consideration by filing and approving a discharge petition on the chamber floor. A third of deputies or one-fourth of the Senate can request such a petition and a simple floor majority is

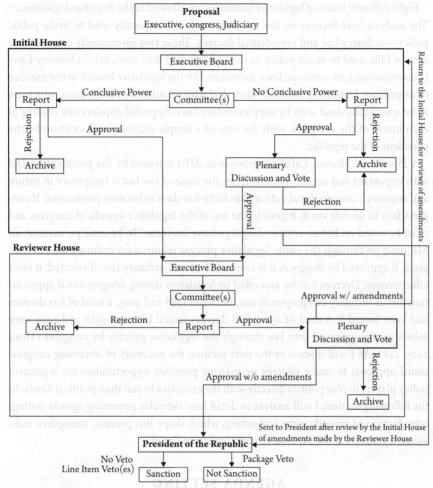

Figure 3.2. *Legislative Process for Bills in Brazil*
Source: Hiroi (2005, 56)

required to approve it. After being voted on, it is forwarded to the reviewing house if approved. In the reviewing house if it is amended, it is returned to the originating house to be reconsidered; if it is approved, it is forwarded to the president to be either sanctioned or vetoed. Ordinary laws require simple majorities to pass. If the bill is rejected in either house, it is dismissed entirely from consideration.

Upon receiving a bill of law, the president of the republic may either sanction it or veto it in whole or in part. A presidential veto can technically be issued only on the grounds of unconstitutionality or damage to public interest. In practice, this has been a subjective criterion. Any presidential veto must be issued within fifteen days from receipt of the bill, and congress must vote on it within thirty days if it wants to override the veto. Simple majorities in both houses are sufficient to override a presidential veto. If a bill is sanctioned by the president or if the veto is overridden, then the president needs to promulgate it for it to be effective. This completes the process.

Eight different kinds of legislative initiatives are allowed in the Brazilian legislature.[22] The analysis here focuses on the two that are most frequently used to make public policy—ordinary law and presidential decrees. These two instruments cover at least 90% of bills used to enact policy in the legislature (Hiroi 2005, 81).[23] *Ordinary Laws* (*Leis ordinárias*) are common laws, formulated by the legislative branch in the exercise of its primary legislating function. They deal with all subjects, except those which are to be specifically dealt with by supplementary laws. Approval requires one reading in each house of the congress, with the vote of a simple majority and sanction by the president of the republic.

A *Provisional Measure* (*Medidas provisórias, MP*) is issued by the president to deal with important and urgent matters. It has the force of law but is temporary in nature and requires a congressional vote within forty-five days to become permanent. If congress fails to so vote on it, it goes to the top of the legislative agenda of congress and must be voted on before any pending legislative business. To become permanent, an MP must go through the entire legislative process required for ordinary laws in congress. If approved by congress, it is converted into an ordinary law; if rejected, it loses effectiveness. Decrees can be amended by legislators during congressional appreciation just as ordinary bill proposals can. Between 1988 and 2005, a total of 892 decrees had been issued.[24] A total of 65% of all decrees issued between 1988 and 2001 were subsequently approved into law through the legislative process by congress (Hiroi 2005, 148). As I will discuss in the next section, the necessity of obtaining congressional approval to make decrees permanent provides opportunities for legislative policy players to play politics directly with the executive to suit their political needs. In the following section, I will analyze in detail how the rules governing agenda-setting, introduction of amendments, and voting, which shape this process, strengthen individual legislators at the expense of party leaders in Brazil.

AGENDA-SETTING

In Brazil, the agenda is controlled by a body of freely elected board members comprised of legislators from multiple parties. As I discuss below, this has given legislators a high degree of access to the floor agenda independently of their party leaders. At the same time, party leaders are not able to exercise firm control over the procedures governing passage of bills or debates on them through control over elected board members. Therefore, legislators are able to influence the agenda based on their own initiatives, political acumen, and prestige.

The constitution identifies two formal sets of agenda-setters—the executive and the *Mesa Diretora*, the Governing Board.[25] Both chambers elect members to their own *Mesa* via open elections for two-year terms. While parties register the candidates for these positions, the candidates are then elected by the entire floor, not just their party delegations. The officers elected are a chamber president, two vice-presidents, four secretaries, and two substitutes. The senate president presides over joint sessions. The chamber presidents and other *Mesa* members are all responsible for organizing all plenary activities, including supervising the procedures for passage of bills, amendments, decrees, and motions as well as scheduling time for debates. The president of a chamber is required to "consult" with another legislative body, the *Colégio de Líderes* (College of Leaders), when setting the monthly agenda.[26] The *Colégio* is comprised of the elected floor leaders of all the legislative parties, the majority and minority leaders, and a government-appointed government leader. *Colégio* decisions are made by majority vote where party leaders' votes are weighed by their seat shares in the chambers.[27] It is important to note that the recommendations of the party leaders in the *Colégio* are not legally binding on the presidents and are truly advisory in nature (*Regimento Interno Article 20:32*). The *Colégio* however has little say in the daily agenda of the house (*Ordem do Dia*) which is set exclusively by the president and governing board of each chamber. As I discuss below, the role of the *Colégio* in this process has been a subject of some dispute among scholars of Brazilian legislative politics and has led one school of scholars to argue that party leaders do have a significant role in agenda-setting in Brazil.

Individual legislators may sign up to present a bill directly with the *Mesa* of their chamber. Every deputy and senator has equal and direct access to floor time for this purpose, and party floor leaders do not enjoy any institutional privilege in introducing bills or amendments to the floor. Therefore, deputies and senators can propose bills and amendments without any formal mediation from their party leaders. Furthermore, they can also sign up with the *Mesa* directly in order to speak to the chamber on any subject including legislation proposed by others. As proposers of a bill or an amendment, legislators enjoy preeminence in presenting and debating their own bill. All final decisions on timing and level of urgency accorded to a bill on the agenda, as well as the procedural fate of different bills presented on a single issue, are decided by the boards of each chamber.

The ability to issue presidential decrees, *Medidas Provisórias* (*MP*), gives the executive considerable agenda-setting powers in Brazil. Since the reforms of 2001, presidential decrees can now only be renewed once and must be voted on within forty-five days of being issued. If this voting deadline has not been met, they automatically go to the top of the congressional legislative agenda in order to ensure timely consideration. The president also enjoys the constitutional privilege of requesting urgency (*pedido de urgência*) on any executive initiative. So, for example, if the congress is considering draft proposals that the executive does not favor, he can introduce an alternative draft which jumps the queue in the agenda and must be considered ahead of its rival congressional versions. These privileges provide the president with the ability to influence both the timing and substantive version of bills under consideration in the congress, thus making him an influential agenda-setter.

Scholars have modeled the agenda-setting process this set of institutional arrangements creates as three very distinct processes and associated them with varying levels of agenda powers by party leaders ranging from very strong to very weak. In the first formulation, agenda-setting in Brazil is seen to be a centralized, parliamentary-style process, where the consultations between the executive and party leaders in the *Colégio* allow them to collaborate to control the agenda completely (Figuerido and Limongi 1995, 1999, 2000, 2003). In this characterization, individual congressmen have little independent access to the agenda and must rely on their party leaders to obtain it. The *Colégio* plays a crucial role, and party floor leadership becomes an important political prize for legislators.

In complete contrast, the second formulation of the agenda-setting process characterizes it as an atomistic process where deals must be negotiated constantly between all legislative players and the agenda is dominated by deals struck between the executive and individual legislators (Ames 2001). In this model, party leaders play little to no role in these negotiations and deputies and senators can rely on their own political assets to obtain agenda access, can log roll freely, and have alternative channels of agenda access open to them. The *Colégio* is a marginal player in these negotiations and party floor leadership positions should not be particularly coveted by legislators. In the third model, agenda power is seen to vary between these two realizations conditional on the coalition-building strategy of the executive (Amorim Neto, Cox, and McCubbins 2003; Pereira and Mueller 2004; Santos 2003). When the executive is successful in building a coalition, agenda-setting power is theorized as being wielded by a cartel that primarily includes executive and individual legislators and can include party leaders. When the executive fails in his attempts to construct such a coalition, agenda-setting reverts to the atomistic process described above.[28]

Authors of all three models have offered empirical evidence in support of their arguments. Therefore in order to assess which of these best captures the dynamics of agenda-setting in Brazil, we need to answer three empirical questions: How much are positions on the *Mesa* and *Colégio* coveted by members? How much control do party leaders have over getting their members successfully elected to these positions? What happens to *Mesa* officials or floor leaders if they do not follow the wishes of their party leaders? As I discuss below, evidence shows that while *Mesa* positions are considered desirable and are sought after by legislators, *Colégio* positions are not seen as a significant step up in the professional ladder. Party leaders in Brazil are not able to decisively control elections to positions in either the *Mesa*. Members get elected to these positions on the strength of their personal following and skills and even independently of their party's endorsement. Finally, *Mesa* officials and floor leaders who go against party diktat do not suffer any harsh consequences to their careers. Taken together, these characteristics strongly support the view that party leaders in Brazil do not exert decisive, reliable influence over the legislative agenda of either chamber. Rather, the influence of the *Colégio* has waxed and waned with the prestige and political influence of the individuals who were elected to these positions.

Evidence from electoral contests for *Mesa* and floor leader positions, as well as from interactions between these officials and other congressmenshows that while *Mesa* positions are highly valued in Brazilian politics, the positions in the *Colégio* hold little attraction for either deputies or senators. For example, in a pattern typical of other elections, prominent congressional floor leaders of government and opposition parties such as the PT (Walter Pinheiro), DEM (ACM Neto), PCdoB (Jo Moraes), and PSol (Luciana Genro) chose to run for the position of mayor in various cities in the 2008 elections, while others went on leave to take up positions in the state governments. Legislators thus expressed their preference for moving to local-level executive positions rather than staying in national-level party leadership positions. Similarly, switching parties from the PSDB to PMDB did not prevent Romero Juca from maintaining his position as government leader in the senate because there was no significant interest in preserving this position for a loyal internal party candidate from the PMDB (Fleischer 2008). In an another example, Senator Sergio Machado, serving as floor leader of the PSDB in 2001, preferred to run for state governor and successfully switched parties to the PMDB and obtained its nomination to run for the post of governor (Fleischer 2001).

In contrast, elections for the position of chamber president have been bitterly contested. A recent but not isolated example was the hard-fought contest between Aldo Rebelo of the Communist Party, who was openly backed by President Lula, against Arlindo Chinaglia of the president's own PT party for the position of president of the chamber of deputies. In an election that went to a second round, Chinaglia won 261 to 243 with the support of deputies from the opposition PSDB (Xinhua, February 2, 2007). Rumors that pork inducements had been offered to buy legislative votes abounded on both sides, underlining the importance of this position (Reuters, January 31, 2007). Furthermore, the independent capacity of influential legislators to win these positions independently of their parties and rampant party-switching affected even the ability of parties to stake their claim to nominate the majority candidate for them and their weight in *Colégio* votes.

For example, in October 2006, the PFL won the largest share of seats in the senate, 18, making it eligible to stake a claim for the senate presidency. However, by the time the new congress was sworn in on February 1, 2007, it had already lost its majority status to the PMDB because three senators switched parties primarily to the PMDB. In 1993 and 1995, the largest party in the chamber deputies, the PMDB, suffered from such internal uncertainty that the second-largest party, the PFL, was able to build a coalition to elect the chamber president from among its ranks. As a result of similar political dissension within party ranks, Severino Cavalcanti emerged as the surprise winner in the 2005 contest for presidency of the chamber. These repeated events strongly suggest that in stark contrast to India, aspirants for the most powerful agenda-setting posts in the Brazilian congress do not see themselves succeeding as protégés of their own parties. Hence, they do not tend to act as their agents either. As described in the discussion of the 2007 CPMF bill in chapter 4, this was demonstrated by the refusal of the then senate president, who belonged to the PMDB, to pressure senators to vote with the party line.

Numerous examples such as these demonstrate that party floor leadership is not considered to be a valuable position in Brazil because it is not seen to be influential in influencing legislation or appointments. On the other hand, positions on the governing board are seen to be a source of political influence and prestige and are contested and fought for by legislators. Furthermore, chamber positions can be obtained independently of one's party's wishes and without relying on the support of one's party leaders. Chamber leaders cannot be penalized by party leaders for going against their wishes. The legislators elected to these positions exhibit considerable independence in the exercise of their procedural powers and command influence in their capacity as board members.

Therefore, based on this institutional arrangement, which distributes agenda-setting power among multiple political actors, we expect that individual legislators will be able to successfully access the agenda without party support in Brazil. Independent access to board members allows legislators the strategic space to influence important procedural decisions such as which version of a bill makes it to the agenda and which doesn't, whether or not bills go to committee, the identity of the committees which consider the bill, whether they are voted on in committee, and when a bill is voted on in the plenum. According to hypothesis H_{1a}, we should therefore expect individual legislators to be the channels used by special interest groups for securing access to influence the agenda in Brazil.

AMENDMENTS

In Brazil, legislative rules give individual legislators the ability to modify bills by introducing and debating amendments without party interference. Party leaders on the other hand enjoy no institutional privileges in this regard and are unable to influence the behavior of their legislators in discharging this function. Therefore, according to hypothesis H_{2a}, legislators rather than party leaders should be the policy actors considered influential by interest groups for this function in Brazil and, hence, should be the ones lobbied by them.

In Brazil, amendments that directly affect the substance, scope, implementation, and regulation of policy can be attached to ordinary bills, constitutional rules, presidential decrees, and budgetary appropriations. Once presidential decrees are under congressional consideration, they follow the same procedures as ordinary legislation with the exception that they must be voted on within forty-five days of being issued by the executive. Amendments to these bills can be introduced at various stages of the process for an ordinary bill, including committee and floor consideration. Amendments at the committee stage are submitted directly by legislators to the committee, and amendments at the floor stage are introduced by signing up with the board.[298] Party leaders do not enjoy any institutional privileges that would allow them to expedite the consideration of favored amendments or prevent the introduction of amendments not in their interests. Thus, they exercise little influence on the introduction and passage of amendments.

For example, even the ruling PT party was caught off-guard when, in April 2008, two of their own senators, Tião Vanna and Paulo Palm, successfully introduced amendments to increase the share of the federal budget allocated to health care and to index increases in social security to inflation rates against their party's wishes (Fleischer, April 18, 2008). Despite the important financial repercussions of these amendments, they were passed successfully against the government's wishes because the two PT senators marshaled sufficient opposition votes in favor of it. Furthermore, their careers within their party did not suffer any significant repercussions from this legislative decision.

Budgetary amendments influence spending on issues of interest to various constituencies including business groups. They affect spending on infrastructure and public works projects as well as spending on subsidies, taxes, and other financial measures that can affect the bottom line of firms. Thus the ability to influence them draws the attention and resources of business lobbies. In countries where party leaders are able to influence budgetary amendments, they have provided party leaders with a central source of pork and patronage that can potentially be used to discipline party members (Schofield 2008). Since 1995, however, budgetary amendments in Brazil can only be introduced by legislators (Neto *et al*, 2003; Samuels 2003). Prior to this, party leaders had the power to introduce such amendments but were unsuccessful in getting them approved (Samuels 2003). Since 1995, deputies have been entitled to request budgetary amendments up to roughly 2 million Reais. While the executive has been known to slow down or speed up disbursements as a means of persuasion, party leaders do not figure anywhere in their approval, release, or implementation.[30] Therefore, legislators, not party leaders, exercise influence over them.

Legislators also exercise tremendous influence on policy through their ability to amend presidential decrees. In crucial policy areas such as budgets, policy regarding state-owned enterprises, and administration in Brazil, the executive enjoys exclusive legislative privilege of introduction. In these cases, legislator amendments provide the *only legislative tool* to influence policy outside of the executive office. This is especially relevant for Brazil because a significant share of legislation is enacted through the presidential office. Furthermore, as discussed earlier, decrees are often used by the executive to force congress to consider substantive versions of bills preferred by the executive and to expedite consideration of this preferred version. The ability to influence the substance of decrees using amendments can thus be crucial for business groups. Studies have shown that decrees which have more amendments attached to them enjoy significantly higher success rates in getting approved later as bills (Reich 2002, 13). This attests to the intense bargaining and change they undergo during their passage through congress. Therefore, individual legislators, not party leaders, should provide an important channel through which interest groups can gain influence over executive decrees in Brazil.

Finally, individual legislators also exercise the prerogative of introducing and debating constitutional amendments without party mediation on behalf of or against their efforts. They require 49 votes in the senate and 308 in the house rather than a simple majority in two rounds, but they otherwise undergo a procedure similar to ordinary legislation. Given the extent of social and economic government commitments embodied in the Brazilian constitution, many constitutional amendments directly impact businesses and are a magnet for intense lobbying by them. Here again, party leaders are not able to control the behavior of their members on these amendments. In a recent demonstration of this, on December 13, 2007, the government lost a key vote in the senate on the CPMF (Provisional Contribution on Financial Transactions), which would have allowed it to renew its taxation of financial transactions (Financial Times, December 13, 2007; Fleischer 2007). Some prominent business organizations such as the industrial federation of the city of Sao Paolo, (FIESP) had lobbied intensely against passage of the CPMF bill arguing it would hurt businesses. Others however had lobbied in favor of its passage due to the expected damage the loss of this tax revenue could do to Brazil's fiscal deficit and thus to its credit ratings. Despite the fact that this rejection would lead to a R$40 billion loss in revenue and would hurt popular and high-profile government programs in welfare (the *Bolsa Família* program) and pensions, six senators from the ruling coalition voted against it in defiance of their party whips. Party leaders were unable to control their votes or to penalize them politically even for voting against such a crucial bill.

The above discussion shows that individual legislators have the independent competence to introduce pertinent amendments to ordinary bills, constitutional amendments, decrees, and budgetary amendments. Additionally, party leaders are not able to successfully control the behavior of their members in this regard. Given that individual deputies and senators exercise control over the ability to amend bills, according to hypothesis H_{2a}, interest groups should lobby them in order to exert influence over amendments in Brazil.

VOTING

Parties in Brazil could not expel legislators who voted against the party whip from their chamber mandate till 2008.[31] At the time of this study, therefore, legislators could vote against their party whips without losing their congressional seats. This gave deputies and senators tremendous political and policy leverage as they were able to vote freely in their own interest, form their own legislative coalitions, and log roll independently on their own initiative. This state of affairs was described by Sartori (1993, 13): "Politicians relate to their parties as a *partido de aleguel*, as a rental. They freely and frequently change party, vote against party line, and refuse any kind of discipline on the ground that their constituency cannot be interfered with." Roll call data from Brazil shows that, over time, legislators have been voting independently of their party's wishes when the need arose.[32] Roll call numbers however, *understate* the lack of voting discipline among Brazilian parties for various reasons.

As scholars have noted, roll call analysis suffers from many severe problems.[33] The sample of votes which are subjected to roll call is small and not representative since they are not a random sample of all votes; rather they tend to be votes where party leaders expect to see the most or the least discipline. Crucially, voting represents the last stage in a long, extended bargaining process between various legislative actors including the executive, individual legislators, party leaders, and interest groups (Carubba et al. 2008; Ames 2002). If party leaders or the executive must make significant concessions to legislators in order to persuade them to vote for or against a bill, it signals the high value of that independent vote. In Brazil, this is the typical mode of legislative bargaining.

Deputy Luiz Carlos Santos, government leader to President Cardoso and ex-minister for political coordination, summarizes this legislative reality: " . . . The majority in Congress is reached through negotiations, concessions, exchanges of favors, and patronage. Since there are no solid parties or institutions, the conquered are ad hoc. The fragility of the parties is frightening: only in the last year nearly 130 deputies changed their parties."[34] The severe selection bias that can stem from analysis which does not account for the cost of votes is highlighted by the fact that many bills do not make it to the plenary floor for a vote in a given session or at all because the cost of striking bargains to obtain sufficient votes is too high (Carruba *et al.* 2008; Ames 2002, 189). Analyzing the final vote cast by a legislator without any measure of the cost incurred in obtaining that vote, as roll call analysis does, can therefore be misleading as a measure of voting discipline. Scholars are currently using various measures to try and capture the costs to the executive and to party leaders of buying individual legislative votes. Studies have found that the timing and speed with which appropriations of legislators' budgetary amendments are approved by the executive, for example, are frequently tailored to support those individual legislators who vote with the executive, with or without the consent of their party leaders (Hagopian 2008; Ames 2002). Thus, they support the findings of other scholars who have argued that parties in Brazil are not able to influence the votes of their legislators.

As this discussion indicates, in contrast to India, where party delegations vote in complete unison with party whips because they can be expelled for voting against them, in Brazil legislators make decisions on their votes based on their personal political calculus. When this calculus favors the party's position, they vote for parties; when it does not, they vote against the party. Given this independence, we expect that according to hypothesis H_{3a}, interest groups in Brazil should lobby legislators rather than parties in order to influence votes on the floor.

As the discussion outlines, the institutional rules on agenda-setting, on introduction of amendments, and on voting defections in India and Brazil are very different and *each of them* corresponds to the institutional configuration for party-focused and individual-focused legislative systems, respectively. Therefore, these two countries should provide us with clearly contrasting cases for testing how legislative institutions determine the conditions under which legislative lobbying strategies are more likely to lead to more corruption.

CONCLUSION

This chapter presented and discussed the logic of case selection in the context of the research design employed in this project. The logic of the most-similar case selection strategy adopted for this project requires that the selected cases should be representative of their underlying theoretical categories, and be as homogeneous as possible on other characteristics not central to the theory being tested, while providing the most contrasting values on the key theoretical factors being analyzed. I then presented the institutional details of the two cases which qualified them for selection.

Brazil and India are typical examples of the theoretical categories required for testing the theoretical framework presented in chapter 2. Brazil has agenda-setting, amendment, and voting expulsion rules that favor individual legislators as the influential legislative policymakers. India on the other hand has agenda-setting, amendment, and voting expulsion rules that favor parties as the influential policymakers in the legislature. Thus, these countries provide contrasting values on the three explanatory factors of theoretical interest—legislative rules on agenda-setting, introduction of amendments, and voting defections. This also makes them good representatives of the underlying theoretical categories they are representing—individual-focused and party-focused legislative systems. They are also broadly similar to each other in many socioeconomic, institutional, and political characteristics, which makes them more homogeneous cases. Thus they fit all three criteria required for a most-similar design case strategy and provide a good fit for it. This should facilitate testing the causal mechanism of legislative institutions in both lobbying and corruption while minimizing the impact of other confounding variables. Various within-case strategies are also discussed in order to ensure that the case results are as robust as possible. These countries are also representative of many underlying characteristics of developing country democracies, which are the universe of cases for which this theoretical framework has been developed. As with any case-study strategy, there is a lack of perfect homogeneity due to variations across cases in the sample. Therefore, in order to assess the results of these two cases and their applicability to other cases, within-case analysis will need to be especially attentive to differences in such factors as executive influence and global economic prominence.

As the above discussion of legislative rules in these two countries shows, the Indian case provides us with a typical example of party-centered agenda-setting, amendments, and voting control while Brazil provides us with a typical example of an individual-centered legislative system with individual legislators exerting influence over these three aspects of policymaking. The influential policymakers in the two countries should therefore be very different. According to our hypotheses, we should expect to see party-focused lobbying in India and individual-focused lobbying by business groups in Brazil, and these lobbying behaviors should lead to higher corruption levels in India. Next, chapter 4 tests the theoretical expectations on lobbying behavior with a combination of qualitative and quantitative survey data obtained for these two cases. Chapter 5 uses similar data to test the hypotheses that relate these lobbying patterns to higher corruption levels in India. Chapter 6 then generalizes these results by testing them on a large sample of developing country democracies and discusses how they relate to case results.

4

BRAZIL AND INDIA: LEGISLATIVE INSTITUTIONS AND LOBBYING BEHAVIOR

In chapter 2 I hypothesized that party-focused legislative rules on agenda-setting, amendments, and voting in a country should motivate party-focused lobbying by special interests whereas individual-focused rules should motivate individual-focused lobbying. In chapter 3, I discussed how case analysis using carefully selected cases could be used to test these theoretical predictions in the absence of large-n data on lobbying. Chapter 3 also discussed in detail the institutional configuration that qualified the two selected cases as theoretically appropriate—Brazil to represent the category of individual-focused legislative rules and India to represent the category of party-focused legislative rules. In this chapter I begin the theory testing process by testing the first set of hypotheses linking institutions to lobbying behaviors. Chapter 5 then tests the link between lobbying behavior and corruption.

Hypotheses H_{1a}, H_{2a}, and H_{3a} in chapter 2 framed the causal mechanism that links specific legislative institutions to political corruption, that is, the behavior of business lobbies. Therefore, the first step in testing this two-step theoretical chain is to test whether business groups in Brazil and India respond to these legislative incentives by lobbying political parties in India and individual legislators in Brazil. There are two types of data that are needed to check these hypotheses. First, we need evidence that links institutional design to perceptions of political influence by business groups. Second, we need data that documents how groups strategize based on these perceptions, specifically how they choose their political venue. For this project, I collected and combined three types of evidence to answer these questions—group survey data, open-ended interviews, and analytical narratives of legislative bills.

To the best of my knowledge, the variables on venue choice are currently not available through an existing dataset for any set of countries. Therefore, to operationalize this variable, I collected data on venue choice and perceptions of institutional influence through a systematic survey of business interest groups conducted in 2005–2006 in India and Brazil. This survey provides data on 179 groups in India and 158 groups in

Brazil. These data are used to directly test hypotheses H_{1a}, H_{2a}, and H_{3a} on institutional sources of strategic lobbying behavior. This evidence is supplemented by the perspective gained through open-ended interviews, 45 in India and 47 in Brazil, with political party leaders, members of parliament, journalists, scholars, business interest groups, firms, and social interest groups.

Finally, in order to see how behaviors reported by groups in the survey match their strategic behavior in practice, I trace and analyze the actual lobbying behavior of business groups on key legislative bills in both countries. For India, I analyze the passage of the Patents Amendment Bill 2005 and the Insurance Regulatory Development Authority Bill 1999. For Brazil, I analyze the passage of the Pensions Reform Bill 1999 and the Provision Contribution on Financial Transactions (CPMF) Bill 2007. As I discuss below, these distinct and independent bits of information all support the hypotheses of institutionally motivated patterns of party- and individual-focused lobbying and provide strong robust support for all three hypotheses.

SURVEY DESIGN AND SAMPLE CHARACTERISTICS

From July 2005 through February 2006, I implemented a *multistage, stratified, clustered random* sampling design to administer a survey to organized business interest groups in Brazil and India. This was done with the assistance of local survey teams. The survey questionnaire was designed to elicit information on business interest perceptions of institutional influence and their interactions with legislative policymakers. Only interest groups which had well-defined, fee-paying memberships, who met at least annually, had an officially assigned space, employed staff dedicated to the organization, and had been in existence for at least two years were included in the sampling frame. This was done to ensure that only stable, experienced, and bona fide organizations were surveyed.

Organizations at local, state, and national levels as well as those organized along the lines of a single sector (for example, FEBRABAN representing banks in Brazil), those that are multisector bodies (for example, the Confederation of Indian Industry in India), and those representing specific regions (for example, FIESP representing businesses in the state of São Paolo in Brazil and the Mumbai Chamber of Commerce representing all businesses in the city of Mumbai in India) were included. The questionnaire was made available in English in India but also in Portuguese in Brazil. The interviews were conducted exclusively with high-level managers such as presidents, vice-presidents, directors, chairs, and, where available, government liaison officers and legal counsels at these organizations. This was done to ensure that only officeholders who would be privy to the strategies of that organization were interviewed. The final sample size realized was 179 in India and 158 in Brazil.

Figures 4.1 (a) and (b) summarize the *multistage, stratified, clustered random* sampling design implemented in this survey. First, I divided each country up into regional strata. The strategy was to allocate sample shares to each regional stratum proportional to its GDP contribution to the national GDP as well as to produce a sample representative of the shares of different economic sectors. This was done to ensure a geographically

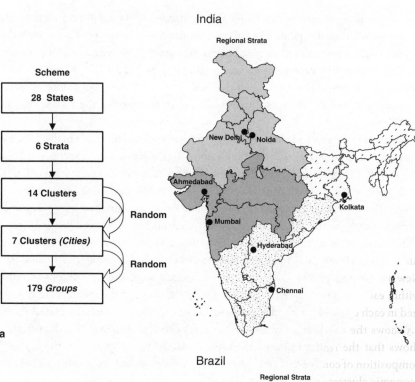

India

Regional Strata

Scheme

| 28 States |
| 6 Strata |
| 14 Clusters |
| 7 Clusters *(Cities)* |
| 179 *Groups* |

Random

Random

a

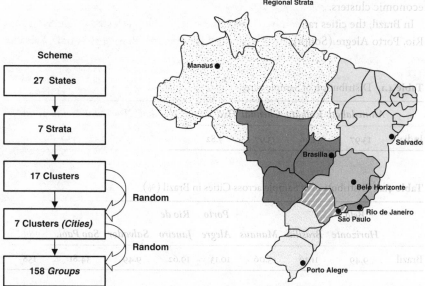

Brazil

Regional Strata

Scheme

| 27 States |
| 7 Strata |
| 17 Clusters |
| 7 Clusters *(Cities)* |
| 158 *Groups* |

Random

Random

b

Figure 4.1. (a) and (b) *Survey Sampling Scheme: Multi-Stage, Stratified, Clustered, Random Sample Design*

and economically representative national sample. Interest organizations tend to locate in state and national capitals. For this reason, the three state capital cities with the highest GDP contributions to a specific stratum were then picked as potential clusters for that stratum. For each stratum, I then randomly picked one cluster out of three. Within the chosen cluster city, I then randomly selected the number of interest organizations assigned to that stratum based on GDP. This yielded the final sample of interviews.

The maps in figures 4.1 (a) and (b) show the geographic definitions of the regional strata for both countries. Due to their commercial significance, the cities of New Delhi and Mumbai in India and the states of São Paolo and Rio de Janeiro in Brazil were themselves defined as strata. India was divided up into 6 strata—North, South, East, West, Mumbai, and New Delhi. Brazil was divided into 7 regional strata—North, Northeast, South, Southeast, Central, São Paolo, and Rio de Janeiro. Within each stratum, the cities randomly selected as the cluster for that strata were Ahmedabad (West), Chennai and Hyderabad (South), Kolkata (East), Mumbai, New Delhi, and Noida (North). Interest groups were then randomly selected within each of these clusters. Table 4.1 shows the share of the 179 interviews realized in each city and is a good approximation of their shares in national GDP. Table 4.3 shows the distribution of interviews across sectors in India. This distribution shows that the realized sample is proportionately representative of the sectoral composition of commercial activity in India and contains interviews from all major economic clusters.

In Brazil, the cities randomly selected as the cluster for each strata were São Paolo, Rio, Porto Alegre (South), Belo Horizonte (Southeast), Brasilia (Central), Salvador

Table 4.1. Distribution of Sample across Cities in India (%)

	Ahmedabad	Kolkata	Chennai	Hyderabad	Mumbai	New Delhi	Noida	Total No.
India	13.97	7.26	13.97	7.82	22.35	29.05	5.59	179

Table 4.2. Distribution of Sample across Cities in Brazil (%)

	Belo Horizonte	Brasilia	Manaus	Porto Alegre	Rio de Janeiro	Salvador	Sao Paolo	Total No.
Brazil	9.49	11.39	5.06	10.13	19.62	9.49	34.81	158

Table 4.3. Distribution of Sample across Sectors (%)

	Agriculture	Manufacturing	Services	Construction	Utilities	Commerce	Total No.
India	6.15	36.87	27.37	6.7	8.38	14.53	179
Brazil	15.82	22.15	32.28	3.16	8.23	18.35	158

(Northeast), and Manaus (North). Interest groups were then randomly selected within each of these clusters. Row 2 of table 4.2 shows the share of the 158 interviews realized in each city and is a good approximation of their shares in national GDP. Row 2 of table 4.3 shows the distribution of interviews across sectors in Brazil. This distribution shows that the realized sample is proportionately representative of the sectoral composition of commercial activity in Brazil and contains interviews from all major economic clusters. Manufacturing and services form the biggest GDP contributors in both countries and are sampled most heavily. Agriculture is overrepresented in Brazil because it has a vibrant agribusiness sector that is very well organized and, hence, overrepresented in the sampling frame.

There are four issues that could have risen in the realized sample and introduced severe biases into the results. *First,* the realized sample could have been biased in terms of sector, size, and economic experience due to nonresponse. However, as discussed above, this is not the case. The realized sample is fairly representative in terms of regional representation, sectors, size, and economic experience. Furthermore, the nonresponse rates are independent of sector identity, cluster, or size. *Second,* the quality of political information revealed by the groups will depend on the exposure and experience of these groups with respect to the political establishment and the policy process. If they only interact rarely with political policymakers, their perceptions will be less reliable. Therefore, it is important to know how frequently groups interact with various parts of the political establishment.

In fact, as figures 4.2 (a) and (b) show, groups report considerable interaction with the political establishment and the policy process in both countries. Thus, lack of experience with institutions should not undermine the reliability of responses. Figure 4.2 (a) shows that in India, 88% of groups report interacting with the legislature at least once a year, 64% every few months, and 32% report interacting as frequently as a few times a month. A total of 85% report meeting with executive office holders at least annually, 56% every few months, while 38% report interactions as high as a few times a month. These interaction patterns indicate that interest group perspectives are informed by considerable familiarity and experience with the policy process in India.

As figure 4.2 (b) shows, the numbers in Brazil are similarly high. The reporting shows that 84% of groups report interaction frequency as high as a few times a month with executive offices, 82% with legislature offices, and 25% with political party officeholders. The share reporting at least annual contact with parties is 43%. Importantly, more than 95% of Brazilian groups report interacting with the legislature at least every few months. Thus, Brazilian interest groups seem experienced and active in engaging policymakers. Open-ended interviews further confirm the investment of effort and resources that groups make in acquiring political information and keeping abreast of political developments. These numbers are consistent with the characterization of business interest groups as among the most experienced policy players in any country (Deardoff 2006; Huber and Shipan 2002). Thus, business interest groups in both countries report interacting frequently and extensively with different parts of the political establishment in both countries.

Third, we need to check whether firms use their personal contacts or go through their interest group of choice in order to exercise influence on policy. In the sample of

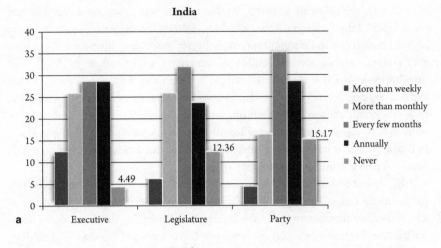

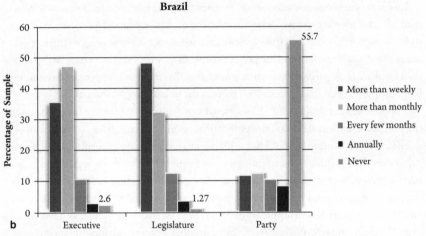

Figure 4.2. (a) and (b) *Frequency of Group Interaction with Political Institutions*

interest groups in India, 71% report that firms go through representative organizations most of the time or always, with only 7.3% reporting that they do so rarely. In Brazil, 87% of sampled interest groups report that firms go through representative organizations most of the time or always, with only 5.2% reporting that they do so rarely.[1] This suggests that firms use interest groups as fora to discuss, analyze, and negotiate strategies on policy on their behalf with policymakers. It is worth recognizing, though, that organizations representing sectors dominated by a few big firms are less likely to fully represent the concerns of smaller firms to policymakers and that big firms may be more likely to lobby policymakers directly. If they do so, these firms should still be subject to the same institutional logic. Thus, they should perceive similar loci of institutional influence and adopt similar venue choice strategies. In order to assess whether or not this is the case, 10% of the sample was drawn from firms rather than interest groups. They report similar patterns of strategic interaction with policymakers.

Finally, theoretically, hypotheses 1_a, 2_a, and 3_a apply not just to economic interest groups but to all kinds of special interests. While business interests tend to be the richest groups in these countries, other social and religious groups also possess resources that are potentially attractive to policymakers and engage them in financial quid pro quos as well. Therefore, to check whether the institutional logic of lobbying holds for nonbusiness groups, I also drew 10% of the sample from labor unions and other civil society groups, organized to represent a range of social interests such as consumer interests, environmental issues, women's issues, and indigenous rights. These groups also report similar institutional interactions on venue choice; however, they are more likely to use nonmonetary resources. The details are discussed later in the chapter.

In addition to the survey interviews, I conducted 45 open-ended interviews in India and 47 in Brazil with a variety of institutional, political, and bureaucratic actors as well as journalists and scholars. These are listed in tables 4.4 and 4.5 Not only did these interviews provide a rich context for the survey data, they also allowed me to ensure the best cognitive match between the concepts and measures employed in the survey instrument and those used by policymakers and special interests.

I now use evidence from both the survey and the interviews to test whether lobbying decisions made by business groups in Brazil and India are consistent with hypotheses H_{1a}, H_{2a}, and H_{3a} and whether these decisions are driven by perceptions of influence over agenda-setting, amendments, and voting dissidence. I also test the explanatory power of alternative factors such as sector, size, age, concentration, and issue type identified by scholars as being the drivers of venue choice by lobbies.

INSTITUTIONS, INFLUENCE, AND LOBBYING: EVIDENCE FROM A SURVEY OF BUSINESS GROUPS

The first set of evidence needed is data that captures interest group perceptions of who commands political influence over agenda-setting, the introduction of amendments, and voting behavior. Before we analyze whether groups choose to lobby parties in the

Table 4.4. List of Open-Ended Interviews in India

Category	City	Code
Political: Party/Legislator	Mumbai	BJP-1
		National Congress Party-1
		Congress (I)-1
	New Delhi	BJP-2
		BJP-3
		Congress (I)-2
		CPI (M)-1
Government Officials	Kolkata	State Government-1
	Mumbai	National Government-1
		National Government-2

(continued)

Table 4.4. *(continued)*

Category	City	Code
		National Government-3
		National Government-4
		State Government-2
		State Government-3
		City Government-1
		City Government-2
	New Delhi	National Government-5
		National Government-6
		National Government-7
Chambers /Associations	Chennai	Manufacturing-1
		Manufacturing-2
		Regional-1
	Kolkata	Manufacturing-3
		Commerce-1
		Regional-2
	Mumbai	Commerce-2
		Finance-1
		Finance-2
		Manufacturing-4
	New Delhi	Regional-3
		Manufacturing-5
		Services-1
		Agriculture-1
Labor Unions	Mumbai	Union-1
	New Delhi	Union-2
Nongovernmental Organization	Kolkata	Development Group-1
	Mumbai	Children's Group-1
	New Delhi	Women's Group-1
Journalists	Mumbai	Financial Paper-1
		Business Paper-1
		Newspaper-1
	New Delhi	Newspaper-2
		Newspaper-3
Academics	Mumbai	Dr. Thomas
		Dr. Desai
	Total No. of Interviews =	45

Table 4.5. List of Open-Ended Interviews in Brazil

Category	City	Code
Political: Party/Legislator	Brasilia	PT-1
		PMDB-1
		PSDB-1
	Sao Paolo	PT-2
		PMDB-2
Government Official	Brasilia	Executive Research Staff-1
		Executive Research Staff-2
		Executive Research Staff-3
		Legislative Staff-1
		Legislative Staff-2
		Legislative Staff-3
		Legislative Staff-4
	Sao Paolo	City Government-1
		City Government-2
	Rio de Janeiro	City Government-1
		City Government-2
Chambers /Associations	Brasilia	Manufacturing-1
		Manufacturing-2
		Agriculture-1
	Manaus	Agriculture-2
		Regional-1
	Rio de Janeiro	Commerce-1
		Manufacturing-3
		Regional-2
	Sao Paolo	Finance-1
		Utility-1
		Manufacturing-4
		Agriculture-3
		Regional-3
Labor Union	Brasilia	Union-1
		Union-2
	Rio de Janeiro	Union-3
	Sao Paolo	Union-4
		Union-5
Nongovernmental Organization	Manaus	Environment-1

(continued)

Table 4.5. *(continued)*

Category	City	Code
		Indigenous Rights-1
	Sao Paolo	Environment-2
		Women's Rights-1
		Health-1
Academics	Brasilia	Dr. David Fleischer
	Sao Paolo	Dr. Fernando Limongi
	Sao Paolo	Dr. José Augusto Guilhon Albuquerque
	Salvador	Dr. Celina Souza
Journalists	Brasilia	Financial Paper-1
		Financial Paper-2
		Newspaper-1
	Rio de Janeiro	Newspaper-2
	Sao Paolo	Financial Paper-3
		Newspaper-3
	Total No. of Interviews =	47

party-focused case, India, and individuals in the individual-focused case, Brazil, we need to verify that perceptions of the policy process are consistent with our theoretical expectations given the institutions in these countries. Additionally, since the ability of parties to control policymaking also depends on their ability to control appointments, especially procedural gatekeepers, data that establishes the degree of party control perceived over legislative appointments is also important. To obtain the relevant information I asked groups the following questions:

(1) Consider the legislative process in 5 stages. Rank *only* the 3 actors you think are most influential at each stage and indicate how influential you think they are at *that* stage using the following scale: 1 (no influence), 2 (some influence), 3 (average influence), 4 (strongly influential), and 5 (decisive influence). The 5 stages presented were: introduction, procedural decisions, committees, amendment and debates, and voting. The list of political actors was: executive's office, procedural officers, government party leaders, opposition party leaders, committees, sectoral and regional caucuses, individual members of parliament, and others.

(2) How important is the following to you in the legislature: the party's control over appointments to important committees and posts.

Figures 4.3 (a) and (b) show the distribution of responses to this question for the actor ranked first. Figure 4.3 (a) shows that in India political parties are perceived to dominate

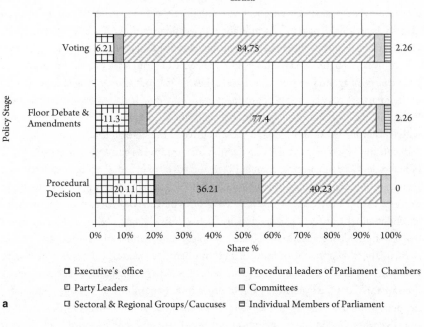

a

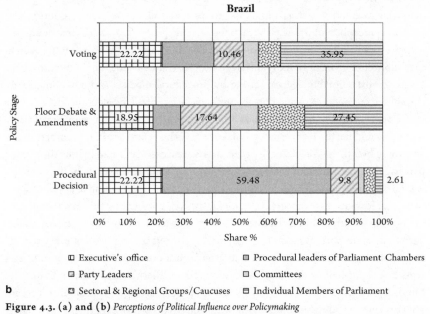

b

Figure 4.3. (a) and (b) *Perceptions of Political Influence over Policymaking*

all three legislative stages while individual legislators are rarely seen to have any influence on legislation at all. Political parties are identified as the most important actors by 40% of groups at the agenda-setting stage, by 77% of groups at the amendments stage, and by 85% of groups at the voting stage. In separate survey questions, groups also report that they see procedural positions and committees as being controlled by party leaders in

India. Hence, the 36% of groups who identify procedural officers as the most influential also report that these officers are seen to be obedient to their parties' wishes. No groups identify individual legislators as influential in agenda-setting in India while barely 2% identify them as most influential at amendment and voting stages.

In contrast, as figure 4.3 (b) shows in Brazil, 60% of groups see procedural officers to be in charge of agenda-setting and also see these legislators as operating independently of their parties. A total of 27% of groups report individual legislators as being the most influential political actors at the amendments stage. Influence at this stage is shared with legislators on committees and the executive in Brazil to an extent not reported in India. As discussed below, this is a reflection that groups see committee and procedural officeholders as being nonpartisan in Brazil and partisan in India. Therefore, parties are seen to dominate this stage through all available channels including committees and procedural officers in India, while in Brazil groups perceived them as policy actors who are independent of their parties. Finally, at the voting stage, 36% of groups in Brazil perceive individual legislators to be the key policy actors while only 10% identify parties as such. These data therefore show that groups perceive political parties as dominating policymaking at all three stages in India. In Brazil, groups perceive all legislators, whether they are rank and file legislators or hold procedural or committee posts, as being independent in their functions and as being the influential policy brokers in Brazil. Additionally, when I consider perceptions of legislative influence reported by groups belonging to different sectors, I find that groups across all sectors in each country share the same perception of where political policymaking power is located in that country.

Legislative rules governing how members elected to legislative posts set the agenda may allow either parties or individual legislators to influence the functions carried out by these posts, notably agenda-setting by procedural officials and amendments by committee members. As argued in chapter 3, parties control the election and behavior of the speaker of the lower house in India, whereas given the rules in Brazil party leaders should fail to exercise much influence over the behavior of the members of the governing board, the *Mesa*. These expectations are clearly reflected in how the groups perceive the importance of party influence over such appointments in both countries. A total of 76% of groups in India consider party control over legislative appointments to be of at least average importance to them with 53% considering this to be significant or very significant. In Brazil, however, most groups do not consider such party influence to be an important factor in policymaking. About 50% report that party control over these legislative positions is of little or no importance to them with only 23% reporting significant or very significant importance. These perceptions underline the trends reported in figures 4.3(a) and (b) at the procedural stage. Procedural officers are seen to exert considerable influence in Brazil and party control over them is not significant. However, in India, the procedural stage sees more direct influence by party leaders as well as more indirect influence through the influence they exert over procedural appointments.

It is important to note that this survey was conducted in Brazil at a time when the Partido *dos* Trabalhadores (the PT) was serving its first term in the government and the presidency. This represented the first time that an ideologically coherent, leftist party known for its party discipline was in power in Brazil. In 2005–2006, when this survey was conducted, business groups were operating in an environment dominated by a government and a legislature run by a disciplined, tight-knit party leadership. Thus the numbers for party influence in Brazil can only be biased upward during this period. The low numbers revealed by the survey for party influence therefore show how low the institutional levels of party influence are in Brazil and are very strongly supportive of hypotheses. Brazil at this point in time therefore provides a much harder test for the theoretical hypotheses in this project.

Figures 4.3 (a) and (b) also provide evidence that puts the influence of legislative rules in the perspective of electoral rules and executive regime. If these institutions determined entirely the strength of political parties in a system and, hence, their influence over policy, we would observe little variation across the various stages in each country. Instead we see that there exists variation in the perception of party influence across stages in both countries. Analysis shows that this variation is not driven by obvious culprits such as lack of access to the preferred target or inexperience on the part of the respondent. This suggests that the structure of the legislative rules governing each stage introduce variation in the relative influence of various policy actors. Thus, they matter in structuring political influence in the legislature and also matter in the political and party system.[2]

Given that the perceptions of party influence over legislative functions of policy-making conform to the expectations given their institutional structure, the next set of evidence required is data that can address the lobbying venue choice—the question of which political actors are lobbied by interest groups in Brazil and India. According to the theoretical framework presented in chapter 2, political parties should be lobbied in party-focused India while individual legislators should be targeted by groups in individual-focused Brazil. In order to elicit information on this venue choice from business groups, I posed the following questions to them:

(3) When your sector wants to influence legislation when it is being designed and passed through congress, who do you prefer to approach to lobby for your sector's position? Individual Legislators = 1 or Political Parties = 2

(4) Indicate the % allocations of the total political contributions made by your sector along the following categories: Between Parties/Individuals.

(5) Consider the lobbying experience of your sector. What % of lobbying effort went into lobbying the following: executive office, political parties, individual legislators.

(6) For the policy of most importance to you (trade, financing, labor, foreign exchange, environment, taxes, other), who did you approach with your concerns. The list of political actors provided was: executive's office, procedural officer, government party leaders, opposition party leaders, committees, sectoral and regional caucuses, individual members of parliament, and others.

These questions were designed with two goals in mind. First, to obtain both perception- and experience-based measures. Second, to put the party–individual choice in full political context by allowing groups to choose from a full range of political actors including the executive. Question # 3 elicits information on a principled preference whereas question # 4 extracts information on actual actions undertaken by respondents. Thus it allows us to obtain both perception- and experience-based measures. Questions # 5 and # 6, on the other hand, only elicit information on actual practice, with question # 6 obtaining information on a specific piece of legislation. Groups were asked to identity a specific bill, amendment, or decree in the issue area they identified as the most important from the list of six issues provided and then respond with respect to their behavior on that specific piece of legislation. The six issue areas listed in question # 6 included those issues routinely identified by businesses as being the most important one in these countries in various surveys.[3]

Furthermore, while questions # 3 and # 4 focused only on the choice between parties and individual legislators, questions # 5 and # 6 allowed respondents to choose from a range of political actors. Questions # 5 and # 6 thus allow groups to reveal choices that include the calculation to use parties or individual legislators as the appropriate conduit to approach the executive or the choice to bypass them and lobby the executive directly. This allows respondents to freely express their perspective of relative influence of the executive vis-à-vis other actors in both systems through their preferences and, without the imposition of any prior expectations, through the design of the question.

This gives us some leverage in addressing how and if differences in the policy role and influence of the executive in parliamentary and presidential systems might affect the choice between parties and individuals in these countries. The received wisdom on executive regimes suggests that the executive should be lobbied considerably more in India, due to its parliamentary nature, compared to Brazil, which is a presidential regime. It also allows us to use a third measure of lobbying strategy, lobbying effort, to check their reported strategy in addition to preference and money. Party leaders should be able to exert control over executive policy actions in parliamentary systems

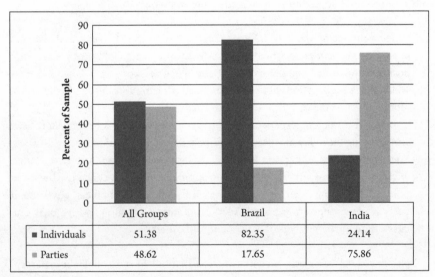

	All Groups	Brazil	India
■ Individuals	51.38	82.35	24.14
■ Parties	48.62	17.65	75.86

Figure 4.4. *Venue Choice by Business Interest Groups—Political Parties vs. Individual Legislators*

and should be used to lobby the executive in India whereas the executive should be lobbied through individuals in Brazil.

Figure 4.4 shows the distribution of responses to question # 3. The graph shows that 82.35% of 158 groups in Brazil lobbied individual legislators while 75.86% of all 179 groups in India lobbied political parties. These data provide very strong support for the hypothesis that parties are lobbied in India and individual legislators are lobbied in Brazil. A simple t-test confirms that the shares of groups lobbying parties and legislators in each country is significantly different. Therefore, these samples of legislative lobbying come from populations employing very different

India

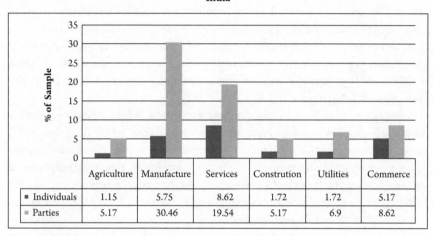

	Agriculture	Manufacture	Services	Constrution	Utilities	Commerce
▪ Individuals	1.15	5.75	8.62	1.72	1.72	5.17
▪ Parties	5.17	30.46	19.54	5.17	6.9	8.62

a

Brazil

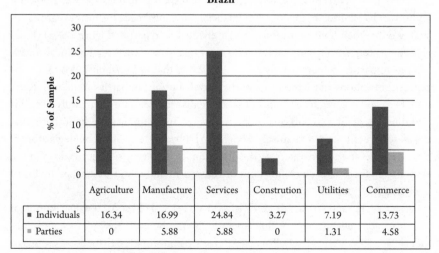

	Agriculture	Manufacture	Services	Constrution	Utilities	Commerce
▪ Individuals	16.34	16.99	24.84	3.27	7.19	13.73
▪ Parties	0	5.88	5.88	0	1.31	4.58

b

Figure 4.5. (a) and (b) *Venue Choice by Business Interest Groups - By Sector*

lobbying strategies. The combined sample for both countries, on the other hand, is almost evenly split and masks this stark difference in legislative lobbying behavior completely.

Figures 4.5 (a) and (b) show the distribution of these responses *by sector* for each country. If lobbying venues are determined by characteristics of the sector the group represents, rather than by its institutional environment, then each sector should demonstrate similar choices in both countries. As figures 4.5 (a) and (b) show, however, this is not the case for any sector. The incentives created by the institutional environment groups operate in dominate those created by the nature of the sector. The choice of political parties as the lobbying venue is the dominant venue for each sector in India. Similarly, in Brazil, the choice of individual legislators is the dominant choice for all sectors. These distributions are statistically different across the two countries for each sector. Further tests of venue choice across groups of similar sizes and geographic and sectoral concentrations show that political institutions rather than these factors dominate the strategic calculus of groups in each country.[4] The distribution of responses to question # 6 shows that groups also exhibit similar differences irrespective of the policy issue they are lobbying on.

However, age does have a significant impact in India, where younger groups are more likely to lobby legislators and are more likely to use information. Interviews reveal that these groups are still building up their resource base and do not have the resources to attract the attention of party leaders successfully. Their reported preferred strategy, however, is also to lobby party leaders. As discussed in chapter 1, extant work on lobbying has largely been built through single country studies of lobbying behavior. These data show that such studies can miss the most significant differences in lobbying behavior across countries, which arise due to national institutional choices rather than due to differences in sector, issue, size, or concentration.

Figures 4.6 (a) and (b) show the distribution of responses to question # 4. The graph shows the distribution of the shares of financial donations made by business groups to parties out of their total allocation across individuals and parties. Figure 4.6 (a) shows that about 56% of groups in India allocate more than 50% of their total political contributions to parties. In contrast, figure 4.6 (b) shows that in Brazil only 23% of groups report contributing more than 50% of their contributions to parties. Wilcoxon Rank Sum tests and median tests confirm that these distributions are statistically different and thus represent different behaviors by groups. This supports the hypothesis that business groups use their financial resources to lobby parties in India but legislators in Brazil. However, the sensitivity of this question led to a very significant drop in the response rate for this question. Only 61 groups in India and 82 groups in Brazil answered this question.

Figures 4.7 (a) and (b), 4.8 (a) and (b), and 4.9 (a) and (b) show the distribution of responses for question # 5 for time spent lobbying the executive, parties, and individual legislators, respectively. This question elicits information that allows groups to account for the perceived relative influence of parties and legislators *in the context of the executive* in the policy process. Thus when groups report lobbying parties and

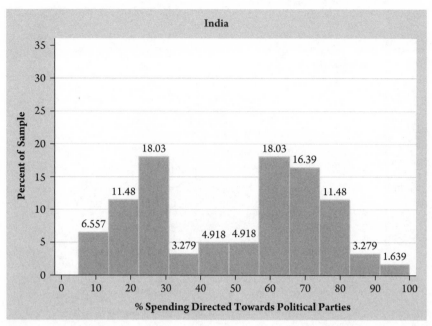

a

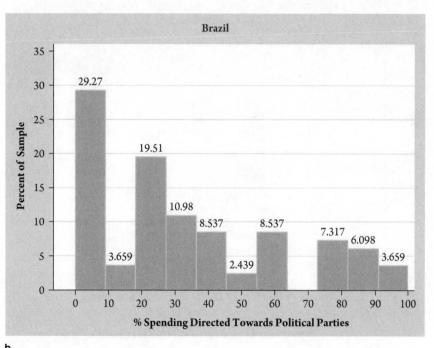

b

Figure 4.6. (a) and (b) *Allocation of Financial Donations by Groups—Across Parties and Individuals*

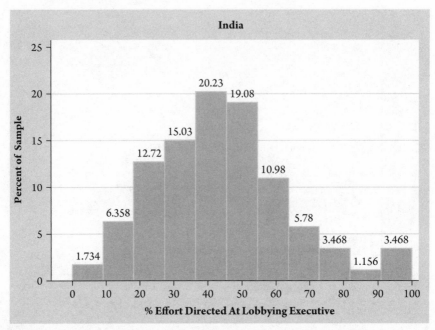

a

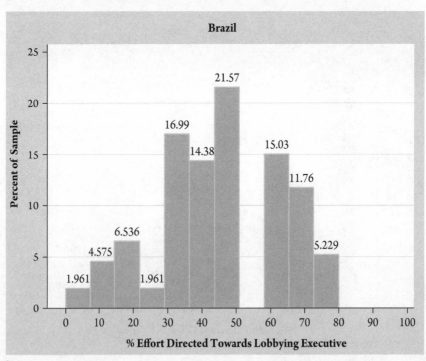

b

Figure 4.7. (a) and (b) *Allocation of Lobbying Effort across Executive, Political Parties, and Individual Politicians—Executive*

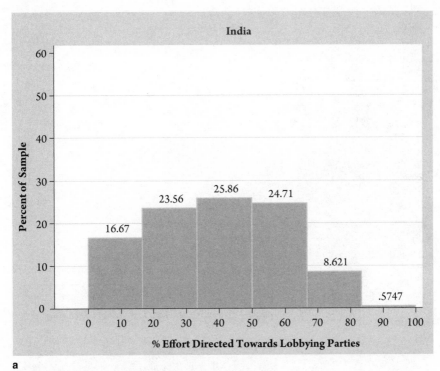

a

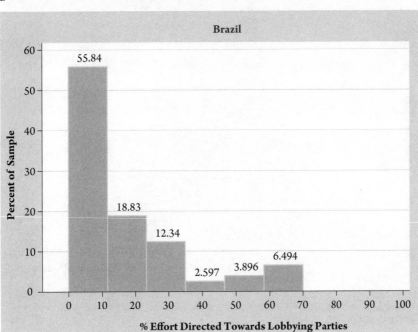

Figure 4.8. (a) and (b) *Allocation of Lobbying Effort across Executive, Political Parties, and Individual Politicians—Parties*

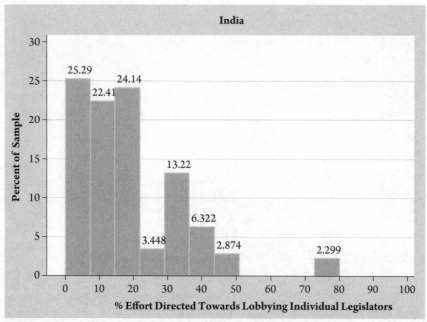

a

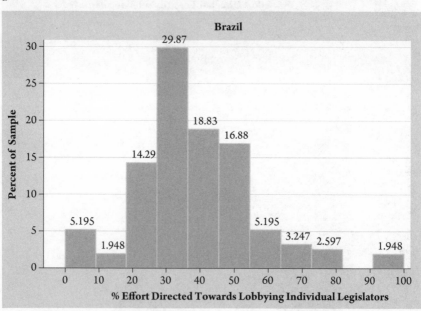

b

Figure 4.9. **(a) and (b)** *Allocation of Lobbying Effort across Executive, Political Parties, and Individual Politicians—Legislators*

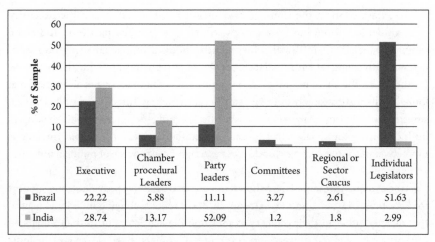

	Executive	Chamber procedural Leaders	Party leaders	Committees	Regional or Sector Caucus	Individual Legislators
▪ Brazil	22.22	5.88	11.11	3.27	2.61	51.63
▪ India	28.74	13.17	52.09	1.2	1.8	2.99

Figure 4.10. *Venue Choice by Business Interest Groups—Across All Institutional Venues*

legislators, they are choosing to lobby these venues in preference to the executive. A total of 34% of groups report spending more than 50% of their effort lobbying political parties in India while only 10% of groups in Brazil report this strategy. On the other hand, while only 2% of groups in India report spending more than 50% of their effort lobbying individual legislators, 30% of groups report doing so in Brazil. Therefore, even accounting for the preference to lobby the executive, groups clearly demonstrate a preference to lobby political parties rather than individual legislators in India and legislators rather than parties in Brazil.

The data show 38% of groups in India and 32% of groups in Brazil report spending more than 50% of their lobbying effort lobbying the executive. A Wilcoxon Rank Sum test shows that these distributions are *not* statistically different. This is also confirmed by tests comparing their medians. These data support the assertion that executive policy influence cannot be derived on the basis of executive regime alone. Rather, legislative institutions have a significant influence on the context and, hence, on the degree of executive influence.[5]

Figure 4.10 shows the distribution of responses to question # 6. This question asks groups for their lobbying strategy with respect to the full set of potential political venues—executive, procedural leaders in the chambers, party leaders from governing and opposition parties, committees, regional or sectoral caucuses, and individual legislators— for the policy that was their top lobbying priority. It also allowed them to specify an actor they had lobbied if he was not included in this list. The response reported the actual action they had undertaken on a specific piece of legislation on their top-ranked issue. The data show 52.09% of groups in India lobbied political parties while only 11.11% of groups did so in Brazil. Only 3% of groups in India reported lobbying individual legislators whereas 51.63% of groups reported lobbying them in Brazil. Also, 28.74% of groups reported lobbying the executive in India while 22.22% reported doing so in Brazil. The distributions of reported venue choice are again statistically different for the choice of parties and individual legislators.

These data confirm the findings of question # 5 that even when the executive is an available option, business groups still choose to lobby parties in India and individual legislators in Brazil. The executive holds a similar rank in group strategies in both countries with similar shares of groups reporting lobbying the executive. Furthermore, the share of groups choosing to lobby the executive is about half that lobbying the institutionally optimal actor in each country. Therefore, despite the pessimism expressed by many scholars that the executive dominates policymaking in both countries, these data show that in fact legislative politics and policymaking is more dynamic, more complex, and serves as a significant source of political influence and intrigue.

As the evidence presented here shows, the survey data above provide strong support for hypotheses H_{1a}, H_{2a}, and H_{3a}. Groups in Brazil report lobbying individual legislators directly either in their capacity as rank and file legislators or in their enhanced capacity as procedural officers and committee members. Business groups in India report lobbying political parties for their policy influence. Importantly, parties play an insignificant role in Brazil and individual legislators play a negligible role in policymaking in India. These theoretical expectations are confirmed by data that measure perceptions as well as data that are based on actual experience of lobbying. These lobbying patterns were also confirmed by both business and political elites in open-ended interviews with the author.

A typical response in Brazil was articulated by the president of an agribusiness association (Sao Paolo-3), as follows: "It is important to cultivate the right people in Congress. Not party men, but men who know business, who understand politics and who will commit to us. If they have experience in our industry that is better but not necessary. Party leaders are not useful, they can't control Deputies, so they can't commit." In India, a regional chamber of commerce (Author interview, Commerce-2) described his experience working for various industry bodies in the following way: "One has to be on good terms with party leaders. MPs come and go and they have little influence unless they are high up in the party themselves. Yes, we wish some knowledgeable members were important party men but it is not so. So, lobbying has to be done with the party if you want to get anywhere." Chapter 5 presents further evidence from these interviews confirming these strategies.

To match these reported behaviors against observed behavior, I now systematically analyze the lobbying strategies employed by interest groups in India on two key bills—the Patents Amendment Bill 2005 and the Insurance Regulatory Authority Bill 1999. This is followed by the analysis of two legislative bills in Brazil, one on pension reform and the other regarding an extension of a tax on financial transactions.

The Patents Amendment Bill 2005

The Patents Amendment Bill 2005 was formulated to reform the original Patents Act of India 1970. The passage of a bill updating patent laws was required in order to satisfy India's obligations as a signatory of the WTO rules on Trade Related Aspects of Intellectual Property Rights (TRIPS).[6] The key principle of moving from a regime that patented the process to one that patents the product had already been established. However, the details of the transition process raised several critical issues. The manner of their resolution would determine which firms would survive in the domestic market and as exporters, the impact on the prices of essential medications in the domestic and global markets, and the future direction of the industry itself in India. Therefore, the stakes were very high for all the stakeholders. As the discussion of the passage of this bill below shows, the political actors lobbied through the entire process were party leaders from various political parties, not individual legislators. Had individual legislators been lobbied, it would have provided evidence against the hypothesis that Indian legislative rules caused parties to be lobbied.

The process of investigating and drafting a new Patent Amendments bill had been taken up in earnest in November 2004 under the UPA coalition government led by the Congress (I).[7] Alliances were formed based on interest rather than national affiliation. Nongovernmental organizations such as the Médecins Sans Frontières, Oxfam, Association of Alternative Medicine, and the Lawyers Collective strategized with the WHO as well as with domestic generic producers, represented by the Indian Pharmaceutical Alliance (IPA), and the domestic producers of new drugs, the Indian Drug Manufacturers Association (IDMA) (MIP News, September 5, 2004). This alliance targeted the leaders of the leftist CPI (M) since the party had consistently opposed TRIPS on principle (People's Democracy, March 27, 2005). Together, these lobbies cooperated with the party to articulate a platform that demanded restricted patentability to prevent firms from using small modifications to evergreen their patents, liberalization of the compulsory license regime to allow exports at cheap prices, extended pregrant opposition rights to limit the exclusive marketing rights of patent applicants during the application period, and the ability to fully exploit the production flexibility provided by TRIPS based on public health concerns. This alliance began mobilizing its supporters in parliament as well as on the streets.

The opposition BJP, which had sponsored the bill when in office, wavered initially and then decided to oppose the bill as well. They represented substantial hurdles for the passage of the bill for two reasons: the UPA alliance did not command enough votes to ensure the bill would pass, and the BJP and the CPI (M) collectively possessed considerable procedural weight in parliament due to their combined seat strength.

The pro-WTO rationalization groups such as the Organization of Pharmaceutical Producers of India, which is dominated by foreign originator firms, various OECD governments, and multinational firms, lobbied the ruling Congress (I) leaders in support of the bill. This alliance pushed to retain the specific provisions in the draft that expanded the domain of patentable inventions, restricted the scope for compulsory licensing, and restricted the principles on which patent applications could be challenged during the application period. In the face of stiff resistance from its coalition allies and the opposition in parliament, the government postponed introducing the bill and promulgated a temporary Ordinance to meet the January 1, 2005 WTO deadline. This measure contained the provisions favored by the pro-WTO groups lobbying it.

In December 2004, the CPI (M) presented to the Congress party leadership a list of twelve amendments to the bill they had proposed. No private amendments were proposed or scheduled. The next two months saw intense lobbying of party leaders by both industry lobbies as well as the executive. While the government lobbied party leaders from both the left parties and the BJP, it did not approach individual legislators to seek their vote despite the fact that it only needed to get a few extra votes for passage (Press Trust of India, March 16, 2005). Neither did any of the industry lobbies. Intense interparty negotiations led the government to concede seven of the twelve amendments demanded by the CPI (M). When the bill was finally introduced to the floor on March 18, five key amendments were still outstanding and its prospects still looked uncertain (Financial Express, March 24, 2005).

The BJP moved procedural amendments in both houses requesting the setting up of expert committees to delay passage and threatened to walk out if these were defeated. The left party as well refused to support the bill as it stood and demanded negotiations on the five amendments the congress had failed to include. None of the nineteen MPs who participated in this debate belonged to a constituency representing commercial pharma interests, and none had links with any of the nongovernmental organizations that were lobbying on this issue. The list of speakers was made up entirely of party leaders from the governing and opposition alliances. Over the weekend the Congress party conceded two more amendments to the CPI (M). On Monday, March 21, discussions on the bill and a resolution disapproving it were both deferred amid political uncertainty.

The next day, the government conceded three more of the CPI (M)'s twelve amendments and four amendments demanded by international players. It also agreed to convene an expert committee to consider the two further CPI (M) amendments. Despite these concessions, the opposition BJP tabled a resolution disapproving the bill. After five hours of raucous debate, this resolution was voted down and the entire BJP contingent of legislators walked out to a man (Lok Sabha Bulletins, March 18–23, 2005). In the clause by clause voting over the next two hours, not a single member present crossed party lines to vote for or against the bill. On the next day the bill was passed by the upper chamber as well, again along strictly partisan lines.

The lobbying on this bill demonstrates four things. First, that the entire debate and legislation process was dominated by party leaders. Procedural decisions such as changing of the business agenda and the committee procedures to be followed, the introduction of amendments, and the outcome of the votes on the amended bill were controlled throughout by parties. Second, no individual legislator went against the party line through actions on any of these functions. Even MPs from the constituencies where these firms were concentrated did not show any independent initiative or take the lead on any legislative action on this crucial bill. Third, all interest groups, not just business lobbies, identified and lobbied parties, not MPs, as their points of influence. Lastly, the executive as well only lobbied party leaders and did not canvass individual legislators for their support.

The Insurance Regulatory Bill 1999

Similar dynamics were demonstrated even more strongly in the lobbying that took place on the Insurance Regulatory and Development Authority Bill 1999. In this case, there was considerable dissent within the ranks of the two biggest parties, the Congress (I) and the BJP, and within the ruling and opposition party coalitions. If ever there was a situation where an individual MP might find the value of his legislative vote skyrocket for lobbies, this was it. Party leaders, business lobbies, and trade unions were all potentially competing against each other for the votes of individual MPs. Yet, business lobbies targeted party leaders, not individual MPs, and left it up to the party leaders to muster their troops. The outcome proved them right. When the bill finally came to a vote, every member of parliament voted strictly along party lines.

The 1999 IRDA bill was introduced by the BJP-led NDA coalition government in October 1999.[8] It sought to grant statutory status to the interim Regulatory Authority and end the public-sector monopoly of the insurance sector by privatizing it. Two major coalitions of interest groups assembled on this issue. The proprivatization camp argued that privatization would benefit the Indian consumer by providing an array of efficient, competent services at reasonable costs and by providing domestic financial markets with funds to invest in development projects, especially in the infrastructure sector. Its members included groups representing domestic business sectors such as shipping, the foreign business community such as AIG, financial market lobbies, and several influential peak business associations such as the Confederation of Indian Industry.

The opposition argued that foreign companies would increase premiums, focus on the lucrative urban segments of the market at the expense of rural markets, and invest the capital they raised abroad or invest it in high-return ventures rather than low-yield infrastructure projects. It included both the extreme left in the form of the CPI (M) and the extreme right in the form of the RSS as they opposed foreign ownership in the insurance sector on principle. Concerns about profitability and resulting potential job losses motivated the All India Insurance Employees Association (AIIEA), representing 80% of insurance employees, and the All India Employees Union, representing all public-sector employees, to join forces with this coalition of interests.[9] Both camps lobbied intensely using money, information, media campaigns, mass demonstrations, and paralyzing industrial strikes.

What makes this issue a particularly revealing test for our purposes is that it created ideological splits among rank and file legislators in both the BJP and the Congress party, and among their leaders as well as among the ruling and opposition party coalitions. While Congress party leaders Sonia Gandhi and P. Chidambaram stated they would support the bill, their co-partisans P. Shiv Shankar (the deputy Congress leader in the Lok Sabha) and Sharad Pawar (an influential party leader from Maharashtra) joined antiprivatization rallies outside parliament (Diwanji 1998). They were joined there by allies of the ruling BJP coalition—the AIDMK, the Telugu Desam, and the National Conference parties. Senior BJP figures such as Uma Bharati, Shanta Kumar, and K. R. Malkani publicly opposed their own government's policy. In an unprecedented move, seventy-five BJP MPs announced that they did not support the insurance bill. A commentator summarized the BJP's dilemma: "They probably thought that the government is more important than the party, and the party itself more important than the Sangh Parivar from which it draws its strength. It is this miscalculation that is responsible for the furore over the bill."[10]

Trade unions on the left and the right formulated a strategy novel to India—that of lobbying individual legislators. This was premised on beliefs that the severity of party fissures made legislators open to outside pressures. The unions threatened to canvass against individual legislators who voted for the bill in their constituencies come next election (Frontline, July 1999). Business lobbies, on the other hand, approached party leaders in the BJP and the Congress and did not undertake delegations to rank and file legislators at all. These coalitions produced competing amendments to the bill that favored their own demands. In effect, this provides us with a counterfactual experiment, since the trade unions adopted a strategy that had not been observed before. If in fact lobbying individuals is optimal given India's policymaking institutions, we should expect to see this strategy succeed.

After hectic consulting between various party leaders on the terms of the amendments, the bill was finally presented for voting on December 2, 1999, three months after its introduction into parliament. The BJP government announced in parliament that they would include four amendments favored by the Congress Party (UNI News, December 2, 1999). These concessions, however, did not meet the demands of many Congress (I), CPI (M). and BJP MPs. As the vote drew near, there was increasing suspense on whether various parties would issues whips and whether their MPs would defy them. At the end of the show, when the voting finally commenced, all members voted strictly along party lines. So strong was this trend that only one of the CPI (M)'s amendments was subjected to a division; all the others were negatived purely by voice votes. With cross-party voting failing to materialize, the CPI (M) and its allies realized their position on the issue had been defeated. They walked out of the chamber again, to the last member. The amended bill was then approved by the lower chamber. On December 7, strict partisan voting in the Rajya Sabha ensured passage there as well.

This case provides us with a counterfactual experiment in that one coalition of interests lobbied individuals. The failure of this experiment was not the passage of the bill but rather the failure of the alliance built on individual votes to materialize on the legislative floor. While rhetoric was freely expended by legislators from the BJP and the Congress sympathetic to unions, they did not translate words into costly amendment or voting decisions that could jeopardize their careers. Business lobbies correctly anticipated the ex-ante ability of party leaders to maintain discipline among their legislators. Therefore, lobbying individuals proved to be an institutionally suboptimal strategy in India and lobbying parties was proven optimal.

This segment of the chapter revealed two key features about the policymaking process in the Indian legislature and lobbying by business groups. First, as indicated earlier, legislative rules in India allow political parties—rather than individual legislators—to formally control agenda-setting and introduction of amendments as well as to expel party dissidents who defy the party whip in the legislature.[11] Second, hypotheses 1a, 2a, and 3a on the link between institutional rules and lobbying behavior are strongly supported by evidence from two sources: lobbying behavior demonstrated by business groups on two specific pieces of legislation, and data from a survey of business groups in India. The next chapter looks at evidence that this lobbying behavior by business groups leads to higher levels of political corruption in India.

To see whether the trends reported by business groups in the survey correspond to actual behaviors in Brazil, I now consider in detail the lobbying process that played out over two important pieces of legislation there—the Pensions Reform Bill 1999 and the CPMF Bill 2007.

The Pensions Reform Bill 1999

The 1988 Brazilian constitution included some of the most generous pension benefits for public-sector employees in the world, including those for legislators and judges. The disastrous fiscal impact of this scheme was manifested at national, state, and municipal levels of government since each was responsible for paying benefits to its own employees. By 1997, about 20% of federal revenue was spent on pension benefits (Ministério da *Previdência Social* 2005).[12] By 1990, the first pension reform proposals had already made their way to the government agenda under Collor. These proposals were framed by professional associations, not parties (Pinheiro 2004, 9). On March 17, 1995, President Fernando Henrique Cardoso introduced a bill to the lower house, the chamber of deputies, to reform various aspects of the pension system including making it a subject of ordinary law. In December 1998, after four years of legislative trench warfare, a considerably watered-down version of the bill without many key provisions was passed.

The two sides of the debates on pension reform in Brazil pitted those who were direct beneficiaries of its generosity against those who were footing the bill for it. The business groups opposed to the original constitutional pension provision thus included the Brazilian Banking Federation, the Brazilian Stock Market Institute, the National Confederation of Industry (CNI), and various associations representing pension funds (Bassini 1997, 30–37; Mello 1997, 304–306; Valderrama 1997, 2–10). These groups agreed with most of the government's reforms, which included establishing a minimum age for retirement, calculating benefits based on years of contribution not service, lowering payroll taxes paid by firms, harmonizing public- and private-sector pensions, eliminating special pension provisions for certain civil servants, imposing taxes on beneficiaries, reducing the income threshold covered by these schemes, and various levels of privatization of pensions. They were joined in some of these demands by the conservative labor union, *Força Sindical*. Broadly speaking, this camp wanted a shift from a pay as you go system to one where pensions were capitalized and privatized, and an end to the special privileges extended to narrow sections of civil employees. This group identified the expenditure side of the pension scheme as the source of its problems.

The opposition on the other hand identified the revenue side of the scheme as the source of pension problems. They argued that deficits in funding the scheme emerged from tax evasion, fraud, mismanagement and corruption in the administration of funds (Pinheiro 2004, 11). This alliance included various labor unions such as the leftist *Central Única dos Trabalhadores* (CUT) the General Workers' Confederation (CGT) and various employee associations such as the Movement of Retired Public Servants, the Association of Auditors of Social Security Contributions, the National Confederation of Social Security Workers, and the Brazilian Federation of Retired Workers and Pensioners (Silva 1997, 13–17; Cavalcanti 1997, 5–10; Pressuto 1997, 16–19; Schmitt 1997, 22–27; Cota 1997, 11–16). These groups were vehemently opposed to any changes relating to benefit reduction, minimum age requirements, taxing of benefits, and changes to the special privileges of public servants. Both sides approached legislators of all parties as a strategy of putting together cross-party alliances in their own favor.

When the bill was first introduced to congress in March 1995, Cardoso's alliance commanded a majority in both the chamber and the senate, and by 1996 this had soared to over 70% in both chambers. The leftist opposition held only 100 seats in the chamber and over 10% of senate seats at its peak. Despite this overwhelming majority, the government had to engage in various negotiations and dispense appointment and funding favors to legislators from its own ranks and opposition parties in order to muster the 308 votes needed to pass a constitutional amendment. The initial comprehensive bill it submitted was aimed at revamping the entire benefits system, but the only component that survived to the next stage was directly related to pensions. It was further decimated in the special committee constituted on pensions reforms (CESP) where the government faced both substantive and procedural hurdles from powerful legislators holding the posts of the chair and the reporting officer. Sensing the imminent loss facing the government, in February 1996 the president of the chamber, deputy Luis Eduardo Magalhães, a member of the ruling alliance, exercised his prerogative and pulled the bill out of committee consideration and directed it to the floor for consideration. When the vote was finally held on March 6, the proreform alliance could only get 294 votes. While they gained several votes from opposition congressmen, 96 of their own deputies contributed to the 190 votes cast against the bill. The bill failed to pass.

This defeat was followed by hectic lobbying of legislators by the executive, by party leaders, and by interest groups. The proreform alliance made promises of pork and threats of legislative retaliation to legislators as it bargained over provisions in the bill with deputies. Labor unions held massive rallies across the country to put pressure on their supporters. A much weaker bill finally passed the house floor on March 21, with 351 deputies voting in favor of the bill and 139 against it. Thirty-eight deputies from the governing alliance still voted against it. Many important provisions were subsequently introduced as amendments and also saw little success for the ruling parties. Party leaders were unable to impose party discipline since they could not expel these members from the chamber for voting against party leaders despite controlling a range of carrots as members of the coalition in office.

The government had better success in the senate where it commanded 61 of 80 seats. It restored measures on lowering proportional retirement and retirement salaries and on setting a minimum qualifying retirement age, but it failed to convince its senators to change pensions into a subject of ordinary legislation as opposed to a constitutional amendment (Pinheiro 2004; Hiroi 2005). This substitution bill was then reconsidered by the chamber of deputies in October 1997. Seventy-five legislators from the PMDB and the PPB, parties in the governing coalition, publicly stated their intention to vote against it. In response, the executive unleashed the full extent of its budgetary resources to buy legislative support. For example, in the last month before the vote, deputies from the PFL, PSDB, PMDB, and PPB had received 50%, 58%, 43%, and 48% of the total authorized budgets for their amendments, respectively (*Folha de São Paulo*, February 13, 1998, 1–4). The executive branch supplemented this with further financial inducements up to the final hours before the floor vote on February 12, 1998 was held by releasing extraordinary funds targeted at dithering legislators (*O Globo*, February 12, 1998, 3).[13]

When the vote was held in February, protestors from various groups marched onto the plenary floor itself. The escalation of public lobbying efforts by interest groups, and the impending impact of the 1997 Asian financial crises on Brazil, led the government to postpone the final vote. Its strategy of using amendments and DVSs to pass key provisions in the interim failed as it lost successive votes. In December 1998 the final version of the bill shorn of most of its fiscally beneficial measures was passed. This ensured that the issue stayed alive on the reform agenda of business groups for the future. In 2003, President Lula now in government, introduced another pension reform bill aimed at reviving the defeated measures of the 1998 bill, but it underwent a similarly tortuous, long and politically hard-fought process where parties were again ineffective and legislators dominated the process.

The contrast with India is striking. As the discussion makes clear, party leaders were unable to exercise influence in controlling the procedural path of the bill, the substance of the various drafts, the timing, or the outcome of voting. Legislators followed their own preferences in performing these legislative functions. Both business groups and labor unions identified legislators with influence over specific stages of the bill's passage and lobbied them using information, protests, and media coverage. This pattern was echoed by the executive who also chose to forgo lobbying party leaders in preference to directly lobbying legislators for their votes. Despite the *Partido dos Trabalhadores'* (PT) prior reputation as an ideologically coherent and disciplined party, this pattern was repeated for the 2003 Pension Reform Bill under President Lula. The lobbying behavior exhibited here by business lobbies, NGOs, firms, state institutions, and the executive is fairly representative of lobbying practices in Brazil. While this example represents a bill on a single issue, the results from the survey of Brazilian business groups provide strong support that these lobbying strategies are widely employed by business interest groups in Brazil.

The CPMF Bill 2007

The CPMF (Provisional Contribution on Financial Transactions) was a temporary charge levied on all banking online, except for share trading in the stock market, withdrawals from retirement, unemployment, wages, and transfers between current accounts of the same title. It was approved for the first time in 1993 and subsequently renewed in 1996, 1999, 2001, and 2004. It next came up for renewal in 2007 to extend the tax till 2011. During that time the size and scope of the levy varied, ranging as high as .38%, with its revenue being allocated to a number of different social and economic programs including programs supporting families in poverty, health care, education, and public employee and rural worker pensions.[14] By the time the bill came up for renewal in 2007, it was expected to finance R$40 billion or 10% of total government spending in 2008.[15] Renewing this tax required two rounds of approval in each chamber, and the requirement for passage was a 2/3 supermajority because the tax itself was a constitutional amendment. The fact that it had to go through two rounds in each chamber provides us with a very nice window into the efficacy and importance of party leadership in the Brazilian legislature's leaders and legislators.

The set of interests who were against it were primarily the industrial and commercial sectors of the economy, whose cause was spearheaded by two influential associations—FIESP and Fecomericio, the associations for industry and commerce for the state of Sao Paolo. These groups argued that the tax was irrational, distortionary, and had led to a frequent lack of capital for investment.[16] Instead of cutting spending, they advocated that the government focus on cutting costs and improving efficiency.[17] These interest groups lobbied influential senators and deputies from all parties for their votes and allied publicly with the political opposition headed by the PSDB and including the DEM, PPS, and the PV.[18]

The set of interests that favored the renewal of the CPMF included groups who would be direct beneficiaries, including public employees in the bureaucracy, the armed services, the judiciary, and rural workers. Nongovernmental organizations active in working on issues of poverty, education, and health also strongly supported this amendment. Influential governors from the PSDB, Jose Serra and Aecio Neves, also supported the government's position. Finally, the financial sector was also supportive of the bill because it was concerned that its defeat would return Brazil to an era of fiscal deficits and borrowing and would hurt Brazil's credit rating.[19] This alliance of interests was active in lobbying members of congress and members of the executive.

Given the fiscal importance of the bill, government officials, party leaders, and congressmen were very active in promoting the extension of the tax. President Lula, José Múcio Monteiro (Minister of Institutional Relations), and Guido Mantega (Minister of Agriculture) were each personally involved in negotiations and made substantial concessions to garner favor with on-the-fence politicians. The president went on record the day before the first round claiming that "no party can govern without the CPMF" and urging members of his coalition to vote for it. On September 20, 2007, in the first round in the house, the votes were 338 in favor, 117 against with 2 abstentions.

This round was marked by voting defections by members of both the ruling and the opposition coalitions. This initiated more lobbying by all the interest groups and the parties to sway more votes in the house and the senate. Party disloyalty was met with disapproval. In the words of deputy Paulo Bornhausen, "the party took a position, therefore, it must be followed. There's nothing to question."[20] In a telling set of incidents, deputy Salviano of the PSDB voted for the measure and quit the party. However, this was when the Supreme Court, the STF, ruled that a deputy who switched parties or was expelled by his party for antiparty behavior would lose his mandate as the mandate belonged to his party. After this ruling, Salviano negotiated his return to the PSDB successfully in order to retain his seat in the house.[21]

Concern was rising over the real possibility that the bill might not pass in the senate where the ruling coalition enjoyed a slight majority of 51 out of 80. The executive and party leaders from all parties began lobbying senators from various parties to switch sides or to switch parties. By the time the second round took place on October 9, three senators of the opposition DEM party had switched to the ruling PT. At the same time, the opposition made gains as well, luring five PMDB senators and one PTB senator away from the ruling coalition's line supporting the bill. Despite various threats by party leaders, in the end there were many defections from many parties on both sides of the issue.[22] The house passed the bill in the second round with 333 votes for it, 113 against, with two abstentions. Eighteen deputies from the ruling coalition voted against the bill while another 17 chose to register opposition by not showing up for the vote. The government was supported by 13 different parties including those from its base (PT, PSC, PHS, PT, and PC do B) as well as a hodgepodge of ideologically distinctive parties (PSB, PTB, and PMDB).[23] In the opposition, 36 deputies voted for the bill and 22 missed the vote. All of the seven amendments opposition deputies had introduced were defeated as well.

Given that the ruling coalition lacked a supermajority, lobbying by all parties became intense. By October 19, the government admitted that it did not have enough votes and started negotiating with opposition parties. At the same time, it continued its efforts to persuade senators to switch parties with promises of budgetary amendments and state positions. The opposition mounted a similar campaign and honed in on senators such as Pedro Simon (PMDB-RS) and Jarbas Vasconcelos (PMDB-RS) who were known to oppose the bill. Under this onslaught, the PT and the executive agreed to release R$4.3 million in amendments for members of the PMDB and R$2.3 million for senators from its own party. In early November, government negotiators accepted opposition demands regarding exemptions for poor families and a commitment for introducing a larger tax reform bill but were turned down by the PSDB party leadership.[24] The government reacted by vowing to "seek dialogue directly with individual senators."[25] Despite these high stakes, however, parties were not willing to expel members who voted against them. In fact, as the PMDB leader stated, "The PMDB also said that the closure of issue of the bench PMDB is a political gesture. That is, the party will not punish the senators who do not follow the decision of the bench."[26] Even the speaker of the chamber, an ally from the PMDB, refused to vote for such a measure to pressure party members.

The government's efforts however were insufficient and they could not persuade enough senators to constitute the required supermajority. On December 13, the senate rejected the extension of the CPMF by 4 votes. Four members of the ruling coalition voted against the measure ensuring its defeat.[27] Immediately, after the vote, a party leader from the ruling coalition stated that none of the defectors would be punished by their party.[28] In January, the government responded to the revenue shortfall by using a presidential decree to impose new taxes on financial institutions and corporate earnings and cutting funding to party caucuses. The opposition subsequently challenged the constitutionality of this decree in the Supreme Court. In 2009, the government was again circulating a revised version of a CPMF bill for passage.

As this case shows, despite the fiscal ramifications of the bill for the economy and for core programs of the ruling coalition, party leaders were unable to discipline their own members to vote with them in either the house or the senate. Opposition parties suffered a similar fate. Parties across the spectrum faced threats of losing the votes of their own members and were actively trying to win that of other parties. The executive was actively adopting similar strategies and using the assets of office in its efforts. Interest groups were involved directly in all of these actions and various groups from the business and social sets of interests lobbied deputies and senators from various parties. In contrast to India, this entire process is marked by a basic operating assumption made by all the players involved that party strength in the chambers did not say anything about what the final votes would be. Whether it came to votes or amendments, individual members were the ultimate prize, not their party leaders.

CONCLUSION

This chapter tested the expectations generated in chapter 2 on the lobbying behavior for Indian and Brazilian business groups based on the design of their legislative institutions. Hypotheses H_{1a}, H_{2a}, and H_{3a} are strongly supported by evidence from three sources: data from a survey of business groups, open-ended interviews with various participants, and lobbying behavior demonstrated by business groups on two specific pieces of legislation. As expected, business groups in India perceive parties as being formally in control of agenda-setting and introduction of amendments. At the same time, parties are seen to control the voting behavior of their members as they have the institutional authority to deprive members of their legislative seats should members defy the party whip. Accordingly, business groups choose to lobby parties in preference to individual legislators in India who are perceived as having little sway over policymaking. In contrast, interest groups in Brazil identified individual legislators as being the influential policymakers in Brazil and perceived parties as having little influence over agenda-setting, amendments, or voting. In line with these expectations, they rationally lobby individual legislators rather than parties.

These hypotheses on lobbying venue choice were confirmed by soliciting data on both perceptions and actual experiences. In addition to eliciting information on preferences, the survey also obtained data on the actual strategies adopted by business groups on a specific piece of legislation in a policy issue of salience to them. This allows one to verify that stated preferences are consistent and not driven by unobserved factors and to account for the political salience of other factors. Since both countries are considered to have strong executives, groups were asked to report their lobbying strategy in the full context of alternative political venue choices including the executive. The preferences revealed through the actual strategy adopted on a specific policy issue show that even when groups have accounted for the influence of the executive as they evaluate it, they still have a pronounced preference for parties in the party-focused system, India, and for individuals in the individual-focused system, Brazil. Furthermore, access to the executive is obtained via parties in India and via legislators in Brazil.

These data also show that other factors identified by many theories such as sector identity, size, geographic concentration, and age do not explain significant variation across countries. Business groups from similar sectors in Brazil and India make very different political choices in their lobbying strategies, and these choices are dictated by the characteristics of the institutions governing their policy environment not their sectors. Similarly, groups lobbying on different policy issues within each country adopt similar strategies, whereas groups who are lobbying on similar issues across countries lobby different actors, thus choosing the strategy that is institutionally optimal for their country. These reported behaviors are also confirmed in the manner in which specific policy bills were passed in both countries.

Next, chapter 5 focuses on establishing the second link in the causal chain of figure 2.1—the link from these institutionally inspired legislative lobbying behaviors to corruption levels. If the causal mechanism identified in this project is correct, then party-focused lobbying should lead groups to observe higher levels of political corruption in India compared to the individual-focused lobbying case in Brazil. The chapter uses data from the same set of surveys and interviews to show that this is indeed the case.

5

BRAZIL AND INDIA: BUSINESS LOBBYING
AND CORRUPTION

Chapter 4 presented evidence testing the first step of the causal link between institutions and corruption, namely, the link between legislative institutions and lobbying. This chapter presents evidence on the second link, that between lobbying and corruption. Hypotheses H_{1b}, H_{2b}, and H_{3b} state that when agenda-setting, amendments, and rules on voting defections give political parties control over these key dimensions of policymaking, ceteris paribus, lobbying should lead to higher political corruption. Hence, the institutional design of these legislative institutions defines the conditions under which legislative lobbying is more likely to lead to higher political corruption. As I argued in chapter 2, under strong parties, higher political corruption also leads to higher overall corruption because strong parties are successfully able to control delegation decisions. This allows them to co-opt extralegislative institutions such as the bureaucracy, the judiciary, and the police to support their delivery of policy outcomes to business donors thus increasing the extent of corruption and hence, generating higher levels of corruption in party-focused countries.

In this chapter, I test these hypotheses using a combination of data from the surveys and interviews conducted in Brazil and India for this project, secondary data provided by other scholars, anecdotal examples, and, finally, survey data from the International Country Risk Guide (ICRG), Transparency International (TI), and the World Bank (WB). These distinct and independent bits of evidence all strongly support the hypothesis that institutionally induced, party-directed lobbying leads to higher corruption levels in India relative to the corruption levels realized by individual-focused lobbying in Brazil. I first present evidence that legislative lobbying by business interests is a significant source of political finance and corruption in both these cases, and I then demonstrate that it leads to higher political and aggregate corruption in India. The next three sections present evidence that shows the differences in the dynamics of financial demand and party capacity to supply it that connect stronger parties to relatively higher levels of corruption in India compared to Brazil. Finally, I use time-series data from the ICRG, TI, and WB to show that aggregate corruption levels in India are higher than in Brazil as well as higher than the average level of corruption in all individual-focused systems in the sample. Corruption levels in Brazil are not just lower than in India but also lower than the average for all party-focused countries in the sample.

BUSINESS INTERESTS, LEGISLATIVE LOBBYING, AND CORRUPTION

In order to assess the role legislative lobbying plays in driving relative corruption levels in these two countries, we need to first establish (a) how important business finance is in each country as a source of political revenue, (b) whether legislative lobbying constitutes an important financial investment for business interests, (c) whether money spent on legislative lobbying is contributed legally or illegally by businesses, and finally d) whether business contributions, both legal and illegal, are directed to parties or individual legislators. Then we can move on to compare the patterns and levels of corruption in these two countries.

Evidence from reported donations, interviews with business and political elites, and research by scholars shows that business is the *dominant* source of political finance in both Brazil and India as is the case in many developing country democracies around the world. Data from the Tribunal Superior Eleitoral (TSE) in Brazil shows that the bulk of political contributions are made by business interests (Claessens 2008, 561; Samuels 2001).[1] Even the leftist Partido dos Trabalhadores (PT) party with the ability to successfully raise funds through contributions levied on party members has run up deficits and has had to increasingly rely on business allies for money (Fleischer 2007; Samuels 2001; Mainwaring 1997). Donations by voters and members have been steadily falling and are no longer sufficient to meet political expenses required to support political careers in either country. These trends are confirmed by political party leaders and deputies in interviews (PMDB-1, PSDB-1, PT-2). Political financing in India has followed a similar trajectory; donations by voters and members have fallen and declining memberships have yielded lower revenues as fees (Jalan 2007; Sridharan 2006, 323; Mitra 1999; Malik 1989). Fees imposed by party leaders on members holding office have also not been able to meet increasing expenses (Venkatesan 1999; Suryaprakash 1993). Business interests have therefore increasingly come to provide the lion's share of party finances during the entire political cycle in India (TI 2007; Sridharan 2006; Bryan and Baer 2005, 70; IDEA 2003; Kumar 2001; Mitra 1999). Party leaders and business leaders confirmed these trends in interviews with the author and stressed the increasing strategic importance of business interests as a reliable and increasing source of political finance.

In order to understand the extent to which the design of legislative institutions influences corruption, it is crucial to investigate the extent to which business groups spend on legislative lobbying. The second crucial bit of information we need is to know whether legislative lobbying is strategically important enough to business groups that they would reserve a significant share of their political donations for use at this stage of the political cycle as opposed to election campaigns. If lobbying at the legislative stage does not provide interest groups with the requisite strategic influence, they will not withhold funds from campaign contributions to spend on it.

To obtain systematic data to test whether legislative lobbying was a significant financial investment by groups in these countries and to test whether legislative corruption was higher in India relative to Brazil, I asked business interests surveyed in these two countries the following questions:

(1) Indicate the % allocations of the political contributions made by your sector along the following categories:
   • Between election campaigns and legislative terms
(2) To what extent have the following forms of corruption had an impact on businesses in your sector:
   • Sale of parliamentary votes on laws to private interests—No Impact, Minor Impact, Significant Impact, Very Significant Impact, Don't Know, Not Applicable.

Figures 5.1 and 5.2 show the distributions of responses to these questions. Figure 5.1 shows that in both countries business interests devote a considerable share of their financial resources to lobbying during the legislative term. In Brazil, 60% of groups report spending *more than 50%* of their total political contributions on lobbying during the legislative term. In addition, 88% report spending at least a third of their total political expenditures on lobbying. In India, 43% of groups report spending *more than 50%* of their total political contributions during the legislative term while 66% report spending at least a third of their expenditures on lobbying. These data show that in both countries business interests spend a very significant share of their resources on legislative lobbying.

Figure 5.2 shows the distribution of responses to question (2) on legislative corruption for 172 groups in India and 157 in Brazil. A total of 58.98% of groups in India report parliamentary corruption to be at least a significant source of corruption in India, and only 5.77% report no impact. In contrast, 32.2% of groups in Brazil report at least significant corruption and 17.2% report no impact. These data show that corruption levels in legislative policymaking reported by groups in India are *significantly higher* than those reported in Brazil. Tests comparing the means and medians of these distributions confirm that the two distributions of legislative corruption are significantly different and that the probability of drawing a higher corruption level is higher in India relative to Brazil. Therefore, corruption in the legislative process, while high in both countries, is significantly higher in India than in Brazil.

As discussed earlier in chapter 2, while ideology and the concern for stability undoubtedly play some part in their political calculations, business interests contribute to election funds primarily to buy the goodwill of parties and politicians during their terms in office. Therefore we expect that the locus of legislative power should also influence patterns of campaign contributions. However, in order to understand campaign finance patterns, scholars have focused heavily on the incentives that structure the demand side of political finance as defined by electoral rules at the expense of rules that determine the supply side, that is, legislative policymaking rules.

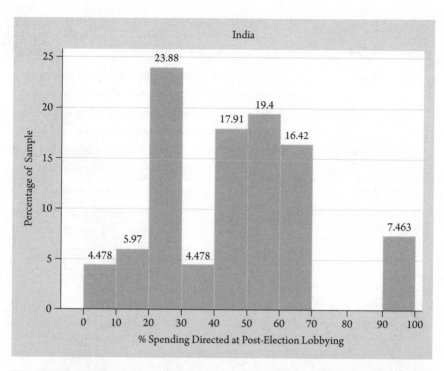

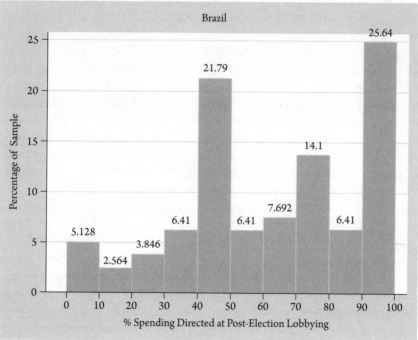

Figure 5.1. *% of Political Spending Directed at Legislative Lobbying vs. Election Campaigns*

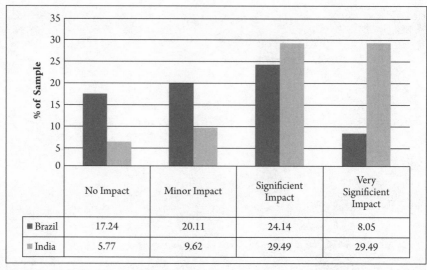

	No Impact	Minor Impact	Significient Impact	Very Significient Impact
■ Brazil	17.24	20.11	24.14	8.05
▪ India	5.77	9.62	29.49	29.49

Figure 5.2. *Sale of Parliamentary Votes*

Both Brazil (state districts, open-list PR) and India (SMD plurality) have electoral rules that should create candidate-centered incentive systems. Recall from chapter 3 that the Carey-Shugart index compiled by Johnson and Wallack (2008), which takes into account the electoral rules (plurality, open list PR, closed-list PR), district magnitude, ballot, and pooling of votes. This index ranks Brazil as a 7 and India as a 10 on a 1–13 scale where 13 indicates the most individual-centered electoral system. According to these scores, interest groups should be directing money to individual candidates in *both* countries. If, however, as argued earlier, campaign financing is heavily influenced by group perceptions of legislative influence, groups should donate to parties in India but not in Brazil. Furthermore, as discussed in chapter 2, since parties require more money to run election campaigns and prefer receiving money over other resources, groups in India should be experiencing *higher* campaign corruption as well compared to groups in Brazil. In order to see whether campaign finance was directed to parties and caused more corruption in India, I asked the following questions:

(3) To what extent have the following forms of corruption had an impact on businesses in your sector:
  • Illegal contributions by private interests to *party* election campaign funds—No impact, Minor Impact, Significant Impact, Very Significant Impact, Don't Know, Not Applicable.
(4) To what extent have the following forms of corruption had an impact on businesses in your sector:
  • Illegal contributions by private interests to *individual* election campaign funds—No Impact, Minor Impact, Significant Impact, Very Significant Impact, Don't Know, Not Applicable.

Table 5.1. Perceptions of Corruption across Institutions, Parties, and Politicians

	Brazil		India	
	% Reporting corruption is significant or very significant	*% Reporting corruption not significant at all*	*% Think corruption is significant or very significant*	*% Reporting corruption not significant at all*
#3. Party Campaign Funds	41.7	12.21	62.0	6.9
#4. Individual Campaign Funds	51.8	11.63	31.15	9.6
#8. Political Patronage	53.1	23.0	78.5	12.7
#9. Bureaucratic Corruption	40.0	18.4	71.3	5.2
#10. Judicial Corruption	41.6	28.9	49.7	32.6
#11. Party Corruption	35.2	44.8	87.3	8.2

Table 5.1 shows the distribution of responses to questions (3) and (4) reporting significant or very significant corruption and no impact from corruption at all. The data show that 41.7% of 158 Brazilian groups report at least significant impact while 62% of 172 Indian groups report such levels of corruption through party campaign financing. These numbers clearly show that groups report experiencing higher levels of party corruption during election campaigns in India compared to Brazil and lower levels of individual corruption during election campaigns. When asked about corruption through individual campaign financing practices, 51.8% of Brazilian groups and 31.15% of Indian groups report at least significant impact. Thus, business groups suffer from higher levels of corruption through demands to finance individual election campaigns in Brazil compared to India. Both these trends are consistent with the responses of the surveyed groups, reported in chapter 4, asking them how they allocated their total budgets between parties and candidates. Additionally, if we compare these two dominant channels of corruption in campaign finance, a higher share of respondents in India, 87.3%, report experiencing at least significant levels of party corruption compared to Brazil where 51.8% report such experiences with individual campaign donations.

While these resources may, theoretically, be contributed legally or illegally, discussions in open-ended interviews confirm that a significant share of the resources contributed by lobbyists at any stage is illegal and influence-seeking. Such transactions are conducted "off the books" in both countries and payments are made in cash (Mitra 1998, 115; Fleischer 1997, 302). In a 2002 survey of 92 Brazilian firms, Abramo (2003) similarly found that more than half of all firms who were asked for electoral finance were explicitly promised policy favors in exchange for firm donations by the legislators requesting them. Deputies use their powers to sponsor amendments to appropriate pork-barrel projects that direct public money to generous donors (Samuels 2002, 851). The importance of being able to influence these stages of the policy process, and the advantage of doing it through individual congress members, was summarized by the legislative liaison of a prominent manufacturing association in Brazil as follows: "We choose Deputies we like, then we meet with our Congressmen frequently, sometimes every week in session. They give us information, we give them information. Money also exchanges hands, under the table, but we only pick people who know our industry or they are smart and can move things."[2] These findings are consistent with those of other scholars who find that "the bulk of campaign finance in Brazil is service-induced" (Samuels 2001, 42). As the survey data and the opinions of group leaders show, political funds are directed toward individual legislators in Brazil. Frequently this is done illegally and with the specific intention of buying influence with the recipient.

These trends are also clearly observed in the legal contribution patterns and in the corruption scandals that come to light in the media in the two countries. Donations by businesses go to legislators in influential positions, as in the examples of Mesa members or members on the Budgetary, Agriculture, Finance, and Taxation committees (Fleischer: February 19, 2007; Samuels 2001, 36). In a pattern typical of most Brazilian corruption scandals, in 2007, federal deputies Marina Maggessi (opposition Partido Popular Socialista Party), Simão Sessim (government-allied), and Senator Romeo Tuma were named by the federal police as being on the bankroll of the gambling industry in Rio during both their election campaigns and their tenure in office. Police claimed that the gambling industry had bankrolled the election campaigns of these congressmen with the expectation that they would sponsor the introduction of a bill legalizing gambling in Brazil and lobby other deputies to drum up the necessary votes (LatinNews.com, April 19, 2007; Xinhua April 20, 2007). These were widely seen as the schemes of individual legislators rather than of their parties, and the individuals were picked based on their geographic affiliations as well as their perceived corruptibility. No party leaders were seen to be involved at any stage.

In India, the strategic rationale for lobbying parties at both the legislative and electoral stages was articulated very clearly in interviews. For example, the expectation of a legislative quid pro quo was emphasized by the director of a manufacturing sector chamber (Author Interview, Manufacturing-4): "At election time, the party leaders come or they call and ask for so much. How can you say no? The local MPs are of no use unless they are party leaders, you have to make the party happy or you are done for. If parties are not happy with you, you will experience all sorts of problems when you have an issue after election time, it does not matter who is in power."[3] The chairman of another influential chamber in the service sector (Author Interview, Finance-2) stated, "Policy issues, bureaucratic hurdles, legislation . . . this is all handled by parties. You cannot expect something for nothing, so you must pay when they ask. Election campaigns are important but donations are needed at all times and when you are stuck in something, you cannot say no."[4]

This raison d'être to make political donations in amounts and forms that violate legal provisions on corporate financing of political activities was poignantly demonstrated by the failed financing experiment conducted by a leading business house of India, the Tatas. In 1998, the Tatas set up a corpus fund to finance political parties before and after elections in order to reduce the practice of political corruption and introduce transparency into business financing of politics (Indian Express, January 28, 1998). The distribution of funds was to be supervised by a neutral board of eminent citizens in line with the purely secular principle of seat shares. All business chambers and firms were invited to contribute. The scheme failed spectacularly and was closed down at that time. The reason for the failure of this novel experiment was articulated by Vijay Kalantri, then president of the All India Association of Industries (Indian Express, January 30, 1998): "As most of the corporate funds to the politicians are donated in black, that too expecting some quid pro quo, I doubt whether the Tata fund would get even Rs. five from other companies." In the event, not even Tata's own subsidiaries contributed to this fund. Other corruption scandals such as the Hawala scandal and the Fodder scam show similar trends, with party leaders rather than legislators being the recipients of business largesse.[5]

As these figures and opinions show, business lobbying is directly tied to corruption in India via corrupt legislative lobbying practices and service-induced campaign contributions directed toward political parties. This incident is representative of the general view held by business elites that parties are the only viable game in town for influencing legislation and hence are the primary targets of both legal and illegal political financing by business lobbies. In Brazil, in contrast, lobbyists emphasized the importance of identifying and cultivating appropriate legislators during the election and legislative stages. These strategic calculations by lobbies confirm the findings of the systematic data obtained from the survey.

To summarize, business lobbies in both countries consider the legislative stage to be of great strategic policymaking importance and reserve a substantial share of their resources for this stage of the political cycle. Furthermore, campaign financing patterns are substantially influenced by calculations of postelectoral influence over policymaking. As the examples discussed above and survey data demonstrate, lobbying directed at the systemically optimal actor in these countries raises political corruption levels significantly in both these countries. The next section discusses why party-directed lobbying in India leads to higher rather than lower *overall* corruption there compared to Brazil.

IMPERATIVES OF PARTY FINANCE AND CORRUPTION

In chapter 2, I argued that lobbying in party-focused systems is subject to 4 dynamics that lead to higher corruption throughout the system and link higher political corruption to higher systemic levels of national corruption. The two demand-side dynamics were the vast scale of financial demands faced by parties and their preference for fungible resources such as money over functionally nonsubstitutable resources such as information. These higher demands were met only in countries where parties were strengthened by legislative institutions so that they could command party discipline in the policy process and control legislative outcomes. In these countries parties used their legislative influence to manipulate delegation authority in order to co-opt the bureaucracy and the judiciary into their corruption networks. This allowed them to peddle influence at these institutions, to integrate them to raise graft from the state and citizens, and to finesse financial accountability requirements and protect donors. In this section, I show that we find all four dynamics active in India.

In contrast in Brazil, the evidence shows that information has more value as a lobbying resource. The "price" of influence is lower since it is targeted at the individual level, and state institutions are abused for personal enrichment in an idiosyncratic fashion by ambitious individuals rather than systematically by parties. These characteristics lead us to expect not just the higher levels of political corruption in India demonstrated by the survey data presented above but also higher levels of aggregate national corruption there compared to Brazil. The final section will present data comparing aggregate corruption levels in these two countries with each other and with the average levels of corruption in the theoretical comparator categories of all party-focused and individual-focused countries in the sample to see if this hypothesis of higher corruption in party-focused systems is rejected or not.

Scale of Party Expenses

The first reason to expect party financial demands made to lobbies to be higher in party-focused systems, I argued in chapter 2, was the higher variety and scale of expenditures parties have to incur to stay competitive in a political environment characterized by interparty rather than intercandidate competition. Parties undertake many expenses, such as maintaining and running party organizations and buying legislative votes, that are not borne by individual legislators. The scale of these and other expenses overwhelms any efficiency gained by centralizing election expenditures into party-dominated campaigns. As the discussion below shows, parties in India are subject to all of these spending compulsions, which increases the quantum of funds they must raise from business donors considerably compared to the funding needs faced by legislators in Brazil.

Given the illicit nature of these funds in both countries, it is impossible for researchers to get exact figures that would allow a direct comparison of the scale of their expenditures. Therefore, with all its caveats, the best direct comparison available is to obtain the opinions of informed elites on the prevalence of corruption among these political actors in the two countries. Questions 3 and 4 discussed earlier elicited responses on the experience of business groups with demands for illegal campaign finance for party and individual campaigns. This is clearly an imperfect indicator of such expenses since it only covers business groups. However, it has two key advantages. First, as the biggest source of illegal campaign funds in both countries, business's perspective should be well-informed and represent a significant share of the fundraising practices in both countries. Second, the data thus obtained should be more directly comparable across these two countries and allow us to draw more credible comparisons. As shown in table 5.1, corruption reported due to demands by parties exceeded those reported by individual campaigns in India while the reverse is true for Brazil. Furthermore, the share of respondents reporting significant or very significant corruption through parties in India was much higher than corruption through individuals in Brazil. This supports evidence from other sources, anecdotal evidence on fundraising, and expenditures.

Parties in India structure the basis of political competition at all levels of political competition ranging from local to national elections. Even the prominent candidates in India rely crucially on public popularity of their party's label (Keefer and Khemani 2009). This requires them to finance the organizational infrastructure required to support elections, tenure in office, publicity, outreach, training, constituency service, and the party organization at each of these levels (Suryaprakash1993; Mitra 1998; Shourie 2007; Sridharan 2001). While the most popular candidates may be able to raise sufficient funds to finance their own elections, most candidates for office in India are supported heavily by party funds. As Mitra (1998, 115) states, "Most parties also bear a substantial share of their candidates' poll-related expenses, for few politicians can afford to pledge the large amounts needed to successfully contest an election."

In contrast, it is the candidates in Brazil who bear responsibility for financing their own elections, supporting their own work in office, hiring their own staffs, and doing outreach and constituency service in their districts. As Mainwaring (1999, 149) points out, "Candidates bring their own campaign teams with them. The party neither dictates how campaigns should be run, nor provides much help in running or financing campaigns." And Samuels (2001, 34) similarly remarks on the "the general absence of national party influence over the distribution of campaign funds in Brazil." While parties in Brazil also maintain organizational infrastructure at various levels, they do not fill the same roles or serve the same functions that parties in India do.

Under Article 38 of law 9096 on parties, political parties in Brazil receive a share of public funds to underwrite party expenses in proportion to their vote shares, and these are paid monthly to parties. These funds barely cover the operating expenses of small parties and are not believed to form a significant share of expenses for bigger parties (LatinNews Daily, March 27, 2007). Consider that the entire sum of public funds made available for all parties in 2007 was $60 million whereas election expenses alone in 2006 were estimated at $427 million (OPB 2007). Therefore, these funds have not made a significant dent in expenses for any but the smallest parties and they do not reflect the demand structure for political financing in Brazil. These contrasting environments of political competition reflect the difference in the scale of political expenses incurred under the two systems. The expenses that must be financed in Brazil are largely those of legislators.[6] However, not all candidates expect to raise nor do they raise significant funds in their careers, which reduces the corruption we would expect from decentralized political spending.

In Brazil, groups only target select legislators based on specific personal characteristics including their general competence, their legislative reputation, their familiarity with relevant issues, their access to the executive, their personal background, and their personal ideology as well as the positions they hold in the chambers.[7] This situation was summarized by a deputy of the Partido do Movimento Democrático (Author interview, PMDB Brasilia-1) as follows: "If you have a reputation for getting things done, money comes your way. Industry and business people will pay for a deputy who is smart and committed. So, it is not necessary to look to party leaders for money or other types of support. You can be totally independent." In the survey, 65% of groups reported that the ideology of the targeted legislator was either strong or decisive determinants in their decision to lobby that specific legislator and 64% reported that the legislators' chances of holding an important legislative chamber post were either strong or decisive determinants in their of legislators to lobby. Being targeted by other interest groups (55%) also attracted their attention to particular legislators. However, only 27% of groups cared enough about the party affiliation of their legislators to be concerned about changes in their party affiliations. Other studies confirm as well that many legislators fail to attract lobbyist attention because they are judged wanting on these dimensions (NIS 2001, 7). Therefore, only a subset of the entire potential set of all congress members is targeted by lobbies.

Additionally, since competition for business funding takes place in a competitive market compared to that of parties, legislators must additionally be good bargains in terms of price. This constrains their ability to bargain. Parties in India, on the other hand, operate in an oligopolistic influence market where they can charge higher prices for their products. Brazilian legislators, furthermore, need only raise enough revenue to meet their personal campaign, staff, and legislative needs, not those of their co-partisans. This reduces the frequency and scale of financing that business interests must undertake to buy and exercise influence in Brazil. Both factors reduce the impact decentralized funding has on aggregate corruption levels.

This is evident from the scale of operations and the expenses that have been visible in these two countries.[8] Two recent studies of vote-buying illustrate this difference. A study in India estimated that as much as 20% of the Indian electorate's votes might have been subject to cash bribes in 2008 and that while some vote-buying was arranged by individual candidates, the dominant form of organization and financing was by political parties (Mint, September 22, 2008). In contrast, studies from the 2002 and 2006 elections reveal that about 3% and 8% of Brazilian voters, respectively, were offered cash and other bribes for their votes in these elections (Trasparencia Brasil 2007). These studies also found that vote-buying in Brazil was organized and paid for by the candidates competing for those seats rather than by their parties.

Parties in India also raise considerable funds to run and maintain their organizations in between elections and to amass a war chest for buying MPs and their votes in parliament (Suryaprakash 1993; Mitra 1998; Sridharan 2001; Jalan 2007; Shourie 2007). Many of the most egregious corruption scandals, including the 1993 vote-buying scandal for which Prime Minister Narashimha Rao was first convicted in 2000, are associated with the necessity to raise such funds. While legislative vote-buying certainly took place in Brazil before 2004, it was not organized and financed as a partisan investment in Brazil until very recently. As I discuss later, it is only with the advent of a stronger party like the PT in Brazil that the state itself has come to be exploited as a source for rent by the party to finance legislative vote-buying there.

Party Preference for Fungible Resources

In chapter 2, I argued that a second dynamic that leads to higher levels of political corruption in party-focused systems is the stronger preference for fungible resources such as money, which can be transferred across functions and jurisdictions by parties over less transferable resources such as technical information. Money will still be highly valued by individual politicians in Brazil (Samuels 2002, 851). However, information should be valued more highly by them relative to India because the utility of such information to an individual's career is much higher than to a party's prospects. Legislators can leverage political knowledge and technical information at both the electoral and the legislative stages to raise money and build better campaigns. This difference in the relative preferences for money over information of the dominant policy player should lead groups in Brazil to employ information *more often* than money for lobbying policymakers relative to India. In India, the reverse should hold true, with lobbyists preferring to use money over information as the currency of influence due to its higher political value there.

These preferences and practices are supported strongly by data obtained on the perceptions and actual lobbying behavior of interest groups through the two-country survey. Question # 5 below elicits information about the group's perception of how politically valued different resources are. Question # 6 elicits information on the actual resources employed by the group as part of their lobbying strategy on a policy issue of high concern to them. Figures 5.3 and 5.4 report the distribution of responses to questions # 5 and # 6 below:

(5) The following questions ask you why your choice for lobbying would choose to represent your sector's interests rather than some other sector's interests:
   (a) Scale of your political contribution to his party
   (b) Scale of your political contribution to that individual legislator
   (c) Your technical knowledge on policies relating to your sector
   (d) Your technical knowledge on issues of national concern
(6) For the policy issue most important to you (trade, financing labor, environment, foreign exchange, taxes), which tool did you find most useful—technical information, political contributions, media publicity, demonstrations for or against the policy, other.

Figure 5.3 (a) shows that distribution of responses to question (5) for 157 groups in Brazil and 173 groups in India. Financial contributions to parties are valued by the recipient in both countries but tend to be decisive more often in India. Contrast this with the value perceived of individual contributions reported in figure 5.3 (b). The contrast with a) is striking. Financial donations to individual politicians are rarely seen to be influential in India, only 14% report average or above influence. However, in

Brazil these financial contributions are considered to be highly valued and about 74% of groups report it as being at of at least average influence. These two figures paint a very clear picture of where groups see their political investment paying off.

To see how this compares with the political value of information, consider figure 5.3 (c), which show the distribution of political value for sector-specific technical information, and figure 5.3 (d), which shows the distribution for technical ability on issues of national concern. Both figures show that the ability of groups to provide valuable technical information is more highly valued as a currency for influence in Brazil

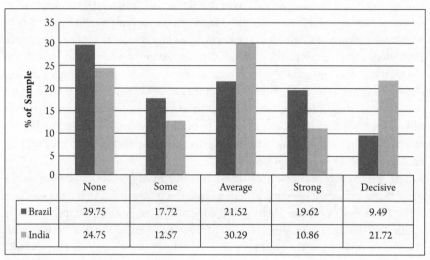

	None	Some	Average	Strong	Decisive
■ Brazil	29.75	17.72	21.52	19.62	9.49
▦ India	24.75	12.57	30.29	10.86	21.72

a

(a) Financial Contributions to Parties

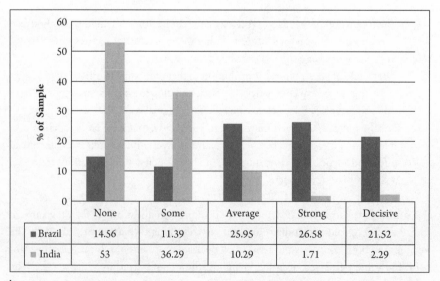

	None	Some	Average	Strong	Decisive
■ Brazil	14.56	11.39	25.95	26.58	21.52
▦ India	53	36.29	10.29	1.71	2.29

b

(b) Financial Contributions to Individual Legislators

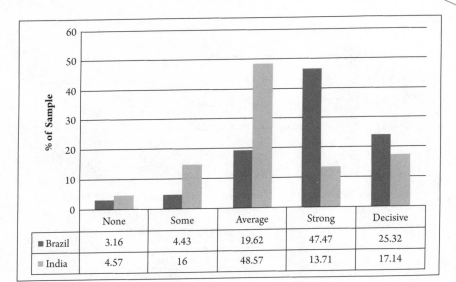

c

(c) Technical Ability of Group on Sector-Related Issues

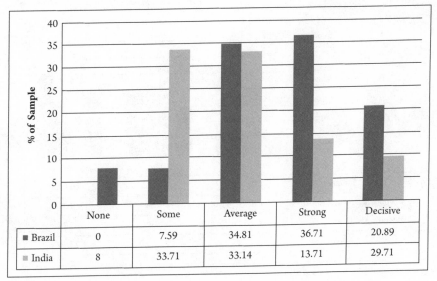

d

(d) Technical Ability of Group on National Issues

Figure 5.3. (a), (b), (c) and (d) *Perceptions of Sources of Group Influence: Money vs. Information*

compared to India. In Brazil 72% of groups report sector ability as being strong or decisively important while in India the figure is only 31%. Similarly, 57% of groups in Brazil report ability on national issues to be strongly or decisively valued by policy-makers and only 23% report this in India. Statistical tests show that the means and medians of the distributions for each of these variables are significantly different for the two countries. Therefore, collectively these data show clearly that money is seen to

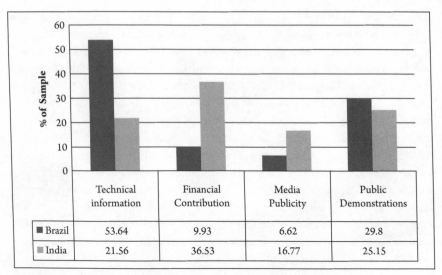

	Technical information	Financial Contribution	Media Publicity	Public Demonstrations
■ Brazil	53.64	9.93	6.62	29.8
▦ India	21.56	36.53	16.77	25.15

a

(a) All Groups: Brazil and India

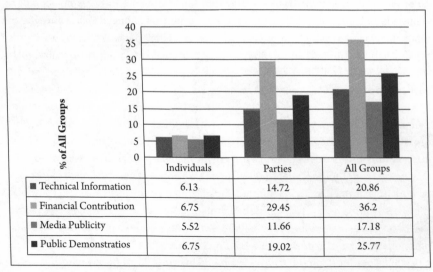

	Individuals	Parties	All Groups
■ Technical Information	6.13	14.72	20.86
▦ Financial Contribution	6.75	29.45	36.2
■ Media Publicity	5.52	11.66	17.18
■ Public Demonstratios	6.75	19.02	25.77

b

(b) Tool Chosen Conditional on Venue Lobbied—India

be more persuasive as a means of influence by groups in India compared to Brazil while information is seen to be more influential in Brazil than in India.

Question # 6 elicited information on how lobbies respond to these political valuations of the various resources at their command. Groups were asked to report on the actual strategy they had employed in practice on a specific policy issue of importance to them. Figure 5.4 (a) shows that groups respond to the valuations they see by using money more frequently in India and information in Brazil. While 53% of 158 Brazilian

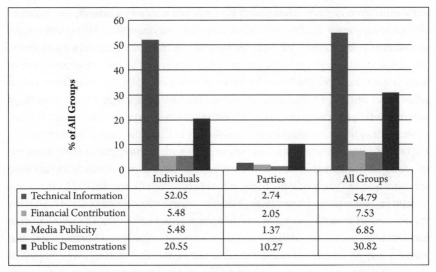

	Individuals	Parties	All Groups
■ Technical Information	52.05	2.74	54.79
■ Financial Contribution	5.48	2.05	7.53
■ Media Publicity	5.48	1.37	6.85
■ Public Demonstrations	20.55	10.27	30.82

c

(c) Tool Chosen Conditional on Venue Lobbied—Brazil

Figure 5.4. (a), (b) and (c) *Choice of Lobbying Tool Employed for Policy Issue Ranked #1 by Groups*

interest groups report using technical information, only about 21% of 176 Indian groups do. Conversely, while 36% of groups reported using financial contributions to buy influence, only 10% of Brazilian groups reported employing money. These differences in the means and medians of the distributions for the two countries are statistically significant. Business groups therefore respond rationally to the "market" they see for influence and use the resource they perceive has the most political value in their system.[9]

This can be seen even more clearly in figures 5.4 (b) and (c), which identify the tool used by groups conditional on their choice of lobbying venue. Figure 5.4 (b) shows that when groups in India lobby parties they are more likely to use money over any other resource. Whereas for the few groups that choose to lobby individual politicians, the difference between using money or information is not statistically significant. Similarly, in Brazil, as figure 5.4 (c) shows, when groups lobby individuals they over-whelmingly use information over other resources. But when they lobby parties the difference between money and information is not very significant. These data show that there is a preference for money by parties and that lobbies respond to it by making more frequent use of money to lobby parties in India. Therefore, corruption through this dynamic is higher in India compared to Brazil.

Influence-Peddling and Party Machines

In chapter 2, I argued that legislative institutions also create higher and more pervasive corruption in party-focused democracies by allowing parties to systemically capture the state apparatus through legislative delegation. By exercising partisan control over state institutions such as the bureaucracy and the judiciary, they can peddle influence at the policy design, implementation, and oversight stages to raise business funds. Additionally, parties can use these institutions to steal directly from state coffers and to extract rent from citizens through graft networks managed by captive bureaucrats. These linkages can raise corruption levels and extend political corruption into the sphere of ordinary citizens. They can also raise corruption by lowering the norms of behavior among public officials and extending political protection to collaborators. I present evidence in this section that this is the case in India.

In contrast, while collusion between individual ministers, legislators, and bureaucrats can happen frequently in countries with weak parties, such interactions are fundamentally different in their nature and scale. The lack of systemic co-optation of the bureaucracy, the judiciary, and the police limits the extent to which political corruption can corrupt other parts of the system and keeps overall levels of corruption in the country relatively lower compared to a party-centered system. The Brazilian case discussed illustrates these dynamics and demonstrates that the levels, channels, and nature of corruption are very different in the two countries.

According to the theoretical framework, *levels* of bureaucratic and judicial corruption should be higher in India relative to Brazil and, importantly, the *correlations* between political corruption and bureaucratic corruption as well as between political corruption and judicial corruption should be significantly higher in India as well. In order to test whether this is the case, I asked business groups the following questions:

To what extent have the following forms of corruption had an impact on businesses in your sector:

(8) Political patronage (politicians hiring friends and relatives into official positions)
(9) Bribes to public officials
(10) Sale of arbitration court decisions to litigants
(11) Illegal contributions by private interests to political parties

Bureaucratic corruption is operationalized using two measures here—the first captures the payment of bribes to public officials (question # 9) and, the second captures the political manipulation of bureaucratic appointments to positions (question # 8). Judicial corruption is operationalized as the sale of court decisions (# 10). Political corruption is operationalized using three distinct questions: on party corruption (question # 11), corruption through party campaign finance (question # 3), and, corruption through individual campaign finance (question #4). Table 5.1 presents data on responses regarding levels of corruption of each type in the two countries. Table 5.2 presents the correlation between the responses to the questions on bureaucratic, judicial, and political corruption.

Table 5.1 shows that bureaucratic, judicial, and party corruption are all reported by business groups to be higher in India compared to Brazil. In India 71.3% report bureaucratic bribe-taking, 78.5% report patronage, and 49.7% report judicial corruption as having a significant or very significant impact on them. In Brazil these numbers are significantly lower at 40%, 53.1%, and 41.6%. Wilcoxon Rank Sum tests on each of these

Table 5.2. Correlations between Political and Officials Corruption

1	2	3	4	5
Correlation Between Variables (x,y)	Survey Question Numbers	Correlation in Brazil	Correlation in India	z-statistic– Statistical difference in correlations[1]
Patronage, Party Corruption	8,11	0.38	0.75	-24.78*
Bureaucratic Corruption, Party Corruption	9,11	0.23	0.82	-39.91*
Judicial Corruption, Party Corruption	10,11	0.36	0.38	-0.93
Sale of Parliamentary Votes, Party Corruption	2,11	0.39	0.79	-28.53*
Patronage, Party Campaign Finance Corruption	8,3	0.18	0.67	-27.20*
Bureaucratic Corruption, Party Campaign Finance Corruption	9,3	0.21	0.64	-23.57*
Judicial Corruption, Party Campaign Finance Corruption	10,3	0.19	0.22	-1.35
Sale of Parliamentary Votes, Party Campaign Finance Corruption	2,3	0.25	0.77	-31.86*
Patronage, Individual Campaign Finance Corruption	8,4	0.53	0.72	-13.73*
Bureaucratic Corruption, Individual Campaign Finance Corruption	9,4	0.61	0.30	17.28*
Judicial Corruption, Individual Campaign Finance Corruption	10,4	0.24	0.13	4.93
Sale of Parliamentary Votes, Individual Campaign Finance Corruption	2,4	0.68	0.29	22.95*

*Indicates statistical significance at the 5% level.

1. See Kanji (1999) for test details.

questions show that the distributions of the two countries for bureaucratic corruption, patronage, and judicial corruption are indeed statistically different. While the
distributions for judicial corruption are statistically different, this difference is lower
than that in bureaucratic corruption. Finally, 87.3% of groups in India and 35.2%
in Brazil identify party corruption as a significant or very significant problem. The
difference in the distributions of party corruption is statistically significant as well.
These data therefore support the hypotheses that corruption in extralegislative public
institutions, specifically the bureaucracy and the judiciary, is higher in India than in
Brazil.

Table 5.2 shows the correlations between these various kinds of corruption including
party corruption, legislative corruption as proxied by sale of parliamentary votes
(question # 2), party and individual campaign finance corruption, bureaucratic
corruption, patronage, and court corruption. Column 1 lists the two variables whose
correlation is being considered and column 2 in table 5.2 shows the survey questions
these variables correspond to. Columns 3 and 4 show the values of correlation between
the variables listed in column 1 for Brazil and India, respectively. Column 5 shows the
value of the z-statistic calculated to test whether the difference in the correlations
between those variables for the two countries is statistically significant.

We can see that the correlations between party corruption and sale of parliamentary
votes, bureaucratic corruption, and patronage are very high in India at .79, .82, and .75.
Whereas in Brazil these values are .39, .23, and .38, respectively, all are less than .50
indicating weak correlations. Furthermore, the strength of these correlations is significantly different for the two countries. The z-statistic values in table 5.2, column 5,
show that the difference in these correlations between the two countries is significant
for all forms and types of corruption but not for judicial corruption.

The difference between the two countries in the correlation between party and
judicial corruption is not significantly different and it is weak in both countries at .36
in Brazil and .38 in India. This result does not align with the theoretical discussion
above so it is important to explore what the potential reasons for it might be. The
possible explanations include the following: there is no causal link between judicial
and party corruption; or there is a causal link but it is not captured due to poor operationalization of the concept in this question or due to factors affecting the capacity
to operationalize it. Later in this section, I will bring additional evidence to bear on
this question to see which of these explanations is valid. Briefly, I will argue that these
results might be due to the positive image of the Supreme Court in India; it also may
be due to the higher exposure of judicial corruption in Brazil and the consequence of
the wording of the survey question, which did not allow respondents to discriminate
between judicial corruption at different levels.

This survey evidence supports the discussion above that bureaucratic corruption is
strongly correlated with party corruption levels in India. If parties themselves are
strong, they are more likely to integrate these state institutions into their networks
raising the overall level of corruption in that country. Thus, by manipulating these
state institutions, parties are able to translate legislative strength and discipline into a
mechanism that generates increasing returns to their influence over the legislative

process. In contrast, when parties are weak, as in Brazil, systemic corruption in these state institutions goes down. These data indicate that there are systematic differences in the degree to which these institutions are politically tied in their behavior. These perceptions held by business groups are echoed by other segments of society as well. As discussed below, they are supported by evidence found by other scholars; from secondary evidence from the behavior of parties, politicians, and public officials; and in the open-ended interviews conducted by the author.

Public officials in India including the bureaucracy, police services, and the judiciary are routinely evaluated as being very corrupt by citizens and businesses and rank among the most corrupt in the world (TI 2007, 2008; National Integrity Report 2003; WBES 2005; WEF 2009). While some of the bribes exchanged in their corrupt transactions undoubtedly just involve greedy officials lining their own pockets, the more pervasive form of systemic administrative corruption has been created and sustained by political parties. Chandan Mitra, a senior journalist, observes in his work on corruption in India (1998, 115), "The collection of illegal funds by the organization obliges the party as a whole to perpetuate corruption once it in power, through suitable alteration of government policies or questionable award of contracts, to repay their patrons and keep the route to future supply of resources open." Das (2002, 195) echoes this assessment: "In India, the functional distinction between bureaucratic and political corruption has all but disappeared." Direct political interference to influence policy implementation, transfers of recalcitrant officials to suit donor needs, and the establishment of a hierarchical system of graft with party leaders at the top have led to the complete co-optation of state institutions into partisan revenue schemes.

The constant stream of corruption scandals involving collusion between political leaders and public officials has been documented in various studies by scholars, policymakers, and politicians themselves.[10] Two academic studies by Mitra (2006) and Iyer and Mani (2008) are especially insightful. In a 1998–1999 survey of 161 elites, including political leaders, administrators, and police officers from four regions, Subrata Mitra (2006, 266) found that the most frequently cited reason by these elites for the ineffectiveness of the bureaucracy (35% of respondents) and the police (38% of respondents) was their politicization. Furthermore, when queried about the nature of the particular problems political leaders brought to the attention of administrators, 86% of Mitra's (2006, 101) respondents said it was sometimes or frequently related to political party considerations. These numbers show that the politicization of the bureaucracy is driven primarily, though not exclusively, by considerations of parties and their supporters. Former head of the central bank Bimal Jalan (2007, 167) summarizes the situation: "Any party that comes to power is inclined to appoint favored bureaucrats in sensitive positions who are expected to carry out the wishes of its party leaders, irrespective of their merits or legality. If a bureaucrat does not comply, he or she is likely to be transferred immediately to another position in another location. . . . Corruption becomes unavoidable, both to avoid transfers as well as to secure remunerative postings by corrupt officials."

This ability to transfer uncooperative officials who are not willing to show such consideration and install more malleable cooperative officials in their place is a political trait that is highly valued and sought after by business supporters. In a comprehensive study of 4000 officials of the Indian Administrative Service from 1980 to 2004, Iyer and Mani (2009) found that political parties routinely transferred bureaucrats around, almost at will, and did so in order to suit their partisan goals. They found that the probability that an officer would be transferred to a different jurisdiction in any given year was 49%. Only 56% of officers remained at their initial posting for more than a year, and the average tenure of an official in a district was a mere sixteen months! Consequently they find that officials chose to invest their time and energy currying favor with influential party leaders and their clients rather than discharging their public responsibilities, developing their skills, or denouncing corruption by others. Even technocratic bureaucrats must work constrained by these political considerations. Hence, the utility of technical information declines since it can no longer be used to improve policy or to further one's career. This is another reason that information is less valued as a lobbying tool in party-focused systems.

These numbers demonstrate the extent to which parties use their networks to peddle influence in India and do so successfully. While party members indulge their own corruption schemes on the side, these are tolerated only in the context of party needs. As Mitra (1998, 115) describes, "While politician do raise funds to further their personal fortunes, the bulk of the amounts garnered illicitly by them is undoubtedly taken by the party for election purposes." The result of such partisan co-optation has been a seamless system of collusion between public officials, including the police and the judiciary, and political parties for the purpose of facilitating business–political exchanges of mutual financial benefit, for stealing from state coffers, and for raising money from citizens through bribe-extortion rings (Verma 2005; Krishnan and Somanathan 2005; NIS Report 2003; Das 2002; Mitra 1999). Regulatory bodies, which are staffed primarily by retired or current civil servants, have thus also been drawn into the ambit of collusive partisan behavior both through political appointments and through selective legislative delegation (Bhattacharya and Patel 2005, 455). Such extensive institutional control has also allowed corrupt state officials running their own petty rackets to flourish as long as they have cooperated with the party on their schemes (Das 2001; Jalan 2007). Thus, parties in India have successfully leveraged legislative influence into an accelerating production function for raising rents. As a consequence, corruption levels are high and corrupt behaviors pervade the entire state apparatus resulting in pervasive corruption.

While the bureaucracy in Brazil hardly enjoys a reputation for efficiency or honesty (Abramo and Speck 2001, 12; TI 2003, 5), it is not perceived to be as corrupt as India's. Evidence from various sources indicates that the politicization of the bureaucracy is not a widespread phenomenon in Brazil (Abramo 2001; Fleischer 2007; TI 2003; Alston et al. 2009). Nepotism has been an issue of some concern for political positions but not for career bureaucratic or judicial appointments (Abramo 2001, 19; Taylor 2008, 153). The rampant transfer of honest or uncooperative bureaucrats, a commonly used tool in India, has not been a big concern in Brazil (NIS 2001, 6; Alston et al. 2009). Similarly, the systematic undermining of the bureaucracy and its co-optation into patronage and graft networks by party machines in pursuit of revenue is not a common phenomenon (Taylor 2009; Alston et al. 2009). Thus, Taylor (2009, 152) states, "Although many government bureaucracies are power unto themselves . . . the top down monopoly of political power is absent in the broad political system, even though—as in other democracies—some public posts may offer the chance of monopoly rents to mid-level bureaucratic officeholders who control the regulatory approvals or other bureaucratic bottlenecks in a specific domain."

Thus opportunities for petty corruption by individual public officials clearly exist and frequently lead to corruption, but the bureaucracy itself as an institution has not been transformed into an extension of the political establishment's influence-peddling machinery. As a result of this political autonomy and technical competence, the Brazilian bureaucracy has been considered "as a fairly successful case" in the context of developing country democracies (Alston et al. 2009, 133).

This is clearly reflected in the ability of public institutions, including the police and the judicial systems, to pursue corruption charges filed against high-profile officials and politicians. For example, when the federal police announced the names of those arrested in a national scam involving public procurement, Operation Razor (*Navalho*), the bureaucrats they charged were all political appointees. None of the permanent bureaucratic staff were involved (Fleischer 2007: May 17, 2007). Plots to obtain policy favors have been hatched and implemented by business lobbies in collusion with individual legislators and ministers deemed appropriate targets rather than with party leaders in such capacity. The *Sanguessugas* example discussed in detail below illustrates what has been the typical modus operandi of corruption scandals involving bureaucrats and politicians in Brazil. Individual politicians and business interests have typically targeted and recruited specific officials for a *particular* corruption scheme because of their suitability for that scheme rather than engaging them as part of a more permanent ongoing relationship.

Considered one of the biggest corruption scandals in Brazil, the *Sanguessugas* or "Bloodsucker" scandal of 2002–2004 investigated up to a third of all congress members for corruption. This scheme involved getting legislators to authorize the purchase of overpriced ambulances for their districts through the use of budgetary amendments that entitled them to a certain amount of district-level expenditure (*Véja*, July 26, 2006). Participants were recruited on the basis of their personal relationships with each other and their perceived corruptibility. Legislators from nine parties, which spanned the ideological spectrum, were recruited to participate in this scheme based on these individual characteristics.[11] These deputies in turn recruited specific officials in the concerned ministries at the central and district levels to participate in their plans and to share in the payoffs. As commentators and investigators in Brazil observed, party leaders were not invited to participate, were not implicated as the puppetmasters in it, and were not even considered to be in the know about the operation of this scam (Mercopress, August 11, 2006; *Véja*, July 26, 2006). The funds appropriated went into building the personal fortunes of individual politicians rather than toward party coffers. Public opinion polls showed similar assignment of blame by voters, with 30% linking Congress rather than political parties to corruption (Mercopress, August 11, 2006).

While this pattern of collusion has undoubtedly led to corruption in Brazil, it is not typically identified as a systemic problem by businesses. In a 2003 study of 92 firms conducted by Transparency International and Kroll, the author found that the correlation between the likelihood of corruption by procurement officials and parliamentarians was 0.26, that between customs officials and parliamentarians was 0.31, and that between bank officials and parliamentarians was .28. These numbers show weak correlations and indicate weak politicization of agencies that are typically seen to be among the *most corrupt* by Brazilian businesses (TI 2003, 3). Bureaucratic agencies emerged from the military period with a reputation for being captured, especially in the initial transition to democracy (Geddes and Neto 1992). However, in recent times the bureaucracy— especially the regulatory agencies—have demonstrated considerable political independence and have refused to accommodate their requests and maintained their apolitical status (Fleischer: February 19, 2007; Alston et al. 2009; Taylor 2009).

This modus operandi is thus very different from that observed in India, where the partisan fundraising network of graft extends from low-level bureaucrats to the political party leaders at the top. Weak political parties have therefore constrained the extent to which the political establishment has been successful in incorporating state institutions into influence-peddling networks.[12] While individual legislators have sometimes found willing public collaborators to exploit their influence, in Brazil we do not observe the kind of routine exploitation of state institutions seen in India.

Similarly, the judiciary, which was constitutionally given considerable independence, has successfully maintained it over the years (Alston et al. 2009; Fleischer 2007; Taylor 2008; Brinks 2005; Santiso 2003). Taylor (2008, 44) describes the operational status of the Brazilian judiciary, "Brazil's federal courts are strongly independent of the elected branches. Judicial decisions are made without undue concern for the executive or legislative branches' reaction; compliance with court decisions by public bureaucracies is largely expected; and recent history suggests that no retaliation is to be expected in terms of court budgets or general administrative freedom." Despite expensive policy disagreements, such as on the CPMF tax discussed in chapter 4, no governments or congresses have successfully used the legislature to roll back the constitutional autonomy granted to the judiciary over their budgets and appointments (Hammergren 2007; Taylor 2008; Alston et al. 2009). Their internal management system is controlled by the judiciary itself, and no legislative changes have attempted to install political interference in recruitment, retention, or dismissals (Hammergren 2007; Brinks 2005). In this political environment, the corruption scandals that have come to light have involved petty corruption by individual judges who struck bargains directly with litigants or with individual legislators who were linked to influential litigants rather than grand corruption involving routine cover-ups of fraud perpetrated by parties and businesses connected to them (Taylor 2008, 43).

This difference is also manifested in the manner in which the judicial and police systems have been politically manipulated in India but not in Brazil. Brazilian police officials, known for petty corruption, have rarely been implicated in political corruption schemes and have been able to undertake investigations and expose corruption schemes (Abramo 2001:, 13). For example, in the Bloodsucker scandal discussed above, the Brazilian police were able to investigate these allegations without official interference from political authorities, a luxury rarely afforded to Indian police officials. This has been typical of political and judicial corruption scandals there as well. For example, when federal judge Rocha Mattos was found to be blatantly favoring the ex-governor of Sao Paulo in his case distribution, the Superior Court of Justice suspended him, conducted an investigation of his financial assets, and found them to be excessive given his income (Fleischer 1997, 312). A spate of successful operations by the police, such as Hurricanes I, II, and III; Themis; Anaconda; and Razor, have caught many public officials, including judges, engaging in corruption without drawing any political interference.

Again, what is notable is that the schemes uncovered were either those of petty corruption by judges and police or of collusion between them and a few individual legislators rather than of systemic political exploitation of captured state institutions. These trends reflect the fact that these state institutions are politically independent and not used for influence peddling by political principals. These perceptions are also supported by the 2006 Transparency International study of 92 Brazilian firms, which found that few firms associated judicial corruption with political corruption by parliamentarians, the correlation between the two being just .34. On the other hand, Indian police officials and public prosecutors, also known for their petty corruption, have been routinely plagued by political interference and manipulation at every stage of the implementation process and are widely seen as arms of the political establishment (Lok Satta 2007, 29; Verma 2005; Das 2001; Ribeiro Committee Report 1998).In chapter 2 I argued that in party-focused legislative systems, the likelihood of partisan capture of the judiciary would be very high. In such systems, parties could use their legislative powers to enact rules that undermine judicial independence by politicizing control over a variety of tools such as appointments, budgets, dismissals, and by reducing the powers of the judiciary to challenge the executive. This would lead to increased corruption through two channels – parties would use their influence over the judicial system to deliver legal favors to business interests, and judicial officials would be more likely to engage in petty corruption in exchange for extending legal protection to political leaders and their clients. In India we find strong evidence for both but with an interesting caveat. While the Indian Supreme Court has maintained a high level of independence and largely enjoys a reputation for honesty, the lower courts have been widely associated with high levels of political and petty corruption (Transparency International 2007; Jalan 2007; Bhushan 2007; Mehta 2005; Sathe 2002; Mitra 1998).

The legislative picture of de jure rules on the judiciary is mixed and hence a mixed picture of de facto judicial independence has emerged. Control over judicial budgets and dismissals are exercised by the executive and legislative branches and, the judiciary has only been given limited powers of judicial review. Over time the power to appoint judges to lower courts was appropriated by the Supreme Court but this power is now being contested between the political establishment and the Supreme Court. This system of political control has resulted in a judicial system where lower level courts have been integrated into partisan networks of influence peddling but the Supreme Court has managed to avoid political interference from authorities. Both police and judicial officials in lower courts are frequently pressured to drop investigations, lose evidence, present weak cases for prosecution, dismiss cases, postpone judging them indefinitely, and issue light penalties (Mehta 2005, 183; Verma 2009; Das 2001, 193; Mitra 1998). The ability to exercise political influence in lower courts and obtain such desirable outcomes, has therefore increasingly made these courts the object of considerable business attention and involved these courts in partisan networks of corruption as well (Jalan 2007; Mehta 2005; Sathe 2002; Baxi 2000; Mitra 1998). As Jalan (2007, 101) notes, this has resulted in "a horizontal spread of corruption among other public institutions, including parts of the judiciary, parts of the media and some independent professions."

Additionally, lower court officials have been able to indulge in purely petty corruption to benefit themselves as well since the involvement of political parties in corrupt transactions has created a reciprocal relationship of immunity between courts and political parties. Judges in lower courts have become increasingly active as policymakers on various issues (Mehta 2005, 168; Baxi 2000). This has created increasingly lucrative opportunities for corrupt judicial officials to engage in deals with business interests which benefit them personally (Bhushan 2007; Mitra 1998). Selective judicial laxity in pursuing pending legal cases against political elites has facilitated such petty corruption. Due to their collusion with political interests, they have however largely escaped investigation and prosecution for such behaviors despite the best efforts of civil society groups and a free media to draw attention to such behaviors (Transparency International 2007; Mehta 2005; Shourie 2007; Jalan 2007). By 2009 only three judges in India had ever been investigated on charges of corruption, only one was brought up for a parliamentary vote on impeachment, and as of this date, no judge has ever been convicted of corruption in India (Bhushan 2007). The complicity of political parties in corruption and the potential threat of judicial action against them on corruption charges have therefore provided judiciary with a great measure of insurance against political action aimed at the judiciary's own corruption. As a result of such petty corruption and of influence peddling on behalf of parties, judicial corruption in India is widely evaluated as being very high (Transparency International 2007; World Economic Forum 2004-2005; Jalan 2007; Shourie 2007).

The data from the 2005 author survey of business groups in India presented mixed evidence on judicial corruption. While the survey responses reported significantly higher corruption in courts in India relative to that in Brazil, the correlation of judicial corruption with party corruption was not significantly different for the two countries as predicted in chapter 2. As discussed earlier, the survey data on the correlation between judicial and party corruption in India was found to be weak (.38) and not significantly different from that in Brazil (.36). I suggested several possible explanations for this: there is no causal link between judicial and party corruption; or there is a causal link, but it is not captured in this data due to poor operationalization of the concept in the survey question or due to factors affecting the capacity of a perceptions-based survey to operationalize the concept. The question included in the two-country survey on the sale of court decisions was not worded in a manner that made a clear distinction between corruption in the supreme and lower-level courts, that is, it did not specify the source of corruption as high court judges, supreme court judges, lawyers, or clerks. Responses to this question therefore may be reflecting a composite of the entire system or some mix of perceptions of both levels. This might explain why business responses to this question in India did not differ significantly from the distribution of responses in Brazil, where judges are evaluated as being corrupt on their own account.

Given the evidence of high lower-level judicial corruption from other surveys as well and studies of the judiciary in India, the likely possibilities seem to be the following: only capture of lower-level courts is high and hence lower-level corruption is high, capture of the entire system is low due to independence in judicial appointments, and increased lower-level judicial corruption is due to high petty corruption by individuals. My choice of wording unfortunately does not give me data suitable for discriminating between these arguments. As the discussion above indicates, secondary evidence does support the link between political and judicial corruption at lower levels in India, I cannot however conclusively falsify or support the hypothesis that party control in India leads to a politically captured and corrupt judicial system at all levels *based on the survey data alone*. Future research will hopefully capture these nuances and allow clear falsification of the partisan judicial corruption thesis.

Recent political events in Brazil also offer us a stronger test of the impact of legislative institutions on corruption in an individual-focused country. The leftist PT, which was in power at the time of the survey, was regarded as the most disciplined party in Brazil when it came to power for the first time in 2004. At that time it was considered to be a highly disciplined and ideologically coherent political party. Its tenure in office since then offers us a good test of whether and how much strong parties can be affected by the design of individual-focused legislative incentives and, in turn, how much that can affect corruption in the system. In 2004, for the first time, a PT presidential candidate, Lula de Silva, won the presidential elections. Despite not having a legislative majority initially, his coalition successfully weaned away legislators from the other parties who switched their party affiliations while retaining their legislative seats. This was a familiar trend in Brazilian politics. However, in 2005, the details of a scandal that came to be known as the *Mensalao* or "big monthly payments" scandal, involving the purchase of legislative votes, started emerging and showed a new face of Brazilian corruption.

In an interview with the *Folha de São Paulo*, deputy Roberto Jefferson revealed that the PT was involved in an elaborate scheme that paid legislators from other parties a monthly sum to vote with the governing coalition. While the sale of legislative votes in itself was not a new phenomenon in Brazil (Geddes and Neto 1997; Fleischer 1997), two things made this particular version of it new to Brazil. First, the PT organization itself systematically organized and managed the scheme with senior PT leaders such as José Genoino (president of the Workers' Party), Delúbio Soares (treasurer of PT), Antonio Palocci (finance minister), and José Dirceu (chief-of-staff) being directly implicated in the logistics and eventually resigning or being expelled (CPI 2005). Second, the money to finance this operation was raised by the PT through systematic exploitation of state resources using the party machinery's control of state offices. The party manipulated funds from public contracts given to an advertising firm and allocated to the post office among other sources (BBC, December 1, 2005).

This scandal demonstrated how a disciplined party like the PT was forced to adjust to the institutional incentives it faced in the legislature, once it was in power. Its own members were subsequently discovered to be accepting bribes to vote with the government and with parties in opposition as well (*Carta Capital*, January 2006). What is striking about this is not that legislative office was exploited by unscrupulous politicians but that it was systematically exploited by an unscrupulous *party*. In contrast to earlier abuses of state resources (Geddes and Ribeiro Neto 1992), this increased the range of the state and public offices that were co-opted into this corruption scheme. An experienced participant, Martus Tavares, commented on the change in the level of corruption when he observed, "Merit was thrown into the rubbish bin. . . . They simply decided to occupy the government machine. I'm a career diplomat. I worked with four previous presidents and I have never seen anything like it."[13] Thus the advent of a strong party, whose strength was based on ideological coherence, immediately changed the dynamics of corruption in a way that increased the level of political corruption as well as the overall level of corruption in the system. The party, in turn, was affected adversely by the individual-focused incentives of the legislature and experienced a considerable deterioration in the discipline and loyalty demonstrated by its legislators and members.

Transparency, Creative Accounting, and Donor Protections

As discussed in chapter 2, of the three dimensions of accountability, lack of accountability within parties is the most serious because it severely limits the extent to which parties can be accountable to the state and the public. This dimension is seriously challenged in party-focused systems due to two reasons: state capture of the authorities responsible for enforcing financial accountability and the technical complexity of party accounts. As discussed below, this difference can be observed clearly in the Brazilian and Indian cases. Both countries have similar regulations requiring parties and candidates to identify major donors by name and amount and to file detailed reports of all their income and expenditures (Knack and Djankov 2009; IDEA Handbook 2003, 185–222). The consensus among experts in both countries is that the bulk of political finance flowing through the system is illegal. Despite these similarities, the success authorities have achieved in detecting and punishing violations by them are remarkably different.

In 1994, in the wake of the Collor de Melo presidential corruption scandal, Law No. 8713 was passed requiring parties and candidates to submit detailed balance sheets listing contributors and expenses to the electoral courts. Since then, these reports have been filed on a regular basis by parties and candidates and disclosed publicly through a national database. The relevant state institutions, the Supreme Electoral Court (TSE), the Office of the Comptroller General (CGU), the local courts, and the police authorities are largely free of political interference and sufficiently empowered to initiate investigations into corruption scandals under their jurisdictions. As a result, all of these Brazilian authorities have been able to successfully identify and prosecute many cases of financial fraud by politicians at every level. Between 2002 and 2006, 623 politicians, including federal deputies, senators, governors, mayors, city council members, and state deputies, were stripped of their mandate or resigned in anticipation of such expulsion for electoral fraud.[14] Between 1999 and 2007, the electoral tribunal (TSE) successfully investigated 215 politicians which included deputies, senators, governors, mayors, and municipal representatives for vote-buying and revoked their electoral victories (*Estadão de Hoje*, September 29, 2007). In 2007, the TSE investigated the ruling PT party for not disclosing a $250,000 donation by Cisco Systems (LatinNews, October 24, 2007). This political independence and capacity to pursue corruption cases has also put a damper on the incentives of judges and policemen to collude and strike ad hoc deals with individual legislators on these cases since chances of their arrest and prosecution are higher as well.

While congress members continue to try to pass legislation that would allow them many privileges in prosecution, these numbers indicate the relatively strong ability of Brazilian state institutions to pursue corruption cases successfully. Therefore, legislators cannot count on enjoying effective immunity from prosecution if they are caught and cannot offer such protection as an incentive to potential donors. Furthermore, legislators have been active in investigating and prosecuting fellow legislators on corruption charges as well. Hardly a year has gone by without at least one parliamentary inquiry commission being constituted to conduct a corruption inquiry into allegations against congress members (NIS 2001, 9). Individual legislators relying on their personal networks cannot count on being protected from such inquiries if they are caught up in such allegations. Both factors serve as a disincentive to engage in high levels of corruption.

An important piece of this successful enforcement structure in Brazil is the lower technical ability required to successfully identify violations and to acquire information on them in the first place. This is logistically and technically more feasible in Brazil since the bulk of political finance flows through individual-level accounts rather than national or regional party accounts, making them easier to audit. It is important to recognize that this discussion does not imply that Brazilian political finance is transparent and accountable. Indeed most observers view political accounts and the donations database with some suspicion, and the number of politicians who have been able to evade detection is surely not small. However, it does allow us to understand which *systemic* elements of the financial infrastructure affect transparency and can increase it, even in a country with all the structural and institutional weakness endemic to developing democracies such as Brazil.

The rarity and high profile of cases that have been prosecuted in India, on the other hand, highlight the systemic sources of this difference. Despite the legal requirement to submit detailed accounts of donations, expenditures, and tax returns since 1978, with the exception of the left parties, *none* of the major political parties did so till 1995 (IDEA 2007; Sridharan 2006). In that year, parties were forced to do so by a public interest lawsuit filed by an NGO. Current party reports are incomplete, do not provide detail sufficient for auditing, do not correspond to observed expenditures, and are widely considered to be inaccurate (IDEA 2007; Sridharan 2006). Yet, investigations have been exceedingly rare and prosecutions are almost unheard of. The authorities responsible for monitoring the behavior of political parties and candidates at all stages in the political cycle—namely the Election Commission of India (ECI) and the two institutions most closely associated with political investigations, the Central Bureau of Investigation (CBI) and the Central Vigilance Commission (CVC)—have neither the resources nor the political independence to pursue these cases aggressively (Das 2001, 52, 118). The result, as a recent study (Bryan and Baer 2005, 71) noted, has been that "India's legislation on party finance is rendered nearly useless by the lack of an effective monitoring and enforcement mechanism. The Election Commission should be aided and supported in its work to make elections and campaigns more legitimate."

Capture of these institutions by parties in India has prevented them from enforcing existing rules and imposing the legally mandated penalties even in the most blatant and public cases of violations. During a 2008 vote of confidence against the sitting UPA government, opposition members of parliament publicly waved millions of rupees they claimed the governing coalition had used to bribe them, and they produced a videotape of the alleged attempt (New York Times, July 22, 2008; Livemint.com, August 4, 2008). The speaker of the house took possession of the videotape and initiated a parliamentary inquiry into the sources of this money and into the incident itself. The case is yet to be resolved as of 2010. Similar videotapes of party leaders accepting bribes from various business firms and dealers during and after elections have routinely appeared in India but never resulted in any corruption convictions. Most cases have been buried in the Indian legal system and will not come to trial for years. The regularity with which such incidents come to light demonstrates that despite the limited institutional resurgence of the ECI as a result of a one-man crusade, its authority has been largely exercised in preventing only the most blatant violations of lesser political mortals.

The task of authorities has been considerably harder due to the higher technical burden they face in monitoring complex party accounts as well as due to the lack of resources they are systematically subjected to. The lion's share of political funds in India is donated to parties, not individual politicians. Theoretically, therefore, the political system has the potential to be subject to all the abuse in accounting, reporting, and enforcement of party-focused systems. For example, in a survey of party leaders and candidates conducted during the 1999 elections, Sridharan (2001) found that that the estimates of campaign and party expenses given by party leaders and candidates differed by as much as Rs.1080 million.[15] The members of a national-level parliamentary committee formed to review the working of the Indian constitution in 2001 summarized this strategy followed by parties (NCRWC 2001, Article 6.4): "Very little is known about finances of political parties. In fact, secrecy is maintained even within a party. Only a few leaders at the higher level know the truth about the total funds and expenditure. Parties do not publish statements of accounts, income and expenditure, though financial matters are discussed at conventions and conferences or in meetings of higher bodies like working committee or the executive committee."

In another systematic study of 34 parties in India, the authors (IDEA 2007, 86–87) found that "parties have not developed the practice of accounting for all the income they receive and they declare only very small amounts as their income." Evidence from interviews, reports and investigations confirm that such strategies are deliberate and conducted in the context of partisan capture of legal and police systems. Author interviews with party leaders and rank and file members in India confirmed that party leaders choose not to cultivate a formal bookkeeping system or an internal audit mechanism that would integrate party information about finances. Different branches of parties withhold information from each other while national-level leaders rarely share information outside of their inner circle. This multiplicity of expenditure levels and types allows party leaders to conceal expenditures more easily and raises the technical skills required of authorities to successfully detect such violations. Protection for these activities has been obtained and maintained by manipulating all the tools of delegation—appointments, dismissals, transfers of bureaucrats, and control over the budgets of these agencies (Mitra 1998; Das 2001; NIS 2006; Jalan 2007; Shourie 2007; TI 2008). Indian parties have indeed successfully strategized to exploit these opportunities, raising corruption levels there substantially.

This has led to some of the most damaging consequences of state capture by parties, as political and business elites have been emboldened to indulge in blatant violations of financing regulations secure in the knowledge that they are protected by partisan patrons who can pull the required bureaucratic and legal strings. The political financing system at large in India remains opaque and largely immune to any legal challenges and a primary source of corruption there. This reality has been recognized in India for a long time. Numerous bodies such as the Law Commission 1999, NCRWC 2001, and the Santhanam Committee 1999 have repeatedly suggested that in addition to compulsory maintenance of the accounts, there should be open acceptance of company donations by the parties, obligatory auditing of their accounts by an agency appointed by the Election Commission, public disclosure of all accounts. and also that this should be done explicitly at every level of party organization. At the moment, these agencies do not have the technical or legal capacity to enforce existing rules, thus designing new rules seems a fruitless exercise.

In contrast, Brazilian auditors face an easier task in monitoring and auditing individual-level expenses. Significantly, though, they have been provided more resources and have not suffered from systemic political capture and manipulation like the Indian agencies have. As a result, financial malfeasance has been detected and punished more frequently in Brazil, and both parties and candidates show significantly more adherence to the rules than we see in India. These dynamics are part of the mechanism that only parties are able to employ in generating increasing returns to their tenure in office. Therefore, the ability to protect donors and fudge accounts successfully should also lead to relatively higher corruption in India compared to Brazil. The next section presents time-series evidence from both countries that these supply side dynamics result in much higher corruption levels in India compared to Brazil and also apply to the category of individual-focused countries.

In chapter 2, I hypothesized that the level of corruption is likely to be higher in countries where business groups directly lobby political parties, such as in India, and lower in those countries such as Brazil where business groups lobby legislators. The analysis in chapter 4 demonstrated that legislative lobbying is directed toward parties in India due to its party-focused legislative institutions and toward individual legislators in Brazil due to the individual-focused character of Brazilian legislative institutions. The data and analysis in this chapter demonstrates that legislative lobbying is a significant source of corruption in both countries but more so in India. The discussion so far in this chapter has focused on presenting strong evidence that the four dynamics of supply and demand believed to link stronger parties to higher corruption are present in India, absent in Brazil, and functioning in the manner expected theoretically. Finally, the discussion above shows that political, bureaucratic, and judicial corruption and patronage are closely linked in India and that these links generate higher returns for parties there but not in Brazil. All these pieces of evidence lead us to expect that overall corruption should be significantly higher in India compared to Brazil.

CORRUPTION LEVELS IN BRAZIL AND INDIA

I now present evidence that, as expected, these dynamics result in creating higher levels of corruption in India relative to Brazil and relative to the comparator category here, individual-focused systems. I conducted three main exercises on the corruption data available for these cases. *First*, I simply assessed the annual level of corruption from 1984 to 2004 for each of three widely used cross-national measures of corruption—the International Country Risk Guide (ICRG) index of corruption, the Transparency International (TI) corruption perceptions index, and the corruption index from the World Bank (WB). *Second*, I compared the average level of corruption in India to the average corruption level in Brazil where political parties do *not* control the agenda or the introduction of amendments and also lack the institutional power to expel party dissidents who defy the party whip. *Finally*, I compare the levels of corruption in India to that of other democracies from the developing world where parties do not have agenda-setting, amendment, or expulsion powers. I compare the levels of corruption in Brazil to its comparator category—the sample of developing country democracies where institutions give parties control over all three functions. Given the predictions in hypotheses 1b, 2b, and 3b in chapter 2, I anticipate that corruption in India will not only be high but also relatively higher than the level of corruption in Brazil. I also expect it to be higher than the average level of corruption in all developing democracies where parties do not control the policymaking process in the legislature.

The three measures of corruption that I employ, the ICRG, TI, and WB corruption indices, are generated by questions posed on corruption as perceived by domestic and/or multinational business groups in the countries in which they run their business operations. Although, as I discuss in detail in chapter 6, different methodologies are employed to generate each of the three corruption measures, they are positively and highly correlated with each other. This indicates that all three corruption measures employed here are consistent, capture the same underlying phenomena, and are reasonably reliable. For these reasons they have been the most widely used measures in studies of corruption. They are available for different time periods and for different sets of countries, and they use different scales. The ICRG measure of corruption is available for 150 countries from 1984 to 2004, the TI corruption measure for roughly 130 countries from 1995 to 2004, and the WB corruption measure for 200 countries from 1998 to 2004. For ease of interpretation I rescaled these indices such that higher numbers indicate higher levels of corruption for all of them. The ICRG index now goes from 0 to 6, the TI from 0 to 10, and the WB from 0 to 5.

Based on the rescaled ICRG corruption index, figures 5.5 (a), (b), and (c) illustrate for India and an annual average for the 29 individual-focused democracies in the sample where political parties do *not* control agenda-setting or introduction of amendments, nor do they have the institutional power to expel party dissidents who defy the party whip. The (a) annual ICRG corruption level from 1984 to 2004, (b) shows the annual average TI corruption measure from 1995 to 2004 and (c) shows the annual WB corruption measure from 1995 to 2004. Similarly, figures 5.6 (a), (b), and (c) show for Brazil and the annual average for the 31 party-focused democracies in the sample the ICRG levels 1984 to 2004 in figure 5.6 (a), the annual TI corruption level from 1995 to 2004 in figure 5.6 (b), and the annual average WB corruption levels from 1995 to 2004 in figure 5.6 (c).

It is clear from each of the figures in figures 5.5 (a), (b), and (c) that the level of corruption has been extremely high in India during the last two decades. The mean corruption level in India as measured by the ICRG index is 4.5 during 1984–2004, using the TI index is 7.6 during 1995–2004, and it is 4.1 using the WB corruption index for 1998–2004. Furthermore, the level of corruption in India with respect to the ICRG

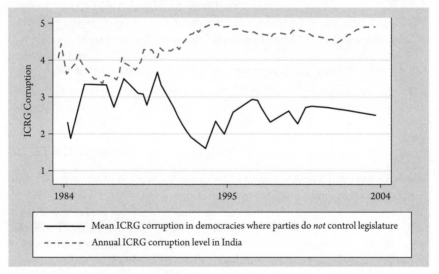

a

(a) ICRG Corruption Index

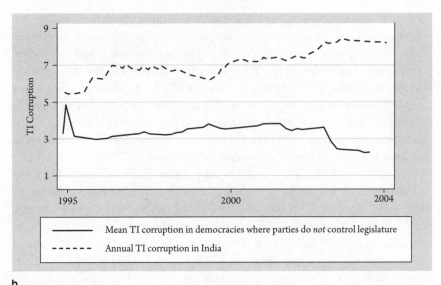

b

(b) TI Corruption Index

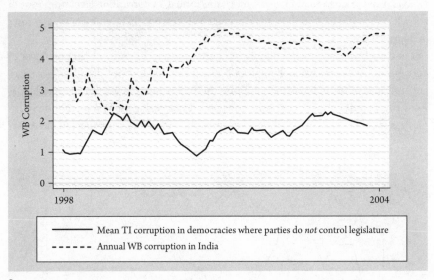

c

(c) WB Corruption Index

Figure 5.5. **(a), (b) and (c)** *Corruption Levels in India vs. Individual-Focused Developing Democracies in Sample*

index consistently remains above 3.4 on the 0 to 6 scale, higher than 7.5 out of a maximum of 10 on the TI scale and higher than 4 on a scale with a maximum of 5 for the WB index, all of which are clearly very high.

In Brazil, the average scores for the three indices over the same time periods were 3.45 for ICRG, 6.5 on the TI index, and 3.2 on the WB index. Figure 5.6 (a) reveals that

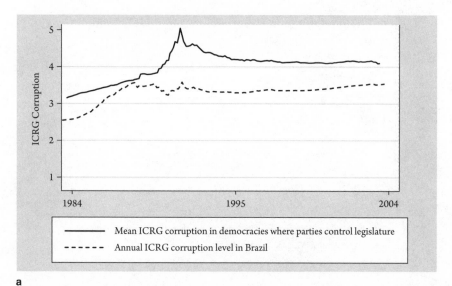

a

(a) ICRG Corruption Index

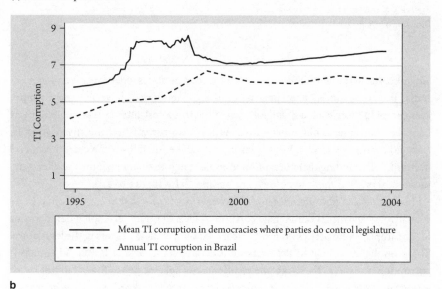

b

(b) TI Corruption Index

the level of corruption in Brazil with respect to the ICRG index remains consistently between 3.1 and 3.9 on the 0 to 6 scale. In the TI index in figure 5.6 (b), Brazil's level of corruption lies approximately above 6 out of a maximum of 10 for much of the 1995–2004 period. In the WB corruption index in figure 5.6 (c), Brazil's corruption level is at or slightly above 3 on a 0 to 5 scale.

When compared to Brazil—a "similar" developing country where political parties do *not* (but where individual legislators do) control agenda-setting and introduction of

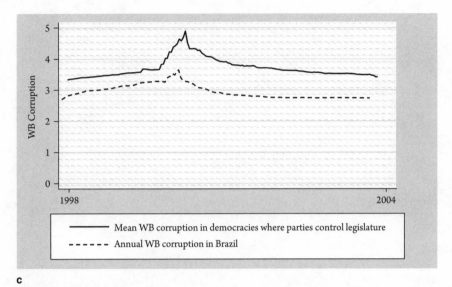

c

(c) WB Corruption Index

Figure 5.6. **(a)**, **(b)** and **(c)** *Corruption Levels in Brazil vs. Party-Focused Developing Democracies in Sample*

amendments in the legislature—one finds that corruption is indeed relatively higher in India. The *average* level of corruption in India, as mentioned above, is *higher* than the average corruption level in Brazil for each of the three corruption measures employed here. Furthermore, a difference-of-means test also reveals that the mean (that is, average) corruption level in India is statistically higher than the mean corruption level in Brazil.[16] The finding that corruption in India is higher than Brazil thus confirms my theoretical predictions in hypotheses 1b, 2b, and 3b for these two cases.

Finally, one also finds unambiguously in figures 5.5 (a)–(c) that corruption in India is relatively *higher* than the average corruption level in other developing democracies in the sample where parties do not control the policymaking process in the legislature. These results are robust to the measure used and stand for the ICRG, TI, and WB corruption measures. Therefore, the results are not specific just to Brazil but hold with respect to the theoretical category of cases represented by Brazil. Similarly, figures 5.6 (a)–(c) show that using any of the three measures of corruption, corruption in Brazil is *lower* than the average corruption levels in developing democracies where parties are institutionally endowed with agenda-setting, amendments, and expulsion powers. This supports the hypotheses with respect to India as well as with respect to the category of theoretical cases that it represents.

CONCLUSION

From the preceding discussion, it is thus clear that the level of corruption in India, a country where political parties institutionally control policymaking dynamics in the legislature, is not only high but also relatively higher than corruption in Brazil where parties do not control various aspects of the legislative policymaking process. This is an encouraging result as it supports the predictions in hypotheses 1b, 2b, and 3b for these cases. Furthermore, in conjunction with the results in chapter 4, these detailed case studies support lobbying as a significant cause of these higher levels of corruption in India, the party-centered case, relative to Brazil, the individual-centered case. In addition to the survey, I also provided evidence of demand for illegal finance by parties' and businesses' role in supplying them from open-ended interviews with business groups, trade unions, party leaders, journalists, and scholars, as well as from secondary sources including work by other scholars. This cumulative body of evidence suggests that the causal story posited above is indeed plausible for these cases.

The evidence shows that the two dynamics leading to higher demand—scale and type of expenses and preference for money over information—do work to raise the scale of financial demands in India over that observed in Brazil. The evidence on the political links with the bureaucracy and the judiciary shows that the two dynamics on the supply side—capture of state institutions and higher ability to hide and protect fundraisers—both work to raise corruption as well. Therefore, evidence from the survey, the interviews, and from secondary sources shows that party leaders in India exploit their legislative influence over policy outcomes to raise funds at all stages of the policy process including design, implementation, and oversight. This raises the level of political corruption and extends it to the wider society through captured state institutions. In Brazil, legislators are able to cash in their influence over policy design in the legislature, leading to political corruption, but they do not have the political structure or support to extend this ability to exploit policy implementation or oversight for funds. Furthermore, not all legislators attract the attention of rich lobbies due to competition between legislators. Thus, both the extent and hence, level of corruption in Brazil is lower compared to India.

Another method for testing whether it is the legislative strength of parties that is leading to higher corruption is to consider what happens when we observe one of the following experiments: the rules change to allow legislators more authority in a party-focused system or the rules change to allow parties more control in an individual-focused system. Brazil in fact provides us with a recent instance of the latter.

As discussed in chapter 3, laws on party switching have varied over time in Brazil. While legislators were free to switch parties during the democratic period from 1946 to 1964, they lost this right once the military came to power (Fleischer, September 29, 2007). When the return to civilian rule was instituted in the late 1980s, the right of legislators to switch parties without losing the legislative mandate was restored. The next two decades witnessed rampant party-switching by legislators. Surveys showed that while legislators believed that co-partisans should express more party loyalty in their voting behavior, they were not willing to support a change in the rules to allow it (Hagopian 2004). Party protocols allowed parties to expel members from the party for any behavior deemed antiparty by party leaders but this did not strip these legislators of their legislative mandate. This allowed deputies and senators to switch parties freely and importantly to vote against their party line with impunity. Thus, legislators could and did vote against their party line freely even when the party whip announced that the "question has been closed" (*fechar a questão*).

Finally in March 2007, in response to these trends, key political parties including the PSDB, DEM (ex-PFL), and PPS filed an injunction request asking the TSE, the supreme electoral tribunal, to strip 23 deputies from these parties who had switched parties of their legislative mandate and allow parties to nominate their alternates to these seats. These deputies had been elected through the electoral lists of these parties in 2006 and subsequently switched parties. Ruling in favor of the parties would therefore give the mandates of these seats to parties rather than to the deputies elected on them. In November 2007, the Supreme Court of Brazil (STF) issued its decision favoring the parties, and by October 2008, the TSE changed its rules to accommodate this decision. In accordance with Resolution TSE 22,610/2007, any political party interested in retaining its mandate after expelling a member can file a petition announcing the loss of an elected position as a result of party disaffiliation without just cause with an electoral judge.[17] The causes considered just for a member to disaffiliate himself from a party without losing his mandate were incorporation or fusion of a party, the creation of a new party, the substantial change or the reiterated deviation from the party program, and serious personal discrimination. The TSE is responsible for processing and judging the relative petition of a federal mandate. The Ministry of Public Elections may file a similar request with the TSE as well.

This rule has now given Brazilian parties the right to expel members from the party for voting against the party whip should the party choose to do so. Thus it is similar to the power that parties have in India and in many other countries as listed in table 2.1. The response to this change has been seen as positive by many Brazilian scholars. Pereirra (2009) describes how significant this change is: "Extremely positive. Not for the loss of the mandate itself, which is something regrettable. But above all, because it changes the dialogue between the party leadership and parliamentarians. Now the party can—as in any country in the world seriously—to close the question in relation to certain points. . . . The resolution of party loyalty was essential to strengthen the democratic system itself."[18]

The impact of this law is beginning to be felt with legislators now changing both their party switching and their voting behaviors. For example, while 198 deputies switched in the 49th Congress and 169 in the 50th, this dropped to 51 amid the uncertainty in 2007, and only one deputy switched parties in all of 2008 (*Câmara dos Deputados*). A similar trend is now beginning to be observed in voting where party leaders are choosing when to exercise this strategic prerogative to expel members and when to allow them free votes. If the theoretical framework here is correct, then we should expect to see parties becoming somewhat stronger in Brazil, some diversion of lobbying resources toward parties, and eventually some increase in corruption. Since agenda-setting and amendments still favor legislators, only time will tell which of these three rules is more influential in influencing their behaviors and those of lobbies. This experience also provides an excellent experiment to study the relative value of these three rules in determining the totality of party influence over members.

Unfortunately, given the secrecy that surrounds acts of corruption and the paucity of cross-country data on lobbying behaviors, it is difficult to empirically substantiate the causal story supported in these cases for a larger set of countries at this micro-level. However, it is possible to test the implication—that countries which have party-centered legislative institutions such as India's should experience higher levels of corruption than those which have individual-focused legislative institutions similar to Brazil. The next chapter, chapter 6, systematically tests these hypotheses on a time-series cross-section dataset of 64 countries over twenty years. This large-n analysis gives us the tools to test these results across countries exhibiting a wide range of social, economic, and political characteristics to see if these results can be generalized beyond these two cases. I find strong and robust support of these hypotheses.

6

LEGISLATIVE INSTITUTIONS, PARTY CONTROL, AND CORRUPTION: THE EMPIRICAL EVIDENCE

The main argument of this book is that if legislative rules in developing democracies allow political parties to control the policymaking process via drafting and passage of bills in the legislature, then business groups will directly lobby political parties to influence policies, and this lobbying of political parties, in turn, will lead to an increase in corruption. In particular, the theoretical arguments in chapter 2 generated hypotheses 1b, 2b, and 3b, which predict how party control of policymaking dynamics in the legislature affects corruption. These hypotheses specifically posit that party control of agenda-setting in the legislature and the introduction of amendments to bills on the legislative floor, as well as control over expulsion of party members that vote against the dictates of the party whip, have a positive impact on corruption. As discussed in chapter 2, according to the research design implemented in this project, chapters 4 and 5 tested the validity of the two-step causal mechanism by analyzing how differences in legislative rules in the selected cases, Brazil and India, led to variation in the lobbying venue choice of business groups in these countries and, hence, to variation in their levels of corruption.

The two case studies revealed that since Indian political parties formally control agenda-setting and amendment-making and moreover have the ability to expel party "dissidents," corruption in India is higher than in Brazil. Compared to India, corruption in Brazil is lower because individual legislators (rather than policy parties) control policymaking dynamics in the legislature. Hence, comparing the Brazilian case to the Indian case provided some initial evidence for the prediction in hypotheses 1b, 2b, and 3b. Furthermore, the case studies also corroborate the causal mechanism that accounts for the link between party control of policymaking in the legislature and higher levels of corruption. While these case studies are useful for assessing the causal mechanism that accounts for the link between party control of policymaking in the legislature and corruption, the findings from the case studies cannot be realistically generalized to all other democracies in the developing world.

Therefore, in this chapter, I implement large-n tests for hypotheses 1b, 2b, and 3b, which link legislative institutions to corruption outcomes. I statistically test how formal party control of policymaking processes in the legislature (that is, hypotheses 1b, 2b, and 3b) influences corruption on a time-series cross-sectional (hereafter TSCS) data set of 64 democracies across the developing world between 1984 and 2004. As described below, the TSCS data set that I employ for the statistical tests is quite comprehensive. Thus, it enhances considerably the generalizability of the empirical findings obtained from the cases. Furthermore, I use a variety of well-known measures of corruption to test the hypotheses of interest to ensure that the results that I obtain are not driven by any particular features specific to a particular measure of corruption.

The rest of this chapter is organized as follows. In the first section, I provide a summary of existing empirical studies on corruption and briefly explain how the empirical analysis in this chapter contributes to this literature. This is followed by a description of the data that is used to test the theoretical model's central predictions. After doing so, I describe the operationalization of the dependent variable, independent variables, and control variables for the empirical specification. I then briefly discuss the statistical model that I estimate to test the relevant hypotheses on this sample. The fourth section provides an analysis of the results derived from the data, and this is followed by a brief discussion of robustness tests as well as diagnostic checks. The chapter concludes with a summary of the main findings from the empirical tests.

PREVIOUS EMPIRICAL RESEARCH

The empirical literature on the determinants of corruption is vast. I lack the space in this chapter to discuss extant empirical studies on the causes of corruption in detail. But I provide a brief summary of the current empirical literature on corruption. This discussion is important because it presents the alternative theories of corruption that explain corruption in the literature. In order to robustly test the theoretical framework presented in this book, I explicitly control for the variables that these existing empirical studies identify as determinants of corruption in my statistical analysis.

Stated briefly, the literature on the causes of corruption can be divided into four main categories. The control variables in my empirical model are drawn from each of these. These categories are as follows: (i) economic and demographic determinants of corruption, (ii) the impact of political institutions on corruption, (iii) the effect of legal systems on corruption, and (iv) cultural influences on corruption. I discuss the empirical literature on each of these four categories below.

Economic and Demographic Determinants

Scholars believe that a wide range of economic variables influence the level of corruption across countries. GDP per capita is commonly used to explain corruption (Damania, Fredriksson, and Mani 2004; Persson, Tabellini, and Trebbi 2003; Van Rijckeghem and Weder 1997; Treisman 2000). This is because corruption is conceptualized as an inferior good, thus the demand for corruption falls as income rises. Additionally, higher GDP per capita implies that more resources are available to combat corruption. Not surprisingly, scholars generally find that higher GDP per capita has a negative and significant effect on corruption, even though Kaufmann, Kraay, and Mastruzzi (1999) and Hall and Jones (1999) question the causal relationship between corruption and income.

The size of government, operationalized as total central government expenditure as a percent of GDP, is also put forward as a determinant of corruption. If countries exploit economies of scale in the provision of public services—thus having a low ratio of public services per capita—those who demand these services might be tempted to bribe bureaucrats "to get ahead of the queue." Furthermore, a large government sector may also create opportunities for corruption. Empirical studies by Fisman and Gatti (2002) and Bonaglia, de Macedo, and Bussolo (2001) find quite interestingly that the size of government has a negative impact on on corruption, while others like Ali and Isse (2003) report the opposite.

According to various authors, another economic variable that also explains corruption is trade openness, that is, the ratio of the sum of exports and imports to GDP. For example, Herzfeld and Weiss (2003), Fisman and Gatti (2002), Frechette (2001), and Treisman (2000) report that more trade openness leads to less corruption. In particular, higher levels of trade openness typically imply lower tariff and nontariff import restrictions. Lower trade barriers curtail bureaucratic restrictions, such as necessary licenses to import, for example, which create opportunities for government officials to demand bribes especially in developing countries. Therefore, more trade openness leads to lower corruption (see Knack and Azfar 2003; Frechette 2006).

Some other economic variables are less frequently considered as determinants of corruption. Inflation, for example, is argued to stimulate corruption as it increases the costs of enforcement against corruption (Braun and Di Tella 2004; Paldam 2002). Some studies also hypothesize that foreign aid should increase corruption since transferred resources from third parties to decision makers who are not accountable may create opportunities for rent extraction (Ali and Isse 2003; Tavares 2003). Knack (2001), however, does not find a significant link between aid and corruption.

Sociodemographic determinants associated with corruption include human capital (proxied by schooling) and population growth. Economists typically find that countries with more human capital have low levels of corruption (Ali and Isse 2003; Alt and Lassen 2003; Brunetti and Weder 2003; Persson, Tabellini, and Trebbi 2003; Rauch and Evans 2000). This is because more education increases the ability of society to control government behavior and to effectively judge the performance of politicians. Intense monitoring of the behavior and performance of politicians by a more educated public makes it difficult for politicians to indulge in corruption.

Apart from education, Knack and Azfar (2003) show that an increase in population is followed by an increase in corruption—a finding also reported by Fisman and Gatti (2002). This finding is usually accounted for by the idea that greater economies of scale in governance allow politicians to extract a larger volume of rent for personal gain. As emphasized by Knack and Azfar (2003), "in large nations, rulers can extract significant resources from the country and pay off the constituencies necessary for them to maintain power." Economic and demographic variables are, of course, not the only factors that influence corruption. Rather several studies suggest that domestic political institutions also affect corruption. I thus turn to briefly discuss studies which argue that domestic institutions matter for explaining cross-national variation in corruption.

Domestic Political Institutions and Corruption

Many empirical studies on the political causes of corruption focus on how differences in political freedom across countries can influence the level of corruption. Using various proxies for political freedom—like civil liberty, political rights, democracy, and age of the democratic regime—these studies generally argue that more political freedom enhances checks-and-balances mechanisms, which (i) increases transparency in public services and (ii) creates incentives for politicians to be less corrupt. Building on this argument, these studies find empirically that greater political freedom indeed reduces corruption (see, for example, Lederman, Loayza, and Soares 2005; Kunicova and Rose-Ackerman 2005; Braun and Di Tella 2004; Chang and Golden 2007; Paldam 2002; Treisman 2000; Ades and Di Tella 1997, 1999). While higher levels of political freedom—broadly conceived—are expected to reduce corruption, scholars suggest that institutional features that are inherent to democratic regimes may positively or negatively influence corruption.

For example, selecting politicians through party lists can obscure the direct link between voters and politicians, thus degrading the ability of voters to hold politicians accountable and leading to higher levels of corruption (Kunicova and Rose-Ackerman 2005; Persson, Tabellini, and Trebbi 2003). Chang and Golden (2007) suggest and find that corruption increases (decreases) with district magnitude under an open-list (closed-list) system in PR (proportional representation) countries. Other scholars suggest that corruption tends to be lower under plurality rule since monitoring of rent seekers in plurality systems is more stringent than under a proportional representation system (Brown et al. 2006; Kunicova and Rose-Ackerman 2005; Chang and Golden 2007). Some studies report that a presidential system promotes corruption through increased competition between the various branches whereas others argue that competition between branches in a separation of powers system reduce corruption (Gerring and Thacker 2007; Kunicova and Rose-Ackerman 2005; Montinola and Jackman 2002). The number of political parties is reported to increase corruption since a higher number of parties in government makes it more difficult for the public to monitor the behavior of politicians (Chang and Golden 2007).

Finally, academics continue to debate the impact of federalism on corruption. Some studies suggest that the impact of federal political systems on corruption can cut in both directions (Lederman, Loayza, and Soares 2005). It may promote the ability of local governments to compete against each other for citizens, which may help in curtailing corruption. But it can also provide authorities with the power to amplify regulations in areas already covered by the central government, therein encouraging corrupt practices. With respect to empirical works on federalism and corruption, several studies find that a federal political structure indeed has a negative effect on corruption (Abed and Davoodi 2000; Gurgur and Shah 2005; Ali and Isse 2003). Kunicova and Rose-Ackerman (2005), however, argue and find that federalism increases corruption, holding other factors constant. Likewise, using a dummy variable for the presence of a federal political system, Damania, Fredriksson, and Mani (2004) and Treisman (2000) find that a federal structure is more conducive to corruption. The reason for this finding, according to Brown et al. (2006, 13), follows from the idea that "as the political pie is divided between a greater number of geographic entities, opportunities to generate political rents increase." In short, it can be argued that the actual effect of federalism on corruption remains an open empirical question.

The Legal System and Corruption

Most scholars agree with the idea that the quality of the judicial system matters for explaining corruption. A weak judicial system is likely to have a positive effect on corruption. Many studies have thus employed the ICRG index of the rule of law to test how the strength or lack thereof of the judicial system across countries influences corruption (Brunetti and Weder 2004; Ali and Isse 2003; Leite and Weidmann 1999). The ICRG index of the rule of law reflects the degree to which the citizens of a country are willing to accept the established institutions to make and implement laws and adjudicate disputes. This index also measures the extent of decision-making autonomy for courts across countries. Studies in this issue area almost always find that a strong rule of law helps to reduce corruption (Brunetti and Weder 2004; Ali and Isse 2003).

In addition to the rule of law, some studies also claim that the type of legal system in developing countries—which is determined by their historical, specifically colonial, background—matters for corruption. For instance, Treisman (2000) suggests that corruption is lower in developing countries that follow the British legal system. La Porta et al. (1999), however, report that corruption in countries with a German or Scandinavian legal origin is lower than in countries with a Socialist or French legal origin. Given these studies, I control for variables that capture the rule of law and the type of legal system across countries in the empirical model. The operationalizations of these "legal" control variables are described below. At this stage, I turn to briefly discuss certain cultural variables (identified by scholars) that may potentially influence corruption across countries.

Culture

Last but not least, some studies hypothesize that culture, broadly defined, also influences corruption. In particular, scholars focus on the potential impact that three main "cultural" variables have on corruption. First, studies find that ethnolinguistic homogeneity, for example, is negatively related to corruption (Ali and Isse 2003). In a heterogeneous and fragmented society, the probability that economic agents will be treated equally and fairly is low. As a result, highly fragmented societies are likely to be more corrupt than homogenous societies. It is also often argued that countries with a higher proportion of Protestants in the population tend to have lower corruption levels (Chang and Golden 2007; Bonaglia et al. 2001; Treisman 2000; La Porta et al. 1999). The idea here is that Protestant traditions tend to foster an egalitarian community and this leads to lower corruption levels.

Another cultural variable used to explain corruption is colonial heritage, which typically captures "command and control habits and institutions and the divisive nature of the society left behind by colonies" (Gurgur and Shah 2005, 18). The evidence on the relevance of this variable for corruption is, however, mixed. Some studies find that countries that have been colonialized tend to suffer from more corruption (Gurgur and Shah 2005; Herzfeld and Weiss 2003; Tavares 2003). Other researchers, however, find that former British colonies have lower levels of corruption (for example, Treisman 2000). Persson et al. (2003) measure the influence of colonial history by partitioning all former colonies into three groups, namely British, Spanish-Portuguese, and other colonial origin. They conclude that former British colonies tend to be less corrupt.

Each of these categories of variables identifies explanatory mechanisms that form the basis of alternative theories of corruption. Given the complex, multicausal nature of corruption, it is necessary to explicitly incorporate these explanations in the empirical specifications to robustly and appropriately test the theoretical framework offered in this book. Therefore, as discussed below, in order to test the explanatory power of legislative institutions in the full context of alternative theories, I include control variables which operationalize these alternative factors in my empirical analysis.

THE DATA

The predictions in hypotheses 1a–3b presented in chapter 2 suggest that legislative rules in democracies across the developing world influence the level of corruption via a two-step process. The first step in each of the three hypotheses (that is, hypotheses 1a, 2a, and 3a) suggests that business groups are more likely to directly lobby political parties rather than individual legislators when legislative rules in developing democracies formally allow parties to (i) control agenda-setting, (ii) introduce amendments to bills on the legislative floor, and (iii) expel party members when their voting behavior deviates from the dictates of the party whip. Because lobbying of political parties, as opposed to individual legislators, leads to more corruption, the second step (hypotheses 1b, 2b, and 3b) of the three hypotheses posits that legislative rules which allow parties to control agenda-setting, introduce amendments, and expel party members that vote against party-sponsored bills will have a positive impact on the level of corruption.

Testing the prediction in hypotheses H_o,1a, 2a, and 3a on a large-n time-series, cross-section dataset is unfortunately not feasible considering the paucity of observable data on whether business groups lobby political parties or individual legislators in developing democracies. Hence, as outlined in chapter 2, I exploited the institutional variation in legislative rules across two similar developing democracies—Brazil and India—to assess the predictions in hypotheses 1a, 2a, and 3a. In particular, as described in chapters 4 and 5, I combined case study and survey methodology when using the Brazil and India cases to empirically evaluate these hypotheses.

In contrast to the absence of data on lobbying "venue-choice" by business groups, there exists a variety of time-series, cross sectional (hereafter TSCS) datasets on corruption in developing countries. The corruption data (described below) provide one with an opportunity to test hypotheses 1b, 2b, and 3b across a variety of institutional configurations and socioeconomic, legal, and cultural profiles. Given that hypotheses 1b, 2b, and 3b focus on democracies in the developing world, I require a sample of developing nations that are democratic to test whether or not party control of agenda-setting and amendment-making and the ability of parties to expel dissidents positively influences corruption in developing democracies. Hence, I first put together a sample of 64 democracies in the developing world that were observed between 1984 and 2004 to test hypotheses 1b, 2b, and 3b that explore the link between party control of the policymaking process via drafting and passage of bills in the legislature and corruption.

The number of countries in the sample and the sample's start- and end-dates are determined primarily by the availability of country-year data on corruption and by the availability of sources on the three legislative rules under study for this set of countries. To identify developing countries as democracies for my sample, I used two well-known measures of democracy. The first is the Polity score of democracy developed by Gurr and his colleagues (Jaggers and Gurr 1995; Gurr, Jaggers, and Moore 1989). This measure emphasizes five institutional factors that distinguish democracies from autocracies: (i) the competitiveness of the process through which a country's chief executive is selected, (ii) the openness of that process, (iii) the extent to which there are institutional constraints on a chief executive's decision-making authority, (iv) the competitiveness of political participation within a country, and (v) the degree to which binding rules govern political participation within it. To measure regime type, Jaggers and Gurr (1995) create an 11-point measure of a state's democratic characteristics (DEMOC) and an 11-point measure of its autocratic characteristics (AUTOC). They then derive a variable, REG = DEMOC- AUTOC, which takes on values ranging from -10 to 10. Following several existing studies in political science, I define country-years for which REG ≥ 6 as "democratic" country-years.[1] That is, countries in the sample are classified as democratic regimes for years in which REG ≥ 6 for these countries. The empirical results reported later in this chapter remains robust when the following thresholds from the Polity democracy score are used to classify country-years as democratic: (i) REG ≥ 3, (ii) REG ≥ 4, and (iii) REG ≥ 5.

Using the Polity criteria for democracy as described above leads to a sample of 64 democracies in the developing world for which data on corruption is available from 1984. Table 6.1 lists the developing countries that are included in my sample as democratic as well as the years in which they were observed as democracies according to the Polity criteria.

For robustness tests, I used the Przeworski et al. (2000) dichotomous measure of democracy to classify developing countries as democratic or not for each country-year in my sample. According to Przeworski et al. (2000), a country is defined as a democracy if the chief executive is elected, the legislature is elected, there is more than one

Table 6.1. List of Countries in Sample

	Years observed as democracy		*Years observed as democracy*		*Years observed as democracy*
Albania	1992–2004	Guatemala	1986–2004	Pakistan	1988–1999
Argentina	1984–2004	Guyana	1992–2004	Panama	1989–2004
Armenia	1991–2004	Haiti	1994–2004	Papua New Guinea	1984–2004
Bangladesh	1991–2004	Honduras	1982–2004	Peru	1984–1989
Barbados	1984–2004	Hungary	1991–2004	Philippines	1986–2004
Benin	1991–2004	India	1984–2004	Poland	1989–2004
Bolivia	1984–2004	Indonesia	1999–2004	Romania	1990–2004
Brazil	1984–2004	Jamaica	1984–2004	Russia	1991–2002
Bulgaria	1990–2004	Korea (South)	1988–2004	Rwanda	1998–2004
Chile	1990–2004	Latvia	1991–2004	Sierra Leone	1996–2004
Colombia	1984–2004	Lithuania	1991–2004	South Africa	1990–2004
Congo	1992–1996	Madagascar	1993–2004	Slovak Republic	1993–2004
Costa Rica	1984–2004	Malawi	1994–2004	Sri Lanka	1989–2004
Czech Republic	1990–2004	Mali	1992–2004	Surinam	1991–2004
Dominican republic	1984–2004	Mauritius	1984–2004	Taiwan	1995–2004
Ecuador	1984–2004	Mexico	1999–2004	Thailand	1992–2004
El Salvador	1984–2004	Namibia	1990–2004	Trinidad and Tobago	1984–2004
Estonia	1991–2004	Nepal	1991–2004	Turkey	1984–2004
Ghana	1999–2004	Nicaragua	1984–2004	Uganda	1984–1986
Grenada	1984–2004	Niger	1993–1995	Ukraine	1991–2004
		Nigeria	1999–2004	Uruguay	1985–2004
				Venezuela	1984–2001
				Zambia	1991–2004

Note: The years listed in the column for "Years observed as democracy" is based on REG≥ +6 in the Polity score for democracy. Note that the years listed in the column for "Years observed as democracy" match closely with democratic country-years in the Przeworski et al. (2000) sample.

political party, and alternation in power occurs between political parties. Data for operationalizing this variable has been drawn from Przeworski et al. (2000), Cheibub and Gandhi (2004), and Norris (2008). Thus for each year, a country is coded as 1 for democracy if it satisfies all the four criteria described above and is coded as zero otherwise. Using the Przeworski et al. (2000) definition of democracy, I obtain a relatively smaller sample of 60 developing democracies during the 1984–2004 time period. These countries are also included in the list in table 6.1.

MEASURING THE DEPENDENT VARIABLE

The dependent variable in hypotheses 1b, 2b, and 3b is the level of corruption. As discussed in chapter 1, operationalizing the level of corruption across countries poses a formidable empirical challenge as corruption is difficult to define empirically. As discussed in the introduction, corruption is notoriously difficult to measure since the illegality of bribe-taking implies secrecy. Further, cultural differences across countries make it hard to investigate corruption without taking country-specific features into account. Notwithstanding these problems, the extant empirical literature on corruption (that was summarized above) primarily employs three measures of corruption: the International Country Risk Guide (ICRG) data on corruption, the Transparency International (TI) index of corruption, and the poll-of-polls corruption data from the World Bank (WB). To ensure that my results are not driven by any particular measure of corruption, I employ all three measures of corruption to test hypotheses 1b, 2b, and 3b.

A key advantage of the three corruption measures mentioned above is that the operational definition of each of these three measures closely matches the definition of corruption that I employ in my theoretical chapter (see chapter 2). Specifically, in chapter 2 and in the preceding case study chapters, I defined political corruption as a phenomenon where business groups provide funds (that is, bribes) to political parties or individual politicians/legislators to gain "favors," patronage, and contracts. It is impossible to obtain large-n data on actual (illegal) financial amounts offered by business groups to political actors. Political corruption is then systemically linked to total corruption through the degree of influence peddling and state capture in that country, which brings bureaucrats and other public officials into its ambit as well. Party-focused systems, I argued, will draw other public institutions into their networks and lead to higher levels of overall corruption as well relative to individual-focused systems. Hence, the corruption measures that I require for the empirical tests should to some extent capture the degree of or at least the perceived degree of financial links between business groups and politicians/political parties as well as the consequences of this relationship for corruption in the rest of the system through the corrupt links between political and public officials.

As described below, each of the three measures of corruption that I employ for the tests largely operationalizes the conceptual definition of corruption that is posited in the book's theoretical chapter. I systematically define each of these measures below. Each of them individually constitutes the dependent variable in separate empirical models.

The first measure that I use is the International Country Risk Guide (ICRG) corruption index that has been developed by Political Risk Services, a private international investment service. The ICRG data on corruption covers almost 150 countries since the beginning of the 1980s, thus making it the largest panel dataset[2] that is available for purchase. The ICRG corruption data is derived from expert-based assessments of political, economic, and financial risks. Corruption is one of the 12 political risk components, with scores ranging between 0 and 6, where a higher score means less corruption.[3] Corruption is captured via "actual or potential corruption in the form of excessive patronage, nepotism, job reservations, 'favor-for-favors,' secret party funding, and suspiciously close ties between politics and business."

The continuous ICRG index of corruption varies from 0 to 6, with higher values denoting less corruption. To facilitate interpretation of the statistical results that I obtain from the empirical models, I invert the 0–6 ICRG index and rescale it from a scale of 0, implying low corruption, to a scale of 6, implying high corruption. The rescaled ICRG index that I use for my statistical tests is labeled as *ICRG Corruption*. An important advantage of *ICRG Corruption* over the other two available measures that I employ (described below) is the fact that it is available for a long time period and for a large sample of countries.[4] In fact, the ICRG corruption measure is available for all 64 developing democracies in my sample from 1984 to 2004. Another advantage of the ICRG corruption measure is that it has been widely used by scholars which makes any results more directly comparable to other research in this field (see, for example, Ades and Di Tella 1999; Knack and Keefer 1995; Fisman 2001). Furthermore, the *ICRG corruption* measure is positively and highly correlated with at least two other well-known cross-national measures of corruption. The two additional corruption measures that I use for robustness tests are two widely used indices of perceived levels of corruption across countries: (i) the Corruption Perceptions Index constructed by Transparency International (TI) and (ii) the poll-of-polls corruption data designed by Daniel Kaufmann and his team at the World Bank (WB).

The Transparency International (TI) index, which is also called the Corruption Perception Index (CPI), contains data on corruption for approximately 130 countries since 1995/1996. Stated broadly, the Corruption Perceptions Index produced by TI measures the "perceptions of the degree of corruption as seen by business people, risk analysts and the general public." To measure perceptions of corruption, TI primarily computes the average of a number of different surveys that assess perception of each country's corruption level in a given year.[5] More specifically, at least three primary surveys or sources should be available for a country to be included in the calculation of CPI. Computed by Lambsdorff on behalf of the TI since 1995, the CPI aggregates various perception-based indicators of corruption to a new continuous 0–10 index where a higher score means less corruption.

The index is constructed via two steps. First, standardization of the primary data is done by a sequential procedure: matching percentile and ß-transformation.[6] This is done to tackle the differences in scaling system among the primary sources as well as in the distribution of data, and also to ensure that the resulting index lies between 0 and 10. The latter is to handle the tendency of the standard deviation to attenuate over time. In the second step, the final index is computed as the unweighted average of the standardized and transformed data (Lambsdorff 2002, 2003b, 2004). Taken together, these two steps lead to the 0–10 (roughly) continuous TI corruption score for several countries since 1996.

Similarly to the *ICRG corruption* measure, I rescale the TI corruption index from 0 to 10 where 0 implies no corruption and 10 denotes extremely high levels of corruption. I label the rescaled Transparency International corruption index as *TI Corruption*. A critical advantage of the TI 0–10 index of corruption is that it is available for all the developing democracies in my sample. Further, since TI has also calculated corruption ratings since 1995, there is some time-series variation in the corruption score reported for each country. In figure 6.1, I illustrate in a map the mean TI corruption level classified according to four categories—high, moderate, low, and very low—for all 64 developing countries in my sample. This figure clearly reveals that there is considerable variation in corruption across countries in the sample. The TI data, however, is only available between 1995 and 2004 for the developing democracies in the sample. Consequently, when I use the TI corruption data as an alternative dependent variable to test hypotheses 1b, 2b, and 3b, the size of my TSCS sample shrinks to some extent.

The third measure of the dependent variable that I use is the poll-of-polls corruption data from the World Bank (Kaufmann and Kraay 2002; Kaufmann et al. 1999, 2006, and 2007). Corruption is one of the six components of the Kaufmann et al. governance index. Reporting corruption data since 1996, this index covers almost 200 countries and territories and draws upon 40 data sources produced by more than 30 different organizations. To aggregate the various corruption indicators, Kaufmann et al. (1999, 2002) use a latent variable approach in which the observed perception indicators

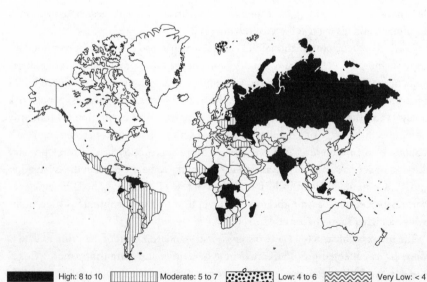

| ■■■ High: 8 to 10 | ‖‖‖‖ Moderate: 5 to 7 | ▒▒▒ Low: 4 to 6 | 〰〰 Very Low: < 4 |

Figure 6.1. *Transparency International's Rescaled [1 (low) to 10 (high)] Average Corruption Score for Developing Democracies (1995–2004) in Sample*

of corruption are expressed as a linear function of the latent concept of corruption plus a disturbance capturing perception errors and sampling variation in each indicator. This operationalization procedure produces a continuous index of corruption that ranges between -2.5 (most corrupt) and +2.5 (least corrupt). I invert and then rescale this particular World Bank measure from 0 (least corrupt) to 5 (most corrupt) to aid interpretation of my statistical results. This variable is labeled as *WB Corruption*. Data for WB Corruption is available for all the countries in my sample from 1998 to 2005.

Panel A in table 6.2 reports the descriptive statistics for the three corruption measures described above, while Panel B of this table reports the correlation between these three measures. The descriptive statistics reveal that the mean of *ICRG Corruption, TI Corruption*, and *WB Corruption* in the sample of developing democracies is 3.35, 4.36, and 2.52, respectively. The descriptive statistics also suggest that each of the three corruption measures is characterized by substantial variation. Panel B in table 6.2 indicates that there exists a high degree of correlation between the three corruption measures. For instance, the correlation between *ICRG Corruption* and *TI Corruption* is 0.84 and highly significant, while the correlation between *ICRG Corruption* and *WB Corruption* is 0.79 and significant at the 1% level. The correlation between *TI Corruption* and *WB Corruption* is 0.93 and significant at the 1% level. In short, even though there are differences in the method used to operationalize the three indicators of corruption mentioned above, they are primarily measuring some features of corruption that are common to all three measures.

OPERATIONALIZING THE INDEPENDENT VARIABLES

To test hypotheses 1b, 2b, and 3b, one needs to operationalize three independent variables. These three variables should capture whether or not political parties in developing democracies (i) control agenda-setting by introducing drafted bills in the legislature (the independent variable in hypothesis 1b), (ii) control introduction of amendments to legislative bills (the independent variable in hypothesis 2b), and (iii) have the institutional power to expel party members who vote against the diktat of the

Table 6.2. Descriptive Statistics of Corruption Measures and Correlation

Panel A	Mean	Std. deviation	Min	Max
ICRG Corruption	3.35	1.50	2.01	5.49
TI Corruption	4.36	2.22	1.12	10.00
WB Corruption	2.52	1.02	0.42	4.87
Panel B	ICRG Corruption	TI Corruption	WB Corruption	
ICRG Corruption	1.00			
TI Corruption	0.84*** (0.15)	1.00		
WB Corruption	0.79*** (0.21)	0.93***	1.00	

party whip (the independent variable in hypothesis 3b). Below I further describe each of the three variables that operationalize (i), (ii), and (iii).

In chapter 2, I suggested that formal legislative rules in some but not all democracies across the developing world allow political parties to formally make a proposal to the legislature by introducing a drafted bill for deliberation on the legislative floor. In developing countries where political parties are not allowed to introduce a drafted bill, individual legislators typically have the institutional authority to formally make proposals to the legislature by introducing drafted bills for discussion on the legislative floor. As emphasized in the literature on legislative bargaining in comparative politics,[7] the introduction of drafted bills on the legislative floor by either individual legislators or political parties de facto allows the relevant political actor that introduced the bill to engage in agenda-setting.[8] Therefore, to test the prediction in hypothesis 1b, the dummy independent variable *Agenda-Setting* is coded as 1 when the legislative rule formally permits political parties to introduce drafted bills to the legislature and is coded as 0 otherwise. Observe that when *Agenda-Setting* is equal to 0, it implies that individual legislators rather than political parties control the introduction of drafted bills in the legislature. Since hypothesis 1b predicts that party control of agenda-setting via introduction of bills on the legislative floor has a positive impact on corruption, I anticipate that the estimate of *Agenda-Setting* will be positive in the empirical model where the level of corruption is the dependent variable. The data sources that are used to code this variable are briefly listed below and then described in detail in Appendix A of this chapter.

Legislative rules in democracies across the developing world also institutionally permit either political parties or individual legislators to introduce amendments to bills that are being discussed on the legislative floor. Note that the introduction of amendments will provide the relevant political actor—in this case either the political party or the individual legislator—the ability to influence the substance of the bill that has been introduced in the legislature for potential implementation as policy. Thus to test hypothesis 2b, the second independent variable *Bill Amendment* is set equal to 1 when the legislative rule formally allows political parties to introduce amendments to bills being deliberated on the legislature floor and is coded as 0 otherwise. When *Bill Amendment* is equal to 0, it implies that individual legislators rather than political parties control introduction of amendments of bills in the legislature. Because hypothesis 2b predicts that party control of the introduction of amendments to legislative bills positively influences corruption, I anticipate that the estimate of *Bill Amendment* will be positive in the specification where the level of corruption is the dependent variable. The data sources that are used to code this variable are also described below.

After a bill is introduced and modified via amendments in the legislature, legislators/party members from different political parties vote for or against the bill. Prior to voting, leaders of each political party in the legislature usually issue a party whip that directs (or "orders") party members to vote along party lines.[9] In other words, if leaders of say political party "X" support a particular bill that has been introduced and modified in the legislature, then they will issue a party whip that will direct party members to vote for the bill. Note, however, that even though each political party may issue a whip before party members vote for or against a bill, there is no guarantee ex-ante that every individual party member will follow the party whip when voting. The cost of disobeying the party whip varies across countries. After legislators vote for or against bills, legislative rules in some (but not all) developing democracies allow party leaders to expel party members, that is, dissidents who failed to follow the party whip when voting. In such countries the cost of voting against the party line is thus very high. Expulsion of dissidents (when permitted by legislative rules) is feasible since each party member's action of voting for or against a bill is observable to all actors—including the leaders of his or her party—in the legislature.

To test hypothesis 3b, I code the dummy variable *Expel Dissidents* equal to 1 when legislative rules in a democracy formally allow political parties to expel dissidents who fail to follow the party whip when voting; it is coded 0 otherwise. Based on the prediction in hypothesis 3b, I expect that *Expel Dissidents* will have a positive influence on the level of corruption. A large number of primary and secondary sources, slightly more than 40, have been used to code the three independent variables: *Agenda Setting, Bill Amendment,* and *Expel Dissidents.* Since it is not feasible to list all these forty sources here, I systematically list them all in Appendix B to this chapter.

These sources have been categorized into five main groups: General sources, followed by sources that contain information for each of the four independent variables in developing democracies: Africa, Asia, Latin America, and Eastern and Central Europe and the former Soviet Union. A brief examination of the descriptive data for the three independent variables—*Agenda-Setting, Bill Amendment,* and *Expel Dissidents*—reveals that there is substantial variation in each of them in the dataset. For example, as illustrated in figure 6.2, political parties have the institutional power to introduce

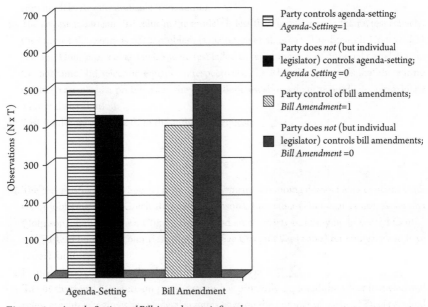

Figure 6.2. Agenda-Setting *and* Bill Amendments *in Sample*

legislative bills and thus engage in agenda-setting in about 54% of the total number of observations in the TSCS sample of 64 democracies from 1984 to 2004; in the remaining 46% of the observations, however, political parties cannot (but individual legislators can) introduce bills for deliberation on the legislative floor. Figure 6.2 shows that political parties are formally allowed to introduce amendment to bills in 43% of the observations in the sample, but not in the remaining 57% of the observations where individual legislators can introduce amendments to bills. Figure 6.3 shows that legislative rules permit political parties to expel dissidents who vote against the party whip in 58.2% of the observations, but not in the remaining 41.8% of the observations in the TSCS sample.

Is there a systematic difference in the number of observations of party control of the legislative policymaking process between presidential and parliamentary democracies in my sample? Similarly, is there a systematic difference in the number of observations of party control of the legislative policymaking process between countries with a majoritarian electoral system and developing countries with a proportional representation (hereafter PR) electoral system? Figure 6.4 reveals that there is no real difference in the number of observations of party control of *Agenda-Setting* and *Bill Amendments* between presidential and parliamentary democracies in the sample. This figure also shows that the number of observations that capture the institutional ability of political parties to expel dissidents is similar between presidential and parliamentary democracies. The illustration in figure 6.5 shows that there is no substantial difference in the number of observations of party control of *Agenda-Setting* and *Bill Amendments* between countries with a majoritarian electoral system and those with a PR electoral system. The only discernible difference in figure 6.5 is that the number of

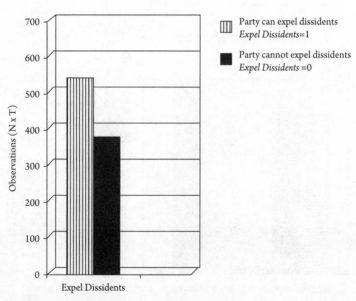

Figure 6.3. Expel Dissidents *in Sample*

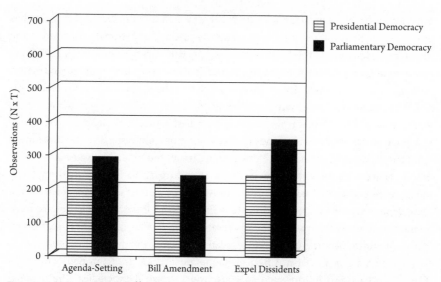

Figure 6.4. *Party Control of (i)* Agenda Setting, *(ii)* Bill Amendments, *and (iii) Party Ability to* Expel Dissidents *in Presidential and Parliamentary Democracies*

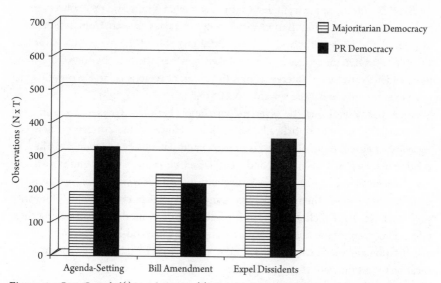

Figure 6.5. *Party Control of (i)* Agenda Setting, *(ii)* Bill Amendment, *and (iii) Party Ability to* Expel Dissidents *in Majoritarian and PR Democracies*

observations in which political parties can expel dissidents in PR democracies is visibly higher than in majoritarian countries in my sample.

These figures show that there exists considerable variation in the nature of the legislative rules found within parliamentary and presidential executive regimes and within plurality and proportional electoral systems. It is not the case that party-focused legislative rules are invariably found only in parliamentary systems while individual-focused rules are inevitable in presidential systems. This tremendous institutional variation has not received attention in either the corruption or the party strength literatures. The theoretical argument in this book is that this variation is very significant in generating different degrees of party strength and, hence, in motivating different lobbying behaviors and corruption levels. The empirical task in this chapter is to address whether this variation matters for understanding either of these phenomena and whether it does so in the manner that the theoretical argument posited in this book claims.

More interestingly, one also finds regional variation with respect to the three independent variables in the dataset. For example, 31% of the total observations in which political parties are institutionally allowed to introduce legislative bills are from developing democracies in Asia, 25% are Latin American democracies, 23% are from the new democracies in Central and Eastern Europe, and the remaining 21% are from democracies in Africa. 22% of the observations in which only political parties are allowed to introduce amendments to legislative bills are from developing democracies in Asia, 29% are from Latin American democracies, 25% are from democracies in Central and Eastern Europe, and 24% are from African democracies. The regional distribution of observations in which rules permit political parties to expel dissidents are slightly skewed toward Asian democracies. In particular, about 35% of the observations for *Expel Dissidents* = 1 are from developing democracies in Asia, 23% of observations for these variables are from Latin American democracies, 22% are from democracies in Central and Eastern Europe, and the remaining 20% of the observations for this variable is from democracies in Africa. Taken together, the distribution of the three independent variables of interest across the different regions is largely proportional and not substantially skewed toward any one region.

Simple tests reveal that the bivariate correlation between *Agenda-Setting* and *Bill Amendment* is 0.61 and statistically insignificant. However, the correlation between *Agenda-Setting* and *Expel Dissidents* is only 0.32 and statistically insignificant. The correlation between *Bill Amendment* and *Expel Dissidents* is merely -0.27 and statistically insignificant as well. Since *Agenda-Setting* and *Bill Amendment* have a correlation of 0.61, I do not include them in the same empirical specification to avoid collinearity problems. Rather, I include them in separate empirical models when testing their effect on corruption, that is, I incorporate *Agenda-Setting* and *Expel Dissidents* in one specification and then include *Bill Amendment* and *Expel Dissidents* in a separate specification to test their effects on corruption.

As an initial empirical exercise, I checked the mean *ICRG corruption* level across different permutations and combinations of the three independent variables. These descriptive results reported in table 6.3 show that the mean ICRG corruption level is the highest in the relatively few countries where political parties control *Agenda-Setting* and *Bill Amendment* and where parties have the ability to expel dissidents. Conversely, the mean ICRG corruption level is the lowest in (again, the few set of) countries where political parties do not control *Agenda-Setting* and *Bill Amendment and* where parties do not have the ability to expel dissidents. These two descriptive results are supportive of the theoretical framework. Given the discussion in chapter 2 of this book, I would anticipate that levels of corruption are likely to be the highest (lowest)

Table 6.3. Mean of ICRG Corruption

	Bill Amendment = 1; Expel Dissidents = 0	Bill Amendment = 0; Expel Dissidents = 1	Bill Amendment = 0; Expel Dissidents = 0	Bill Amendment = 1; Expel Dissidents = 1
Agenda-Setting = 1	3.74	4.56	4.12	5.09
Agenda-Setting = 0	4.23	3.45	2.89	4.60

in developing democracies where political parties (do not) control key aspects of the policymaking process in the legislature. I now turn to briefly list and describe the control variables that are included in the empirical models.

THE CONTROL VARIABLES

As discussed earlier, existing empirical studies of corruption have identified a litany of economic and demographic, political, legal, and cultural variables that may influence the level of corruption. I follow these studies and incorporate key controls in my specification that may potentially influence corruption. To describe the controls as systematically as possible, I first list below the economic and demographic control variables. This is followed by a brief description the political, legal, and cultural control variables in the specification.

Economic and Demographic Controls

The following economic and demographic variables are incorporated in the specification:

- *Log GDP per Capita*: This is operationalized as the natural logarithm of per capita GDP (PPP adjusted). Data for this variable is drawn from the World Bank (2006) and IMF (2006h). Based on extant studies of corruption—that were discussed earlier—the coefficient of *Log GDP per Capita* is expected to be negative.
- *Log Inflation*: Measured as the log of inflation for each country-year. The coefficient of this variable is expected to be positive in the specification. Data for this variable is drawn from the World Bank (2006) and IMF (2006).
- *Trade Openness*: Operationalized as the ratio of the sum of exports and imports to GDP for each country-year. Data to operationalize this variable is taken from the World Bank (2006). The estimate of *Trade Openness* is expected to be negative.

- *Size of Government*: This variable is operationalized as total central government expenditure as a percent of GDP. It is expected to have a positive effect on corruption in the empirical specification. Data for this variable is from the IMF (2006) and the World Bank (2006).
- *Log Population*: Measured as the log of population for each country-year. This variable is expected to have a positive effect on corruption. Data for this variable is from the Penn World Tables (2006).
- *Education*: Measured by the percent of the secondary school gross enrollment rate for male and female citizens in the population. *Education* is expected to have a negative effect on the level of corruption. Data for *Education* is from Barro and Lee (2002) and is updated based on the relevant data from World Bank (2006) and Norris (2008).

Political Controls

The political control variables in the specification include:

- *Presidential Democracy*: Dummy variable that is coded as 1 if the country in question is a presidential democracy. Following extant studies, this control is predicted to have a positive impact on corruption. Data for this variable is taken from the World Bank's *Database of Political Institutions* (DPI) (2008).
- *Democracy Age*: This is a count variable that captures the amount of years of uninterrupted democratic rule for each country in the sample. The estimated coefficient of *Democracy Age* is expected to be negative. Data to construct this variable is taken from World Bank's DPI (2008), Przeworski et al. (2000), and Cheibub and Gandhi (2004).
- *Magnitude* x *Open List–PR*: Chang and Golden (2007) suggest that greater district magnitude has a positive impact on corruption in PR countries with an open-list system. *Open List–PR* is a dummy variable that is equal to 1 for countries with a PR electoral system in the sample that employ the open-list system for elections (data for *Open List–PR* is from the World Bank's DPI (2008)). The variable *Magnitude* (which is essentially equal to the mean district magnitude) is operationalized as the average number of legislators elected to the lower house from each district. Since *Open List–PR* is a dummy variable, I interact *Magnitude* with *Open List–PR* to account for Chang and Golden's (2007) claim in the specification. Data for *Magnitude* is from the World Bank's DPI (2008). *Magnitude* x *Open List–PR* is expected to have a positive effect of corruption.
- *ENLP*: Effective number of political parties in the legislature, which, following the extant literature (see Golder 2004), is operationalized using the Hirschman-Herfindahl index of the effective number of political parties in the legislature. The variable *ENLP* is expected to have a positive influence on corruption. Data for this variable is from Cheibub and Gandhi (2004) and Norris (2008).

- *Federal*: Dummy variable that is coded as 1 if the country in question is a federal democracy. Since scholars disagree on whether federalism has a positive or negative effect on corruption, *Federal* may have a positive or negative effect on corruption. Data for *Federal* is from the World Bank's *Database of Political Institutions* (DPI) (2008).

Legal Control Variables

The following variables that pertain to the strength and type of legal system in each country in the sample are controlled for in the empirical model:

- *Legal_UK*: This is operationalized as a dummy variable that is coded as 1 for countries in my sample that follow the British common law system. Data for *Legal_UK* is from La Porta et al. (1999) and Norris (2008). I anticipate that this variable will have a negative effect on corruption in the specification.
- *Rule of Law*: This variable is purchased from the ICRG dataset that has been put together by the Political Risk Services Group. In the ICRG dataset, the *Rule of Law* is a 0–7 index that captures the strength, robustness, autonomy (from political interference), and quality of the judicial system for each country-year from 1984 to 2002. Higher values of this index indicates a stronger, more autonomous, and competent judicial system. Based on extant studies in the literature, I anticipate that the estimate of *Rule of Law* will be negative in the specification.

Cultural Control Variables

Based on the empirical corruption literature that was discussed earlier, the following "cultural" (broadly defined) control variables are also incorporated in the specification:

- *Ethno-Linguistic Fractionalization* (ELF): I use a widely available measure of ethnic and linguistic fractionalization, which is itself put together as an average of five different indices (see La Porta et al. 1999, Alesina et al. 2003, Persson and Tabellini 2002). The ethno-linguistic fractionalization measure that I use is measured as a continuous 0–1 variable and is drawn from Banks (2003) and Przeworski et al. (2000). Following extant studies, I anticipate that ELF will have a positive impact on corruption.
- *Protestant*: This is operationalized as the share of the population with a Protestant religious tradition. Data for this variable is gathered from Banks (2003), Przeworski et al. (2000), and Boix (2003). *Protestant* is predicted to have a negative impact on the dependent variable.
- *Colony_UK*: Dummy variable that is coded as 1 for countries in my sample that were colonized by the British. This variable is expected to have a negative effect on corruption. Data for *Legal_UK* is from Przeworski et al. (2000).

The summary statistics for the three key independent variables and the control variables listed above are provided in table 6.4.

For robustness tests, I included additional control variables that, according to the extant empirical literature, may influence corruption. The results from the robustness tests that are conducted after incorporating these additional controls are discussed later in this chapter. At this stage, I turn now to describe below the statistical methodology employed for the empirical analysis to test hypotheses 1b, 2b, and 3b on the sample listed in table 6.1.

STATISTICAL METHODOLOGY

The bounded nature of the three corruption measures, which individually constitute the dependent variable in separate models, demands special consideration when choosing the appropriate statistical model to test hypotheses 1b, 2b, and 3b. Specifically, the existence of a finite *ceiling* for each corruption measure—that is, 6 for the

Table 6.4. Summary Statistics of Independent and Control Variables

	Mean	Std. deviation	Min	Max
Agenda-Setting	0.56	0.31	0	1
Bill Amendment	0.53	0.41	0	1
Expel Dissidents	0.39	0.27	0	1
Log Inflation	-2.17	1.12	-6.94	4.82
Log Population	13.79	1.85	8.73	18.679
Log of GDP per Capita	3.86	4.07	1.91	11.25
Size of Government	15.56	5.97	2.97	43.46
Trade Openness	65.53	47.20	6.32	206.71
Education	51.39	31.44	7.16	92.35
Democracy Age	9.6	5.2	1.0	19
Magnitude	12.54	26.71	0.68	123.45
Open List–PR	0.52	0.24	0	1
Federal	0.56	0.49	0	1
ELF	0.48	0.25	0.002	0.88
Rule of Law	-0.09	1.00	-2.50	+2.29
ʾony_UK	0.33	0.47	0	1
ʾʹ	0.41	0.52	0	1
	3.85	2.02	1.23	13.86
	0.56	0.73	0	1
	11.96	18.54	0.0	86.15

ICRG measure, 10 for TI, and +2.5 for the WB measure—places an upper bound on the plausible theoretical range in the level of corruption across countries. This, in turn, increases the possibility that the observed dependent variable, the level of corruption, may be *right-censored*, that is, censored from above. The problem of right-censoring is a potentially serious one, since the theoretical range of the level of corruption in the population (of countries) may extend well beyond the upper limit of each corruption measure employed here. Two reasons, in fact, suggest that right-censoring of the corruption measures employed here may indeed be an issue that needs to be addressed.

First, there is the possibility that right-censoring may have occurred in the corruption measures employed here in this sample. In fact analysis of the data show that the mean corruption score for each of the three corruption measures moves toward their highest level from the late 1990s or first two years of this century, more technically, observations of the level of corruption across countries in the sample *cluster* toward the upper bound for each corruption measure, which is an indication of censoring of higher values of corruption or, in other words, right-censoring. Given the proximity of the mean level of corruption for all three measures to their respective maximum value, one must consider a statistical model that will account for the bounded nature of each corruption measure and the attendant problem of censoring to avoid inconsistent estimates.

Second, it is plausible that the upper end of each corruption measure may have failed to capture the possibility that the corruption level is, in reality, higher than the value recorded for each country's corruption score in the ICRG, TI, and WB index. Two possibilities could account for the aforementioned problem. For one, scholars and policy analysts have suggested that corruption levels increased exponentially in developing countries during the 1990s primarily because of the dubious and nontransparent manner in which privatization of public companies was done in many developing countries.[10] Indeed, even institutions such as the World Bank have acknowledged that privatization of public enterprises during the 1990s substantially enriched many politicians and officials in developing countries.[11] Because the corruption measures are bounded from above, it is plausible that they may have failed to sufficiently capture the exponential increase in corruption levels across countries in my sample, therein exacerbating the right-censoring problem mentioned above. Additionally, scholars who collect survey data to operationalize perceptions of corruption tend to find that survey respondents often *understate* the level of corruption (see, for example, Lambsdorff 2004). This implies that the actual level of corruption in developing countries may, in reality, be higher than those perceived by survey respondents since these respondents may be systematically understating corruption levels. If the level of corruption is indeed higher than what is being captured in the corruption indices, then this suggests as well that the corruption measures employed here are likely to suffer from the problem of right-censoring.

Since the dependent variable that I employ for the tests is potentially right-censored, I estimate a Tobit "right-censored" model that accounts for potential right-censoring (that is, censoring from above) of the dependent variable in the estimation process.[12] When estimating the statistical model on my sample, I also need to account for unobserved heterogeneity and serial correlation since I use a time-series cross-section dataset (as described earlier) to test hypotheses 1b, 2b, and 3b. Following recent studies that have assessed the efficacy of Tobit models with fixed effects on panel datasets[13], I estimate the Tobit right-censored model on my sample with country fixed effects and a lagged dependent variable. Doing so allows me to correct for unobserved heterogeneity and serial correlation in the data. The Tobit model (with fixed effects and a lagged dependent variable) that I employ is briefly described formally in Appendix A of this chapter. To check the robustness of my results, I also estimate some lagged dependent variable (hereafter LDV) regression models with country fixed effects and panel corrected standard errors (Beck and Katz 1995) to test the main hypotheses of interest. Since introducing the lag of the dependent variable in the specification may weaken the explanatory power of the estimated coefficients (see Achen 2000), I also estimate Prais-Winsten models with PCSEs and country fixed effects. Estimation of the Prais-Winsten models with fixed effects and PCSEs did not substantially or significantly in the statistical sense alter any of the results obtained from the Tobit right-censored and LDV models. Thus to save space I do not report the results from the LDV and the Prais-Winsten models, which instead are available upon request. Finally, given that it is possible to obtain spurious correlations between data series that are trended, I also include a control for a linear time trend to purge these effects from the estimates.

THE EMPIRICAL RESULTS

Results from the Tobit Right-Censored Models

To begin with, I initially estimated some simple Tobit right-censored models with country fixed effects and a few controls for each of the three measures of corruption (the dependent variable) employed here: *ICRG Corruption*, *TI Corruption*, and *WB Corruption*. Recall from an earlier discussion that the two independent variables *Agenda-Setting* and *Bill Amendment* are statistically correlated with each other to some extent in the data. Hence to avoid collinearity problems, I include *Agenda-Setting* and *Expel Dissidents* in one specification to estimate their impact on corruption, while in a separate specification I incorporate *Bill Amendment* and *Expel Dissidents*.[14]

The results in the six models in table 6.5 (models 1 to 6) are obtained from estimating the Tobit right-censored model with fixed effects for the Polity-defined sample of democracies with the (i) *ICRG corruption* measure as the dependent variable (models 1 and 2, table 6.5), (ii) *TI corruption* measure as the dependent variable (models 3 and 4), and (iii) *WB corruption* measure as the dependent variable (models 5 and 6).

The estimated coefficient of the independent variable *Agenda-Setting* is positive and ~~cant~~ at the 1% level in the relevant Tobit models in table 6.5. This provides initial ~~for~~ hypothesis 1b. Likewise, the estimate of the other two independent ~~Bill~~ *Amendment* and *Expel Dissidents*—is also positive and highly significant Tobit models in table 6.5. The positive and significant coefficient of *Expel Dissidents* thus also provides preliminary statistical support hypotheses 2b and 3b, respectively.

Table 6.5. Basic Tobit Right-Censored Model Results

| | Democracy Sample based on Polity Criteria | | | | | |
	ICRG Corruption Model 1	ICRG Corruption Model 2	TI Corruption Model 3	TI Corruption Model 4	WB Corruption Model 5	WB Corruption Model 6
Lagged Dependent Variable	.1936***(.0540)	.2762***(.0863)	.3170***(0.0801)	.2541***(.0657)	.0632(.7556)	.3385***(.0774)
Agenda-Setting	.3132***(.0911)		.3857***(.0905)		.4051***(.1265)	
Bill Amendment		.2321***(.0249)		.1581***(.0326)		.2155***(.0292)
Expel Dissidents	.2044***(.0049)	.2725***(.0042)	.2084**(.1107)	.1541***(.0703)	.1496***(.0297)	.1289***(.0345)
Economic Controls						
Log GDP per Capita	−.2826***(.0612)	.2270***(.0498)	−.2438***(.0382)	−.1932***(.0407)	−.1558***(.0276)	−.1191***(.0322)
Trade Openness	.1651(.7411)	.1984(.8233)	.3467(1.417)	.2142(.965)	.2423(.2858)	.1792(.2140)
Political Controls						
Presidential	.0246**(.0122)	.0341**(.0170)	.0153**(.0092)	.0178*(.0112)	.0041**(.0015)	.0060**(.0028)
Open List (PR)	.0654(.1107)	.0863(.1384)	.0994(.2233)	.0262(.2055)	.0133(.0800)	.1361(.0904)

(continued)

Table 6.5. (continued)

| | Democracy Sample based on Polity Criteria | | | | | |
| | ICRG Corruption | ICRG Corruption | TI Corruption | TI Corruption | WB Corruption | WB Corruption |
	Model 1	Model 2	Model 3	Model 4	Model 5	Model 6
Other Controls						
Rule of Law	−.0137*** (.0052)	−.0240*** (.0075)	−.0422*** (.0124)	−.0761*** (0.0039)	−.0355*** (.001)	−.0182** (.0080)
Time Trend	.0031*** (.0010)	.0065** (.0032)	.0078*** (.0024)	.0059*** (.0021)	.0040*** (.0015)	.0038*** (.0021)
Constant	.6051*** (.0235)	.8077*** (.0342)	.3203*** (.0416)	.2975*** (.0519)	.0158*** (.0047)	.0133** (.0064)
Log Likelihood	-5052.06	-5129.07	-4311.3	-5247.06	-4635.72	-4711.12
Fixed Effects	Yes	Yes	Yes	Yes	Yes	Yes
N	877	812	480	457	362	315

Notes: ***, ** denotes significance at 1%, and 5%, respectively. Cell entries are maximum-likelihood estimates with robust standard errors in the parentheses. Each model has been estimated with country fixed effects that have not been reported to save space.

In models 7 and 8 of table 6.6, I report the results from estimating the *complete* specification of the Tobit right-censored model with fixed effects for the Polity-defined sample of democracies and with the *ICRG corruption* measure as the dependent variable. The effect of *Agenda-Setting* is positive and significant at the 1% level in model 7. This result statistically corroborates the prediction in hypothesis 1b when the *ICRG Corruption* measure is used as the dependent variable. The estimates of the other two independent variables—*Bill Amendment* (see model 8) and *Expel Dissidents* (see models 7 and 8)—are also positive and highly significant. The positive and significant coefficient of *Bill Amendment* and *Expel Dissidents* thus statistically corroborates the prediction in hypotheses 2b and 3b, respectively.

While the estimated coefficients of the three independent variables in models 7 and 8 statistically support hypotheses 1b, 2b, and 3b, they do not provide enough information about the substantive effect of the independent variables on corruption. To get a better sense of the substantive effect of the independent variables, I first compute from model 7 the substantive impact that *Agenda-Setting* has on the *ICRG Corruption* measure when the *Agenda-Setting* dummy is changed from 0 to 1, while all other variables in model 7 are held fixed at their respective means in the sample. This exercise reveals that when the *Agenda-Setting* dummy is increased from 0 to 1, the level of *ICRG Corruption* increases from by 0.47 points in the 0 to 6 ICRG scale (see table 6.7). In percentage terms this implies that when the *Agenda-Setting* dummy is increased from 0 to 1, the level of *ICRG Corruption* increases by almost 11.2%, which is substantial. Moreover, the aforementioned substantive effect is statistically significant at the 5% level, as illustrated in figure 6.6. The reported marginal effect of *Agenda-Setting* on

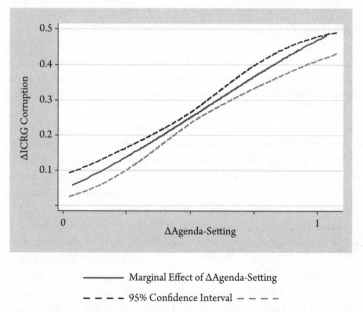

———— Marginal Effect of ΔAgenda-Setting

– – – – 95% Confidence Interval – – – – –

Figure 6.6. *Marginal Effect of 0 to 1 Change in Agenda Setting on ΔICRG Corruption with 95% Confidence Intervals*

ICRG Corruption in table 6.7 and the commensurate illustration in figure 6.6 thus provides strong substantive and statistical support for the claim in hypothesis 1b.

I similarly calculated the substantive effect of *Bill Amendment* on *ICRG Corruption* from model 8. When the *Bill Amendment* dummy is increased from 0 to 1, while all other variables in model 8 are held fixed at their respective mean, *ICRG Corruption* increases by 9%. As indicated in table 6.7 and figure 6.7, this substantive effect is statistically significant as well. When *Expel Dissidents* is increased from 0 to 1, while all other variables in model 8 are held fixed at their respective mean, *ICRG Corruption* increases by 10.5%. This particular substantive effect is also significant at (at least) the 10% level as indicated in table 6.7 and in the illustration in figure 6.8. The reported marginal effect of *Bill Amendment* and *Expel Dissidents* in table 6.7 thus substantively corroborates hypotheses 2b and 3b.

As an initial test of robustness, I checked whether the results obtained from the *ICRG Corruption* measure remain consistent when I employ two other alternative measures of corruption for the dependent variable: *TI Corruption* and *WB Corruption*. The results in models 9 and 10 in table 6.6 report the estimates from the Polity-defined sample of developing democracies when the *TI Corruption* measure serves as the dependent variable. Models 11 and 12 in Table 6.6 present the estimates from the Polity-defined sample of developing democracies when the *WB Corruption* measure serves as the dependent variable. The estimated coefficient of each of the three independent variables—*Agenda-Setting, Bill Amendment,* and *Expel Dissidents*—is positive and highly significant in the models listed above. This suggests that the results from

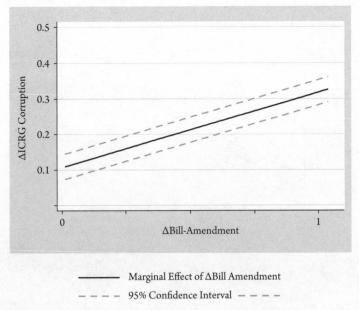

Figure 6.7. *Marginal Effect of 0 to 1 Change in* Bill Amendment *on* ΔICRG Corruption *with 95% Confidence Intervals*

Table 6.6. Tobit Right-Censored Model Results: Complete Specification

	ICRG Corruption Model 7	ICRG Corruption Model 8	TI Corruption Model 9	TI Corruption Model 10	WB Corruption Model 11	WB Corruption Model 12
			Democracy Sample Based on Polity Criteria			
Lagged DV	.1746***(.0246)	.1321***(.0482)	.1281***(.0375)	.1879***(.0592)	.1769***(.0440)	.1868***(.0494)
Agenda-Setting	.3181***(.1371)		.3659**(.1870)		.4189***(.1221)	
Bill Amendment		.1120**(.0063)		.1214***(.0320)		.1073***(.0051)
Expel Dissidents	.0971***(.0217)	.0944***(.0226)	.0805***(.0242)	.0712***(.0189)	.0665**(.0102)	.0576***(.0126)
Economic Controls						
Size of Government	.1322(.1536)	.1155(.1350)	.1042(.1237)	.1218(.1343)	.1198(.1254)	.1389(.1156)
Log GDP per Capita	-.1208**(.0600)	-.1194***(.0506)	-.1143***(.0365)	-.1251***(.0440)	-.1087***(.0537)	-.0306***(.0147)
Education	-.1752(.3377)	-.1057(.1206)	-.1754(.1221)	-.1337(.1890)	-.1295(.1759)	-.1355(.1882)
Log Population	.0637(.0433)	.0287(.0247)	.0312(.0252)	.0521(.0592)	.0239(.0298)	.0211(.0534)
Trade Openness	.0749(.1132)	.0945(.1289)	.0910(.1260)	.0987(.1247)	.1192(.1240)	.1152(.1177)
Log Inflation	.0375(.0701)	.0214(.0629)	.0925*(.0519)	.0483(.0806)	.0131(.0339)	.0037(.0218)
Political Controls						
Federal	.0163(.0175)	.0185*(.0107)	.0154*(.0098)	.0145(.0159)	.0103*(.052)	.0165**(.0081)
Democracy Age	-.0114(.0135)	-.0140(.0126)	-.0167(.0188)	-.0112(.0133)	-.0115(.0120)	.0190(.0153)
Presidential	.0196*(.0115)	.0165*(.0097)	.0147*(.0090)	.0172*(.0105)	.0132*(.077)	.0148*(.0083)
ENLP	.0085***(.0031)	.0046***(.0015)	.0147**(.0070)	.0122**(.060)	.0124***(.039)	-.0177***(.0060)

(continued)

Table 6.6. (continued)

	Democracy Sample Based on Polity Criteria					
	ICRG Corruption Model 7	ICRG Corruption Model 8	TI Corruption Model 9	TI Corruption Model 10	WB Corruption Model 11	WB Corruption Model 12
Magnitude x Open List (PR)	.0189*** (.0067)	.0158*** (.0034)	.0123*** (.0039)	.0107** (.0040)	-.0208** (.060)	-.0194*** (.006)
Magnitude	.1252 (.2177)	.1981 (.2544)	.1811 (.2571)	.1825 (.2077)	.2341 (.2519)	.2644 (.2123)
Open List (PR)	.0121 (.0138)	.0149 (.0127)	.0122 (.0136)	.0138 (.0144)	.0131 (.0197)	.0126 (.0237)
Other Controls						
Rule of Law	-.2526*** (.0749)	-.1948*** (.0523)	-.2236*** (.0479)	-.2147*** (.0664)	-.2126*** (.0749)	-.2409*** (.0898)
Colony_UK	.0036 (.0030)	.0027 (.0029)	.0041 (.0040)	.0055 (.0068)	.0016 (.0035)	.0022 (.0024)
Legal_UK	.0651 (.0740)	.0742 (.0956)	.0677 (.0842)	.0770 (.0564)	.0210 (.0637)	.0092 (.0048)
ELF	.0084 (.0095)	.0079 (.0056)	.0091 (.0085)	.0094 (.0093)	.0115 (.0140)	.0092 (.0096)
Protestant	-.0216 (.0599)	-.0307 (.0512)	-.0281 (.0334)	-.0170 (.0264)	-.0361 (.0215)	-.0237 (.0152)
Time Trend	.0191*** (.0114)	.0123*** (.0039)	.0055*** (.0020)	.0167*** (.0082)	.0107*** (.0040)	.0086*** (.0041)
Constant	.6215*** (.2765)	.8478*** (.3155)	.8505*** (.3193)	.4851*** (.2301)	.4720** (.2353)	.5118** (.2391)
Log Likelihood	-7983.91	-7784.02	-7903.06	-7234.21	-7144.56	-7928.62
N	837	795	475	402	301	287

Notes: *, **, *** denotes significance at 10%, 5%, and 1%, respectively. Robust standard errors reported in parentheses. Each model in the table has been estimated with country fixed effects that are not reported in the table because of space constraints.

Table 6.7. Substantive Effects from Models in Table 6.6

Effect of . . .	ΔICRG Corruption
0 to 1 Change in *Agenda-Setting* in Model 13 when all other variables in specification are held at their mean in the sample	0.47 [0.32, 0.68]
0 to 1 Change in *Bill Amendment* in Model 14 when all other variables in specification are held at their mean in the sample	0.30 [0.19, 0.42]
0 to 1 Change in *Expel Dissidents* in Model 13 when all other variables in specification are held at their mean in the sample	0.36 [0.25, 0.51]

Notes: Numbers reported in the parentheses show the upper and lower limit 95% confidence interval of the estimated marginal effect of change in each of the independent variables on ICRG corruption.

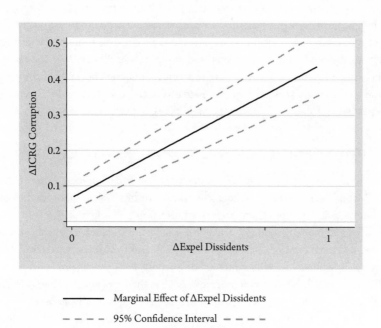

Figure 6.8. *Marginal Effect of 0 to 1 Change in* Expel Dissidents *on ΔICRG Corruption with 95% Confidence Intervals*

models 7 and 8 remain robust when the *TI Corruption* and *WB Corruption* measures are used to operationalize the dependent variable in the empirical model.[15]

Unlike the strong statistical support for hypotheses 1b, 2b, and 3b, the estimates of some but not all control variables in each specification in table 6.6 is weak and/or insignificant. For example, the estimates of *Trade Openness, Log Population.* and *Log Inflation* are consistently insignificant in these two tables. Similarly, the *Size of Government* and *Education* is also insignificant in the models. However, the estimate of *Log GDP per Capita* is negative and highly significant in all the models in table 6.6, which is not surprising. The political control variables fare better in the specifications compared to the economic controls. For instance, the coefficient of *Presidential Democracy* is weakly significant at the 10% level but positive in all the reported models. This finding supports Kunicova and Rose-Ackerman's (2005) claim that the level of corruption tends, on average, to be higher in presidential democracies.

The estimate of *ENLP* and *Magnitude* x *Open List--PR* is positive and highly significant in each empirical model. This substantiates the claims put forth by Chang and Golden (2007) that a higher number of political parties has a positive impact on corruption and that greater district magnitude positively influences corruption in PR countries with an open-list system. The estimate of the *Federal* dummy is at best mixed. In some of the reported models, the estimate of *Federal* is positive and weakly significant. This appears to support Kunicova and Rose-Ackerman's (2005) idea that federal (and thus decentralized) political systems tend to foster corruption. However, the statistical insignificance of the *Federal* dummy in the other models suggests that the influence of this variable on corruption may not be substantial. With respect to the remaining controls, we find that the *Rule of Law* has a negative and statistically significant effect on all three corruption measures in table 6.6. This result is interesting but hardly novel given that many previous studies report a similar finding. The estimated coefficient of *ELF* and *Protestant* are in the predicted direction but statistically insignificant in all the models. Finally, the estimate of *Colony_UK* and *Legal_UK* is surprisingly positive but statistically insignificant in the specifications.

ROBUSTNESS TESTS AND DIAGNOSTIC CHECKS

The estimates reported in table 6.6 are derived from tests conducted on the Polity-defined sample of developing democracies. Do the results remain robust in the sample of developing democracies that are chosen according to the Przeworski et al. (2000) criteria for a democratic regime? Furthermore, do the results remain robust when I include additional control variables in the specification? Models 13 to 18 in table 6.8 report results estimated on the sample of developing democracies that meet the Przeworski et al. (2000) criteria for democracy between the years 1984 and 2004, and from specifications which include some additional controls. Specifically, in models 13–18, I follow the extant empirical literature on the determinants of corruption described in the previous section and include the following additional controls: a dummy variable for the *Plurality* electoral system, a dummy variable for countries whose legal origins are German (*Legal_German*), a 0–100 index of *Media Freedom* that is taken from the Freedom House (2007) data source, and the variable *Natural Resource Endowment* that operationalizes the fraction of GDP produced in the Mining and Quarrying sectors and in the production of oil for each country-year.

The control *Plurality* is included in the specification because, as emphasized earlier, Kunicova and Rose-Ackerman (2005) suggest that this electoral system variable is likely to have a negative impact on the level of corruption. Note that to minimize problems of collinearity, I drop the variable *Magnitude* in the models where the dummy *Plurality* is incorporated. This is because *Magnitude* and *Plurality* are statistically correlated with each other. The index *Media Freedom* is incorporated in the specification

Table 6.8. Robustness Tests: Tobit Right-Censored Model Results

	Democracy Sample Based on Przeworski et al. Criteria					
	ICRG Corruption Model 13	ICRG Corruption Model 14	TI Corruption Model 15	TI Corruption Model 16	WB Corruption Model 17	WB Corruption Model 18
Lagged DV	.1713***(.0357)	.1348***(.0246)	.1824***(.0439)	.2437***(.0779)	.2254***(.0431)	.2167***(.0479)
Agenda-Setting	.2721**(.0857)		.1236***(.0044)		.3237**(.0454)	
Bill Amendment		.1885***(.0244)		.1751***(.0311)		.1233***(.0064)
Expel Dissidents	.0725***(.0268)	.0618***(.0240)	.0689***(.0184)	.0771***(.0240)	.0588***(.0207)	.0616***(.0302)
Economic Controls						
Size of Government	.1125(.1221)	.1242(.1323)	.1133(.1284)	.1279(.1701)	.1406(.1265)	.1353(.1662)
Log GDP per Capita	-.0144***(.0039)	-.0128**(.052)	-.0164***(.0050)	-.0049***(.0012)	-.0124***(.009)	-.0108**(.0032)
Education	-.1432(.1132)	-.1141(.1236)	-.1322(.2536)	-.1871(.1905)	-.1255(.1350)	-.1476(.1715)
Log Population	.0172(.0855)	.0197(.0801)	.0110(.0463)	.0125(.0387)	.0139(.0405)	.0211(.0537)
Trade Openness	.0282(.0324)	.0229(.0318)	.019(.0310)	.0349(.0421)	.0307(.0352)	.0226(.0265)
Log Inflation	.1089(.1217)	.1288(.1334)	.1076(.1122)	.1174(.1216)	.1540(.0886)	.1059(.0821)
Political Controls						
Federal	.0451(.0712)	.0342(.0612)	.0289(.0256)	.0223(.0450)	.0216(.0354)	.0136(.0337)
Democracy Age	-.0379(.0701)	-.0881***(.0245)	-.0863(.1384)	-.0483(.0806)	-.1317***(.0219)	-.0616(.0599)
Presidential	.0103*(.0062)	.0167**(.0100)	.015*(.062)	.0208*(.0124)	.0116*(.0067)	.0165*(.0112)
ENLP	.0106**(.0058)	.0223***(.0057)	.0361*(.0175)	.0266***(.0127)	.0117**(.0043)	.0105**(.0032)
Plurality Rule	-.0113*(.0065)	-.0151*(.0094)	-.0126*(.079)	-.0185*(.0107)	-.0149*(.0080)	-.0122**(.0068)

(continued)

183

Table 6.8. (*continued*)

Democracy Sample Based on Przeworski et al. Criteria

	ICRG Corruption Model 13	ICRG Corruption Model 14	TI Corruption Model 15	TI Corruption Model 16	WB Corruption Model 17	WB Corruption Model 18
Open List (PR)	.0136 (.032)	.0189 (.0177)	.0141 (.0186)	.0122 (.0141)	-.0166 (.0154)	.0117 (.0126)
Other Controls						
Rule of Law	-.1762*** (.0563)	-.1170*** (.0501)	-.2039*** (0.0614)	-.1846*** (.0361)	-.1072*** (.0351)	-.1161*** (.0339)
Media Freedom	-.0125 (.0316)	-.0118 (.0219)	-.0207 (.0789)	-.0377 (.0296)	-.0165 (.0322)	-.0544 (.0339)
Colony_UK	.0543 (.0732)	.0112 (.0190)	0.0148 (0.0163)	.0349 (.0623)	.0395 (.0718)	.0380 (.0557)
Legal_UK	-.0437 (.0568)	-.0283 (.0598)	-.0212 (.0427)	-.0388 (.0442)	-.0271 (.0213)	-.0135 (.017)
ELF	.0077 (.0064)	.0065 (.0058)	.0040 (.0036)	.0045 (.0039)	.0022 (.0027)	.0043 (.0032)
Protestant	-.0025 (.026)	-.0023 (.018)	-.0010 (.012)	-.0011 (.065)	-.0022 (.0021)	-.0037 (.0038)
Legal_German	.0315 (.0330)	.0514 (.0455)	.0406 (.0433)	.0314 (.0263)	.0283 (.0225)	.0318 (.0341)
Natural Resource Endowment	.1019 (.0912)	.0931 (.0808)	.1125 (.0761)	.1433 (.1304)	.1307 (.1452)	.1214 (.1052)
Time Trend	.0257*** (.0112)	.0144*** (.0039)	.0128** (.052)	.0164*** (.0050)	.0049*** (.0012)	.0124*** (.009)
Constant	.2335*** (.0744)	.2598*** (.0711)	.2126*** (.0453)	.2378*** (.0337)	.3165*** (.0532)	.2378*** (.0544)
Log Likelihood	-4079.88	-5012.34	-4158.12	-4219.36	-3799.25	-4147.68
N	882	453	341	775	420	307

Notes: *, **, *** denotes significance at 10%, 5%, and 1%, respectively. Robust standard errors reported in parentheses. Each model in the table has been estimated with random effects.

since Adserà, Boix, and Payne (2000) and Brunetti and Weder (2003) suggest that corruption may be significantly lowered by the diffusion of daily newspapers and greater independence of the media in a democratic context. Similarly, La Porta et al. (1999) report that corruption is lower in countries with a German legal origin compared to those with a social or French legal origin. Therefore, I anticipate that the estimate of *Plurality, Media Freedom,* and *Legal_German* will be negative in the empirical model. The variable *Natural Resource Endowment* is included in the model as well since Leite and Weidmann (1999) suggest theoretically and find empirically that greater reliance on a country's endowment of natural resources tends to have a positive impact on corruption.

The variable *Agenda-Setting* continues to have a positive and highly significant effect on *ICRG* Corruption (model 13), TI *Corruption* (model 15), and *WB Corruption* (model 17) in this sample. Similarly, both *Bill Amendment* and *Expel Dissidents* have a positive and highly significant effect on each of the three measures of corruption in the relevant models in table 6.8. Thus the estimated coefficient of the three independent variables in models 13–18 statistically confirm the predictions in hypotheses 1b, 2b, and 3b for the Przeworski et al. –defined sample of democracies and in specifications where I included additional controls. In contrast to the estimates of the independent variables in table 6.8, the estimated coefficients of the "additional" control variables— that is, *Media Freedom, Natural Resource Endowment,* and *Legal_German* are statistically insignificant in the empirical models in this table. The control *Plurality* is, however, significant in the empirical models in this table.

In addition to the results reported in models 7–18 in tables 6.6 to 6.8, I also estimated additional empirical models for the Polity-defined and Przeworski et al.–defined sample of democracies after adding variables in the model including a continuous variable that captures the amount of foreign aid as a ratio of GDP (*Foreign Aid*) and a dummy variable for democracies in the developing world that employ the French legal system (*Legal_France*). I do not report the results from the models with these additional controls to save space. But including these additional controls did not substantively or significantly alter any of the main results presented earlier.

Diagnostic tests conducted for the empirical models revealed that *none* of the models suffer from severe multicollinearity, serial correlation, or omitted variable bias and that the residuals are normally distributed.[16] I also check whether each of the three independent variables in my empirical analysis are potentially endogenous to any of the three measures of corruption used here even though I do not theoretically expect that the level of corruption determines any particular choice of legislative rules, the three dummy independent variables of interest here. To be safe, however, I conducted two simple tests to check the potential endogeneity problem mentioned above.

First, I implemented a variant of the Granger causality test designed for panel and TSCS data by Hurlin and Venet (2003) to assess the potential endogenous relationship between each of the three measures of corruption used here and each of the three independent variables in the empirical tests. F-test statistics from Hurlin and Venet's (2003) testing procedure reveals that neither the *ICRG,* the *TI,* nor the *WB corruption* measure statistically influence any of the three independent variables. Second, I also estimated several Markov transition Probit models in which I separately estimated the effect of each of the three measures of corruption used here on each of the three independent variables in the empirical analysis. In particular, in three separate Markov transition Probit models I separately estimated the effect of *ICRG Corruption*, *TI Corruption*, and *WB Corruption* on the dummy variable, *Agenda-Setting*. I repeated this exercise for the other two variables *Bill Amendment* and *Expel Dissidents*. Results from the Markov transition Probit models that are not reported here to save space clearly reveal that the three measures of corruption do *not* statistically influence any of three variables: *Agenda-Setting*, *Bill Amendment*, and *Expel Dissidents*. Results from Hurlin and Venet's (2003) test and the Markov transition models described above thus indicate that the results reported in tables 6.6, 6.7, and 6.8 are not only robust but also not plagued by endogeneity problems.[17]

CONCLUSION

The empirical results presented in this chapter are encouraging since they reveal that party control of policymaking dynamics in the legislature indeed has a positive influence on corruption. More specifically, the estimates from the empirical models presented in tables 6.6 to 6.8 and figures 6.6 to 6.8 show that when legislative rules formally allow political parties to control the introduction of drafted bills and thus influence agenda-setting in the legislature of developing democracies, the level of corruption increases substantially. Likewise, formal party control of the introduction of amendments to legislative bills statistically has a positive effect on the level of corruption in the sample of sixty-four developing democracies that are observed between 1984 and 2004. Finally, the results suggest that when political parties have the institutional power to expel dissidents who go against the party whip when voting on legislative bills, then corruption also increases significantly in the statistical sense. The key findings summarized above are robust to specification changes such as inclusion of additional controls and to different measures of the dependent variable, the level of corruption.

The statistical findings in this chapter thus provide strong empirical support for the implications that emerge from the theoretical arguments that explain why party control of the process of policymaking via bills in the legislature positively influences corruption. Since the quantitative results are inferred from a fairly comprehensive sample of sixty-four democracies from the developing world between 1984 and 2004, the key empirical findings reported here are thus quite generalizable across space and time. Furthermore, the quantitative study reveals that certain important economic control variables—such as trade openness and the size of government—do not have a statistically substantial impact on corruption once I account for how party control of policymaking dynamics in the legislature influences corruption. At the same time, however, one finds that key political controls, such as the dummy variable for presidential democracies and the effective number of political parties, statistically have a positive impact on corruption, as predicted in extant studies.

Put together, the case studies of Brazil and India presented in the earlier chapters and the large-n empirical analysis in this chapter show that the causal story described in chapter 2 suggests that legislative rules that enhance party control of the policymaking process in the legislature affects not only the lobbying behavior of business groups but also the level of corruption. The two case studies, in particular, suggest that that business groups are more likely to directly lobby political parties rather than individual legislators when legislative rules in developing democracies formally allow parties to control agenda-setting, introduce amendments to bills on the legislative floor, and expel party members when their voting behavior deviates from the dictates of the party whip. Because business groups lobby political parties instead of individual legislators when rules allow parties to control policymaking dynamics via the drafting of bills in the legislature, we observe higher levels of corruption as shown empirically in this chapter. What are the substantive implications of the empirical findings presented in the two case studies and in this chapter for academics and for policymaking? I attempt to answer this question in the concluding chapter of this book.

7

CONCLUSION

Robert Reich (2008), U.S. secretary of labor under Bill Clinton, argues that market forces have increasingly used money to achieve their goals politically, creating corruption. The result, he claims, is that "supercapitalism" has replaced "democratic capitalism," leading to an imbalance in the political provision of private and social goods. In contrast, Edward Busek, the vice-chancellor of Austria and the Special Coordinator for the Stability Pact for Southeastern Europe (Financial Times, April 2, 2008), argued that unless the business community organized and lobbied actively for its policy preferences, governments would not act to improve their policy design or implementation. "The business community must find ways to influence policy development," he urged. The MPs in the Czech parliament agreed with him that lobbying was "an important part of a modern political system" and a desirable element of society that could be conducted in an ethical manner (Donath-Burson and Marstellar 2005). However, Vaclav Klaus in his premiership of the Czech Republic in 1997 echoed Reich's fears when he stated that he wanted to "dissolve dangerous lobbying, rent-seeking, protectionist organizations, pressure groups and so on" (quoted in O'Mahoney 2003:, 190).

The intensity of this debate regarding the nature of the relationship between business lobbying and corruption in rich countries with considerable experience of markets and democratic politics, and in the context of established legal and judicial systems and free media underlines the deeper consequences of this relationship for the stability and prosperity of developing countries without these institutional advantages. These differences in opinions regarding the necessity of a close relationship between business and politics for social and economic progress, and, its potential costs to society, has a venerable intellectual history dating back to Tocqueville. The following conclusions reached by two recent studies on corruption and lobbyists summarize the reasons why policymakers, scholars, and citizens in contemporary democracies are still struggling with this dilemma:

Despite the popular association of lobbyists with corruption, it would be very difficult for government officials to conduct the public's business without lobbyists. . . . lobbyists serve an invaluable function in democratic governance. They provide useful information and expertise to government officials on any given matter. They represent interests that may be adversely and unintentionally impacted by a poorly deliberated public policy. And they translate into understandable terms everything from scientific data to public opinions. Just as importantly, lobbyists then inform their employers and clients of the actions of government officials, helping hold the government accountable and assisting to effectuate compliance with the laws. (Report on Lobbyists, Government and Public Trust, OECD 2009, 18)

    Failure to curb undue influence lays the foundations for a kleptocratic state, stunted economic and political development, and, perhaps most perniciously, a citizenry that loses trust in a fair democratic bargain, with dramatic consequences for the viability of the entire political and economic system. (Global Report on Corruption, Transparency International 2009, 39)

However, countries such as Estonia, Taiwan, and Chile are examples showing that the benefits of positive business influence do not have to come at the cost of high corruption and that this balance can be managed productively. The key is to understand which factors are more likely to skew this relationship toward the practice of corrupt behaviors making a country more prone to corruption and to design reforms to constrain them accordingly. In this book, I have identified one such conditioning factor that has received surprisingly little attention in the corruption literature—the design of policymaking legislative institutions.

In the rest of this chapter I first put the findings of this book in theoretical and empirical perspective and then discuss its scope and limitations in addressing the relationship between business lobbying and corruption. Next, I discuss how these findings expand our understanding of corruption as a multicausal phenomenon, allow us to identify the dynamics underlying varieties of corrupt behaviors, and provide some insights into designing better anticorruption measures. This is followed by a discussion of this book's contributions to the theoretical and empirical literature on comparative lobbying and on lobbying regulations intended to curb corrupt practices. I conclude by discussing some implications.

DISCUSSION OF FINDINGS

To address the complex puzzle of corruption, this book started with three questions. Why do some developing democracies experience much higher levels of corruption than others? How is the behavior of business interest groups related to corruption? How do legislative institutions governing the policy process promote or restrain corruption through the rules of engagement they provide to political and business actors? The analysis in this book shows that one of the important reasons that some developing democracies experience more corruption than others is because of the *manner* in which legislative institutions structure how business and political elites groups engage with each other to influence policy.

Legislative institutions are important in incentivizing more or less corrupt behaviors by business and political elites because they establish incentives that make certain corruption prone lobbying strategies more effective than others. Legislative lobbying can be a potentially important source of corruption in any developing country democracy, but there are specific institutional conditions that magnify its significance as a source of corruption. Specifically, when legislative institutions on agenda-setting, introduction of amendments, and antiwhip voting privilege party control of legislative policymaking, groups lobby parties and corruption is higher relative to countries where parties do not enjoy these institutional privileges and individual legislators are lobbied instead. The high ability of parties to leverage their influence over the legislative policy process to supply their greater financial demands therefore leads to higher corruption.

The channels through which corruption due to legislative lobbying takes place, and the additional institutions that get co-opted into supporting these corrupt exchanges, are distinct in the two types of legislative systems. Money flows are centralized and constructed vertically in party-focused systems with significant flows originating from a large share of captured state institutions. In individual-focused legislative systems, money flows are decentralized with few vertical flows beyond the legislators concerned, and state institutions will only be sporadic, ad hoc originators of such revenue streams flowing to individual legislators. Therefore, the patterns of corruption that occur in the two systems are distinct and will require different anticorruption tactics.

The empirical results in chapters 4 and 5 strongly support the mechanism of legislative lobbying as a source of corruption in both countries and the *difference* in legislative lobbying patterns as a significant source of *difference* in their corruption levels. They also confirm the distinct patterns of corruption they create in the two types of systems. The results in chapter 6 generalize these theoretical implications beyond the two cases by providing robust empirical support for the links among these three legislative rules and corruption levels in developing democracies. Since the quantitative results are inferred from a fairly comprehensive sample of sixty-four democracies from the developing world between 1984 and 2004, the key empirical findings reported here are quite generalizable across space and time.

The quantitative analyses also find that several economic control variables—such as trade openness and the size of government—that have been identified as important in many studies do not have a statistically substantial impact on corruption once party control over legislative policymaking has been accounted for. At the same time, however, these results confirm current findings that key political variables such as the presence of a presidential system and the effective number of political parties have a statistically significant positive impact on corruption.

Collectively, the case studies of Brazil and India and the large-n empirical analysis in chapter 6 support the causal story that legislative rules which enhance party control of the policymaking process in the legislature affect the level of corruption a country experiences by affecting the lobbying behavior of the business groups there. In party-focused countries, the benefits of business lobbying come at a very high price. Whereas in countries with institutions that incentivize individual-focused lobbying patterns, the benefits of lobbying are accompanied by significantly lower levels of corruption. Therefore the answer to solving the dilemma posed by this relationship should rest partly on how political control over its legislative policy process is structured. I now discuss how these findings influence our understanding of corruption, lobbying, and the role that party systems play in connecting the two.

CORRUPTION

Scholars have exhaustively demonstrated that corruption is a complex, multicausal phenomenon. Thus, I do not argue here that legislatively induced lobbying is the only significant source of corruption in developing countries. Rather, I argue that legislative institutions are a frequently *overlooked* source of corruption with considerable explanatory powers. Since larger shares of political funds are increasingly coming from business interests seeking to influence policy, an understanding of the institutional policymaking incentives that shape their lobbying strategies should provide valuable insights into corruption in these countries. I find that when legislative rules allow parties to control agenda-setting, corruption is higher by 11.2%; when parties control the amendments process, corruption is higher by 9%; and when legislative rules allow parties to strip dissident voters of their legislative mandate, corruption goes up by 10.5%. Collectively, the adoption of these three legislative rules alone can cause corruption to increase by almost 30% in a country. These effects are substantial in the context of a multicausal phenomenon. The results hold after controlling for various institutional and socioeconomic sources of corruption including electoral rules, federalism, executive regime type, income rules of law, and freedom of media, and they hold for all three measures of corruption used widely by scholars.

Recall from chapter 6 that these three legislative rules showed considerable variation within each category of electoral rule and executive regime and are only weakly correlated with them. While agenda-setting and amendments show moderate correlation, the voting expulsions rule is not even moderately with either agenda-setting or amendments. These empirical results therefore provide strong support for the argument that legislative institutions are an additional, frequently overlooked, and important source of corruption. Understanding how these legislative rules create incentives that support or oppose those created by these other institutions therefore allows us to expand our understanding of how the full array of institutional choices countries make—electoral, executive, federal, and legislative—affects corruption.

As scholars of corruption have long noted, one of the most significant variables missing from the analysis of corruption are political parties (Shugart 1999; Bull and Newell 2003; Kunicova 2006; Lambsdorff 2006). The analysis here speaks to this concern directly by analyzing the impact of legislative institutions and of special interest groups on the relationship between party leaders and party members. Many scholars have argued that in systems with strong parties, corruption will be lower. Far-sighted leaders use party discipline to ensure corruption-free behavior by their members in order to attract voters (Manow 2005). Corrupt party leaders concentrate rent-extraction in their own hands to prevent overgrazing of common pool party assets by members, thus lowering aggregate corruption (Gerring and Thacker 2004, 2008; Rasmussen and Ramseyer 1994; Shleifer and Vishny 1993). Furthermore, these scholars have argued that parties can achieve economies of scale in campaigning and organization which lowers corruption as well when parties are strong. In contrast, other scholars have argued that strong parties increase corruption (Mueller 2006; Bull and Newell 2003; Bleichinger 2002). The findings in this book support the second argument. To the extent that higher legislative policy influence strengthens party leaders, the results here show that stronger parties raise corruption in developing country democracies.

The prediction of higher corruption from strong parties in this book stems from a different view of the role party leaders play in "managing" political assets such as state resources and institutions. Rather than providing a fixed common pool of resources that can be overgrazed, these results suggest that party assets resemble inputs into a rent production process. High legislative discipline allows party leaders to use these political inputs to produce a higher volume of the existing influence products but also to create *new* influence products. Far from lowering corruption by preventing corrupt behaviors by its members, party strength allows party leaders to use party members and public officials more *creatively* and thus more *productively* to extract higher rent from their legislative tenure. Furthermore, since only parties represented in the legislature have access to the legislative process, the market for legislative policy influence parties run will operate as an oligopoly rather than the competitive market that will be run by legislators in an individual-focused system. This will allow party leaders to charge higher prices than those that can be demanded by legislators operating in their competitive influence market.

Consider the following two examples of corruption discussed in chapter 2. In Romania, a new corruption scheme was implemented when political parties used their influence over bank officials to systematically identify firms in debt and then offered to reschedule their debt via legislation for a financial consideration (OSI 2002; Bryan and Baer 2005). These parties leveraged their ability to influence and control legislation to invent and pull off a new, complex, multi-institutional corruption scam geared to a specific consumer market—debtor firms. Similarly, in Indonesia, parties first used their influence to ensure some public contracts were awarded to real collaborating firms and then set up front firms which jointly extracted rents from the state using party-generated "business proposals" (Mientzner 2007). This new scheme was also designed with the explicit cooperation of specific partners—business firms—and the rents were realized as a joint effort by creative party managers and businesses. Here, parties used their influence over bureaucratic appointments and budgets to co-opt state administrations into approving these scams.

In both cases, parties leveraged their legislative influence to create a valuable new influence product for a business market that was willing to pay for it. Since individual legislators do not command such influence networks, they cannot ex-ante guarantee the legislative approval necessary to enact such complex schemes or extend their influence beyond the legislature to systemically use other state institutions for this purpose. Thus, they have less leverage to produce more of existing influence products and to create new influence products and cannot extract similar levels of rents from legislative office as parties. While some individual legislators may sometimes strike such ad hoc deals on a limited basis with corrupt state officials, they do not have the influence to construct a comparable rent machine. Whereas the stronger party influence is, the higher the ability of parties to create such new products will be when they control legislation. This suggests that the partisan corruption rent-production function in party-focused countries may be characterized by increasing returns to party strength.

Scholars of collective action theory stress that structural factors such as the scale of the production function affect the nature of the solution reached in collective action problems especially in terms of its distributional and welfare consequences (Ostrom 2009, 202; Marwell and Oliver 1993; Hardin 1976). In the party-focused case, increasing returns to party control over legislative policy would yield increasing returns to its members as well. Since individual legislators in a party-focused system cannot match the party's "technology" for producing corrupt rents, they have the incentives to cooperate rather than defect from the collective solution. As a result, rent production, though centrally managed, results in higher and more pervasive *aggregate* corruption in these countries. The strong empirical results from the analysis in this book suggest that this model of increasing returns in production might be a better fit than the fixed common pool model typically applied to study the role of party leaders. Future work should aim at theoretically fleshing out these implications for micro-mechanisms and testing them empirically.

Collectively, these results suggest that any reforms aimed at containing corruption must account for the nature of the political and policy incentives offered by legislative institutions. The findings in this book support those who have argued for strengthening regulation of parties to promote intraparty democracy and enabling institutions, members, and civil society groups to act as checks on party leaderships (Carothers 2008; Johnston 2005). Strengthening parties in countries with high corruption levels will lead to even higher and more pervasive corruption. As chapter 2 argued, even personally incorruptible party leaders may be compelled to engage in unethical practices in order to fund the various tasks a strong, successful party must perform in order to deliver performance to its voters, its financiers, and to its own members. Contrary to the expectations in the literature, rather than expelling all or even most corruption-prone members, leaders of strong parties may choose to punish only those who exhibit too much initiative in enriching themselves at the expense of the party, those who cross acceptable levels of corruption, or those who get caught and become public relations liabilities. Indeed, successful exploitation of state- or local-level resources may be seen as a promising trait that contributes to the making of a rising star within a party. The rise to party leadership positions by such leaders would lead to much higher levels of rent extraction as it would combine the goals of higher levels of top-down corruption with the means of more efficient policymaking and influence-peddling powers of strong parties.

The evidence in this book therefore argues that anticorruption efforts must work within the institutional context of a country if they are to gain a footing in a country's political environment and sustain their momentum. Creating anticorruption bodies, which have the authority and the technical skills to audit individual accounts and to strip those found violating regulations, is a strategy that is more technically feasible and more politically sustainable in countries with individual-focused systems. These reforms should therefore be at the core of anticorruption efforts in these countries. Empowering parliament to initiate investigations and lift the immunity of individuals is also more likely to succeed in such environments. While these trends are clearly evident in Brazil, as I argue above, there are theoretical reasons to expect them to succeed in other individual-focused countries as well. The Carter Center, for example, is currently helping develop such programs in many Latin American countries which have such institutional configurations and are reporting some improvements already (Fontana 2007).

However, as these findings suggest, focusing auditing efforts on individual accounts in a party-focused country will miss most of the financial action taking place. The emphasis in these countries should be on empowering individual party members to be more institutionally engaged with their party leaders so transparency is increased, on incentivizing parties to build policy capacity to increase the value of information in lobbying, and, most importantly, on boosting the technical capacity of existing electoral and auditing bodies and civil society groups. Thus, efforts by the World Bank to train parliamentarians in the practice of budgetary supervision, committee work, and policy networking with other parliamentarians is a more promising anticorruption strategy in party-focused systems (World Bank 2008, 11–12). Similarly, efforts aimed at installing mandatory online party bookkeeping systems, training officials in the accounting skills required to use them for detection, and public dissemination of reports and auditor evaluations by NGOs is more likely to reveal financing inconsistencies and make them politically costly. Programs in Latin America, Thailand, and Cambodia based on training party officials and auditors in reporting practices are seeing some success (Fontana 2007).

Finally, efforts should be made to explicitly incentivize parties to create and build reputations based on their policy knowledge and expertise thus raising the value of information relative to money in these systems. This could be done by extending technical and administrative support to help parties develop intraparty groups composed of party members with the technical skills and policy experience necessary to engage in policy analysis, and by developing mechanisms to publicize the positions and policy analyses produced by these groups to voters, interest groups, and donors through various means including NGOs and the media. If parties experience electoral payoffs from their policy reputations, they are more likely to promote and invest in party members who have these skills and to value groups who can provide them with technical information and skills.

This could potentially make parties accessible and attractive to professionals who have felt alienated from politics by corrupt leaderships and change intraparty culture to some extent. It can also work to raise voter knowledge and expectations as they receive technically competent policy analyses from competing parties and give more weight to these factors in their voting behavior. It may also encourage more groups to lobby using information and their technical expertise because information becomes a more politically valuable commodity in such a political environment. In the long run, this may also incentivize parties to invest more resources in building their electoral base on their policy reputations rather than in vote-buying. Foreign donors such as the OAS, UNDP, USAID, and various party foundations who are currently funding party development in these countries are well positioned to initiate such efforts.

COMPARATIVE THEORY OF INTEREST GROUP BEHAVIOR

Scholars of interest group politics have investigated how institutions affect the choice of venues (Walker 1991; Cowhey and McCubbins 1993; Rockman and Weaver 1993; De Figueirdo and de Figuerido 2002; Holyoke 2003; Naoi and Krauss 2009) and the choice of tactics and tools (Austen-Smith 1993, 1994; Wright 1996; Hojnacki and Kimball 1998; Yackee and Yackee 2006; Hall and Deardorff 2006). The dominant theoretical and empirical focus in the special interest lobbying literature has been on the United States, a few Western European countries and to some extent European Union (EU) lobbying. Most comparative efforts have focused on how electoral rules (Persson and Tabellini 2004; Grossman and Helpman 2000; Naoi and Krauss 2009) and parliamentary and presidential regimes influence lobbying behaviors (Rockman and Weaver 1993; Cowhey and McCubbins 1993). Recent work has begun to extend this investigation to study how legislative institutions drive these choices (Feldman and Bennedssen 2002, 2006; Iaryczower et al. 2006; Hall and Deardorff 2006). This book contributes to this literature by specifying which legislative rules matter in influencing these choices and why.

While agenda-setting rules have received some attention, amendments and, especially, the ability of parties to expel antiwhip voters have not received much attention as influential determinants of lobbying strategies in the literature. The evidence in chapter 4 shows clearly that the amendments and voting stages are considered important to policymaking by business lobbies and the ability to influence policy through these actions is prized by them. Their lobbying strategy is therefore rationally driven substantially by their perception of which political principals can exert influence over these policymaking stages. Furthermore, these data also show that appointed positions in the legislature, such as procedural officers and committees, are assessed and targeted by lobbies in the context of these three rules. Since acquiring these positions requires legislative approval, groups target the political principals exercising that influence in a particular legislature. Thus the appointees themselves are rarely targeted for influence in party-focused India since they are not seen to be independent sources of influence. Whereas in Brazil, where parties do not wield such strong legislative influence, legislators are seen as being largely nonpartisan independent appointees and are frequently targeted by interest groups at these points as well.

These findings also speak to the literature on determinants of lobbying tools. Work primarily within the context of lobbying in the United States has explored how lobbying choices regarding the choice of tools, especially money and information, are made (Austen-Smith 1993, 1994; Wright 1996; Dahm and Porteiro 2004; Bennedson and Feldman 2005; Hall and Deardorff 2006). Whether interest groups use lobbying to influence the preferences of like-minded political principals (Deardorff and Hall 2006) or policymakers on all sides of the issue that they consider politically useful (Holyoke 2003), and whether they do so to persuade them to change their preferences (Austen-Smith 1993; Wright 1996) or to just buy their support (Hall and Deardoff 2006; Stokes 2005), I have argued that the *choice* of political venue is the dominant influence on the choice of tool. Party-directed lobbying is far more likely to be implemented using money than information compared to individual-focused lobbying strategies. The data on choice of tools presented in chapters 4 and 5 strongly support this claim.

These institutionally motivated venue and tool choices dominate the lobbying patterns of both countries and do not vary by group characteristics such as sector, size, concentration, or age. Thus, business groups from the two countries from similar sectors, of similar size and concentrations and of similar age, show little similarity in venue choice or tool choice. These two cases strongly support the theoretical framework on determinants of these lobbying behaviors but they can only be treated as suggestive and must be complemented with large-n analysis of lobbying as more data becomes available.

These findings of preferences in venue choice and tool choice also have implications for the nature and composition of the interest group community in a country. Party-focused lobbying requires higher resources and should privilege bigger groups and the building of group alliances. If a few big groups come to dominate the interest group community of a country, the extent to which public policy is skewed by parties to favor them might be higher and/or more persistent compared to the policy bias afforded them in individual-focused systems. Therefore party-focused systems may, under these conditions, sometimes produce less public-regarding policies compared to individual-focused countries and/or produce more stable and high levels of private-regarding policies.

These implications need to be developed and explored further and provide fertile ground for future theorizing and empirical work. The findings in this book thus add to the body of theoretical work on comparative lobbying and to the very small body of comparative empirical work on this topic. They also add to the unfortunately small number of studies exploring special interest group behavior in developing countries.[1] This project is one of a handful to provide such detailed data and empirical findings on institutional interactions and lobbying choices for lobbies in any developing democracies.

Finally, these findings speak to the literature on the choice of lobbying politicians or bureaucrats (de Figuerido and de Figuerido 2002; Davis 2003, 2004; Naoi and Krauss 2009) and to the emerging strand of work studying the relationship between lobbying and corruption (Harstad and Svensson 2009; Kaufman and Vicente 2008; Chari et al. 2007; Campos and Giovannoni 2007, 2008; Damania et al. 2004). The findings here add further nuance to their work by incorporating the impact of other key features of legislative organization that affect the behavior of organized interests. The theoretical framework in this book builds on prior results of the delegation literature to specify the conditions under which the relationship between politicians and bureaucrats will lead to higher corruption—when party-focused institutions allow political principals to incorporate bureaucrats into their influence-peddling networks. The choice of lobbying political principals or bribing bureaucrats is embedded in this context and must be analyzed within it. If bureaucrats are co-opted by parties, this choice is a false dichotomy since money will flow from the bureaucrats to the political principals. If they are not, then bureaucrats and legislators may offer genuinely independent choices. As chapters 4 and 5 showed, this fits the empirical patterns of lobbying and corruption observed in the two cases discussed in this project and also is consistent with anecdotal evidence from other countries. This suggests that this research question must be embedded in the delegation literature theoretically.

Empirically, the detailed data from the two case studies allow me to address some of the problems scholars have faced in studying lobbying and its relationship to corruption albeit for only two countries. Chapter 4 presented detailed evidence on the institutional interactions of business lobbies with different political players, the executive, parties, legislators, their choice of political venue, and their choice of tools. Chapter 5 presented detailed evidence on the relationship between lobbying strategies, varieties of corrupt behaviors, and corruption levels. These data show that lobbies discriminate between different channels of political corruption, in other words, between party- and legislator-based bribing and that their strategy to bribe bureaucrats may be a function of which type of political principal they choose to bribe. It shows that lobbying strategy significantly affects bureaucratic corruption levels, but the magnitude of this effect depends on which political principal is lobbied. Bribery in the bureaucracy was strongly associated with bribery in the political establishment in India but not in Brazil. This is reinforced by the strong association seen between party corruption and patronage in party-focused India and the absence of this association in Brazil. This evidence supports the view that the institutional conditions governing the policy process influence whether lobbying political principals and lobbying bureaucrats, through legal or illegal means, are seen as substitutes or complements. Cross-country testing of these relationships should prove useful in refining these relationships further theoretically and establishing which of them hold universally.

Given its potential for driving corruption, what are the options for regulating lobbying behaviors? The universe of countries that have adopted regulations to regulate political lobbying is rather small and includes the United States, the United Kingdom, Germany, Canada, the EU, Chile, Peru, Lithuania, the Czech Republic, Hungary, and Poland (Malone 2004; OECD 2008; McGrath 2008; Evanson 2008). These countries demonstrate the range of models that have been tried so far in order to reduce the impact on corruption. The UK regulation targets the lobbied, the MPs, rather than the lobbyists. This decision was reached after previous attempts to define a lobbyist failed to yield satisfactory consensus (OECD 2008, 59). This new policy has been regarded as being somewhat successful (OECD 2008, 61). The United States, Germany, and Canada on the other hand require lobbyists to register and report their actions. While these regulations have been considerable improvements over the past, they have also been accompanied by many political scandals in all these countries. While they have made more transactions transparent, it is unclear whether they have improved the share of transactions that are transparent (OECD 2008, 71). Australia for example legislated lobbying regulation in 1983 and then revoked it in 1996 due to its unenforceability (Malone 2004, 6). Lastly, the EU has chosen to incentivize groups to register themselves and disclose some basic information. This approach has also revealed mixed results (Warner 2007). The mixed success of efforts to regulate lobbying and make it more transparent in countries with strong legal traditions and stable institutions does not augur well for developing countries, which generally do not enjoy these advantages.

Since 2005, a number of Eastern and Central European countries have adopted regulations that fall into one of these philosophies. Other than Hungary, where scholars report some success, these efforts have largely failed to increase the transparency of lobbying or reduce their impact on corruption (McGrath 2008; Open Society Institute 2002). For example, the Czech Republic followed the UK model and tried to regulate the lobbied, the legislators, but with little success (Open Society Institute 2002, 365). Lithuania was the first country in this bloc to legislate regulation of lobbyists in 2000 but by 2004 these efforts had led to the registration of exactly 7 lobbyists (McGrath 2008, 25). Poland passed a controversial bill in 2006 that created a register and imposed some disclosure and led all of 11 lobbyists to register by 2007 (Warsaw Business Journal 2007).

The Latin American experience is even more discouraging. While a number of countries have contemplated lobbying regulation on numerous occasions, few such as Chile and Peru have actually adopted it (TI 2004). The experience of Argentina is emblematic of the problems these countries face in this endeavor. After 11 bills aimed at regulating lobbying were rejected in congress between 1990 and 2000, the Anti-Corruption Office adopted a participatory process to write the twelfth version in 2001 with the help of various civil society groups (Johnson 2008, 90). After completing this consultation process to design and establish a registry of lobbyists, it then decided that "since there is no tradition or profession of lobbyists in Argentina, a register would have been useless."[2] The increasing prevalence of lobbying in these countries along with the lack of transparency on their operations underlines the need to create regulatory options that can be applied successfully to other developing county contexts.

These experiences suggest that certain principles could be borrowed from many of these approaches. They highlight the importance of introducing transparency and the critical role of civil society watchdogs. The EU approach to incentivize lobbies to disclose by providing carrots such as access and information seems more viable than requiring lobbyists to do so as merely a legal obligation. Individual legislators who are independent of each other's political fortunes in individual-focused systems may be more likely to punish violations when they are detected than party members whose fates are tied to that of their co-partisans in party-focused systems. While regulating the lobbied seems more promising and feasible for individual-focused countries, where the MPs would be the ones disclosing, regulating disclosure of donations by parties remains an issue especially for effective enforcement in party-focused systems. The provision of roll call data could facilitate discovery of such connections, but it is not quite clear how such a politically consequential tactic could be imposed on an institution unless politicians and parties themselves are willing to be scrutinized.

Funding civil society groups to perform watchdog functions, and training them to audit, interpret, and publicize this information in an accessible form to voters, the media, and the authorities, seems like the most promising approach. These groups have the advantage that they can combine the roles of monitoring the donor and the recipient sides of these transactions. As scandals are exposed, it is more likely to put pressure on political parties and politicians to limit their transgressions, to be more transparent, and to build a regulatory framework which the political establishment and the business elites have bought into. Currently however, developing democracies lack groups capable of performing these watchdog functions. Training them requires immediate attention from reformers.

IMPACT OF LEGISLATIVE INSTITUTIONS AND LOBBYING ON PARTIES AND PARTY SYSTEMS

Scholars have increasingly stressed the importance of analyzing how parties behave and evolve between elections in developing an understanding the evolution of party systems (Laver and Benoit 2003; Desposato 2004, 2006; Heller and Mershon 2002, 2008; Janda 2005; Volden and Carruba 2004).[3] Understanding how legislative rules affect party strength allows us to understand the influence of some of these interelection factors on party systems. Recent work, particularly on party switching (Mershon and Shvetsova 2009; Heller and Mershon 2001, 2005; Benoit and Hayden 2001), consolidation of government (Agh 1999; Deiermeir and Merlo 2000), and coalitions (Martin and Vanberg 2004; Lupia and Strom 1995), has increasingly emphasized the impact of legislative rules on party systems (Filippov 2002, 2004; Olson 1994, 1998). As these scholars point out, party–member relations are in constant flux and are the outcomes of strategic calculations by both leaders and their members at all points in the political cycle, not just elections. This book adds to this literature by (a) identifying and analyzing the impact that the design of specific legislative rules has on these calculations directly, and (b) by explicitly integrating how the response of special interests to these legislative incentives magnifies the impact of these institutional rules on intraparty relationships.

The degree of proparty behavior exhibited by legislators between elections is influenced by their personal idealogical and policy preferences as well as their party's. Additionally, the party's ability to influence policy outcomes, a legislator's ability to contribute to that influence, the party's ability to provide valuable appointments and resources to him and its impact on his reelection chances will affect a legislator's loyalty to his party (Heller and Mershon 2008, 912; Desposato 2006, 64; Laver and Benoit 2003, 231). Since legislative rules exert significant influence over all these aspects of political careers, they should exert significant influence over legislator attachment to partisan goals and affiliation.

By exerting influence over the agenda and over amendments, party leaders can deprive a legislator of the opportunity to address constituent policy concerns, direct pork to them, and build his personal reputation within the party, with interest groups, and with voters. All of these have significant consequences for the political careers, rent accumulation, and reelection chances of both office-seeking and policy-seeking party members. Thus they allow party leaders to impose variable costs for a range of political misdemeanors by members. Additionally, the ability to strip members of their mandate gives party leaders the nuclear option of imposing the ultimate cost on members, depriving them of their only guaranteed stint in office—their current term.

Such legislative abilities strengthen parties in three direct ways. First, by strengthening party control over policy, they strengthen party control over the political and policy rewards members can reap from favorable outcomes as well as over the penalties. Thus, they enhance party control over member behavior. Second, by strengthening control over policy outcomes and member behavior, they centralize the rent-generating process in the hands of party leaders. Thus, members must be loyal in order to share in the party's booty and gain from office. Third, policy-seeking rich donors contribute to party coffers rather than to those of individual legislators. This makes rank and file legislators more dependent on parties for resources essential to their careers. Where parties do not have such institutional influence, legislators will have the flexibility to choose whose preferences dominate their strategic calculations—the party's, constituents', or their own. In systems where party leaders do have such powers, they exert considerable powers over the interelection behaviors of their legislative delegations. This implies that parties should be much more likely to exhibit stability between elections when these three rules favor them. Party-focused legislative rules may also be more conducive to creating voter accountability for parties since members cannot be blamed for the failure of attempts to legislate. These implications should be developed further and tested in future work.

SCOPE AND LIMITATIONS OF FINDINGS

As Kaufmann et al. (2006, 73) state, "Because corruption is by its nature an illegal activity, direct measures of its prevalence do not exist." The operational reality of corruption precludes the possibility of using objective proxies such as number of corruption cases filed or convictions, the amounts of money involved, or the number of corruption stories reported in the media (TI 2009; Lambsdorff 2006; Gerring and Thacker 2004, 2008; Bull and Newell 2003; Kang 2002; Rose-Ackerman 1999; Homes and Meier 1988). Best practice in the field to conduct cross-country studies of corruption has therefore been to use the three subjective measures of corruption: the ICRG, the WB, and the TI indices used in this book. Concerns about using these measures relate to the various biases that perceptions might be subject to and to the reliability of using perception-based measures of corruption as opposed to experience-based measures (Knack 2007). However, these three measures possess some critical advantages: they capture de facto prevalence of corrupt practices; they draw more heavily from informed respondents such as business firms and experts; they are provided along with estimates of their reliability, allowing scholars to assess the limitations inherent in their use; and they combine the perspectives of all key stakeholders in society.[4]

Political corruption is inherently not a phenomenon that most public citizens directly participate in as they would in incidents of petty corruption, such as bribing the police or health care officials. However, they do observe its prevalence. Therefore using experience-based measures of corruption does not help us investigate political corruption with more accuracy, but using perception-based measures allows us, with some noise, to measure political corruption levels. The advantages of this study are that in the country surveys, I was able to obtain *both* perception- and experience-based measures from the respondents, business groups, who are by far the most important and frequent participants in the conceptually relevant transactions with political agents involving grand corruption.

As chapter 4 showed, business groups meet with policymakers from different parts of the political establishment with great regularity. Thus, their perceptions of both political and overall corruption are more likely to be informed by their direct experiences and hence should be more reliable. This supports the argument scholars have made that business interests tend to be among the most informed, experienced, and sophisticated observers and consumers of politics and of political opportunities to influence policy outcomes in most countries (Evans 1992; Deardorff 2006, 69; Nownes 2006; Huber and Shipan 2009, 2). As the results from the WEF (2003, 2005) survey showed among developing democracies, this also places them in the pantheon of most knowledgeable participants in corruption transactions. Their perceptions, therefore, should be informed measures of petty and grand corruption.

For Brazil and India, I was able to obtain both experience- and perception-based measures through various questions that related to the impact of corruption groups felt through different channels as well as to the share of contributions they actually made to different actors. These data allowed me to evaluate how reliable perception-versus experience-based measures are in capturing political corruption as well as the strength of the relationship between political and overall corruption for these two countries. The perception- and experience-based measures were consistent, strongly correlated, and differed systematically in the strength of the correlations between petty and grand corruption in line with theoretical expectations for these two cases. In the context of current data, these findings support the use of these corruption indices for large-n analysis. To the extent that real behavior is based on perceptions, decisions by politicians, parties, firms, citizens, NGOs, international agencies, and governments will be driven by these assessments of corruption (Kaufmann 2006, 2008; Lambsdorff 2006). These three measures, TI's CPI index, the World Bank index and the ICRG index, therefore still present researchers with the best available data to assess the *level* of corruption as defined by the *extent* or pervasiveness of corruption and to conduct cross-country analysis over any period of time.

One of the strengths of the analysis presented here is the analysis of nuanced data on corruption and lobbying through the two case studies. By analyzing and empirically testing the micro-level incentives and behaviors relating institutions to corruption via lobbying for the two cases, this book is able to go further in its direct analysis of causal mechanisms than many large-n works are able to. However, two cases, no matter how strongly supportive of the theoretical framework, cannot be considered definitive tests of any hypotheses. As I discussed in chapter 3, despite their similarities in many aspects, Brazil and India are also different from each other and from other developing democracies on dimensions that may matter for understanding corruption in its entire complexity. The TSCS analysis allows us to control for these differences when testing the hypotheses linking legislative institutions to corruption. Since the quantitative results are inferred from a fairly comprehensive sample of sixty-four democracies from the developing world between 1984 and 2004, the key empirical findings reported here are quite generalizable across space and time.

However, in order to test the hypotheses linking institutions to lobbying and lobbying behaviors to corruption with the same level of rigor, we need lobbying data from a large panel of countries which vary in their electoral systems, executive regimes, federal character, per capita income, economic openness, literacy, rule of law, and civic and media freedoms among other factors. Until such time as detailed cross-country group-level data on lobbying behaviors becomes available to scholars, the gradual accumulation of detailed case studies by various scholars might be the most feasible way forward in this research program.

As discussed in the introduction, developed country democracies and authoritarian systems were both explicitly excluded from the scope of this study. Developed country democracies are characterized by stable consolidated institutions, higher institutional capacity, professionalized bureaucracies, and strong legal rule of law. Political parties evolved under very different political conditions in these countries and their organizations and operations are rarely governed by constitutional provisions on party laws (Janda 2005). These political differences are accompanied by freer media and higher per capita incomes. Stronger legal systems and the availability of public money to fund parties and candidates change the nature and the severity of the problem facing business and political elites as well. All of these factors combine to create very different stakes and thus a very different environment for politics compared to developing countries.

While similar institutions may facilitate similar actions in these countries, the costs and consequences of these actions could be very different. For example, while separation of powers and an active federalist structure present in the United States are believed to have increased the incentives for corruption there as well, the presence of a professional judiciary willing to prosecute any political player has in turn ensured that the realization of this potential has been capped at a substantially low level (Glaeser and Goldin 2005, 11). These differences suggest that the strategic solutions for similar problems and their probability of success may well be very different across developed and developing countries. Since cross-country group-level data on lobbying is unavailable for developed countries as well, this question cannot be explored empirically by testing the hypotheses from this book for this set of countries. Theoretically, these differences may or may not be significant enough to warrant a different theoretical approach. The strong results in this book, and the pervasive presence of corruption scandals and rich, well-organized business interests in developed democracies, suggest that the study of the influence of legislative lobbying on corruption should provide rich grounds for future research on these countries.

In the case of authoritarian systems, there exists tremendous diversity in the institutional configurations of these countries (Gandhi and Przeworski 2007). Therefore, any analysis of institutional factors in establishing lobbying can only be applied to countries which have legislatures and must account for differences in how they are constituted. Additionally, these legislatures may or may not have any real policy powers or influence even when they have been constituted (Wright 2008). Factors which influence the existence of legislative institutions in the first place may be directly related to factors that influence business lobbying. In addition, the party system as such may operate under very different rules and only certain parties may be allowed to exist or to compete for legislative positions (Janda 2006). Legislative positions may be appointed by the dictator or the dominant party without any grassroots input. Without a well-specified theoretical framework that addresses the issues of legislative politics and parties in these systems, one cannot proceed to an institutional analysis of lobbying behavior and its relationship to corruption in authoritarian regimes. An analysis of corruption in these countries is undoubtedly a question of considerable academic and policy interest but it goes well beyond the theoretical purview of the current framework and requires an entirely new one.[5]

IMPLICATIONS

The results in this book provide strong evidence that legislatures can exert significant influence on important political and policy outcomes even in developing democracies. They support work by other scholars who have argued for a more nuanced analysis of the impact of legislative institutions on various outcomes (Przeworski et al. 2000; Persson and Tabellini 2000; Haggard and McCubbins 2001; Nacif and Morgerstern 2002; Laver 2006; Cheibub 2007). This project also provides a new dataset on legislative rules that can be used to study their effect on other outcomes of interest to political scientists beyond corruption. One of these interesting questions is: Are strong parties desirable in developing democracies?

Scholars have argued about the tradeoffs of having a system with high interparty competition versus one with high intraparty competition.[6] The central tradeoff is argued to come from the logic that higher intraparty democracy weakens parties themselves as institutions (Joubert 2006; Desposato 2006; Montinola 1999). The findings in this book speak directly to this debate by presenting evidence on the desirability of strong parties in developing countries and on the institutional tools required to create them.

Proponents argue that higher internal party democracy is more inclusive, which promotes more political participation from citizens and also promotes better monitoring of party behavior by its members (Carothers 2006; Scarrow 2005, 12–14). Opponents argue that too much internal democracy handicaps the ability of party leaders to be representative, responsive, and decisive (Desposato 2006; Montinola 1999). In the context of developing countries with nascent party systems, proponents have argued that the ability to penalize members for antiparty behaviors by expelling them helps parties build strong party brands and stabilize party systems(Montinola 1999; Kreuzer and Pettai 2003; Booysen 2006). This in turn should encourage programmatic party competition and better policy programs. The analysis and rules on one such antiparty behavior—party switching—has been central to this debate since those rules directly affect the cost party members pay for exercising free will in the context of no internal democracy. The findings in this book add to this debate by analyzing the impact of another such rule—party ability to expel dissident voters from the party.

The empirical results here show that enhancing party control by reducing the ability of members to vote freely in environments that are not democratically consolidated at the institutional or civic level has a significant cost—higher corruption. In the absence of strong legal checks and balances, parties can use such party strength to exploit all the assets and influence they gain from office. While the party system may exhibit more stability, and party competition may indeed coalesce around a few strong parties, this is of dubious value since the parties themselves may not be public-minded. Higher party competition among these parties will not necessarily reduce corruption or produce public welfare–enhancing policies strong parties have been associated with if these parties use some of those rents to buy votes or to buy enough muscle to effectively outflank opposition to them. These findings thus support the position of those who have argued that systems which promote intraparty democracy, rather than making party members the obedient footmen of party agendas, produce better politics and policymaking. Furthermore, these findings also suggest that other benefits that strong parties are automatically expected to deliver through interparty competition—such as programmatic competition and representative parties with deep roots in society—might be doubtful as well.

Party-directed lobbying can also promote a culture of policy disengagement and low policy knowledge by politicians, which can have much deeper and longer-term effects on the party system. As the data on India show, the result of strong parties are legislators whose ideological or policy preferences are irrelevant in signaling the party brand to interest groups. These groups rarely care about the ideology or competence of the legislators but focus largely on the intentions and ideology of party leaders. Legislators receive little technical information directly from interest groups and enjoy no electoral premium for investing in their policy skills. Their party leaders may or may not put enough value on their policy expertise for it to be an asset, especially in the context that interest groups can supply party leaders with such knowledge. Strong policy preferences may even be a liability for backbenchers rather than an asset as far as party leaders are concerned Thus, these MPs have little motive for investing time and scarce resources into acquiring information and expertise even on policy issues of importance to their constituents.

This could discourage the accumulation of human capital at the heart of the country's policymaking center, depriving constituents of knowledgeable advocates for their local interests, and is more likely to lead to poor-quality policies. On the other hand, individual-focused systems reward legislators who invest in policy knowledge by attracting more money and resources to them. These incentives seem more likely to create a political elite that is better informed and engaged with the policy debates of the time. The characteristics needed to succeed in strong party-systems, on the other hand, do not seem to encourage the emergence and consolidation of programmatic parties.

Furthermore, in party-focused lobbying systems, elected legislators have to be more responsive to their party's needs rather than to their voters, which makes them both less representative of and less responsive to their voters. If party leaders choose to distort policy outcomes to favor their donors rather than the public, legislators have less capacity to stop them. Especially in developing democracies where alternative sources of political finance are hard to find, this is more likely to create parties that are less connected to society at large and are captured by social and business elites. Their policy agendas may also be more vulnerable to being hijacked by a few entrenched interests in such systems.

The result can be more social damage since the party's capacity to implement such distortionary policies is higher than that of individual legislators. Foreign aid directed at strengthening parties in such systems will thus further damage the political systems of these countries and make them even less accountable to members and voters (Carothers 2001). Furthermore, corrupt and strong parties that privilege party loyalty so disproportionately over ideological affinity and policy skills are more likely to attract instrumental politicians who see political office as the means to a good life rather than as public service. This can lower the image and dignity of political life in the public mind and discourage more ideological and public-spirited people from entering into politics, thus affecting the very fabric of the country's political life. Party programs are more likely to be the programs of a few elite leaders, rather than being representative of the preferences of a larger set of politically engaged citizens. Such democracies can therefore fall into a vicious trap where the party system is dominated by a few strong parties composed of instrumental, rent-seeking leaders and members who are disconnected from society, less accountable to it, and professionally inaccessible to its higher-minded citizens.

Lastly, these findings speak to the discussion of how party laws influence party systems and whether the presence of party laws explains differences between parties in developed and developing country democracies. Based on an analysis of 1,101 party laws, Janda (2005, 23) notes that while party laws are rarely part of the constitution in developed democracies, they are frequently so in developing country democracies. Given that these laws determine important aspects of the form, substance, and operations of parties, they have the potential to exert significant effects on their behavior and on the evolution of party systems in these countries. Muller (2002, 262), for example, calls them "the most direct form of state intervention in party politics." Given the constitutional status of these rules, it is also harder to change them once they are in place. By influencing these aspects of party organization and operations, party law can also influence the degree of democracy present and the direction in which it is being changed (Carothers 2006, 194). The ability to expel members from the party, which is constitutionally enshrined, is one such party law. Thus understanding its effects can help us understand one of the ways in which party law can impact party and political behavior in society and the nature and type of democracy being built.

APPENDIX A

The Tobit "Right-Censored" Model

As emphasized earlier in chapter 6, the dependent variable *Corruption* (ICRG, TI, and WB)—denoted as y_{it}—may be potentially censored from above (specifically 6 in the ICRG case, 10 for the TI measure, and 5 for the WB measure). In order to account for the right censoring problem in the dependent variable when estimating the empirical model—while retaining the OLS assumption of normally distributed errors—I employ the Tobit model (Maddala 1983; Tobin 1958) with a lagged latent dependent variable. This model is formally defined as:

$$y_{it} = \begin{cases} y_{it}^* = x_{it}\beta + \gamma y_{it-1} + \varepsilon_{it} & \text{if} \quad y_{it}^* < \theta \\ \theta_y & \text{if} \quad y_{it}^* \geq \theta \end{cases} \tag{5.1}$$

where y_{it}^* is the dependent variable, θ is the threshold for right censoring, y_{it-1} is the lag of the observed dependent variable, $t = 1, \ldots, T$ and $i = 1, \ldots, N$. The vector of explanatory variables is given by x_{it} with β as its associated vector of coefficients. Since the data is TSCS, I estimate the Tobit model (with a lagged dependent variable) via fixed effects.

APPENDIX B

List of Primary and Secondary Sources Used
to Code Independent Variables

B.1 GENERAL SOURCES:

Arthur S. Banks, *Political Handbook of the World* (New York: McGraw-Hill, various years)

Arthur S. Banks, Alan J. Day, and Thomas C. Muller, *Political Handbook of the World 1997* (New York: McGraw-Hill, 1997)

Inter-Parliamentary Union (Parline Database, http://www.ipu.org/parline-e/parlinesearch.asp)

Keesing's Contemporary Archives (London: Keesing's Limited, various years)

Library of Congress Country Studies (http://lcweb2.loc.gov/frd/csquery.html)

Library of Congress Portals to the World (http://www.loc.gov/rr/international/portals.html)

Regional Surveys of the World (London: Europa Publications, various years)

Valentine Herman, *Parliaments of the World: A Reference Compendium* (New York: DeGruyter, 1976)

Inter-Parliamentary Union, *Parliaments of the World: A Comparative Reference Compendium,* 2nd ed. (Aldershot, UK: Gower House, 1986)

Gerhard Loewenberg, Peverill Squire, and D. Roderick Kiewiet, eds., *Legislatures: Comparative Perspectives on Representative Assemblies* (Ann Arbor: University of Michigan Press, 2002)

Worldmark Encyclopedia of Nations (1995), CAPEL (various years)

Inter-Parliamentary Union's website at http://www.ipu.org/parline-e/parlinesearch.asp.

B.2 AFRICA:

Michael Bratton and Nicolas Van de Walle, *Political Regimes and Regime Transitions in Africa: A Comparative Handbook* (East Lansing: Department of Political Science, Michigan State University, 1996)

Marion Doro, ed., *Africa Contemporary Record: Annual Survey and Documents* (New York: Africana, various years)

Shaheen Mozaffar, "Africa: Electoral Systems in Emerging Democracies," in Joseph Colomer, ed., *The Handbook of Electoral System Choice* (New York: Palgrave, 2003)

Dieter Nohlen, Michael Krennerich, and Bernhard Thibaut, eds., *Elections in Africa: A Data Handbook* (Oxford: Oxford University Press, 1999)

B.3 ASIA:

Dieter Nohlen, Florian Grotz, and Christof Hartman, eds., *Elections in Asia and the Pacific: A Data Handbook* (Oxford: Oxford University Press, 2001)

Nizam Ahmed, "In Search of Institutionalisation: Parliament in Bangladesh," in Philip Norton and Nizam Ahmed, eds., *Parliaments in Asia* (London: Frank Cass, 1999)

Chong Lim Kim and Seong-Tong Pai, *Legislative Process in Korea* (Seoul: Seoul National University Press, 1999)

Philip Norton and Nizam Ahmed, eds., *Parliaments in Asia* (London: Frank Cass, 1999)

Rommel C. Banlaoi and Clarita R. Carlos, *Political Parties in the Philippines: From 1900 to the Present* (Makati City, Philippines: Konrad Adenauer Foundation, 1996)

Choe Yonhyok, *How to Manage Free and Fair Elections: A Comparison of Korea, Sweden, and the United Kingdom* (Goteburg: Goteburg University, 1997)

B.4 LATIN AMERICA:

Grace Ivana Dehesa, "Gobiernos de Coalicion en el Sistema Presidencial: America del Sur" [Coalition governments in presidential systems: South America] (doctoral dissertation, European University Institute, Florence, 1997)

Dieter Nohlen, ed., *Enciclopedia electoral Latinoamericana y del Caribe* [Electoral encyclopedia of Latin America and the Caribbean] (San Jose, Costa Rica: Instituto Interamericana de Derechos Humanos, 1993)

Political Database of the Americas (http://www.georgetown.edu/pdba/english.html)

Arturo Valenzuela, "Party Politics and the Crisis of Presidentalism in Chile" In The Failure of Presidential Democracy Vol.2 Editors J. Linz and A. Valenzuela (Baltimore, MD: Johns Hopkins University, 1994)

Abdo I. Baaklini, *The Brazilian Legislature and Political System* (Westport, Conn.: Greenwood, 1992)

Octavio Amorim Neto and Eric Magar, "Veto Bargaining and Coalition Formation: A Theory of Presidential Policymaking with Application to Venezuela" (paper delivered at the 22nd International Congress of the Latin American Studies Association, Miami, 2000)

Daniel Chasquetti, "Multipartidismo, coaliciones y estabilidad democratica en America Latina" (Master's thesis, Universidad de la Republica, Montevideo, Uruguay, 2001)

Bonnie Field, "Frozen Democracy?" (paper delivered at the 22nd International Congress of the Latin American Studies Association, Miami, 2000)

Argelina Cheibub Figueiredo, "Government Performance in Multiparty Presidential Systems: The Experiences of Brazil" (paper delivered at the 18th IPSA World Congress, Quebec City, 2000)

Andres Mejia-Acosta, "Weak Coalitions and Policy Making in the Ecuadorian Congress (1979–1996)" (paper delivered at the Annual Meeting of the Latin American Studies Association, Miami, 2000)

Peter Siavelis, *The President and the Congress in Postauthoritarian Chile: Institutional Constraints to Democratic Consolidation* (University Park: Pennsylvania State University Press, 2000)

Michelle Taylor-Robinson, "Candidate Selection in Costa Rica" (paper delivered at the 23rd International Congress of the Latin American Studies Association, Washington, D.C., 2001)

Michelle Taylor-Robinson and Christopher Diaz, "Who Gets Legislation Passed in a Marginal Legislature and Is the Label Marginal Legislature Still Appropriate? A Study of the Honduran Congress," *Comparative Political Studies* 32 (1999): 590–626

N. Guillermo Molinelli, M. Valeria Palanza, and Gisela Sin, *Congreso, Presidencia y Justicia en la Argentina* (Buenos Aires: Temas Grupo Editorial, 1999)

Boletin Electoral LatinoamericanoVarious years.

B.5 EASTERN AND CENTRAL EUROPE AND FORMER SOVIET UNION

Attila Ágh and Sandor Kurtan, *The First Parliament (1990–1994): Democratization and Europeanization in Hungary* (Budapest: Hungarian Centre for Democracy Studies, 1995)

Thomas F. Remington, *The Russian Parliament* (New Haven, Conn.: Yale University Press, 2001)

George Tsebelis and Tatiana Rizova, "Presidential Conditional Agenda Setting in the Former Communist Countries," *Comparative Political Studies* 40 (10): 1155–1182.

Peter Kopecký, "Parliaments in Central and Eastern Europe: Changing Legislative Institutions." *Czech Sociological Review* 3 (2005): 361–373

Peter Kopecký, "Power to the Executive! The Changing Executive-Legislative Relations in Eastern Europe," *Journal of Legislative Studies* 10, nos. 2–3: 142–153

NOTES

Chapter 1

1. The figures the WEF (2003) survey obtained are representative of other studies on business perceptions of these countries. The findings showed that 69.3% rated Taiwan as satisfactory on the level of illegal corporate corruption as opposed to 30.1% in Argentina, 44.6% rated legal corruption levels by corporations as satisfactory compared to 16.2% in Argentina, while 57% in Taiwan rated public-sector corruption as being low enough to be satisfactory compared to Argentina where only 21.8% thought so.

2. See Rose-Ackerman (1999, 2006), UNDP (2001), World Bank (2006), OECD (2008), and Transparency International (2009) for discussions of various aspects of these behaviors around the world.

3. Some scholars go further and define corruption as a violation of not just legal but also social norms (Gerring and Thacker 2004, 300). However, social norms are culturally defined which makes this a difficult concept to compare internationally. Furthermore, as I discuss next, given the measurement problems inherent in measuring corruption this poses a formidable problem in quantifying corruption that results from a violation of just social norms.

4. State capture refers to "the action of individuals, groups, or firms both in the public and private sectors to influence the formation of laws, regulations, decrees, and other government policies to their own advantage" (World Bank 2000, xv). Patronage and nepotism refer to "favoritism shown to narrowly targeted interests by those in power in return for political support" (World Bank 2007, 3). Bureaucratic corruption is defined as "the intentional imposition of distortions in the prescribed implementation of existing laws, rules, and regulations to provide advantages to individuals in and/or outside government through illicit, nontransparent means" (World Bank 2000, xvii).

5. Scholars have found that at the country level political or grand corruption tends to be heavily correlated with overall levels of corruption (Lambsdorff 1999). In this book, I will argue that grand and petty corruption behaviors are *systemically* correlated, either strongly or weakly, as a function of the *type* of political agent who dominates the political and policy life in a country. In countries where these behaviors are strongly correlated, corruption levels will be high, otherwise they will be low. In chapter 2, I lay out the precise causal links that lead to these distinct outcomes.

6. Some researchers have made a distinction between the use of legal and illegal lobbying tools by associating them with legal and illegal corruption. They define legal corruption as "the manipulation of formal legal processes to produce laws (and thus legally sanctioned rules) that benefit private interests at huge expense to the general public" (World Bank 2007, 9). Legal corruption therefore involves the use of legal lobbying tools, such as legal campaign

contributions, and formal official exchanges between lobbyists and government officials. Lobbying using illegal tools is then classified as illegal corruption. The few efforts at measuring the relationship between the two "types" of corruption show that the correlation between them is in fact very strong at 0.86, i.e., countries that have high illegal corruption are the ones also experiencing more legal corruption (WEF 2005, author's calculations).This is not a meaningful distinction in most developing countries where weak rule of law typically makes the marginal cost of substituting between legal and illegal lobbying resources negligible for most elites. However, this is a false dichotomy even in developed countries as the distinction between "legal" and "illegal" forms of corruption has been regarded more frequently as a reflection of regulatory convenience rather than substantive intent (WEF 2007, 90).

7. See Mauro (1995), Bardhan (1997), Krueger (1997), Rose-Ackerman (1999, 2005, 2006), Treisman (1999, 2007), Lambsdorff (2006), and Gerring and Thacker (2004, 2008) for discussions of the various strands of these two literatures connecting higher economic competition and political competition to lower corruption.

8. See for example, TI Global Corruption Report (2008), Knack (2006), Rose-Ackerman (2007), and Kaufman and Vicente (2008).

9. See Transparency International (2009), Austin and Tjernström (2003), Bryan and Baer (2005), USAID (2003), and IFES (2008). I discuss the key findings from these studies in the first section of chapter 2.

10. See, e.g., Mauro (1995), Keefer and Knack (1995), Svenssen (2000), Gupta et al. (2002), Ali and Isse (2003), World Bank (2005), Lambsdorff 2006, and Treisman 2007 for a discussion of various aspects of these issues. Chapter 6 provides a detailed discussion of this literature.

11. See Montinola and Jackman (2002), Seligson (2002), Rose-Ackerman (1999), Theobald (1982), and Tulchin and Espach (2000).

12. This impact can be felt not just through higher costs of doing business but also through other channels such as lower productivity, lower bureaucratic quality, bias in public investment such as education and infrastructure, etc. See Lambsdorff (2006) for further discussion.

13. See Transparency International Annual Report (2004) for details of these corruption cases.

14. For example, around 2005 Poland, Lithuania, and Hungary all introduced legislation requiring all entities who lobbied the legislature to register with the government and to declare various details of their interactions with officials. These efforts were widely regarded as a failure with 7 out of a potential 200 to 300 lobbyists registering in Lithuania (McGrath 2008, 25) and 11 by 2007 in Poland (McGrath 2008, 26). Hungary saw 652 lobbyists register and enjoyed slightly more success (McGrath 2008, 23). Needless to say, this is only the tip of the iceberg and does not begin to reveal the matter in its entirety.

15. For example, the support of business elites were considered a significant reason as to why the military could successfully overthrow a civilian government in 1964 in Brazil, and why democracy returned to it as well (Kingstone 1997).

16. See OECD (2008), McGrath (2008), and Malone (2004) for some discussions of these efforts.

17. See Mauro (1995), Montinola and Jackman (2002), Gerring and Thacker (2004, 2008), Svensson (2005), Lambsdorff (2006), and Treisman (1999, 2007) for a detailed discussion of these findings.

18. See Adsera et al. (2000), Djankov et al. (2002), Montinola and Jackman (2002), Gerring and Thacker (2004, 2008), Svensson (2005), Lambsdorff (2006), and Treisman (2000, 2007) for detailed discussion of the literature.

19. The identity of the colonizing country shows up as significant in some studies because scholars argue it is strongly correlated with the type of legal system that a colony adopts on independence (La Porta et al. 1999). Countries however frequently incorporate a combination of local and colonial legal elements into their legal code making them hard to classify accurately. For example, Nigeria combines English common law with the Sharia while Cambodia combines elements of French legal systems with Confucian principles.

20. Party strength refers to the capacity of party leaders to control the behavior of their members in all political arenas. It is thus characterized by "a high degree of internal party unity, external differentiation and, centralized control" (Gerring and Thacker 2008, 27).

21. See Lederman (2001), Panizza (2001), Persson et al. (2003), Montinola and Jackman (2002), Chang and Golden (2004), Damania et al. (2004), Gerring and Thacker (2004, 2008), Kunicova (2005), and Kunicova and Rose-Ackerman (2005).

22. Panizza (2001) finds that moderate parties and stronger individualism experience lower corruption. Lederman (2001), Kunicova (2005), and Gerring and Thacker (2004, 2008) find that presidential systems experience higher corruption, while Adsera et al.(2000) find presidentialism lowers corruption.

23. Myerson (1993) for PR, Persson and Tabellini (2000) for presidential, Montinola and Jackman (2002) for interjurisdictional competition, and Testa (2003) for intercameral competition.

24. For example, see Treisman (2000, 2007), Kunicova and Rose-Ackerman (2005), Lederman et al. (2005), and Chang and Golden (2007) for a discussion of these arguments. They are discussed in more detail in chapters 2 and 6 of this book.

25. While Damania et al. (2004) find federalism reduces corruption, Treisman (2000), Adsera (2000), and Panizza (2001) find no effect of federalism on corruption. Kunicova (2005), Kunicova and Rose-Ackerman (2005), and Gerring and Thacker (2004, 2008) on the other hand find evidence of higher corruption in federal countries.

26. See Treisman (2007), Svensson (2003), Montinola and Jackman (2002), and Lambsdorff (2006) for discussions based on empirical analysis using datasets that cover most countries for almost three decades.

27. For example, while Norway, the Netherlands, and Ireland are widely regarded as largely free of corruption, corruption scandals frequently make headlines in Germany, France, the United States, and Japan often with prominent political entities at the center. Bull and Newell (2003) have examples of many developed countries; Warner discusses the EU.

28. Adsera et al, (2000) differentiates executive regimes by also looking at cases where presidents are elected by assemblies not just directly, Montinola and Jackman (2002) consider legislative effectiveness, and Kunicova (2005) looks at the legislative ability of presidents. All find significant effects.

29. For results obtained from political elites see IDEA (2003); for business elites see Heller (2000) and Kaufman (2004); for NGOs see TI (2006, 2009).

30. Closed-list systems are believed to provide the strongest incentives to cultivate party-based reputations especially in the context when votes are pooled and district magnitude is large (Carey and Shugart 1995). Plurality and open-list systems are believed to be the most individual-prone systems whose impact is exacerbated if there is no pooling and districts are

small. Centralized nomination procedures further strengthen party incentives while decentralized selection norms would strengthen individualistic incentives (Gallagher and Marsh 1988; Carey and Shugart 1995; Bowler, Farrell, and Katz 1999; Hazan 1999). Research so far has also failed to find strong support for nomination procedures as an independent disciplinary tool producing legislative cohesion (Shomer 2009). Here, too, the value of centralized nomination is effective only if it controls access to a valued brand name.

31. Cowhey and McCubbins (1995); Moe and Caldwell (1994); Huber and Shipan (2002, 2009).

32. See Bennedson and Feldman (2001, 2005).

33. See cross-country studies of parliamentary systems by Liebert (1995) and Norton (1999) and studies by OSI (2002), Johnson (2008), Hrebenar (2008), and Evanson (2008)

34. Lobbying can make bribery of bureaucrats unnecessary if lobbyists succeed in having political policymakers change the rules of implementation (Harsstad and Svenssen 2009; Campos and Giovannoni 2008) or it can facilitate bribery by undermining law enforcement at implementation stages (Damania et al. 2004). When lobbying and corruption are substitutes, higher lobbying is accompanied by lower corruption. In the second formulation, they are complements, hence higher lobbying will be accompanied by higher corruption. This particular framing of the relationship between the two does not allow for corruption through political channels and lobbying through bureaucratic channels, which does not accord with empirical reality of bureaucratic lobbying and political corruption practices by interest groups. Furthermore, it does not embed the capacity of political principals to change the nature, type, and conditions of delegation in their institutional context. These studies measure lobbying by using a dummy variable that captures whether or not a surveyed firm belongs to an association or chamber, i.e., membership is akin to lobbying. Empirically therefore these results are constrained by the lack of good proxies for measuring aspects of lobbying. These studies undeniably offer an encouraging start to the endeavor of understanding one of the links between business lobbying and corruption. For the reasons stated above, though, they are limited in the extent to which they can engage the broader theoretical and empirical questions regarding the links between all forms of lobbying and corruption.

35. See Morris-Jones (1976), Mezey (1983, 1996), Blondel (1973, 2001), Cox and Morgernstern (2002), and Loewenberg et al. (2002) for the range of the discussions of these assumptions and how they hold up to current performance.

36. See, e.g., Döring (1995), Rasch (1995), Milner (1997), Heller (2001), Cox (2002), Volden and Craig (2004), and Cox and McCubbins (2008).

37. Heller (2001), Martin and Vanberg (2004), Martin (2005).

38. See Harstad and Svensson (2009), Kaufman and Vicente (2008), Chari et al. (2007), Campos and Giovannoni (2007, 2008), and Damania et al. (2004).

39. I discuss in detail the insights of these two literatures on bureaucratic and judicial delegation in chapter 2. See Epstein and O'Halloran (1994), Bawn (1997, 1999), Huber and Shipan (2002, 2006), Mishra (2006), Bendor and Meirowitz (2004), Buscaglia (2001), Hammergren (2007), McCubbins and Rodriguez (2008), Ginsburg (2008), and Vanberg (2008) for these arguments

40. See Landes and Posner (1975), Epstein, Knight, and Shvetsova (2002), Iaryczower et al. (2006), and Hammergren (2007) for a flavor of these arguments. I discuss them in more detail in chapter 2.

41. A new set of single-country studies has begun to fill in this gap. See Frye (2001) for Russia, Evanson (2008) for Czech Republic, McGrath (2008) for overview of several Eastern and

Central European countries, Hrebenar et al (2008) for Lithuania, Johnson (2008) and Jones (1995) for Argentinaand Kennedy (2004) for China. There are very few countries that require and enforce lobbying registration and reporting. Thus datasets such as for the U.S. case are rare even among developed country democracies.

42. These rankings hold using the Transparency International Corruption Perception Index, the World Bank Corruption Index, the ICRG Corruption Index, and surveys of businesses conducted by the World Economic Forum and World Bank.

43. See Jones (2002) and Spiller and Tommasi (2008) for Argentina, and Haggard and Noble (2001), Wang (2005), and Tsai (2009) for Taiwan.

44. See Cheng and Haggard (2001), Chu (2001), Tsai (2009), Taipei Times (2004), and Taiwan Today (2006).

45. Spiller and Tomassi (2008), Johnson (2008), and O' Donnell (1996).

46. Carothers (2001), Scarrow (2006), Schmitter (2001), Johnston (2006), and Hagopian (2009).

47. Scholars have conducted wide research on corruption in developed democracies. See, e.g., Glaeser and Goldin (2006) for studies of corruption in the United States, Bull and Newell (2003) for corruption in OECD democracies, and Warner (2007) for corruption in the EU.

48. Montinola and Jackman, (2002), Seligson (2002), Rose-Ackerman (1999), Theobald (1982), and Tulchin and Espach (2000).

49. They cited the persistent and high level of corruption resulting from the relationship between business and political agents as the source of their dissatisfaction with and dismissal of democracy as a desirable form of governance.

50. See Lowery (2007), Yackee (2004), Holyoke (2003, 2008), and Kollman (1998) for samples of how these factors influence lobbying in the United States.

Chapter 2

1. See Transparency International Global Corruption Report (2009), Kaufman and Vicente (2008), Rose-Ackerman (1999, 2006, 2007), Johnston (2006), Bryan and Baer (2005), Kang (2002), OSI (2002), and Hellman (2000) for discussions of various forms of corrupt relationships between business and political actors.

2. These include the *Handbook of Funding for Political Parties and Elections*, edited by Austin and Tjernström for the International Institute for Democracy and Electoral Assistance, published in 2003; a 2005 study of party financing in 22 countries by Bryan and Baer for the National Democratic Institute; a 2003 study of political financing practices co-authored by Gene Ward, Michael Pinto-Duschinsky, and Herbert Alexander for the USAID; various studies by the International Foundation for Election Studies, the World Bank, and the European Union Research Office; and other studies by individual scholars.

3. Bryan and Baer (2005), OSI (2002), USAID Report on Party Financing (2003), Nassmacher (2003), Zovatto (2003, 97), and Walecki (2003, 78).

4. See Pinto Duschinsky (2001), USAID (2003), Nassmacher (2003), Walecki (2003), Ferdinand (2003), Saffu (2003), Bryan and Baer (2005), and CRINIS (2007).

5. Scarrow (2007), Rose-Ackerman (2006), TI (2004), Bull and Newell (2003), Bleichinger (2002), Nassmacher (2001), and Pinto-Dushinsky (2001).

6. South Africa, Morocco, and Seychelles were the three democracies who could afford to do so. Zimbabwe was the fourth country.

7. For example, out of the 62 nations which had any level of financing for parties, in 15 parties received public support only at election times, in 9 only between elections, while 38 received it in both phases (IDEA 2003, 210–213). The purpose of public funds varied as well with 29 countries earmarking the funds for general party administration expenses, 45 for election campaigns, and 8 for other purposes. Only in 20 countries were funds not specifically ear-marked for some purpose by the state. Various in-kind subsidies are also offered as part of state financing. These indirect subsidies can still leave funding at existential levels for parties, especially smaller parties (OSI 2002, 382). In addition, the marginal strategic value of private finance available to only the party or candidate who has raised it remains unaffected by the availability of state funds. The incentive to keep raising private funds therefore remains strong, especially in the context of weak reporting and disclosure laws and weak legal systems.

8. When new techniques are used in countries that lack adequate supporting infrastructure and facilities, political expenses can rise to surprising levels. For example, the amount parties spent on advertising per voter in Latvia in 1998 was ten times more than that spent in Britain and four times more than in France and Sweden (Voika 2004, 51). USAID (2003), IDEA (2003), and Bryan and Baer (2005).

9. Nownes (2006), Nassmacher (2003), Austen-Smith (1992), and Alexander and Shiratori (1993).

10. USAID (2003), IDEA (2003), and Bryan and Baer (2005).

11. Hard figures even on legal business donations are rare and unreliable due to both the lax nature of reporting and disclosure most countries have adopted on corporate donations and a low enforcement capacity (Rose-Ackerman 2007; Bryan and Baer 2005, 20; USAID 2003, 48). Studies of their importance in political funding have therefore relied on surveys and interviews with relevant elites. See USAID (2003), Nassmacher (2003), IDEA Handbook (2003), Transparency International GCR (2004, 2009), Bryan and Baer (2005), and Rose-Ackerman (2006).

12. See USAID (2006), Bryan and Baer (2005), Walecki (2004), Transparency International Global Corruption Reports (2004, 2008), Austin and Tjernström (2003), and IFES (2002) for discussion of these trends using various types of data, reports, and interviews.

13. Cox (1987, 2000), Gallagher and Marsh (1988), Cox and McCubbins (1993), Döring (1995), Mainwaring and Shugart (1997), Bowler, Farrell, and Katz (1999), Laver (2002, 2006), and Spiller, Stein, and Tommasi (2009). In addition to party discipline, scholars have pointed out that party influence over legislative outcomes can also emerge from the similarity of leader and member preferences and also from the similarity of their motives. Party members vote in response to constituent preferences, party preference, and personal preferences (Kingdon 1984). Preference-based explanations of party discipline argue that when all of these preferences are similar, party leaders will be able to lead legislatively united memberships and deliver policy outcomes (Aldrich and Rohde 1997–98, 2000). They do not address the issue of frequency of such congruence over multiple issues at a given moment in time and the reason such divergence does not affect cohesion. Similarly, if party leaders and members share the same electoral or office goals, legislators may choose to delegate legislative control to party leaders enabling them to control legislative policy outcomes. However, leaders and backbenchers often have different goals, and even when they share some of them they may hold different beliefs on the most effective ways to achieve them (Cox and McCubbins 2000; Fiorina 1997). These factors have led scholars to increasingly emphasize the role that political

institutions play in influencing the ability of parties to enforce discipline. The noninclusive, nondemocratic internal party politics typical of developing democracy parties further reduces the probability of preference- or motive-based influence (Scarrow 2006).

14. Closed-list systems are believed to provide the strongest incentives to cultivate party-based reputations especially in the context when votes are pooled and district magnitude is large (Carey and Shugart 1995). Plurality and open-list systems are believed to be the most individual-prone systems whose impact is exacerbated if there is no pooling and districts are small. Centralized nomination procedures further strengthen party incentives while decentralized selection norms would strengthen individualistic incentives (Gallagher and Marsh 1988; Carey and Shugart 1995; Bowler, Farrell, and Katz, 1999; Hazan 1999). Research so far has also failed to find strong support for nomination procedures as an independent disciplinary tool producing legislative cohesion (Shomer 2009). Here, too, the value of centralized nomination is effective only if it controls access to a valued brand name.

15. If party brand value is even partly linked to the ability of parties to deliver policy via legislative outcomes (Cox 1987; Cox and McCubbins 1993; Laver 2002), then such party switching casts doubt on the ability of parties to protect their label and on the ability of personally oriented legislators to deliver policy. Thus, both electorally strong parties and legislators could be weakened in the legislature.

16. If the role of electoral rules is to construct chains of accountability in the minds of constituents, membership in electoral coalitions should diminish the electoral value of any single party's label.

17. Mutual independence of origin and survival coupled with the competition between presidents and parties for legislative influence have been blamed for the lack of party discipline in presidential systems (Linz 1994; Carey 2007). In contrast, the fusion of the executive and legislative branches and the ability of parliamentary party leaders to turn any legislative vote into a vote of confidence for the government have been identified as keys to disciplinary strength of parties in parliamentary systems. See Huber (1996), Baron (1998), and Diermeier and Feddersen (1998) for these arguments. The premise itself is increasingly contested since studies of party discipline using roll call votes have found that while levels of party discipline are indeed higher in parliamentary systems, their levels in presidential systems are fairly high as well, i.e., lack of party discipline in presidential systems has been neither an endemic nor a crippling feature of presidential systems in practice (Cheibub 2007, 117; Carey 2007).

18. Benedetto and Hix (2007), Cheibub (2007).

19. See Cheibub (2007), Carey (2007), Benedetto and Hix (2007), Laver (2002), and Laver and Shepsle (1991).

20. Shugart and Carey (1992), Jones (1995), and Golder (2006).

21. The credibility of parliamentary party leaders threatening to turn a legislative vote into one of confidence may be low due to several reasons: the policy may not be considered critical enough to merit such drastic action by party members thus causing resentment at its use (Heller 2001, 783), the party may be too unpopular to be willing to face elections at that time (Laver 2006, 124–125), or the party or its coalition may be so divided over a policy as to make it too politically costly (Heller 2001, 782). Frequent use of this procedure to pass policy bills may not be politically costless for party leaders as both voters and party members may consider this undemocratic (Huber 1996, 119).

22. See the February 2008 special issue of the *Journal of Public Administration* for Johnson's chapter on Argentina and Evanson's chapter on the Czech Republic.

23. Since presidents vary considerably on the extent of their legislative powers (Carey and Shugart 1992), this implies that, in many countries, they must frequently rely on the success of their legislative coalition-building efforts to get the votes to pass their agendas. See Cheibub, Przeworski, and Saiegh (2004), Golder (2006), Carey (2007), and Cheibub (2007). Similarly, parliamentary party leaders must pacify internal factions in order to contain any fissures and splits (Hirschman 1970; Panebianco 1988; Laver 2002) and to continuously build coalitions to elect them to power, to support their legislative agenda, and to support their survival (Cheibub 2007; Laver 2002, 202).

24. See Cox and McCubbins (1999, 2006) for the U.S. House; Cox, Matsuyama, and McCubbins (2000) for Japan; and, Cox, Heller, and McCubbins (2008) for Brazil.

25. This discussion draws on constitutional details provided in Zubek (2005), Aleman (2006), and the sources listed in the Appendix for chapter 6.

26. This corresponds to the floor agenda model of Cox and McCubbins (2000). Here the relevant factors driving the final agenda choice will be the preferences of individual legislators and the status quo policy.

27. Furthermore, it allows parties to police the policy behavior of coalition partners in the executive and ensure bargains are enforced (Thies 2001; Martin and Vanberg 2004).

28. Cited in Zubek (2005, 10).

29. Mattson (1995) in Döring (1995) and Heller (2001) provide some examples of these variations.

30. Prior to 2007–2008, parties did not have this ability in Brazil. In 2007, the constitutional court ruled that the legislative mandate belonged to the parties not to legislators and subsequently allowed them to expel members for any antiparty behavior in the legislature including antiwhip voting at the discretion of party leaders.

31. See Johnston (2006), Bryan and Baer (2005), USAID (2003), Bleichinger (2001), and Pinto-Duschinsky (2001) for data and discussion of these trends.

32. See Rose-Ackerman (1999, 2006), Carothers (2001), Bleichinger (2002), USAID (2003), Bryan and Baer (2005), IFES (2008), and Janda (2006) for further discussion of these practices and expenses in developing democracies.

33. Quoted in Bryan and Baer (2005, 18)

34. See Bawn (1999), Ting (2001), Huber and Shipan (2002), Bendor and Meirowitz (2004), and Huber and McCarty (2004); for institutional locus of delegation see Epstein and O'Halloran (1994) and Gailmard (2002); and for appointments see McCarty (2004), Iyer and Mani (2009).

35. See Vanberg (2008), Hirschl (2004), and McCubbins and Rodriguez (2008) for a review of the institutional judicial independence literature. The argument has largely revolved around the impact the separation of powers has on increasing judicial independence (Iaryczower et al. 2006).

36. See Epstein and Knight (1998), Spaeth and Segal (1999, 18), Epstein, Knight, and Shvetsova (2002), and Hammergren (2007, 202–208) for arguments that judicial structure and powers are strongly influenced by the institutional powers of political actors, specifically, by powers inherent in the executive and legislative institutions influence. See Ginsburg (2008) for a discussion of constitutional review; Vanberg (2008) and Hirschl (2004) for discussions on judicial independence; and McCubbins and Rodriguez (2008) for a review of this judicial literature.

37. Institutions also determine political control over the criteria and mode for bureaucratic, regulatory, and judicial appointments and dismissals (Abraham 2000; Moreno, Crisp, and

Shugart 2003; McCarty 2004; Iyer and Mani 2009) as well as the budgets of these agencies (Ting 2001; Russell 2001; Buscaglia 2001; Domingo 2001).

38. See OSI (2002), USAID (2003), Doublet (2004, 53), Walecki (2004, 27), Ward (2004, 39 Bryan and Baer (2005, 21), Johnston (2006, 10), USAID (2006), Grzymala-Busse (2007), and IFES (2008) for examples from across the world.

Chapter 3

1. Case studies have been motivated by various goals including theory generation (George and Bennett 2005; Gerring 2007) and theory testing (Gerring 2007; Fearon and Laitin 2008).

2. An appropriate selection of cases must meet the following criteria: the universe of cases from which these case studies are drawn must be well defined, the selected cases must be typical of the underlying categories they are trying to represent, and there must be unit homogeneity among the cases. The first condition ensures the set of cases to which the results are being applied is transparent so that the results are well understood. The second criterion ensures that the findings of the case studies are generalizable to other cases in their categories rather than being driven by peculiarities of the specific cases selected. The third criterion demands that cases be as similar as possible on features that are not relevant to the theoretical mechanism being tested to ensure that the ability to test the plausibility of the theory itself is maximized.

3. George and Bennett (2005), Gerring (2007), and Fearon and Laitin (2008).

4. See Gerring (2007), Skocpol and Somers (1980), Lijphart (1975), and Przeworski and Teune (1970) for more detailed discussions on these issues.

5. As I discuss later in chapters 5 and 6, the rule regarding party powers to strip the mandate from legislators who vote against the party line was introduced in Brazil over 2007–2008. At the time of this study, however, Brazil fit the parameters required of an individual-focused legislative system on all three legislative rules.

6. Johnson and Wallack (2008) compile a particularism index based on four dimensions of electoral systems (ballot type, vote pooling, number of votes and district magnitude) identified in Carey and Shugart (1995). This index measures how individual-centered an electoral system is on a scale of 1-13 with 13 representing the most personalistic electoral system, According to this index, Brazil is scored as a 7 and India as a 13. Therefore, both electoral systems are ranked on the personalistic end of the spectrum of all electoral system types.

7. See Munck and Ragin quoted in Collier and Brady (2004), George and Bennett (2005), Gerring (2007), and Bennett (2008).

8. Members to the upper house are indirectly elected by an electoral college comprised of Lok Sabha (LS) members and members of all state legislative assemblies. Seats are proportional to combined party seat shares. Two Lok Sabha seats have members nominated to them from the Anglo-Indian community in India by the president, taking the total to 545 seats. Elections to both houses are very competitive. The LS turnover rate has averaged 40–50% in recent elections with an average of 10 candidates running for every seat. The number of parties represented has gone up from a handful in 1962 to 39 in 2007. Candidates may contest as independents. Since 1991, all governments have been coalitions featuring up to 14 parties.

9. Bills are rarely sent back to the lower house by the Rajya Sabha or by the president.

10. Rules of Procedure and Conduct of Business in Lok Sabha (2004), 11–14.

11. Sorabjee (in Kashyap 2003, vii) also comments on how speakers have catered to partisan interests in the exercise of their function regarding defections.

12. Suryaprakash (1993, 292). Author's interview with party leaders from the BJP, Congress (I), SP, and CPI(M).

13. The BAC had 14 sittings totalling over 6.55 hours. Average attendance was 67 and 51%. loksabha.gov.in. Accessed Februrary 21, 2009.

14. See Jalan (2007, 135–139) for more details on this event.

15. They must be submitted at least two days in advance and examined by the secretariat for admissibility. The procedure for tabling of amendments, conditions of their admissibility, etc. is as laid down in articles 117 and 274 of the Constitution, Rules 18, 75, 79–87, 118, 177, 180, and 344–347 of the Rules of Procedure and Conduct of Business in Lok Sabha and Directions 21, 41–45, and 113 of Directions by the Speaker.

16. See chapter 4 for a detailed discussion of the passage of this bill and the politics surrounding it.

17. The 52nd amendment amended articles 101, 102, 190, and 191 of the Constitution. Rules of Procedure and Conduct of Business in Lok Sabha (2004, 174).

18. The initial 1985 version of the Anti-Defection Bill did not disqualify members who left their parties as part of a larger faction comprising at least one-third of the party. This was classified as a split. Party mergers are considered to be legitimate and do not affect membership. However, the rash of factional splits that followed led parties to introduce the 91st constitutional amendment in 2003 to successfully remove this exception.

19. Confidential author interview with senior party leader in New Delhi, July 27, 2005.

20. The current constitution was promulgated on October 5, 1998, and is characterized by its written rigid form. The first required revision of the constitution in 1994 left the constitution largely intact.

21. The Chamber of Deputies has 20 standing committees, and the Senate 8.

22. Article 59 of the Federal Constitution states that the legislative process can be exercised through the following legislative initiatives: constitution (the supreme law), constitutional amendments (Emendas à Constituição), laws that are supplementary to the Constitution (Leis complementares à Constituição; can be federal, state, Federal District, or local laws), ordinary laws (Leis ordinárias; either federal, state, Federal District, or local laws), delegated laws (Leis delegadas; federal), provisional measures (Medidas provisórias), legislative decrees (Decretos legislativos), and resolutions (Resoluções).

23. The range is from a low of 89% during Cardoso's 1995–1998 terms, to a high of 98% during Collor's first term in 1990. Source: Brazil—Senado Federal (1999) (www.senado.gov. br); data provided by Argelina C. Figueiredo and Fernando Limongi. As cited in Neto et al. (2003, 563).

24. Pereira et al. (2008, 8). This number understates the importance of decrees since, until 2001, they could be reissued any number of times. After 2001, each decree is limited to only one reissue. The highest rate at which they were issued was 6.8 per month under Cardoso's second term (2002) and the lowest was 2.9 under a two-year tenure (1990–1992). However, the imaginative interpretation of urgency by Brazilian presidents has seen decrees on issues ranging from the purchase of the vice-presidential car to the introduction of new currency. Therefore, the frequent use of these decrees also overstates their importance for policy.

25. These details draw on two sources—the Internal Rules (Regimento Interno) for the two chambers, and the CEDI report on the Brazilian Legislative Branch.

26. The actual language used is *"organizar, ouvido o Colégio de Líderes, a agenda com a previsão das proposições a serem apreciadas no mês subseqüente, para distribuição aos Deputados"* (Article 17,

I (s) RICD). The original *Colégio* sprang up spontaneously during the 1988 Constitutional process and was instrumental at that stage in negotiations between different parties. This led to its role being formalized in this manner. However, as discussed later in this section, its prominence has waxed and waned since then as a function of the political influence of the individual leaders who have taken up positions as the floor leaders of their party delegations in the chambers.

27. In addition to having the ear of the Chamber Presidents during their consultations on the monthly agendas, party floor leaders may also use their privilege to intercede and speak for a period of 7 to 10 minutes at any time during debates, request a roll call, and cast a symbolic vote on behalf of their party delegation.

28. These arguments rely on two dimensions of political influence—institutionally mandated privileges in the legislative process (discussed above) and the ability to provide pork. Figueiredo and Limongi (2000) argue that legislative party leaders have successfully monopolized the agenda in Brazil because they have been able to discipline their members through their powers to provide patronage appointments in the legislature and outside of it. However, Desposato (2006), Samuels (2003, 2004), and Pereira and Mueller (2000) find that committee appointments, which are the appointments directly influenced by party leaders, are not valued by legislators, while Santos (2002) finds that party loyalty does not influence committee assignments. Ames (2001, 2002) has argued that pork in Brazil is controlled by the executive not by party leaders. Hence, it further undermines party control over legislative behavior and strengthens the ability of the executive to forge alliances with individuals. Neto, Cox, and McCubbins (2003) also base the ability of the executive to construct an agenda cartel to a large extent on his ability to offer pork barrel inducements directly to potential cartel members through budgetary amendments (discussed in the next section in this chapter). This claim is contested by others who argue that party leaders do significantly influence pork distribution (Lyne 2008). Hagopian et al. (2008) suggest that, increasingly, voter demand for programmatic parties is creating value for party labels in Brazil and giving parties a new source of influence.

29. Articles 120, 122, and 165 to 178 of the Regimento Interno govern the conduct of most amendments.

30. Many scholars have focused on analyzing whether the roll call behavior of legislators has been successfully influenced by disbursements of budgetary amendments by the executive (Ames 2002) and by party leaders (Lyne 2008). They have found impact ranging from none (Hagopian 2008; Ames 2002) to significant effects (Lyne 2008; Samuels 2003). As some of these scholars themselves point out and I discuss later, this is not surprising because this is a problematic research design with which to study the impact of executive influence on voting. While roll calls suffer from severe selection biases, disbursements may be targeted at swing voters rather than similarly minded legislators.

31. In 2007, the Supreme Court allowed parties to finally expel legislators who switched parties or engaged in antiparty behavior in the legislature. The legislative mandate was deemed as belonging to the party on whose list the legislators had been elected rather than to the legislator himself. This ruling was seen to give parties the ability to expel dissenting voters from their seat. See Resolution-TSE 22,610/2007, with edition given by Resolution-TSE nº 22,733/2008, available at http://www.tse.jus.br/internet/partidos/fidelidade.htm. Accessed October 18, 2009.

32. In 1998, the most disciplined party based on roll-call analysis was the Communist Party of Brazil (PCdoB), whose members voted with the leader 99.3% of the time, but by 2007 this

had fallen to 87.9%. The party with the least discipline in 1998 was the Brazilian Socialist Party (PSB), whose members followed the whip 81.9% of the time. In 2007 they saw their member voting discipline fall to 70.9%. The Workers Party (PT), which boasted the second highest voting discipline at 99.1% in 1998, saw their discipline fall to 80.2% by 2007. The members of the least disciplined party in the government bloc in 2007, the Progressive Party (PP), voted with leaders 62.2% of the time while the lowest discipline was exhibited by the PPS in the opposition bloc with only 59.5%.

33. See Krehbiel (2000), Londregan (2000), Cox and McCubbins (2005), Desposato (2005), Carey (2007), and Carruba et al. 2008 for detailed discussions of the various issues involved.

34. Quoted in Santos (2004).

Chapter 4

1. While these numbers are high and interviews with firms indicate that they are rising even further, there is no systematic evidence to confirm this through interviews with firms for these two countries. Recall from chapter 2, the only dataset that gets at this systematically is the BEEPS dataset of the EBRD and the World Bank, which surveys twenty-seven Eastern and Central European countries and Central Asian countries. These numbers show that firms report considerable variation in their membership. However, there is no way to explore this for firms in other regions of the world given the current lack of data.

2. As discussed in chapter 2, there is rich literature on the debate about the relationship between electoral rules, executive regimes, and party strength. Yadav (2010a) presents results from two models that impose different theoretical structures on these relationships between executive and parties. Results from a bivariate heteroskedastic probit model, which considers the choice to lobby the executive or the parliament and the choice to lobby parties or legislators, show that the critical factor in driving lobbying decisions is the perception of party strength. Results from a mixed logit which include the executive and parties as alternative choices show that party strength in legislation as perceived accounts for the interaction between executive regime and legislative rules in determining lobbying behavior directed at parties and directed at individuals.

3. Examples may be found in surveys conducted by the World Bank and the EBRD (WBES survey), the World Economic Forum, the IFC 2004 and CII in India, and the FIESP in Brazil.

4. In the interest of space, these results are not presented here. However, an extended discussion of these results can be obtained on the author's website at http://polisci.la.psu.edu/facultybios/yadav.html. Yadav (2010b) presents statistical results from a heteroskedastic probit model, which models venue choice as a function of perceptions of legislative influence over policymaking, ideology, sector, policy issue, size, concentration, and age while controlling for respondent heterogeneity due to experience, location, and education. These results confirm that institutions are significant factors while the other factors are not found to be statistically significant.

5. This supports the argument made by many scholars that while parliamentary and presidential regimes constitute an important source of institutionally derived influence, they do not in and of themselves determine the political distribution of influence independently of other institutions (Shugart and Carey 1992; Rockman and Weaver 1993; Cheibub 2008).

6. When India signed this agreement in 1994, it was given ten years to transition from a patent regime that, broadly speaking, supported process patents into one that supported product

patents. By 2004, India's domestic pharmaceutical industry was ranked fourth in production volume and thirteenth in value globally with total revenue of Rs. 1,900,000, and was the single largest global supplier of several critical medications to developing countries, for example, supplying up to 50% of the HIV-AIDS antiretroviral drugs needed in these countries. This immense success was based largely on the strategy and ability of producing popular medicines using alternative production processes at a fraction of their original cost. By the 1990s, domestic originator firms were competing with multinational titans such as Novartis and Pfizer (Bridges Weekly Digest, March 23, 2005).

7. The first three attempts took place under BJP-led governments in 1999, 2000, and December 2003. After their May 2004 victory, the Congress party set up a four-minister committee to review progress but did not invite any civil society groups for comments (Bridges Weekly Digest, March 23, 2005).

8. The insurance sector in India was nationalized in 1956 (life insurance) and 1972 (general insurance) amid allegations of corruption and mismanagement. As part of the economic reform process, efforts to privatize it were begun in 1993 with the setting up of an interim regulatory authority under the Rao-led Congress government. The following years, from 1995 to 1999, were marked by repeated attempts to introduce a bill on privatization of insurance through the rise and fall of several governments of different ideological hues (UNI, December 2, 1999).

9. From interview with N. M. Sundaram, General Secretary, All-India Employees Union, cited in Rediff, December 11, 1998.

10. Dr. Jay Dubashi, ex–Union Minister of Industry under the BJP, stated, "Insurance reforms won't be easy" (Rediff Business Commentary, December 2, 1999).

11. Surveys of voter preferences conducted by CSDS provide strong support for this as well. Despite remarkably identical evaluations by voters of how little parties and representatives cared about them, and how little they could be trusted, voters preferred to vote for parties by a margin of almost 20% (Kumar 2004, 373–377).

12. The average state disbursement between 1997 and 2001 for twenty-two states exceeded 10% of their revenues.

13. For example, *Folha de São Paulo* (February 12, 1998, 1–10) reported that the Cardoso government promised to release R$22 million for public works projects benefiting *governista* deputies' constituencies. According to *Gazeta Mercantile* (February 12, 1998, A-14), Planning Minister Kandir telephoned a government-owned bank (*Caixa Econômica Federal*) to hasten the liberation of the funds for deputies' budget amendments, resulting in the distribution of more than R$4 million in only two weeks in February. Cited in Hiroi (2005, 117).

14. "Conheça a história da CPMF," *Folha de São Paulo*, August 15, 2007. Available at http://www1.folha.uol.com.br/folha/dinheiro/ult91u320356.shtml. Accessed October 12, 2009.

15. "Governo teme derrota na votação da CPMF no Senado," *Estadão*, October 10, 2007 <http://www.estadao.com.br/nacional/not_nac62948,0.htm>; Accessed October 12, 2009.

16. "Fiesp e Fecomercio comemoram fim da CPMF e defendem controle nos gostos," *Folha de São Paulo*, December 13, 2007. Available at http://www1.folha.uol.com.br/folha/brasil/ult96u354616.shtml. Accessed October 12, 2009.

17. "Fiesp e Fecomercio comemoram fim da CPMF e defendem controle nos gostos," *Folha de São Paulo*, December 13, 2007. Available at http://www1.folha.uol.com.br/folha/brasil/ult96u354616.shtml. Accessed October 12, 2009.

18. The PSDB of course had under Cardoso itself renewed this measure in 1993 and 1999 but now in the opposition benches described it as one of the worst things to happen to Brazil. "Saiba como foi a votação CPMF nos partidos," *Bem Paraná*, September 20, 2007. Available at http://www.bemparana.com.br/index.php?n=43309&t=saiba-como-foi-a-votacao-cpmf-nos-partidos. Accessed October 12, 2009.

19. Juliana Rangel, "Para economista, fim da CPMF deteriora cenário econômico; Bovespa cai," *O Globo*, December 13, 2007. Available at http://oglobo.globo.com/economia/mat/2007/12/13/327582040.asp. Accessed October 12, 2009.

20. Gabriela Guerreiro, "DEM quer expulsar três deputados que votaram a favor da prorrogação da CPMF," *Folha de São Paulo*, September 20, 2007. Available at http://www1.folha.uol.com.br/folha/brasil/ult96u329994.shtml. Accessed October 12, 2009.

21. Governo teme derrota na votação da CPMF no Senado," *Estadão*, October 10, 2007. Available at http://www.estadao.com.br/nacional/not_nac62948,0.htm. Accessed October 12, 2009.

22. "Saiba quem votou 'sim' e quem votou 'não' pela prorrogação da CPMF," *Folha de São Paulo* September 20, 2007. Available at http://www1.folha.uol.com.br/folha/brasil/ult96u330125.shtml Accessed October 12, 2009.

23. "Saiba como foi a votação CPMF nos partidos," *Bem Paraná*, September 20, 2007. Available at http://www.bemparana.com.br/index.php?n=43309&t=saiba-como-foi-a-votacao-cpmf-nos-partidos Accessed October 14, 2009.

24. Gabriela Guerreiro, "PMDB poderá forçar integrantes do partido no Senado a apoiarem CPMF até 2011," *Folha de São Paulo*, October 19, 2007. Available at http://www1.folha.uol.com.br/folha/brasil/ult96u338045.shtml Accessed October 14, 2009.

25. The original statement in Portuguese is as follows, "*Vamos trabalhar no varejo e buscar o diálogo com os senadores,*"aide to the Finance Minister Guido Mantega Fontes, quoted in, "PMDB fecha a favor da CPMF; Renan se abstém em decisão," *Estadão*, November 7, 2007. Available athttp://www.estadao.com.br/nacional/not_nac77056,0.htm. Accessed October 14, 2009.

26. The original statement in Portuguese is as follows, "*O peemedebista disse ainda que o fechamento de questão da bancada do PMDB representa um gesto político. Ou seja, segundo ele, não implica punição aos senadores que não seguirem a decisão da bancada.* quoted in. "PMDB fecha a favor da CPMF; Renan se abstém em decisão," *Estadão*, November 7, 2007. Available at http://www.estadao.com.br/nacional/not_nac77056,0.htm Accessed October 14, 2009.

27. Cristiane Jungblut, "Oposiao derruba a prorrogação da CPMF no Senado. Governo consegue só 45 votos," *O Globo*, December 13, 2007. Available at http://oglobo.globo.com/pais/mat/2007/12/12/327565259.asp Accessed October 14, 2009

28. Folha de Sao Paolo. December 13, 2007. "Alencar diz que prioridade é ajustar as contas para evitar desequilíbrio e volta da inflação" Available at http://www1.folha.uol.com.br/folha/brasil/ult96u354591.shtml Accessed October 14, 2009.

Chapter 5

1. See www.asclaras.org.br to access the detailed figures on political donations for 2002, 2004, and 2006 elections. See Samuels (2001) to get figures for earlier elections. Februaruy 8, 2010.

2. Author's interview, Manufacturing Association-2, Brasilia.

3. Director of a manufacturing association in Kolkata. Interview # Manufacturing-3, July 16, 2005.

4. Director of a service sector association in New Delhi, Services-1, July 22, 2005.

5. See the chapter "Anatomy of the Scam Trinity" in Mitra (1998) for a detailed discussion of these scandals.

6. As I discuss at the end of the chapter, the PT as a party is different from other Brazilian parties because of its greater organizational depth and coherence.

7. See Yadav (2009c) for a detailed study of the determinants of legislative reputations in these systems. The statistical analysis of the data using ordered probit models shows that the set of characteristics that influence legislative reputations in Brazil are personal rather than organizational, whereas in India they are based largely on the reputations of MPs within parties.

8. No one knows the true extent of campaign costs in India or Brazil. Estimates of actual campaign expenses in India range from ten times the official limit as estimated by journalists (Mitra 1998, 116), to fifteen times as estimated by civil society monitoring groups (Lok Satta 2001, 3), to twenty times as estimated by legislators themselves (NCRWC Report 2001, 21; Mint, September 22, 2008). To appreciate how little official figures capture actual expenses, consider that while a survey of candidates and party leaders in the 1999 elections revealed total campaign expenses of Rs. 6050 million for just the BJP and the Congress parties (Sridharan 1999), the total campaign expenses reported officially by *all* parties for the 2004 general elections was merely Rs. 2300 million (ECI 2005; indiatogether.org)! These high numbers and the wide range stem from a variety of legal and illegal campaign expenses. As discussed above, parties must finance the lion's share of both legal and illegal aspects of increasingly expensive campaigns for the party *and* for most of its candidates as well. Official campaign figures in Brazil are also considered to be of dubious credibility by scholars (Fleischer 1997, 2007; Samuels 2001, 2002; Mainwaring 1999; Geddes and Neto 1992).

9. This influence can be estimated using a mixed Logit model where choice of lobbying tool is the dependent variable. Venue choice between parties and individuals, legislative stage of interest group intervention, and issue type are found to have significant influence on lobbying tool choice controlling for sector, city, concentration, size, and group experience. See Yadav (2009d) for details of the estimation and analysis.

10. See the NCRWC (2001) report and the books by Arun Shourie (2003, 2007), Bimal Jalan (2005, 2007), TSR Subramaniam (2001) among others for analyses by political and bureaucratic insiders.

11. Details taken from Lando, Senador Amir. "*Relatório dos Trabalhos da CPMI 'Das Amulâncias.'*", *Comissão Parlamentar Mixta de Inquérito* August 2006, Matais, Andreza. "*CPI dos Sanguessugas denuncia 72 parlamentares; veja lista.*" *Folha de São Paulo* August 10, 2006, Carneiro, Marcelo. "*Era pior do que se pensava: O chefe da mafia dos sanguessugas revela que seu esquema corrompeu sessenta prefeitos e 20% do Congresso e adentrou o gabinete de Humberto Costa.*" *Véja* July 26, 2006. Matais, Andreza. "*Peemedebista pede afastamento de Suassuna do partido.*" *Folha de São Paulo* August 9, 2006. http://www1.folha.uol.com.br/folha/brasil/ult96u81256.shtml. All accessed Februrary 9, 2010.

12. The PT era has begun to deviate from this practice. As an atypically disciplined Brazilian party, its stint in power has been accompanied by an increasing degree of institutional capture by party elites to court business donors. I discuss this change in more detail at the end of this chapter.

13. "Lula is besieged by Brazil's corruption scandal" By Raymond Colitt and Richard Lapper Published: July 22, 2005 03:00 | Accessed February 12, 2010.

14. Cited on page 6 of the September 29–October 5th, 2007 issue of the Brazil Focus by David Fleischer. The figures were released by the MCCE (Movement to Combat Electoral Corruption).

15. A survey of rank and file members belonging to the BJP and the Congress, the two biggest parties, revealed an average stated expenditure of Rs. 85,00,000 per constituency for the Congress and Rs. 65,00,000 for the BJP. On the other hand, party leaders reported an average expenditure per constituency of Rs. 19,00,000 for the Congress and Rs. 20,00,000 for the BJP, respectively. In addition, the party leaderships reported expenditures for central party office and organizational tasks at Rs. 400 million for the BJP and Rs 850 million for the Congress. The total reported by candidates therefore came to Rs. 6050 million for campaigns plus 1250 million for party organizational expenditures. Party leaders, on the other hand, reported a total of Rs. 200 million of campaign finances for the BJP. For the Congress, Rs 1250 million was reported for party expenditures alone. The reported discrepancy between the estimates given of party leaders and members is thus staggering. To put these numbers into perspective, consider that permissible limits on campaign expenditures at the time was Rs. 15,00,000 per constituency per candidate in urban districts and 10 hundred thousand rupees in rural districts. For further details see Sridharan (1999).

16. The difference between the mean corruption levels between India and Brazil in the (i) ICRG index is 1.05 (p=0.000), (ii) TI Index is 0.8 (p=0.000), and (iii) WB Index is 0.9 (p=0.000), respectively.

17. Entire rule available at http://www.tse.jus.br/internet/partidos/fidelidade.htm. Accessed January, 28, 2010.

18. Published interview of Dr. Pereirra, Professor, Curitiba University, published April 7, 2009. Transcript available at http://www.jornalcomunicacao.ufpr.br/node/5747). Accessed February 9, 2010.

Chapter 6

1. See, for example, Mansfield et al. (2000), Collier and Rohner (2007), and Gleditsch and Ward (1997).

2. The complete list of primary sources and surveys that have been used to operationalize the ICRG measure can be found in the reports of Kaufmann et al. (1998) and Lambsdorff (1998).

3. For more details of the survey methodology that ICRG employs to develop their corruption measure see www.prsgroup.com/ICRG_Methodology.aspx Accessed July 10, 2009.

4. As mentioned above, the ICRG index of corruption is available for 150 countries. The 150 countries include not only the developing democracies in my sample but also all democratic OECD countries as well as several autocratic developing countries.

5. For example, the 1998 TI score of corruption for each country is based on 12 surveys from 7 different institutions. As discussed in detail in Lambsdorff (1998), the results of these surveys conducted by TI for each country in a given year are highly positively correlated; in fact the bivariate correlation coefficient among different surveys exceeds 0.8 on average, suggesting that the independent surveys genuinely measure some common features.

6. The standardization mentioned above was done by a simple mean and standard deviation approach before 2002.

7. See, e.g., Tsebelis and Aleman (2005); Tsebelis et al. (2001); and Laver and Shepsle (1996).

8. As emphasized in the extant literature (cited above), two reasons explain why the institutional ability to introduce a drafted bill allows the relevant political actors to engage in agenda-setting. First, political actors strategically use the introduction of bills as a tool to influence the legislative agenda (Tsebelis et al. 2001). Additionally, note that the bills that actors introduce on the legislative floor closely match their preferences (Tsebelis and Aleman 2005; Laver and Shepsle 1996; Tsebelis 2005). This gives them incentives to engage in agenda-setting to ensure that the outcome on the legislative floor does not deviate from their ideal point.

9. For the functions of party whips in democracies see, for example, Kopstein and Lichbach (2005) and Kryzanek (2003).

10. See, for example, Kaufmann and Siegelbaum (1997), Moody-Stuart (1995), Rose-Ackerman (2007), and Goel and Budak (2006).

11. See World Bank (1995, 1996).

12. For technical details of the Tobit "right-censored" model, see Greene (2000). Appendix A provides a summary.

13. A thorough discussion of estimation of the Tobit model with fixed effects for pooled and/or panel datasets is provided in Greene (2003). Additionally, for a technical introduction to the estimation of Tobit models with fixed effects and a lagged dependent variable, see Honore (1993) and Hu (2003).

14. Note, however, that I obtain similar results even if I include all three independent variables in a single specification in the Tobit right-censored and LDV models.

15. I also checked whether the results reported in table 6.6 remain consistent when I employ the LDV regression model (estimated) with country fixed effects and PCSEs to test hypotheses 1b, 2b, and 3b. The estimated coefficient of the three independent variables—*Agenda-Setting, Bill Amendment,* and *Expel Dissidents*—is positive and highly significant irrespective of whether I employ the *ICRG, TI,* or *WB Corruption* measure for the dependent variable. This indicates that the results from the Tobit right-censored model also hold in the LDV regression models. Results available from author.

16. The largest and mean VIF value in the models is less than 10 and greater than 1, respectively; thus multicollinearity is not a problem (Chatterjee et al. 1999). The Breusch-Godfrey LM test and Gourieroux et al. (1982) score test failed to reject the null of no serial correlation in the outcome and selection equations, respectively. The RESET test reveals that there is no omitted variable bias problem and the Jarque-Bera test shows that the residuals approximate a normal distribution.

17. Test results are available from the author on request.

Chapter 7

1. The JPA February 2008 Special Issue on lobbying in developing democracies contains studies of lobbying in the Czech Republic (Evanson), Lithuania (Hrebenar et al.), Argentina (Johnson), India (Yadav), China (Yadav), and an overview of lobbying in several Central and Eastern European countries (McGrath). See Cox and Vas (2000) for Hungary and Frye (2001) for Russia.

2. Farmelo (2003, 18), n. 17. Cited in Johnson (2003, 90).

3. The institutional literature on party systems has primarily explored the effect that electoral rules, executive regimes, and federal systems have on the number of parties (Taagepera and

Shugart 1989; Boix 1999; Lijphart 1999; Chhibber and Kollman 2004) and on party discipline (Carey 2007; Jones et al. 2002; Bowler, Farrell, and Katz 1999).

4. In contrast, investment climate surveys such as Business Environment and Enterprise Performance Surveys and World Business Environment Surveys conducted by the World Bank
and the EBRD focus on firms; Public Expenditure Tracking Surveys by the World Bank/UN
focus only on citizen perceptions and corruption by public officials; and Report Card Surveys also focus on citizen perceptions of petty corruption in public services. Furthermore,
these are available only for a few countries and for very few years.

5. For example, see Chang and Golden (2010) for an application of selectorate theory to the
problem of corruption in autocracies.

6. See Scarrow (2005) and Janda (2005) for discussions of this debate.

REFERENCES

Abed, G. T., and H. R. Davoodi. 2000. "Corruption, Structural Reforms, and Economic Performance in the Transition Economies." IMF Working Paper WP/00/132.

Ades, A., and R. Di Tella. 1997. "The New Economics of Corruption: A Survey and Some New Results." *Political Studies* 45: 496–515.

———. 1999. "Rents, Competition, and Corruption." *American Economic Review* 89, no. 4: 982–992.

Adsera, A., C. Boix, and L. Payne. 2000. "Are You being Served? Political Accountability and Quality of Government." Inter-American Development Bank Research Department Working Paper 438. Washington, DC: U.S. Government Printing Office.

Agh, A. 1999. "The Parliamentarization of the East Central European Parties: Party Discipline in the Hungarian Parliament, 1990–1996." In *Parliamentary Discipline and Parliamentary Government*, Ed. S. Bowler, D. Farrell, and R. Katz. . Columbus: Ohio State University Press.

Agrawal, A. 2000. "Small Is beautiful, but Is Larger Better? Forest-Management Institutions in the Kumaon Himalaya, India." In *People and Forests: Communities, Institutions, and Governance*, Ed. C. Gibson, M. McKean, and E. Ostrom. Cambridge, MA: MIT Press.

Aldrich, J. H. 2008. "Political Parties in and out of Legislatures." In *Handbook of Comparative Politics*. Ed. C. Bois and S. Stokes. New York: Oxford University Press.

Aldrich, J. H., and D. W. Rohde. 1997–1998. "Theories of Party in the Legislature and the Transition to Republican Rules in the House." *Political Science Quarterly* 112: 541–567.

Aldrich, J. H. 1995. *Why Parties? The Origin and Transformation of Political Parties in the United States*. Chicago: University of Chicago Press.

Alem án, E. 2006. "Policy Gatekeepers in Latin American Legislatures." *Latin American Politics and Society* 48, no. 3: 125–126.

Alexander, H., and R. Shiratori. 1994. *Comparative Political Finance among the Democracies*. Boulder, CO: Westview Press.

Ali, M. A., and H. S. Isse. 2003. "Determinants of Economic Corruption: A Cross-Country Comparison." *Cato Journal* 22, no. 3: 449–466.

Alston, L. J., and B. Muellar. 2005. "Pork for Policy: Executive and Legislative Exchange in Brazil." *Journal of Law, Economics, and Organization* 22, no. 1: 87-114doi:10.1093

Alt, J. E., and D. D. Lassen. 2003. "The Political Economy of Corruption in American States." *Journal of Theoretical Politics* 15, no. 3: 341–365.

America's Insider. November 24, 2000. "Campaign Finance Scandal involving Cardoso Could Get Worse." Available at http://www.allbusiness.com/specialty-businesses/713088-1.html. Accessed July 21, 2009.

Ames, B. 2001. *The Deadlock of Democracy in Brazil*. Ann Arbor: University of Michigan Press.

Anderson, C., and Y. Tverdova. 2003. "Corruption, Political Allegiances, and Attitudes toward Government in Contemporary Democracies." *American Political Science Review* 47, no. 1: 97–109.

Anti-Corruption Portal. Brazil Country Profile. http://www.business-anti-corruption.com/normal.asp?pageid=238

Asia Times. 2008. " India's Reforms Look Forlorn." August 8. http://www.atimes.com/atimes/South_Asia/JH08Df02.html. Accessed August 30, 2008.

Austen-Smith, D., and J. Wright. 1992. "Competitive Lobbying for a Legislator's Vote." *Social Choice and Welfare* 9: 229–257.

Austin, R., and M. Tjernström. 2003. *Funding of Political Parties and Election Campaigns.* International Institute for Democracy and Elections Handbook Series. Stockholm: Trydells Tryckeri.

Bardhan, P. 1997. "Corruption and Development: A Review of Issues." *Journal of Economic Literature* 35: 1320–1346.

Bardhan, P. 1993. "Analytics of the Institutions of Informal Cooperation in Rural Development." *World Development* 21: 633–639.

Baron, D. P. 2006. "Competitive Lobbying and Supermajorities in a Majority-Rule Institution." *Scandinavian Journal of Economics* 108, no. 4 (December): 607–642.

———. 2002. "Commentary on "Lobbying and Legislative Organization: The Effect of the Vote of Confidence Procedure." *Business and Politics* 4, no. 2: Article 7. Available at: http://www.bepress.com/bap/vol4/iss2/art7 Accessed on March, 6, 2009.

Bates, R. H., and K. A. Shepsle. 1995. "Demographics and Institutions." Paper presented at the Frontiers of Economics Conference (in honor of Douglass C. North), Washington University, St Louis.

Baumgartner, F., and B. Leech. 2001. "Interest Niches and Policy Bandwagons: Patterns of Interest Group Involvement in National Politics." *Journal of Politics* 63: 1191–1213.

Baumgartner, F., and B. Leech. 1998. *Basic Interests: The Importance of Groups in Politics and Political Science.* Princeton, NJ: Princeton University Press.

Bawn, K. 1995. "Political Control versus Expertise: Congressional Choices about Administrative Procedures." *American Political Science Review* 89: 62–73.

———. 1997. "Choosing Strategies to Control the Bureaucracy: Statutory Constraints, Oversight, and the Committee System." *Journal of Law, Economics, and Organization* 13: 101–126.

Baxi, U. 2000. "The Avatars of Indian Judicial Activism: Explorations in the Geographies of [In]justice" in *Fifty Years of the Supreme Court of India* eds. S.K. Verma and Kusum. New York: Oxford University Press.

BBC. September 4, 2007. Q & A: Brazil corruption scandal. http://news.bbc.co.uk/2/hi/americas/4676435.stm Accessed July 10, 2009.

Bendor, J., and A. Meirowitz. 2004. "Spatial Models of Delegation." *American Political Science Review* 98: 293–310.

Benedetto, G. S. Hix 2007. "The Rejected, the Ejected, and the Dejected: Explaining Government Rebels in the 2001–2005 British House of Commons." *Comparative Political Studies* 40: 755–781.

Bennedsen, M., and S. E. Feldman. 2006a. "Informational Lobbying and Political Contributions." *Journal of Public Economics* 90: 631–656.

———. 2006b. "Lobbying Bureaucrats." *Scandinavian Journal of Economics* 108, no. 4: 643–668.

———. 2002a. "Lobbying Legislatures." *Journal of Political Economy* 110, no. 4 (August): 919–946.

———. 2002b. "Lobbying and Legislative Organization: The Effect of the Vote of Confidence Procedure." *Business and Politics* 3, no. 2: 187–203.

Bhagwati, J. 2004. *In Defense of Globalization.* New York: Oxford University Press.

———, and T. N. Srinivasan. 1982. "The Welfare Consequences of Directly-Unproductive Profit-Seeking (DUP) Lobbying Activities." *Journal of International Economics* 13: 33–44.

Birch, S. 2005. "Single Member District Electoral Systems and Democratic Transition." *Electoral Studies* 24:281-301.

Blondel, J., and M. Cotta, eds. 1996. *Party and Government: An Inquiry into the Relationship between Governments and Supporting Parties in Liberal Democracies.* New York: Macmillan.

———. 1973. *Comparative Legislatures.* Englewood Cliffs, NJ: Prentice-Hall.

Bleichinger, V. 2002. "Corruption and Political Parties." *Sectoral Perspectives on Corruption.* Prepared by MSI for USAID, November 2002. Available at http://www.usaid.gov/our_work/democracy.../sector/politicalparties.doc Accessed April5, 2009.

Boix, C. and M. Slovik 2008. "Foundations of Limited Authoritarian Government: Institutions and Power-sharing in Dictatorships" Unpublished manuscript. Available at http://www.princeton.edu/~cboix/boix-svolik-2009.pdf Accessed March 1, 2010.

Bonaglia, F., J. Braga de Macedo, and M. Bussolo. 2001. "How Globalization Improves Governance." Discussion Paper No. 2992. Paris, France: Centre for Economic Policy Research, Organisation for Economic Co-operation and Development.

Booysen, . 2006. "The Will of the Parties versus the Will of the People? Defections, Elections and Alliances in South Africa." *Party Politics* 12: 727–746.

Bowler, S., D. Farrell, and R. Katz. 1999. *Parliamentary Discipline and Parliamentary Government.* Columbus: Ohio State University Press.

Braun, M., R. Di Tella. 2004. "Inflation, Inflation Variability, and Corruption." *Economics and Politics* 16: 77–100.

Bridges Weekly Trade News Digest. 2005. "Indian Parliament Approves Controversial Patent Bill." Vol. 9, no. 10 (March 23): Available at http://www.ictsd.org/weekly/05-03-23/story1.htm. Accessed October 15, 2008.

Brinks, D. 2005. "Judicial reform and independence in Brazil and Argentina: The beginning of a new millennium?" *Texas International Law Journal* 40: 595–622.

Brunetti, A., and B. Weder. 2003. "A Free Press Is Bad News for Corruption." *Journal of Public Economics* 87: 1801–1824.

Bryan, S., and D. Baer. 2005. *Money in Politics: A Study of Party Financing Practices in 22 Countries.* Washington, DC: National Democratic Institute for International Affairs.

Bull, M. J., and J. L. Newell, eds. 2003. *Corruption in Contemporary Politics.* New York: Palgrave Macmillan.

Buscaglia, E. 2001. *Judicial Corruption in Developing Countries: Its Causes and Consequences.* Prepared for UN Office for Drug Control. Available at http://www.unodc.org/pdf/crime/gpacpublications/cicp14.pdf. Accessed November 23, 2009.

Cain,B., Ferejohn,J. and M. Fiorina.1986. *The Personal Vote, Constituency Service and Electoral Independence.* Cambridge, MA: Harvard University Press.

Campos, N. and F. Giovannoni (2008), "Lobbying, Corruption and Other Banes," London, CEPR Discussion Paper 6962.

Carey, J. 2007. "Competing Principals, Political Institutions, and Party Unity in Legislative Voting." *American Journal of Political Science* 51: 92–1007.

———. 1995. "Incentives to Cultivate a Personal Vote: A Rank Ordering of Electoral Formulas." *Electoral Studies* 14: 417–439.

Carothers, T. 2006. *Confronting the Weakest Link: Aiding Political Parties in New Democracies.* New York: Carnegie Endowment for International Peace.

Carrubba, C. J., and C. Volden. 2000. "Coalitional Politics and Logrolling in Legislative Institutions." *American Journal of Political Science* 44, no. 2: 261–277.

CEBRAP. 1996. *Cadernos de Pesquisa.* no. 5, Outobreo de 1996. Sao Paolo, Brazil: CEBRAP.

CEDI. 2006. *The Brazilian Legislative Branch: Chamber of Deputies.* Brasilia: Center for Documentation and Information, Publications Department.

Chamberlin, J. 1974. "Provision of Collective Goods as a Function of Group Size." *American Political Science Review* 68: 707–716.

Chang, E. C. C, and M. Golden. 2010 "Sources of Corruption in Authoritarian Regimes," *Social Science Quarterly* 91:1-20

Chang, E. C. C, and M. Golden. 2007. "Electoral Systems, District Magnitude and Corruption." *British Journal of Political Science* 37: 115–137.

———. 2003. "Electoral Systems, District Magnitude and Corruption." Paper presented at the 2003 annual meeting of the American Political Science Association, August 28–31, 2003.

Chatterjee, S., B. Price, and A. S. Haidi. 1999. *Regression Analysis by Example.* New York: John Wiley and Sons.

Cheibub, J. 2007. *Presidentialism, Parliamentarism, and Democracy.* Cambridge, UK: Cambridge University Press.

———, and J. Gandhi. 2004. "Classifying Political Regimes: A Six-Fold Measure of Democracies and Dictatorships." Paper prepared for annual meeting of the American Political Science Association, Chicago, September.

———, A. Przeworski, and S. Saiegh. 2004. "Government Coalitions and Legislative Success under Parliamentarism and Presidentialism." *British Journal of Political Science* 34 (October): 565–587.

Chhibber, P. K. 1999. *Democracy without Associations: Transformation of the Party System and Social Cleavages in India.* Ann Arbor, MI: University of Michigan Press.

Claessens, S., E. Feijin and L. Laeven. 2008. "Political Connections and Preferential Access to Finance: The Role of Campaign Contributions" ECGI Finance Working Paper No, 166/2007. Available at http://papers.ssrn.com/sol3/papers.cfm?abstract_id=945196. Accessed November 5, 2008.

Cintra, Antônio Octávio. 2004. "Reforma Poítica: de Volta à Cena e Retorno aos Bastidores." *Inteligência. March:* 119–129.

Collier, P., and D. Rohner. 2008. "Democracy, Development, and Conflict." *Journal of the European Economic Association* 6, nos. 2–3: 531–540.

Cowhey, P. F., and M. D. McCubbins. 1993. Structure and Policy in Japan and the United States. New York, NY: Cambridge University Press.

Cox, G. W., W. B. Heller, and M. D. McCubbins. 2008. "Agenda Power in the Italian Chamber of Deputies, 1988–2000." *Legislative Studies Quarterly* 33: 171–222.

———, and Mathew McCubbins. 2007 [1993]. *Legislative Leviathan: Party Government in the House.* 2nd ed. Cambridge, UK: Cambridge University Press.

———, M. Masuyama, and M. D. McCubbins. 2000. "Agenda Power in the Japanese House of Representatives." *Japanese Journal of Political Science* 1: 1–21.

———. 2000. "Legislative Organization." *Legislative Studies Quarterly* 25: 169–192.

————. 1987. *The Efficient Secret: The Cabinet and the Development of Political Parties in Victorian England*. Cambridge, UK: Cambridge University Press.

Curtice, J. and P. Shively, 2000. *Who Represents us Best? One Member or Many?* Oxford: CREST Working Paper 79. Available at http://www.crest.ox.ac.uk/papers/p79.pdf. Accessed April 25, 2008.

Daamgard, E., and P. Svensson. 1989. "Who Governs? Parties and Policies in Denmark." *European Journal of Political Research* 17: 731–745.

Damania, R., P. Fredriksson, and M. Mani. 2004. "The Persistence of Corruption and Regulatory Compliance Failures: Theory and Evidence." *Public Choice* 121: 363–390.

Davis, C. 2004. "International Institutions and Issue Linkage: Building Support for Agricultural Trade Liberalization." *American Political Science Review* 98: 153–169.

de Figueiredo, R. J. P., Jr. 2002. "Electoral Competition, Political Uncertainty, and Policy Insulation." *American Political Science Review* 96: 321–333.

DeSouza, P. R., and E. Sridharan, eds. 2006. *India's Political Parties*. New Delhi: Sage Publications.

Desposato, S. 2006. "The Impact of Electoral Rules on Legislative Parties: Lessons from the Brazilian Senate and Chamber of Deputies." *Journal of Politics* 68: 1018–1030.

Diermeier, D., and R. Myerson. 1999. "Bicameralism and Its Consequences for the Internal Organization of Legislatures." *American Economic Review* 89: 1182–1196.

Diermeier, D., and T. Feddersen. 1998. "Cohesion in Legislatures and the Vote of Confidence Procedure." *American Political Science Review* 92: 611–622.

Diamond, L., and R. Gunther, eds. 2001. *Political Parties and Democracy*. Baltimore: Johns Hopkins University Press.

Diamond, L. 2003. "Moving Out of Poverty: What Does Democracy Have to Do With It?" Paper presented at World Bank Workshop, "Moving out of Poverty: Growth and Freedom from the Bottom Up," Washington, DC, July 15–16.

Di Palma, G. 1977. *Surviving without Governing: The Italian Parties in Parliament*. Berkeley: University of California Press.

Djankov, S., R. La Porta, F. Lopez-de-Silanes, and A. Shleifer. 2009. "Disclosure by Politicians." Working Paper 14703. http://www.nber.org/papers/w14703. Accessed January 18, 2010

Donath-Burson-Marstellar 2005. A Guide to Effective Lobbying in the Czech Republic. Prague: Donath Burson-Marsteller.

Döring, H. 1995a. "Time as a Scarce Resource: Government Control of the Agenda." In *Parliaments and Majority Rule in Western Europe*. Ed. Herbert Döring. Berlin: Campus Verlag.

Döring, H. 1995b. *Parliaments and Majority Rules in Western Europe*. Mannheim Center for European Social Research. Mannheim, Germany: University of Mannheim.

Election Commission of India. 2004. Statement of Accounts. http://www.eci.gov.in/mis-Political_Parties/Election_Expenses/StatementOfaccounts2004.pdf. Accessed August 21, 2008.

Epstein, D., and S. O'Halloran. 1994. Administrative Procedures, Information, and Agency Discretion. *American Journal of Political Science*, 38: 697–722.

Epstein, D., J. Knight, and O. Shvetsova. 2002. "Selecting Selection Programs." In *Judicial Independence at the Crossroads: An Interdisciplinary Approach*. Ed. S. Burbank and B. Friedman. Thousand Oaks, CA: Sage.

Estado de Sao Paulo. 1997. June 25, 8.

————. 1996. "Líderes ameaçam isolar parlamentares disidentes." May 24: A4.

Fearon, J. and Laitin. D. 2008. "Integrating Qualitative and Quantitative Methods." In *Oxford Handbook of Political Methodology*. Ed. J. Box-Steffensmeier, H. Brady, and D. Collier. New York: Oxford University Press.

Feijin, E. 2005. "Does Campaign Finance Imply Political Favors? The Case of the 1998 Brazilian Elections." http://www1.fee.uva.nl/pp/bin/316fulltext.pdf. Accessed October 18, 2008.

Ferdinand, P. 2003. "Party Funding and Corruption in East Asia: The Cases of Japan, South Korea and Taiwan." In *The Funding of Political Parties and Campaigns*. Ed. R. Austin and M. Tjernström. IDEA Handbook Series. www.idea.int/publications/funding_parties/ Accessed September 23, 2008.

———. 2007. Brazil Focus Weekly Report February 19–February 26. All issues available at http://www.wilsoncenter.org/index.cfm?topic_id=1419&fuseaction=topics.item&news_id=232764. All issues accessed December 6, 2009.

———. Brazil Focus Weekly Report May 17–22, 2007.

Fleischer, D. Brazil Focus Weekly Report September 29–October 5, 2007

Fleischer, D_ 1997. "Political Corruption and Campaign Financing: Brazil's Slow Shift towards Anti-Corruption Laws." Paper presented at 20th International Congress of the Latin American Studies Association (LASA), Guadalajara, México, April 17–19.

Figuerido, A., C., and F. Limongi. 2000. "Presidential Power, Legislative Organization, and Party Behavior in Brazil." *Comparative Politics* 32: 151–170.

———. 1999. *Executivo e Legislativo na Nova Ordem Constitucional*. Rio de Janeiro, Brazil: Editora FGV.

Financial Times. 2008. "Thai PM Declares State of Emergency," September 3.

———. 2008. "Politics: Leftwing Populist Surprises Critics and Emerges as a Wily Survivor." July 22.

———.2008. "Cambodians Set to Endorse Ruling CPP." July 18.

———. 2008. "Financiers Tied to Brazil Vote-Buying Arrested." July 9.

———. 2008. "Ukraine Coalition Threatened with Collapse." June 6.

———. 2008. "Balkan Business Needs Consistency to Ride EU bus." April 2.

———. 2007. "The Great Political Divide at Europe's Heart." October 17.

———. 2007. "Brazil Senate Chief Survives Scandal." September 13.

———.2007. "Ukraine Parliament Clips Yushchenko's Wings." January 12.

———.2006. "Conservatives' Stance Angers Business." December 2.

———.2006. "Prospect of Ping-Pong for Tall-Order Companies' Bill." October 28.

———.2006. "Corruption Scandals Lap at Lula's Ankles." October 26.

———.2006. "Prodi Set to Win Confidence Vote." August 2.

———. 2005. "EU Parliament Shrinks Chemicals Safeguards." November 18.

———.2005. "Koizumi Urged to Drop Poll Threat." August 4.

———.2005. "Taiwan Pension Delay Frustrates Managers." June 26.

———.2005. "Corruption Claims Hit Brazil Markets." June 7.

———.2004. "Brazil Probe Reveals a Decade of Corruption in Healthcare Contracts." June 2.

———.2003. "Late Deal Averts Political Crisis in S. Africa." January 8.

———. 2003. "Judicial Reform Holding Back Business." January 28.

Financial Express. 2008. "Somnath Breaks silence, Says I Am Not Quitting." August 2.

———.2008. "Party's Over: CPM Expels Somnath." July 23.

———.2008. "Is Somnath Right or Wrong? Central Body to Assess Today." July 19.

———.2008. "Two CPM MPs Lash Out at Speaker Somnath Agencies." July 17.

Fisman, R. J., and R. Gatti. 2002. "Decentralization and Corruption: Evidence across Countries." *Journal of Public Economics* 83: 325–345.

Folha de São Paulo. 2000. "Especial, Olho no Congresso." March 22, A-6.

————. 1998. "Base governista é favorecida na distribuição de recursos." February 13, 1–4.

————. 1998. "Câmara aprova emenda da Previdência." February 12, 1–10.

————. 1996. "Ministro apela por fim de privilégios." May 25, A1–4.

————. 1994. September 23, 5.

Frechette, G. R. 2001. "A Panel Data Analysis of the Time-Varying Determinants of Corruption." Paper presented at the EPCS 2001.

Frieden, J. A. 1991. Invested Interests. *International Organization* 45: 425–451.

Frontline. 1999. "The Playing Field Favours Foreign Companies." Volume 16–Issue 16, July 31–August 13, 1999. www.hinduonnet.com/fline/fl1616/16160100.htm http://www.hinduonnet.com/fline/fl1616/16160100.htm

————. "There Is a Political Consensus on Economic Issues." Volume 16–Issue 16.

————. "Stability Is Essential for the Economy." Volume 16–Issue 16.

Gailmard, S. 2002. "Expertise, Subversion, and Bureaucratic Discretion." *Journal of Law, Economics, and Organization* 18: 536–555.

Gallagher, M. and I. Holliday 2003. "Electoral Systems, Representational Roles and Legislators Behaviour: Evidence from Hong Kong" **New Zealand Journal of Asian Studies 5: 107-120**

Gandhi, J., and A. Przeworski. 2007. "Dictatorial Institutions and the Survival of Autocrats." *Comparative Political Studies* 40: 1279–2301.

Ganguly, S., L. Diamond, and M. F. Plattner, eds. 2007. *The State of India's Democracy.* Baltimore: Johns Hopkins University Press.

Gazeta Mercantil. 1998. "Câmara aprova reforma da Previdência." February 12, A14

Geddes, B., and A. Neto. 1992. "Institutional Sources of Corruption in Brazil." *Third World Quarterly* 13: 641–661.

George, A., and A. Bennett. 2005. *Case Studies and Theory Development in the Social Sciences.* Cambridge, MA: MIT Press.

Gerring, J., and S. V. Thacker. 2008. *A Centripetal Theory of Democratic Governance.* New York: Cambridge University Press.

Gerring, J. 2007. *Case Studies Research: Principles and Practices.* Cambridge, MA: Cambridge University Press.

Gerring, J., and S. V. Thacker. 2004. "Political Institutions and Corruption: The Role of Unitarism and Parliamentarism," *British Journal of Political Science* 34: 295-330

Ginsburg, T. 2006. "Constitutional Review." *Oxford Handbook of Comparative Politics.* New York: Oxford University Press.

Glaeser, E. L., and C. Goldin. 2006. *Corruption and Reform: Lessons from America's Economic History.* Chicago: University of Chicago Press.

Gleditsch, K. S., and M. D. Ward. 1997. "Double Take: A Re-examination of Democracy and Autocracy in Modern Polities." *Journal of Conflict Resolution* 41 (June): 361–382.

Goel, R. K., and J. Budak. 2006. "Corruption in Transition Economies: Effects of Government Size, Country Size and Economic Reforms." *Journal of Economics and Finance* 30, no. 2 (ummer):.

Goetz, K., and R. Zuberk. 2005. "Lawmaking in Poland: Rules and Patterns of Legislation." Report Commissioned by Ernst and Young, Poland.

Golden, M., and M. Chang. 2001. "Competitive Corruption: Factional Conflict and Political Malfeasance in Postwar Italian Christian Democracy." *World Politics* 53: 588–622.

Golder, M. 2006. "Presidential Coattails and Legislative Fragmentation." *American Journal of Political Science* 50: 34–48.

Gourieroux, C., A. Monfort, and A. Trognon. 1982. "Estimation and Test in Probit Models with Serial Correlation." In J. P. Florens, M. Mouchart, J. P. Raouit, and L. Simar, *Alternative Approaches to Time Series Analysis*. Bruxelles: des Facultes universitaires Saint-Louis, 169–209.

Gray and Lowery 2004. " A Neoplurliast Perspective on Research on Organized Interests" *Political Research Quarterly* 57:164-175.

Greenberg, S., and J. Rosner. 2006. "Leaders Must Join Voters in the War on Corruption." www. greenbergresearch.com/index.php?ID=1723. September 23, 2009.

Grindle, M., and J. Thomas. 1991. *Public Choices and Policy Change: The Political Economy of Reform in Developing Countries*. Baltimore: Johns Hopkins University Press.

Grossman. G and E. Helpman. 2001. Special Interest Politics. Cambridge,: MIT Press.

Gryzmala-Busse, A. 2007. *Rebuilding Leviathan: Party Competition and State Exploitation in Post-Communist Democracies*. New York: Cambridge University Press.

Gurgur, T., and A. Shah. 2005. "Localization and Corruption: Panacea or Pandora's Box." World Bank Policy Research Working Paper 3486.

Gurr, T. R., K. Jaggers, and W. H. Moore. 1989. "Polity II Codebook." Unpublished manuscript, University of Colorado.

Gurr, T. R., , K. Jaggers, and W. H. Moore. 1990. "The Transformation of the Western State: The Growth of Democracy, Autocracy, and State Power since 1800." *Studies in Comparative International Development* 25: 73–108.

Hall, R., and A. Deardorff. 2006. "Lobbying as Legislative Subsidy." *American Political Science Review* 100: 69–84.

———, and C. I. Jones. 1999. "Why Do Some Countries Produce So Much More Output per Worker than Others." *Quarterly Journal of Economics* 114: 83–116.

Hagopian, F. 2009. "Parties and Voters in Emerging Democracies." *Oxford Handbook of Comparative Politics*. Ed. Carles Bois and Susan Stokes. New York: Oxford University Press.

———, and S. Mainwaring, eds. 2005. *The Third Wave of Democratization in Latin America: Advances and Setbacks*. New York: Cambridge University Press.

———. 2004. "Economic Liberalization, Party Competition, and Elite Partisan Cleavages: Brazil in Comparative (Latin American) Perspective." Paper prepared for the Workshop on the Analysis of Political Cleavages and Party Competition, Duke University, Department of Political Science, April 2–3.

Hammergren, L. 2007. *Envisioning Reform: Improving Judicial Performance in Latin America*. State College: Pennsylvania State University Press.

Hardin, R. 1976. "Group Provision of Step Goods." *Behavioral Science* 21: 101–106.

———. 1982. *Collective Action*. Baltimore: Johns Hopkins University Press.

Harsstad and Svenssen 2009. "Bribes, Lobbying and Development" Available at http://www. kellogg.northwestern.edu/faculty/harstad/htm/bl.pdf. Accessed February 15, 2010.

Heller, W. 2001. "Why Government Gets What It Wants in Parliamentary in Multi-Party Parliaments." *American Journal of Political Science* 45, no. 4: 780–798.

Hellman, J., G. Jones, and D. Kaufmann. 2002. "Seize the State, Seize the Day: State Capture, Corruption and Influence in Transition." World Bank Policy Research Paper 2444. Available at http://www.worldbank.org/ Accessed August 29, 2008.

Helpman, E., and T. Persson. 1998. "Lobbying and Legislative Bargaining." NBER Working Paper No. 6589. Available at http://papers.ssrn.com/sol3/papers.cfm?abstract_id=226313. Accessed July 12, 2008.

Herzfeld, T., and C. Weiss. 2003. "Corruption and Legal (In)-Effectiveness: An Empirical Investigation." *European Journal of Political Economy* 19: 621–632.

Hicken, A. 2009. *Building Party Systems in Developing Democracies*. New York, NY: Cambridge University Press.

The Hindu. July 2, 2008. "Towards Free and Fair Elections in India." http://www.hinduonnet.com/2008/07/02/stories/2008070253151100.htm. Accessed August 28, 2008.

———.2006. "Poll Funding: Consensus Elusive." pp 3.

———. 2002. "Judicial Corruption." Pp 2

Hiroi, T. 2005. "Bicameral Politics: The Dynamics of Lawmaking in Brazil." Dissertation manuscript. University of Pittsburgh.

Hirschl, R. 2004. *Towards Juristocracy: The Origins and Consequences of the New Constitutionalism*. Cambridge, MA: Harvard University Press.

Hirschman, A. O. (1970). *Exit, Voice, and Loyalty: Responses to Decline in Firms, Organizations, and States*. Boston: Harvard University Press.

Hix, S. 2004. "Electoral Institutions and Legislative Behavior: Explaining Voting Defection in the European Parliament." *World Politics* 56: 194-223.

Hix, S. 2002. "Parliamentary Behavior with Two Principals: Preferences, Parties and Voting in the European Parliament." *American Journal of Political Science* 46: 688–698.

Hojnacki, M., and D. C. Kimball. 1998. "Organized Interests and the Decision of Whom to Lobbying in Congress." *American Political Science Review* 92: 775–790.

Holyoke, T. 2003. "Choosing Battlegrounds: Interest Group Competition Across. Multiple Venues." *Political Research Quarterly* 56: 325 – 336

Huber, J. D., and C. R. Shipan. 2006. "Politics, Delegation, and Bureaucracy." *Oxford Handbook of Political Economy*. Ed. Barry Weingast and Don Wittman. New York: Oxford University Press.

———. 2002. *Deliberate Discretion? The Institutional Foundations of Bureaucratic Autonomy*. New York: Cambridge University Press.

Huber, J. 1996. "The Vote of Confidence in Parliamentary Democracies." *American Political Science Review* 90: 269-282.

Hurlin, C., and B. Venet. 2003. "Granger Causality Tests in Panel Data Models with Fixed Coefficients." Manuscript. University of Paris IX.

Iaryczower, M., P. Spiller, and M. Tommasi. 2006. "Judicial Lobbying: The Politics of Labor Law Constitutional Interpretation." *American Political Science Review* 100: 85–97.

IPS News, May 31, 2007. "India: Legal System in the Dock." http://cosmicfantasia.com/alternative-news/world-perspective/india-legal-system-in-the-dock.php. Accessed August 29, 2008.

———. 2006. "Challenges 2005–2006: Corruption in Brazil—Old Tricks, New Dogs." http://ipsnews.net/news.asp?idnews=31688. Accessed October 21, 2008.

Indian Express. 1999. "Touch and Go but IRDA Bill goes Through." December 3.

———. 1998. "No Votes, No Notes for Tata's Election Fund." January 30.

———. 1998. "Tatas Set Up Trust to Fund Parties." January 23. http://www.indianexpress.com/res/web/pIe/ie/daily/19980123/02350514.html. Accessed August 29, 2008.

Inglehart,R. and C. Weltzel 2005. *Modernizaion, Cultural Change and Democracy: The Human Development Sequence*. New York, NY: Cambridge University Press.

Jaggers, K., and T. R. Gurr. 1995. "Tracking Democracy's Third Wave with the Polity III Data." *Journal of Peace Research* 32: 469–482.

Janda, K. 2009. "Laws against Party Switching, Defecting, or Floor Crossing in National Parliaments." Working Paper # 2 presented at the World Congress of the International Political Science Association held in Santiago, Chile, July 12–16.

———. 2005. "Adopting Party Law." *National Democratic Institute.* Available at www.ndi.org. Accessed March 4, 2009.

Janssen, M. A. 2008. "Evolution of Cooperation in a One-Shot Prisoner's Dilemma based on Recognition of Trustworthy and Untrustworthy Agents." *Journal of Economic Behavior and Organization* 65: 458–471.

Jenny, M., and W. Muller 1995. "Presidents of Parliaments: Neutral Chairmen or Assets of the Majority?" In *Parliaments and Majority Rule in Western Europe.* Ed. Herbert Doring. Berlin: Campus Verlag.

Johnston, M. 2006. "Political Finance Policy, Parties and Democratic Development." *National Democratic Institute.* Available at www.ndi.org. Accessed March 6, 2009.

———. 2005. *Syndromes of Corruption: Wealth, Power, and Democracy.* Cambridge, MA: Cambridge University Press.

Johnson, J., and J. Wallack. 2008. "Electoral Systems and the Personal Vote: Update of Database of Particularism." Available at: dss.ucsd.edu/~jwjohnso/espv.html Accessed July 7, 2008.

Jones, E. C. 2004. "Wealth-Based Trust and the Development of Collective Action." *World Development* 32: 691–711.

Jones, M. P., S. Saeigh, P. T. Spiller, and M. Tommasi. 2002. "Amateur Legislators—Professional Politicians: The Consequences of Party-Centered Electoral Rules in a Federal System." *American Journal of Political Science* 46, no. 3: 656–669.

Kang, D. C. 2002. *Crony Capitalism: Corruption and Development in South Korea and the Philippines.* New York: Cambridge University Press.

Kanji, G. K. 1999. *100 Statistical Tests.* London: Sage.

Kapur, D., and P. B. Mehta, eds. 2007. *Public Institutions in India: Performance and Design.* New Delhi: Oxford University Press.

Karvonen, L. 2007. "Legislation on Political Parties: A Global Comparison." *Party Politics* 13 (July): 437–455.

Kashyap, S. C. 2003. *Anti-Defection Law and Parliamentary Privileges.* 2nd ed. New Delhi: Universal Law Publishing.

Katz, J. and B. Sala. 1996. "Careerism, Committee Assignments and the Electoral Connection." *American Political Science Review* 90: 21–33.

Kaufmann, D., and A. Kraay. 2002a. "Governance Indicators, Aid Allocation and the Millennium Challenge." World Bank Mimeo.Available at http://www.irisprojects.umd.edu/ppc_ideas/Revolutionizing_Aid/Resources/typology_pdf/MCA_kauffman_kraay.pdf. Accessed July 18, 2008.

———. 2002b. "Growth without Governance." World Bank Policy Research Working Paper No. 2928. Available at http://elibrary.worldbank.org/content/workingpaper/10.1596/1813-9450-2928. Accessed July 18, 2008.

Kaufmann, D., A. Kraay, and M. Mastruzzi. 1999. "Governance Matters." World Bank Policy Research Working Paper No. 2196. Available at http://info.worldbank.org/governance/wgi/pdf/govmatters2.pdf Accessed July 16, 2008.

———. 2000. "Governance Matters: From Measurement to Action." *Finance and Development* 37, no. 2: 10–13.

———. 2003. "Governance Matters III: Governance Indicators for 1996–2002." World Bank Mimeo.

———. 2005. "Governance Matters IV: Governance Indicators for 1996–2004." World Bank Mimeo.

———. 2006. Introduction in *International Handbook on the Economics of Corruption*. Ed. S. Rose-Ackerman. Northampton: Edward Elgar

Kaufmann, D., and A. Kraay, and P. Zoido-Lobatn. 1999a. "Aggregating Governance Indicators." World Bank Policy Research Working Paper 2195.

———. 1999b. "Governance Matters." World Bank Policy Research Working Paper 2195.

Keefer, P. 2005. "Democratization and Clientelism: Why Are Young Democracies Badly Governed?" *World Bank*, May 15, 2005, Policy Research Working Paper No. WPS3594.

Keefer, P. 2005. "Clientelism, Credibility and the Policy Choices of Young Democracies." Presented at "The Quality of Government: What It Is, How to Get It, Why It Matters," International Conference, Goteborg, November 17–19.

Key, V. O. 1964. *Politics, Parties and Pressure Groups*. 5th ed. New York: Cromwell.

Kingstone, P. R. 1999. *Crafting Coalitions for Reform: Business Preferences, Political Institutions, and Neo-liberal Reform in Brazil*. University Park: Pennsylvania State University Press.

Kingdon, J. 1984. *Agendas, Alternatives and Public Policies*. New York: Harper Collins.

Kitschelt, H., and S. Wilkinson, eds. 2007. "Citizen-Politician Linkages: An Introduction." In *Patrons, Clients, and Policies: Patterns of Democratic Accountability and Political Competition*. New York: Cambridge University Press.

———. 2000. "Linkages between Citizens and Politicians in Democratic Polities." *Comparative Political Studies* 33, nos. 6–7: 845–879.

———, Z. Mansfeldova, R. Markowski, and G. Toka. 1999. *Post-Communist Party Systems: Competition, Representation, and Inter-Party Cooperation*. New York: Cambridge University Press.

Knack, S. 2006. "Measuring Corruption in Eastern Europe and Central Asia: A Critique of the Cross-Country Indicators." World Bank Policy Research Working Paper 3968. Available at http://papers.ssrn.com/sol3/papers.cfm?abstract_id=923275#. Accessed August 22, 2008.

Kochanek, S. 1995. Transformation of Interest Politics in India. *Pacific Affairs* 68, no. 4 (winter): 529–550.

———. 1974. *Business and Politics in India*. Berkeley and Los Angeles: University of California Press.

Kopstein, J., M. I. Lichbach. 2005. *Comparative Politics: Interests, Identities, and Institutions in a Changing Global Order*. New York: Cambridge University Press.

Knack, S., and O. Azfar. 2003. "Trade Intensity, Country Size and Corruption." *Economics of Governance* 4: 1–18.

———. and P. Keefer 1995. "Institutions and Economic Performance: Cross-Country Tests Using Alternative Institutional Measures." *Economics and Politics* 7, no. 3: 207–227.: 5 Jan 5187.

Kreuzer, M., and V. Pettai. 2003. "Patterns of Political Instability: Affiliation Patterns of Politicians and Voters in Post-Communist Estonia, Latvia, and Lithuania." *Studies in Comparative International Development* 38: 76–98.

Kryzanek, M. J. 2003. *Comparative Politics: A Policy Approach*. Boulder: Westview Press.

Kunicova, J. 2006. "Democratic Institutions and Corruption: Incentives and Constraints in Politics." In *International Handbook on the Economics of Corruption*. Ed. Susan Rose-Ackerman. Northampton, MA: Edward Elgar.

———. and Susan Rose-Ackerman. 2005. "Electoral Rules and Constitutional Structures as Constraints on Corruption." *British Journal of Political Science* 35, no. 4: 573–606.

La Porta, R., F. Lopez-de-Silanes, A. Shleifer, R. W. Vishny. 1998. "The Quality of Government." *Journal of Law, Economics, and Organization* 15: 222–279.

Laitin, D. and J. Fearon. 2008 "Integrating Qualitative and Quantitative Methods." In *Oxford Handbook of Political Methodology,* eds. Janet M. Box-Steffensmeier and David Collier Oxford: Oxford University Press.

Lambsdorff, J. G. 2006. "Causes and Consequences of Corruption: What Do We Know from a Cross-Section of Countries?" In *International Handbook on the Economics of Corruption.* Ed. Susan Rose-Ackerman. Northampton, MA: Edward Elgar.

———. 1998. "Transparency International (TI) 1998 Corruption Perception Index, Framework Document." Transparency International and University of Passau.

———. 2000. "Background Paper to the 2000 Corruption Perceptions Index: Framework Document." Transparency International and Gottingen University.

———. 2001a. "Background Paper to the 2001 Corruption Perceptions Index: Framework Document." Transparency International and Gottingen University.

———. 2002. "Background Paper to the 2002 Corruption Perceptions Index: Framework Document." Transparency International and Gottingen University.

———. 2003. "Background Paper to the 2003 Corruption Perceptions Index: Framework Document." Transparency International and University of Passau.

———. 2004a. "Background Paper to the 2004 Corruption Perceptions Index: Framework Document." Transparency International and University of Passau.

———. 2004b. "Corruption Perceptions Index 2004." In *D.Rodriguez, G. Waite, and T.y Wolfe,* eds. Global Corruption Report 2005. Transparency International—Pluto Press, London.

Landé, C. H. 1977. "Introduction: The Dyadic Basis of Clientelism." In *Friends, Followers, and Factions: A Reader in Political Clientelism,* ed. S. W. Schmidt, J. C. Scott, C. Landé, and L. Guasti. Berkeley: University of California Press, xiii–xxxvii.

Langseth, P., and E. Buscaglia. 2002. "Judicial Integrity and Its Capacity to Enhance the Public Interest." UNDP Report CICP-8. Available at http://www.unodc.org/pdf/crime/gpac-publications/cicp8.pdf.

Laver, M. J. 2006. "Legislatures and Parliaments in Comparative Perspective." In *Oxford Handbook of Political Economy.* Ed. Barry Weingast and Don Wittman. New York: Oxford University Press.

———, and K. Benoit. 2003. "The Evolution of Party Systems between Elections" *American Journal of Political Science* 47, no. 2: 215–233.

———. 2002. "Divided Parties, Divided Government." In *Legislatures,* ed. G.

Lederman, D., Loayza, N. and R. Soares. 2005. "Accountability and Corruption: Political Institutions Matter" *Economics and Politics,* 17: 1–35

Loewenberg, P. Squire, and D. Roderick Kiewiet. Ann Arbor: University of Michigan Press.

———, and K. Shepsle. 1996. *Making and Breaking Governments: Parliaments and Legislatures in Parliamentary Democracies.* Cambridge, UK: Cambridge University Press.

———, and N. Schofield. 1990. *Multiparty Government: The Politics of Coalition in Europe.* Oxford: Oxford University Press

Lederman, D., N. V. Loayza, and R. R. Soares. 2005. "Accountability and Corruption: Political Institutions Matter." *Economics and Politics* 17: 1–35.

Leite, C. A., and J. Weidmann. 1999. "Does Mother Nature Corrupt?: Natural Resources, Corruption, and Economic Growth." Working paper WP/99/85, International Monetary Fund, Washington, DC.

Li, Q., and R. Reuveny. 2003. "Economic Globalization and Democracy: An Empirical Analysis." *British Journal of Political Science* 33, no. 1: 29–54.

Liebert, U. 1995. Parliamentary Lobby Regimes. In *Parliaments and Majority Rule in Western Europe,* ed. H. Döring. Frankfurt: Campus-Verlag.

Lindberg, S. 2005. "Consequences of Electoral Systems in Africa: A Preliminary Inquiry." *Electoral Studies* 24:41.–64

Loewenberg, G., P. Squire, and D. Roderick Kiewiet, eds. 2002. *Legislatures: Comparative Perspectives on Representative Assemblies.* Ann Arbor: University of Michigan Press.

Loewenberg, G. S., C. Patterson, M. E. Jewell. 1985. *Handbook of Legislative Research.* Cambridge, MA: Harvard University Press.

Lok Sabha Bulletin-I. March 18–23, 2005. Available at http://164.100.47.132/LssNew/Business/Bulletin2detail.aspx?bull2date=23/03/2005. Accessed November 11, 2008.

Lok Sabha Bulletins. March 18–23, 2005 Available at http://164.100.47.132/LssNew/Business/Bulletin2detail.aspx?bull2date=18/03/2005. Accessed November 11, 2008.

Rules of Procedure and Conduct of Business in Lok Sabha. 11th ed. 2004, 174. http://164.100.47.134/newls/Bulletin2archive.aspx. Accessed on August 22, 2008.

Los Angeles Times. 2004. "Alleged Scandal Rocks Poland." November 30, A-13. http://articles.latimes.com/2004/nov/30/world/fg-scandal30 Accessed June 4, 2008.

Lowery, David. 2007. "Why Do Organized Interests Lobby? A Multi-Goal, Multi-Context Theory of Lobbying" *Polity* 39:29-54.

Lowi, T. 1964. "American Business, Public Policy, Case Studies, and Political Theory." *World Politics:* 677–715.

Macklin R. 2004. *Double Standards in Medical research in Developing Countries.* Cambridge, MA: Cambridge University Press.

Maddala, G. S. 1983, *Limited-Dependent and Qualitative Variables in Economics,* New York: Cambridge University Press

Mainwaring, S. P. 1999. *Rethinking Party Systems in the Third Wave of Democratization: The Case of Brazil.* Palo Alto, CA: Stanford University Press.

Mainwaring, S., and M. S. Shugart, eds. 1997. *Presidentialism and Democracy in Latin America.* Cambridge, UK: Cambridge University Press.

Mainwaring, S., and T. R. Scully, eds. 1995. *Building Democratic Institutions: Party Systems in Latin America.* Palo Alto, CA: Stanford University Press.

Malone, M. 2004. *Regulation of Lobbyists in Developed Countries: Current Rules and Practices.* Dublin, Ireland: Institute for Public Administration.

Manow, P. 2005. "Politische Korruption und politischer Wettbewerb: Probleme der quantitativen Analyse." PVS Politische Vierteljahresschrift, VS Verlag für Sozialwissenschaften. 35: 249–66.

Mansfield, E., H. V. Milner, and B. P. Rosendorff. 2000. "Free to Trade: Democracies, Autocracies, and International Trade." *American Political Science Review* 94, no. 2: 305–321.

Manzetti, L., and C. J. Wilson. 2007. "Why Do Corrupt Governments Maintain Public Support?" In *Comparative Political Studies* 40: 949.

Martin, L. W., and G. Vanberg. 2004. "Policing the Bargain: Coalition Government and. Parliamentary Scrutiny." *American Journal of Political Science* 48, no. 3: 445–461.

Marwell, G., and P. Oliver. 1993. *The Critical Mass in Collective Action: A Micro-Social Theory.* New York: Cambridge University Press.

Mattson, I. 1995. "Private Members' Initiatives and Amendments." In *Parliaments and Majority Rule in Western Europe.* Ed. H. Döring. Berlin: Campus Verlag.

Mauro, P. 1995. "Corruption and Growth." *Quarterly Journal of Economics* 110, no. 3: 681–712.

Maxfield, S., B. R. Schneider, eds. 1997. *Business and the State in Developing Countries.* Ithaca, NY: Cornell University Press.

McCarty, N. 2004. "The Appointments Dilemma." *American Journal of Political Science* 48: 413–428.

McCubbins, M., and D. Rodriguez. 2008. "The Judiciary and the Role of Law." *Oxford Handbook of Political Economy.* Ed. B. Weingast and D. Wittman. New York: Oxford University Press.

Noll, R. G., and B. R. Weingast. 1987. "Administrative Procedures as Instruments of Political Control." *Journal of Law, Economics, and Organization* 3: 243–277.

McGrath, C. 2008. "The Development and Regulation of Lobbying in the New Members States of the European Union." *Journal of Public Administration,* Special Issue, 8: 15–32.

Medical Information Net. 2004. India to Finalize Patent Law Changes. September 5. http://www.news-medical.net/print_article.asp?id=8684. Accessed August 30, 2008.

Mezey, M. L. 1994. "New Perspective on Parliament Systems: A Review Article." *Legislative Studies Quarterly* 19: 429–443.

Mershon, C., and O. Shvetsova. 2008. "Parliamentary Cycles and Party Switching in Legislatures." *Comparative Political Studies,* 41(January): 99–127.

Mill, J.S. 1834. *The System of Logic.* 8th Edition. London: Longmans.

Milner, H. 1997. *Interests, Institutions and Information: Domestic Politics and International Relations.* Princeton, NJ: Princeton University Press.

Mint. September 22, 2008. "Politicians Buy a Fifth of Votes, Shows Study." http://www.livemint.com/2008/09/22082537/Politicians-buy-a-fifth-of-vot.html. Accessed September 22, 2008.

———. 2008. "CBI requires sanction from the ministry concerned to chargesheet officers of the rank of joint secretary and above." August 8. http://www.livemint.com/articles/2008/08/08234534/Charging-exofficers-won8217.html. Accessed August 29, 2008.

Mishra, A. 2006. "Corruption, Hierarchies and Bureaucratic Structure." *International Handbook on the Economics of Corruption.* Ed. S. Rose-Ackerman. Northampton, MA: Elgar

Miskin, S. 2003. "Politician Overboard: Jumping the Party Ship." Parliamentary Library, Commonwealth of Australia, Research Paper No. 4 2002–03 (March 24).

Mitra, C. 1998. *The Corrupt Society.* New Delhi: Viking.

Montgomery, K. A. 1999. "Electoral Effects on Party Behavior and Development Evidence from the Hungarian National Assembly." *Party Politics* 5 (October): 507–523.

Montinola, G. R. 1999. "Parties and Accountability in the Philippines." *Journal of Democracy* 10: 126–140.

Montinola G., and R. W. Jackman. 2002. "Sources of Corruption: A Cross-Country Study." *British Journal of Political Science* 32: 147–170.

Moody-Stewart, G. 1994. *Grand Corruption in Third World Development.* Berlin: Transparency International.

Morgernstern, S., and B. Nacif. 2001. *Legislatures in Latin America.* New York: Cambridge University Press.

Mueller, W.C. 2006. "Party Patronage and party colonization of the state." In *Handbook of Party Politics* Ed. R.S. Katz and W. Crotty. Thousand Oaks: Sage Publications. Pp 189–195.

Munck, G. L. 2004. "Tools for Qualitative Research." In *Rethinking Social Inquiry: Diverse Tools, Shared Standards.* Ed. D. Collier and H. Brady. Oxford, UK: Rowman and Littlefield.

Myerson, R.B 1993. "Effectiveness of Electoral Systems for Reducing Government Corruption: A Game-Theoretic Analysis." *Games and Economic Behavior* 5:118–132.

Naoi, M., and E. Krauss. 2009. "Who Lobbies Whom? Special Interest Politics under Alternative Electoral Systems." *American Journal of Political Science* 53: 874–892.

Nassmacher, K.-H. 2003. *Funding of Political Parties and Electoral Campaigns.* Ed. R. Austin and M. Tjernstrom. IDEA Handbook Series. Stockholm, Sweden: Trydells.

National Commission to Review the Working of the Constitution, Consultation Paper* on Review Of Election Law, Processes And Reform Options Advisory Panel, On Electoral Reforms; Standards in Political Life, Member-In-Charge-Dr. Subhash C. Kashyap, Chairperson-Shri R.K. Trivedi, January 8, 2001, *Vigyan Bhavan Annexe,* Parliament Of India, New Delhi.

Neto, O. A., G. W. Cox, and M. D. McCubbins. 2003. "Agenda Power in Brazil's Camara dos Deputados, 1989–98." *World Politics* 55 (July): 550–578.

Norton, P. 2002. "Introduction" In *Parliaments and Citizens in Western Europe.* : ed. P. Norton, Portland: Frank Cass.

Nownes, A. J. 2006. *Total Lobbying: What Lobbyists Want (and How They Try to Get It).* Cambridge, MA: Cambridge University Press.

Nownes, A., and P. Freeman. 1998. "Interest Group Activity in the States." *Journal of Politics* 60: 86–112.

OECD 2008. Lobbyists, Governments and Public Trust: Building A Legislative Framework for Enhancing Transparency and Accountability in Lobbying. *GOV/PGC/ETH(2007) 4.* Available at www.oecd.org Accessed December 6, 2009.

OGlobo. 1998. "Governo joga tudo pela Previdência." February 12, 3.

Olson, M. and M. Mezey. 1991. *Legislatures in the Policy Process.* Cambridge: Cambridge University Press.

Olson, M. 1965. *The Logic of Collective Action.* Cambridge, MA: Harvard University Press.

Ostrom, E. 2009. "Collective Action Theory." In *Oxford Handbook of Comparative Politics.* Ed. C. Bois and S. Stokes. New York: Oxford University Press.

Ozbudun, E. 1970. *Party Cohesion in Western Democracies: A Causal Analysis.* Beverly Hills, CA: Sage.

Paldam, M. 2002. "The Cross-Country Pattern of Corruption: Economics, Culture and the See-saw Dynamics." *European Journal of Political Economy* 18: 215–240.

Panizza, U. 2001. "Electoral Rules, Political Systems and Institutional Quality." *Economics and Politics* 13: 311–342.

Pecorino, P. 1999. "The effect of group size on public good provision in a repeated game setting." *Journal of Public Economics* 72: 121–134.

People's Democracy. 2005. "Amendment To The Indian Patents Act" Xxix No. 13. http://pd.cpim. org/2005/0327/03272005_patent%2oleft.htm Accessed September 17, 2008.

Pereira, C., T. Power, and L. Renno. 2008. "Agenda Power, Executive Decree Authority, and the Mixed Results in the Brazilian Congress." *Legislative Studies Quarterly* 33, no. 1: 5–33.

Pereira, C., and B. Mueller. 2004. "The Cost of Governing." *Comparative Political Studies* 37, no. 7 (September): 781–815.

Pereira, C., and B. Mueller. 2000. "Uma Teoria de Preponderância do Executivo: O Sistema de comisso~es no Legilsativo Brasileiro." *Revista Brasileira de Ciências Sociais* 15.

Persson, T., and G. Tabellini. 2002. *Political Economic: Explaining Economic Policy.* Cambridge, MA: MIT Press.

———. 2003. *The Economic Effects of Constitutions.* Cambridge, MA: MIT Press.

Persson, T., G. Tabellini, and F. Trebbi. 2003. "Electoral Rules and Corruption." *Journal of the European Economic Association* 1, no. 4: 958–989.

Pinheiro, V. C. 2004. "The Political Economy of Pension Reform in Brazil: A Historical Perpsective." Working Paper Version 07//11/2004. Inter-American Development Bank.

Pinto-Duschinsky, M. 2002. "Financing Politics: A Global View." *Journal of Democracy* 13:69-86, no. 4.

Prakash, A. S. 1995. *What ails Indian parliament: An exhaustive diagnosis.* New Delhi: Indus Publications.

Press Trust of India. 2005. "On Patents Bill, BJP & Left see eye-to-eye." March 16.

Przeworski, A., M. Alvarez, J. A. Cheibub, and F. Limongi. 2000. *Democracy and Development: Political Regimes and Economic Well-being in the World, 1950–1990.* New York: Cambridge University Press.

Putnam, R. D., R. Leonardi, and R. Y. Nanetti. 1998. *Making Democracy Work: Civic Tradition in Modern Italy.* Princeton, NJ: Princeton University Press.Rama, M., and G. Tabellini 1998. "Lobbying by capital and labor over trade and labor market policies." *EER* 42: 1295–1316.

Reich, R. 2007. *Supercapitalism: The Transformation of Business, Democracy, and Everyday Life.* New York: Knopf.

Rauch, J., and P. Evans. 2000. "Bureaucratic Structure and Bureaucratic Performance in Less Developed Countries." *Journal of Public Economics* 75: 49–71.

Rediff.com. December 2, 1999. "Insurance reforms won't be easy" Available at www.rediff.com/business/1999/dec/02insure.htm Accessed December 18, 2008.

———. December 2, 1999. "Lok Sabha passes insurance bill with 4 amendments"

Rediff.com. December 11, 1998. Interview with N.M. Sundaram, General Secretary, All-India Employees Union. Available at http://www.rediff.com/business/1998/dec/11ins1.htm. Accessed August 25, 2008

———. Dr. Jay Dubashi, ex-Union Minister of Industry under the BJP. Business Commentary: "Insurance reforms won't be easy." December 2, 1999. Available at http://www.rediff.com/business/1999/dec/02insure.htm. Accessed on August 25, 2008.

———. December 2, 1999. "Insurance bill puts govt in a bind as SJM, BMS, Sena harden stance" Available at http://www.rediff.com/money/1999/oct/02insubl.htm. Accessed December 15, 2008

———. December 2, 1999 "Why the insurance bill is controversial" Available at http://www.rediff.com/money/1999/oct/28irabil.htm. Accessed December 15, 2008.

———. December 4, 1998. "Uncertainty shrouds insurance bill's fate: Malkani sees foreign pressure on govt." Available at http://www.rediff.com/business/1998/dec/04insure.htm Accessed December 15, 2008.

Reich, R. 2008. Supercapitalism: The Transformation of Business, Democracy, and Everyday Life. New York: Vintage Press.

Rogowski, R. 1992. *Commerce and Coalitions: How Trade Affects Domestic Political Alignments.* Princeton, NJ: Princeton University Press.

Rockman, B. A. and R. K. Weaver. 1992. *Do Institutions Matter? Government Capabilities in the United States and Abroad.* Washington, DC: Brookings Institution Press.

Rose-Ackerman, S. 2007. Measuring Private Sector Corruption. *U4 Brief*, September 2007 # 5. http://www.u4.no. Accessed September 25, 2009

———. 2006. Introduction in *International Handbook on the Economics of Corruption.* Ed. Susan Rose-Ackerman. Northampton, MA: Edward Elgar

————. 1999. *Corruption and Government: Causes, Consequences, and Reform*. New York: Cambridge University Press.

Rudra, N. 2005. "Globalization and the Strengthening of Democracy in the Developing World." *American Journal of Political Science* 49, no. 4 (October): 704–730.

Saeigh, S. M. 2005. "The role of legislatures in the policymaking process." Workshop on state reform, public policies and policymaking processes. Inter-American Development Bank. Washington DC. February 28–March 2.

Samuel, J., and E. Jagadananda. 2003. *Social Watch India: Citizen's Report on Governance and Development*. New Delhi: National Social Watch Coalition,

Samuels, David. 2009. "Separation of Powers." In *Oxford Handbook of Comparative Politics*. Ed. C. Bois and S. Stokes. New York: Oxford University Press.

————. 2003. *Ambition, Federalism and Legislative Politics in Brazil*. New York: Cambridge University Press.

————. 2001. "Does Money Matter? Credible Commitments and Campaign Finance in New Democracies: Theory and Evidence from Brazil." *Comparative Politics* 34, no. 1 (October): 23–42.

Santiso, C. 2003. "Economic reform and judicial governance in Brazil: balancing independence with accountability" *Democratization*, 10:161-180

Santos, F., and L. Renno 2004. "Committee Leadership in Brazil." *Journal of Legislative Studies* 10, no. 1 (spring): 50–70.

Sathe, S.P. 2002. *Judicial Activism in India*. New York: Oxford University Press.

Scarrow, S. 2008. "Political Parties and Democracy in Theoretical and Practical Perspectives: Implementing Intra-Party Democracy." National Democratic Institute. Available at www. ndi.org

————. 2007. "Political Finance in Comparative Perspective." *Annual Review of Political Science* 10: 193–210.

Schlozman, K., and J. Tierney 1986. *Organized Interests and American Democracy*. New York: Harper and Row.

Schmitter, P. C. 1971. *Interest Conflict and Political Change in Brazil*. Stanford, CA: Stanford University Press.

Schneider, B. R. 2004. *Business Politics and the State in Twentieth-Century Latin America*. New York: Cambridge University Press.

Scott, J. C. 1972. *Comparative Political Corruption*. Englewood Cliffs, NJ: Prentice-Hall.

Seligson, M. 2002. "The Impact of Corruption on Regime Legitimacy: A Comparative Study of Four Latin American Countries." *Journal of Politics* 64: 408–433.

Shleifer, A., and R. W. Vishny. 1993. "Corruption." *Quarterly Journal of Economics* 108, no. 3: 599–617.

Shourie, A. 2007. *The Parliamentary System: What We Have Made of It What We Can Make of It*. New Delhi, India: Rupa and Co.

Shomer, Y. 2009. "Candidate Selection Procedures, Seniority, and Vote-Seeking." *Comparative Political Studies* 42 (2009): 945

Shugart, M. 1999. "Presidentialism, Parliamentarianism and the Provision of Collective Goods in Less-developed Countries." *Constitutional Political Economy* 10: 53–88.

Shugart, M., and J. Carey. 1992. *Presidents and Assemblies: Constitutional Design and Electoral Dynamics*. New York: Cambridge University Press.

Singh, N. K. 1999. *The Politics of Crime and Corruption: A Former CBI Officer Speaks*. New Delhi, India: Harper Collins.

Sloof, R. 2000. "Interest Group Lobbying and the Delegation of Policy Authority." *Economics and Politics* 12: 247-274. (2000):

Snyder, J. 1991. "On Buying Legislatures." *Economics and Politics* 3: 93–110.

Smith, R. 2006. *Candidate Strategies and Electoral Competition in the Russian Federation: Democracy without Foundation.* Cambridge, UK: Cambridge University Press.

Søreide, T. 2006. "Corruption in International Business Transactions: The Perspective of Norwegian Firms." In *International Handbook on the Economics of Corruption.* Ed. S. Rose-Ackerman. Cheltenham: Edward Elgar.Spiller,P., Stein, E. and M. Tommasi. 2009. "Introduction" *in Policymaking in Latin America: How Politics Shapes Policies* eds. Stein, E. , M. Tommasi, Spiller,P. and C. Scartascini. Cambridge: Harvard University Press.

Sridharan, E. 1999. "Toward State Funding of Elections in India? A Comparative Perspective on Possible Options." *Journal of Policy Reform* 3: 229–254.

Stevens, R. 1993. *The Independence of the Judiciary: The View from the Lord Chancellor's Office.* Oxford: Oxford University Press.

Stokes., S. C. 2007. "Political Clientelism." In *the Oxford Handbook of Comparative Politics* Edited by Carles Boix and Susan Stokes. New York: Oxford University Press.

Subramaniam, T. S. R. 2004. *Journeys through Babudom and Netaland: Governance in India.* New Delhi: Rupa and Co.

Svensson, J. 2003. "Who Must Pay Bribes and How Much? Evidence from a Cross-Section of Firms." *Quarterly Journal of Economics* 118, no. 1: 207–230.

Swamy, A., S. Knack, Y. Lee, and O. Azfar. 2001. "Gender and Corruption." *Journal of Development Economics* 64: 25–55.

Tanzi, V., and H. R. Davoodi. 1997. "Corruption, Public Investment, and Growth." IMF Working Paper 97/139.

Tavares, J. 2003. "Does Foreign Aid Corrupt?" *Economic Letters* 79: 99–106.

Tavits, M. 2009. "The Making of Mavericks: Local Loyalties and Party Defection." *Comparative Political Studies* 42: 793.

Theobold, R. 1982. "Patrimonialism." *World Politics* 34: 549–558.

Thies, M. 2001. "Keeping Tabs on Partners: The Logic of Delegation in Coalition Governments." *American Journal of Political Science* 45: 580–598.

Ting, M. M. 2001. "The 'Power of the Purse' and Its Implications for Bureaucratic Policy-making." *Public Choice* 106: 243–274.

Transparency International. 2009. *Corruption and the Private Sector.* Available at http://www. transparency.org/ Accessed November 5, 2009.

—— 2008. *Progress Report: OECD Anti-Corruption Convention.* Berlin, Germany: TI Organization Available at http://www.transparency.org/ Accessed November 5, 2009

—— 2007 Corruption in Judicial Systems. Accessed November 5, 2009. Available at ttp://www.transparency.org Accessed November 8, 2009.

—— June 30, 2005. *India Corruption Study To Improve Governance Volume–I: Key Highlights Study.* New Delhi, India: Centre for Media Studies.

—— 2004. Global Corruption Report 2004. Available at http://www.transparency.org/publications/gcr. Accessed November 6, 2008.

—— 2002. Report on Compliance with OECD Anti-Bribery Convention Available at http:// www.transparency.org/publications/gcr. Accessed November 6, 2008

—— Bribe Payers Index. May 14, 2002. Available at www.transparency.org/content/download/2863/17759 Accessed November 7, 2008.

Treisman, D. 2000. "The Causes of Corruption: A Cross-National Study." *Journal of Public Economics* 76: 399–457.

Tsebelis, G., and T. Rizova. 2007. "Presidential Conditional Agenda Setting in the Former Communist Countries." *Comparative Political Studies* 40, no. 10: 1155–1182.

Tsebelis, G., and E. Aleman. 2005. "Presidential Conditional Agenda Setting in Latin America." *World Politics* 57 (April): 396–420.

Tulchin, J., and R. Espach, eds. 2000. *Combating Corruption: Anti-Corruption Policies in Latin America*. Boulder, CO: Lynne Rienner.

UNDP 2008. *A Users' Guide to Measuring Corruption*. UNDP Oslo Governance Center. http://www.undp.org/oslocentre/flagship/users_guide_measuring_corruption.html

UNDP Human Development Report. 2007–08. *Fighting Climate Change: Human Solidarity in a Divided World*. Gordonsville, VA: VHPS.

Vanberg, G. 2006. "Establishing and Maintaining Judicial Independence." In *Oxford Handbook of Law and Politics*. New York: Oxford University Press.

Van Rijckeghem, C., and B. S. Weder. 1997. "Corruption and the Rate of Temptation: Do Low Wages in the Civil Service Cause Corruption?" IMF Working Paper WP/97/73.

Varshney, A. 1997. "Post-Modernism, Civic Engagement and Ethnic Conflict: A Passage to India." *Comparative Politics* 30, no. 1: 1–20.

Venkatesan, V. A. 2001. Move against Defections. *Frontline*. Volume 18–Issue 18, Sep. 01–14, 2001
———. 1999. "Chequered Relations." Volume 16–Issue 16, July 31–August 13, 1999. http://www.hinduonnet.com/fline/fl1616/16160100.htm

Weyland, K. 1992. "The Fragmentation of Business in Brazil." In *Business and Peak Associations in Brazil*," Ed. F. Durand and E. Silva. Miami: North-South Centre.

Wilkinson, S. I. 2001. "Cleansing Political Institutions." Available at http://www.india-seminar.com/2001/506/506%20steven%20i.%20.wilkinson.htm. Accessed July 10, 2009.

Volden, C., and C. J. Carruba. 2004. "The Formation of Oversized Coalitions in Parliamentary Democracies." *American Journal of Political Science* 48: 521–537.

Vora, R., and S. Palshikar, eds. 2004. *Indian Democracy: Meanings and Practices*. New Delhi: Sage Publications.

Warner, C. 2007. *The Best System Money Can Buy: Corruption in the European Union*. Ithaca, NY: Cornell University Press

Washington Post. 2002. "It's Open Season on Argentine Leaders." February 28.

Wei, S.-J. 2000. "Local Corruption and Global Capital Flows." *Brookings Papers on Economic Activity* 2: 303–352.

World Bank 2008. Strengthening Parliaments, Strengthening Accountability. Available at http://siteresources.worldbank.org/PSGLP/Resources/RetrospectiveSTRENGTHEN-INGPARLIAMENTS.pdf?&resourceurlname=RetrospectiveSTRENGTHENINGPARLIAM

World Bank 2005. World Bank Business Environment Survey. Data and Reports Available at http://www.enterprisesurveys.org/ Accessed July 12, 2008.

World Bank. 2004. Knowledge and Innovation for Competitiveness in Brazil. Ed. A. Rodriguez, C. Dahlman, and J,. Salmi. Accessed December 12, 2009. Available at http://siteresources.worldbank.org/EDUCATION/Resources/278200-1215707816170/Knowledge_Innovation_Competitiveness_Brazil.pdf

——— 2000. World Bank Business Environment Survey (WBES). Data and Reports Available at http://info.worldbank.org/governance/wbes/

World Bank and European Bank for Reconstruction and Development. Various years. Business Environment and Enterprise Performance Survey (BEEPS). Available at http://www.ebrd.com/pages/research/analysis/surveys/beeps.shtml. Accessed August 9, 2009.

World Economic Forum Executive Opinion Survey 2004–05. Available at www.weforum.org/en/initiatives/gcp/index.htm. Accessed July 19, 2008.

Wright, J. 2008. "Do Authoritarian Institutions Constrain? How Legislatures Affect Economic Growth and Investment." *American Journal of Political Science* 52: 322–343.

Yackee, J. W., and S. W. Yackee. 2006. "A Bias toward Business? Assessing Interest Group Influence on the U.S. Bureaucracy." *Journal of Politics* 68: 128–139.

Yadav, Vineeta. 2009a. Presidents, Parliaments and Lobbyists: Institutional Dimensions of Strategy Available at http://polisci.la.psu.edu/facultybios/yadav.html

———. 2009b. Legislatures and Venue Choice in Developing Democracies: A Comparative Study Available at http://polisci.la.psu.edu/facultybios/yadav.html

———. 2009c. Party Reputations and Political Careers: An Empirical Analysis Available at http://polisci.la.psu.edu/facultybios/yadav.html

———. 2009d. Money, Information or Friends: What a Lobbyist Needs Available at http://polisci.la.psu.edu/facultybios/yadav.html

INDEX